USA

THE COMPLETE BOOK OF

FORD MUSTANG

EVERY MODEL SINCE 1964½

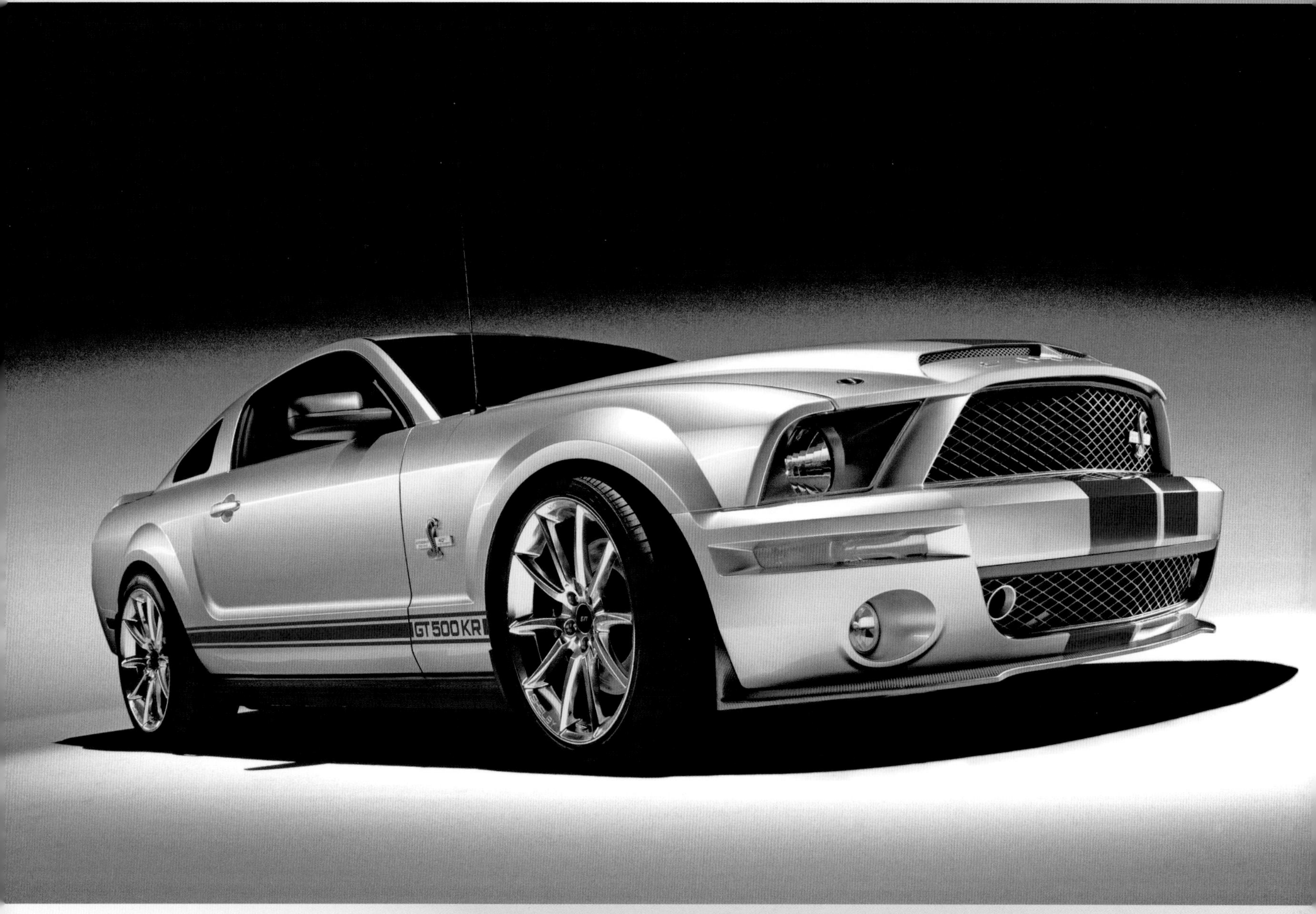

MIKE MUELLER

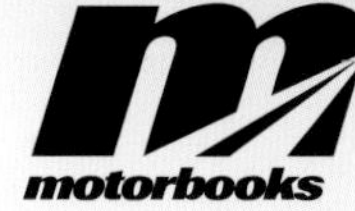

Brimming with creative inspiration, how-to projects, and useful information to enrich your everyday life, Quarto Knows is a favorite destination for those pursuing their interests and passions. Visit our site and dig deeper with our books into your area of interest: Quarto Creates, Quarto Cooks, Quarto Homes, Quarto Lives, Quarto Drives, Quarto Explores, Quarto Gifts, or Quarto Kids.

First published in 2015 by Motorbooks,
an imprint of The Quarto Group, 100 Cummings Center, Suite 265-D,
Beverly, MA 01915, USA. T (978) 282-9590 F (978) 283-2742
QuartoKnows.com

25 24 23 22 21 1 2 3 4 5

ISBN: 978-0-7603-7288-3

Originally found under the following Library of Congress Control Number: 2015932251

Acquisitions Editor: Zack Miller

Cover Designer: Simon Larkin of Larkin Design

Layout Designer: Becky Pagel and Megan Jones Design

Jacket and End Papers Photos: Ford Motor Company

Printed in China

Contents

Acknowledgments

MOTORBOOKS ORIGINALLY TASKED ME WITH producing this epic doorstop some fifteen years back, with the first edition of *The Complete Book of Ford Mustang* culminating in 2007's story. We've since updated it twice, in English that is, for 2011 and then 2015 to mark the arrival of the latest generation, the sixth. A few foreign-language editions also were thrown in (*merci beaucoup* and *danke schoen* right back at ya), temporarily bringing the tale up through 2016.

Now we're trying to modernize yet again, if only temporarily yet again. Flip to the final page here and you should find yourself in 2021, which, if I'm reading my calendar correctly, is presently the present. By the time you read this, however, my words will typically represent old news. Just like me.

In total, I have been producing automotive history books dating back 30 years, over which time I've always tried to deliver thanks to the many people who helped make all this possible. And now's no exception.

Of course I must start with my parents, Jim and Nancy Mueller, if only because they were mostly responsible for "all this." Duh! They made me, right? Ah, but they didn't stop there. Even after strongly suggesting I move out—at 17, sure wish they'd waited until they'd turned 18—they continued watching my back. And occasionally feeding me. And sometimes housing me. And almost always posting my bail. But seriously, as you might guess, Ma was my biggest fan, right up to the end—she succumbed to Alzheimer's in October 2019. Now Pa is battling dementia as well, this after defeating COVID-19 in 2020. I'll remain deeply in their debt all the way to my last day. Already missin' you too, dad.

Forever indebted also applies to the rest of my family, most of whom have long done so much for so little in return. And by "so little," I mean *nada*. My sister, Kathy Young, repeatedly put me up during countless photo junkets around the Midwest that

The author owes endless thanks to his significant other, Erin Welker, and not just because she does editing work for little or no (most likely) pay. Here she clowns at left with longtime friend and part-time supermodel Tawnya Braeutigam during a 2016 photo shoot intended to pair correct (sorta) era apparel and relative vehicle; sock-hopper with Tom and Michelle Grothouse's '56 T-bird, groovier chicster with Joe Moore's '64½ Mustang. How'd the directions get crossed? As Mueller has long told family and friends, "that's what ya get for puttin' me in charge." *Mike Mueller*

resulted in many of the pics following here. As you know well, sis, your contributions to my success rank as priceless, so I won't even begin to try making reparations. Okay with you? Don't answer, because along with my promise to never again move in, you'll also receive this set of Ginsu knives, able to cut the cheese and hold off unwanted guests with equal aplomb.

And let's not forget my brothers, Jim Jr. and David. Year-younger Dave copiloted during many of those junkets, assisting me ably in occasional exchange for maybe a beer or two—or 20. Can't count how much I owe him, either. If not for his inspiration during our teen years, I might've never stumbled into this business. Until then, I'd always wanted to dance. Either that or design shrubbery.

Then there was Jimbo, five years my junior. He didn't just work in the automotive business, he also loved cars with a vengeance, proving that there maybe was something in the water at the Mueller camp back in the day. Or could it have been the lead-painted buckets we used to tote it in? In any case, Jim always had a thing for wheels, regardless of count. Among his toys was a tricked-out Harley, which was so chrome-encrusted, how could that deer have missed it?

On July 31, 2013, Jim's Harley and said wildlife collided on a country route just south of Fisher, Illinois. Neither wore a helmet that day, but fortunately the venison-based lifeform survived and fled the scene before Barney Fife arrived. He remains at large. My brother, on the other hand, opted to lay right where he landed, thank you very much, after regrading the road with his forehead. He remained speechless (a first) for a few weeks while surgeons apparently traded out his banged-up brain for one that actually worked. Following his incredible recovery, he immediately got rid of that hog.

To say he was lucky is akin to . . . well, he was bodaciously lucky. Hell, the doc didn't even need to shave his head prior to surgery. Genetics had already taken care of that.

But all kidding aside again, Jimbo wasn't so fortunate six months later, when doctors discovered a rare gastroesophageal cancer. Yet, despite the bad news, he continued calling, continued helping with my work, continued talking about "beating this thing." I'll never forget our final phone conversation, his jovial front belying his painful struggle, in May 2014. My little brother died about a week and a half later. He would have turned 50 on June 27.

Of course I'll be equally thankful for all my two brothers have done for me, during my career and prior. Funny thing, though: reportedly Nancy Mueller gave birth to four sons. And to date, I've never extended any gratitude towards the youngest of us, Ken, who today occupies the home Ma and Pa built with their own hands outside Champaign, Illinois, nearly 60 years ago. Maybe that's because Kenny apparently knows better than to work for nothing. Dave and Kathy are probably still waiting by the mailbox for their checks. As for my other brother, he who does nothing gets nothing. Not even a false promise.

Upon further review, however . . .

Back in 1983, fresh out of the University of Illinois with a journalism degree, I turned to Kenny in need of a camera to photograph some old car for an unsolicited magazine article I was attempting to force down an unsuspecting editor's throat. He complied, loaning me a 35 mm I've yet to return. Yes, his graciousness changed my life, derailing my plans for postgraduate proctology school and sending me down an incredibly lazy trail masquerading as a freelance automotive journalist. For that I can't help but offer my sincerest appreciation. Now if only all the editors I've ever worked with could say the same. They undoubtedly will never forgive you, Kenny.

Among those who perhaps wish that my youngest sibling was never born is former *Mustang Monthly* editor (and revered pony car whisperer) Donald Farr, who gave this humble scribe his first job in the car magazine biz in 1987. Like Kenny, my old boss never has been thanked sufficiently, so perhaps my family can share their windfall with him once it arrives. Yeah, that'll work.

A great car guy through and through, the author's brother, Jim Mueller Jr., succumbed to cancer on May 23, 2014, at age 49. He's shown here on May 4, 2007, at Tim Mooney Ford-Mercury in Tuscola, Illinois, with the new Mustang his father, Jim Mueller Sr., just bought as a retirement gift to himself. Jimbo only had two words for that 2007 convertible: "Niiii-ice." ***Nancy Mueller***

Another editor who knows a thing or two about how much a Mike Mueller promise is worth is Jessi Schatz, project manager at Quarto Group, parent to Motorbooks. Perhaps with the aid of her two felines, Lily and Pepper, she has somehow managed to keep her wits about her after working with me on two projects over the last year. Congrats and thanks. Furthermore, her boss and mine, longtime Motorbooks editorial shepherd Zack Miller, also deserves both a laurel and hearty handshake for putting up with me far longer than my two exwives combined. But sorry, Zack, I'm already taken. Again.

No, no one was foolish enough to hitch themselves up to this wobbly wagon a third time. But Erin Welker did opt to take me in to raise, first into her Arlington, Texas, home, now here at the present ranch in Kennesaw, Georgia. Still crazy after all these years, she not only holds the title of Best Girlfriend in the History of Girlfriends, she also deserves beaucoup credit for standing by through every day devoid of up-close-and-personal time while I hammer away at these keys. (Know what I mean; nudge, nudge, wink, wink?) I promise, E, someday you'll git yours, and maybe even once again hear those sweet words: "Sure feels like an Arby's kinda night."

Erin additionally earns unending gratitude for loads of editing work, most of it unpaid. And by "most," I mean "all."

Also deserving of a steak and Lowenbrau at my expense is another old friend, John Clor, formerly of Ford's Special Vehicle Team, now enthusiast communication manager at Ford Performance. My queries have rained down on him via email and phone dating back 25 years, but that's what he gets for knowing/loving Mustangs every bit as well/much as Donald Farr.

Lastly but definitely not leastly, I can't forget all of the devoted Mustangers who allowed me to capture their steeds—with my good ol' film-fed Hasselblads—dating back decades now. Though I can't mention your names within these tight confines, I certainly remember who you are. Thanks loads and hope you all like what you see on the following pages.

If not, blame Kenny.

Mike Mueller, May 2021

> "We didn't want to do a retro design," said Dave Pericak during that December 2013 introduction. "We wanted to look forward. We're celebrating 50 years of continuous production and getting ready for the next 50."

Introduction
On Top O' The World

Opposite: Ford's all-new sixth-generation pony car (front and center) was the guest of honor at a humble gathering held April 17, 2014, at the site of the 1964 New York World's Fair to mark the Mustang's 50th birthday. Nearly 100 vintage models also were on hand, demonstrating the long-running legacy in proud fashion.

Below: In August 2018, Ford proudly announced production of its 10 millionth Mustang, a 2019 GT six-speed, in front here. Those 10 million pony cars have rolled through six generations, beginning with numero uno, on the scene from 1964–1973. Succeeding generations spanned 1974–78 (Mustang II), 1979–93, 1994–2004, 2005–2014, and 2015 to present. In back is the Henry Ford Museum's "ceremonial" original Mustang. No one can say for sure if this model actually was first off the production line back in 1964, but its serial number is 100001.

IT WAS A PARTY A HALF CENTURY IN THE making, held simultaneously at two sites at opposite ends of this nation to account for expected overflow crowds arriving from many states, not to mention countries. On April 17, 2014, Ford's beloved pony car turned 50, and Mustang Club of America officials weren't about to let this milestone roll by with simply a lame card and/or corny cake. Same for the parent company in Dearborn.

The one-millionth Mustang rolled off the line in February 1966, and annual production counts surpassed 300,000 up through 1968.

"The excitement of the automotive event of the century is too alluring for the Ford team to miss out on," said Ronald Bramlett, executive director of the MCA's big events, a week before the twin five-day celebrations kicked off on April 16 at the Charlotte Motor Speedway (in Concord, North Carolina) and Nevada's Las Vegas Motor Speedway. In attendance at the eastern extravaganza were Bill Ford and Mark Fields, Ford's executive chairman and chief operating officer, respectively. Mustang chief engineer Dave Pericak was present, too, and Fields did double duty, showing up in Vegas as well. He was joined out west by, among others, Ford's global design v.p., Moray Callum.

Callum also piled up some miles, travelling to a third party held April 17 in Flushing Meadows, New York, at the site of the 1964 World's Fair, an appropriate setting considering that's where Mustang originally debuted. This humbler event was limited to local club members, who displayed their vintage models in the shadow of the iconic Unisphere, the 140-foot-tall stainless-steel representation of Earth that was meant to symbolize global interdependence and mark the beginning of the space age when built nearly 60 years ago. Also showing up at the New York party (as well as the MCA bashes in Nevada and North Carolina) was easily the newest Mustang since the very first, the much-anticipated 2015 model, which had been formally introduced at six sites around the world in December 2013.

Choosing to unveil the breed's next great generation overseas was part of an equally new plan that involved immersing Ford's sixth-gen pony car for the first time in the company's ever-expanding global marketing strategy. While the previous five generations also had shown up before on foreign shores, those export totals were insignificant relative to what product planners now had in mind. More than 100 countries were specifically targeted this time, relying on both left-hand-drivers as well as locale-suited right-hand counterparts.

As *AutoWeek*'s J. P. Vettraino explained in December 2013, "'global' here does not mean Mustangs for oil sheiks on the Arabian Peninsula, or oddball collectors in Japan, or aftermarket right-drive conversions in Australia, or gray-market GT500s in Europe. That global already exists. The new global means [exporting] as many Mustangs as the expanding goldmines of China—and Brazil—will take, as well as delivery from most sanctioned Ford dealers on Earth, even in Southeast Asia or sub-Saharan Africa."

To those ends, 2015's Mustang was fitted with a notable first—Euro-preferred independent rear suspension (IRS)—and was available with a new EcoBoost engine, a turbocharged four that made 310 horses while savoring every drop of precious fossil fuel. At the same time, 2015's GT featured a familiar 5.0L V-8, a fifth-gen carryover now rated

at 435 horsepower, the most standard Mustang power to date.

Next to no bolt was left unwrenched during sixth-gen development, and the works were wrapped up in an exciting package that appeared more than modern. "We didn't want to do a retro design," said Dave Pericak during that December 2013 introduction. "We wanted to look forward. We're celebrating 50 years of continuous production and getting ready for the next 50." Devoted fans nonetheless couldn't miss various familiar touches, including that restored fastback roofline and those traditional three-element taillights in back that still signaled sequentially in a turn, but only in America. "The goal [was] to attract new customers without losing avid enthusiasts," added design director Joel Piaskowski.

Indeed, Ford's latest Mustang represented as sweet a deal as ever seen in the pony field. But isn't that what the breed has been about all along?

From the beginning, Lee Iacocca had envisioned a car that both looked sporty and possessed serious performance potential while remaining affordably practical in base form. From the get-go, impressions were youthful, even sexy, thanks to a distinctive body with its "T-birdesque" long-hood/short-deck layout, complemented by bucket seats and a floor shifter inside. Drivers looked and felt groovy whether they were putting the whip to a mundane six or hot "Hi-Po" V-8.

Above: A Mustang by any other name is still a Mustang, even when exported to Germany. A company there already claimed legal title to the Mustang tag back in the 1960s, so Ford officials used the "T-5" code instead. This T-5 convertible (left) is one of only 151 delivered in Europe in 1967. *Mike Mueller*

Right: History has long credited designer John Najjar with naming the Mustang after North American Aviation's P-51 fighter plane from World War II. But Lee Iacocca says otherwise. In a 2004 *Mustang Monthly* interview, he claimed the tag simply referred to wild horses, not deadly aircraft. *Mike Mueller*

Lee Iacocca never did like the path the Mustang took after 1967. By 1971, Ford's polite pony car had grown into a "fat pig," as he put it. Iacocca's "little jewel," the compact Mustang II, then followed in 1974.

Below: The downsized Mustang II kicked off the breed's second generation in 1974 and immediately won *Motor Trend*'s Car of the Year trophy. But the attraction quickly faded, and not even the flashy 1978 King Cobra (shown here) could prevent the Mustang II's fall from grace.

Iacocca and crew first teased the sports car crowd with a two-seat Mustang I in 1962 then followed with the much more conventional Mustang II concept in 1963, setting the stage for the greatest feeding frenzy ever seen in American automotive history. Taking a regular-production Mustang home early on wasn't easy. Dealers' initial stocks were snapped up immediately, and another 22,000 orders were placed during the first day of public sale, April 17, 1964. A two-month wait for delivery was common, and estimates claimed as many as 4 million potential buyers crammed into Ford showrooms for a gander that first weekend alone.

Mass appeal clearly was Mustang's forte from the outset as Detroit's original pony car represented many different machines to many different people. In most cases early on it was that $2,400 asking price for a six-cylinder model that drew the lion's share of the attention. But the tease of pricier, better-equipped models quickly grew, and sixes soon lost ground in favor of V-8s. A lengthy options list also was present to help further enhance the bottom line.

Although the initial hubbub expectedly died down, sales remained incredibly strong for years to come. The 1 millionth Mustang rolled off the line

A convertible Mustang reappeared in 1983 after a 10-year hiatus. The GT rendition, itself on the shelf since 1969, had made a comeback the year before, bringing with it the hot 5.0-liter High Output V-8. Both the 1983 GT (back) and 1983 convertible shown here feature the HO small-block, then rated at 175 horsepower. *Mike Mueller*

Below: By 1987, the 5.0-liter was producing 225 horsepower, making it one of Detroit's best performance buys. The 1988 GT (shown here) was essentially a carbon copy of its predecessor. *Mike Mueller*

early in 1966, and nearly 300,000 were still hitting the streets annually in 1968.

But an upsizing trend didn't sit that well with purists. First came a bigger, heavier platform in 1967, created primarily to make room up front for more engine. Chevrolet's Camaro and Pontiac's Firebird debuted that year, and both offered optional big-cube V-8s. Ford had no choice but to retaliate, although 1967's 390-powered Mustang still fell flat compared to GM rivals. The muscle Mustang story then took a turn for the better the following year when the 428 Cobra Jet debuted.

Street racers, however, represented just one limited niche market. And while the fastest Mustangs flourished in their own way, the breed as a whole began to slide as the original ideal galloped away from its practical roots. Sales dropped even further after newly hired Ford boss Semon "Bunkie" Knudsen sponsored an even larger, more expensive redesign scheduled for 1971—this time put together to allow installation of a larger, more costly Cobra Jet. But this 429 CJ died after 1971, and Mustang itself also was looking a little terminal in 1972 and '73.

Knudsen grabbed the reins at Ford after quitting General Motors in 1968. Being the disgruntled

Unveiling the 2005 Mustang that January was the real icing on the cake, and it sure looks like the legacy will continue rolling on toward another anniversary.

employee Knudsen stepped over, the ever-ambitious Iacocca had every right to be upset, and he even briefly considered bailing on his company like Bunkie had on his. But the Mustang's proud papa wisely stuck around. Good thinking. In Dearborn, the GM defector almost immediately stomped on toes all the way to the top, never a practice that equates to job security.

Knudsen also pushed Ford products way too hard in a direction contrary to what his new boss had in mind. Bunkie valued racing and performance too highly and further demonstrated this thinking by shepherding the wild, wooly Boss 302 and Boss 429 into play in 1969. In his opinion, Mustang was a factory hot rod first, thus the reasoning behind making more room for more engine within 1971's shell. By then, however, the days of big cubes and mucho horsepower were all but over, a fact not lost on practically everyone in Detroit.

Everyone, apparently, except Knudsen. Incapable of changing lanes, he was fired by Henry Ford II in September 1969, only 19 months after he came onboard. Iacocca finally did reach the top spot in 1970 but then the next year was stuck with a redesigned Mustang he detested. So he tried to turn back the clock in 1974 with his "little jewel," the Mustang II, a compact second-gen pony car that has garnered its fair share of retroactive slings and arrows over the years since its short run.

Although Mustang II sales immediately soared to 1964-like heights, they quickly faded as buyers became disenchanted with the diminutive machine's cramped quarters and wimpy performance. Saving at the pump just wasn't a big enough trade-off.

Resurgence came in 1979 as the more comfortable third-generation Fox-chassis Mustang arrived. Performance and pizzazz quickly went on the rise, evidenced by the return of both the GT in 1982 and a convertible body in 1983. A legacy within a legacy then developed as the 5.0-liter HO V-8 gained strength, becoming one of Detroit's best performance buys in the process.

Ford's Mustang GT and Chevrolet's Camaro Z28 ran neck and neck for supremacy on the street-performance scene during the 1980s. Then the Z28 was fitted with the Corvette's LT1 V-8 in 1993, tipping the scales Chevy's way. When a new GT appeared for 1994 (right), it featured 205 horsepower. Its rival, the 1994 Z28 (left), offered 275 horses. But Ford people got the last laugh after GM cancelled its long-running pony car in 2002, leaving the Mustang to gallop on alone. *Mike Mueller*

What worked so well in 1964 was still attracting buyers in 2007. Various nostalgic touches enhanced the appeal of the fifth-generation Mustang, offered from 2005–2014. The 2007 V-6 convertible at left originally belonged to the author's father, Jim Mueller, Sr., of Champaign, Illinois. It was passed down from dad to son in 2016—to hopefully better preserve it in warmer climes. *Mike Mueller*

While the goal was to roll into the future with a truly new Mustang for 2015, Ford people simply couldn't help but continue to pay tribute to the past. Especially evident was a return to the true fastback body familiar to Mustang buyers in 1965 and '66. To the right of the 2015 model here is a 1966 2+2 Mustang, owned by Tom and Michelle Grothouse, of Arlington, Texas. *Mike Mueller*

Beginning in 2008, Dearborn designers began creating special aviation-themed Mustangs meant to be auctioned off, with proceeds going to the Experimental Aircraft Association to help educate/train young flyers. In back at left is 2011's Blue Angels Mustang, also intended to commemorate 100 years of U.S. naval aviation. In front is 2013's Thunderbirds Edition, which marked the 60th anniversary of the U.S. Air Force's equally famous demonstration team. Ten other special editions have followed this pair, which were caught at rest in 2016 while on display at the National Museum of World War II Aviation in Colorado Springs, Colorado. *Lt. Colonel Rodney Hart, USAF Ret.*

The popular 5.0 engine even survived into a new era as a fourth repackaging followed for 1994, now using the SN95 foundation. But two years later, the aging five-liter pushrod powerplant was replaced by the thoroughly modern 4.6-liter modular V-8 with its overhead cams. An even hotter version of this engine, fitted with dual overhead cams and four valves per cylinder, was created for the Special Vehicle Team's Cobra Mustang, which had debuted in 1993. Thus armed, the DOHC 4.6L SVT Cobra surpassed 300 horsepower in 1996 and was on the verge of topping 400 horsepower in 2003 when SVT marked its ten-year anniversary.

That same year was Ford Motor Company's 100th, and Mustang's own 40th birthday came in 2004. Fortunately those anniversary badges on fouth-gen fenders weren't the only presents unwrapped during the celebration. Introduced that January, the all-new 2005 Mustang was the real icing on the cake. And, like the first SN95 model in 1994, the S197-based fifth generation managed to promise a bright future while still preserving a proud heritage in respectful fashion.

"We weren't just redesigning a car, we were adding another chapter to an epic," explained Ford design exec J Mays. Baby boomers saw a blast from their past while younger buyers were attracted as well to a car that just couldn't be beat, at the price, as far as looks and performance were concerned.

"Mustang attracts two kinds of drivers—those under 30 and those over 30," added Mays with tongue initially planted ever-so-slightly in cheek. "America's most popular nameplate transcends demographics and socioeconomic trends because Mustang is really more than a car. It's an icon that's been woven into the fabric of America for 40 years running."

Beneath the 2005 Mustang GT's hood was a 300-horsepower 4.6L SOHC V-8 fitted with three valves in each cylinder instead of two. Holding those horses was a unitized body/frame stretched out on a 6-inch longer wheelbase, meaning there was notably more room inside for passengers, something sorely missing during previous generations. Two new engines then enhanced fifth-gen appeal in 2011, both featuring up-to-date four-valve DOHC heads. Base models received a 305-horsepower DOHC V-6, while the GT was treated to a born-again 5.0L V-8, this one rated at 412 horsepower, at the time the most muscle by far ever offered as standard fare.

According to Dave Pericak, his team's initial sixth-gen plan involved rolling over the 2014 GT's DOHC V-8 and pairing it with the new turbo four, itself also sporting dual overhead cams operating four valves in each combustion chamber. The V-6 was to remain behind, perhaps due to critics' cries that it didn't offer near enough torque to go along with its impressive 305-horsepower tag. But then came the decision to save the six for a 2015

Right: Mach 1 made a triumphant return after a 17-year hiatus in 2021, now armed with 480 horsepower. At left is the original, introduced for 1969. Mach 1 availability rolled over from the first generation into the second-gen Mustang II run, then was repackaged again during the fourth generation for both 2003 and 2004.

Below: Mustang took to NASCAR tracks in 2011, first on the second-tier Infinity circuit. Competition in the top-shelf Monster Energy Cup series followed in 2019. At right here is Ford's Next Gen NASCAR Mustang, announced on May 5, 2021. Created to both more closely mirror regular-production counterparts and offer ample flexibility for future change—say, a switch to electric drive—the Next Gen racer was slated to debut at the Daytona 500 on February 20, 2022. At left is the most powerful street Mustang to date, the 760-horsepower Shelby GT500

entry-level model, as Pericak explained to *Car and Driver*'s Jeff Sabatini, to "continue to make the Mustang [affordable] to just about anybody who wants one."

And, as mentioned, "anybody" now meant anyone most anywhere on the planet. By 2017, Ford's lastest pony had risen up to claim the title of world's best-selling sports car, which it still firmly clenched as these words met paper in 2021. Twenty-seventeen also was the last year for the cost-conscious V-6 Mustang, indicating that opinions had shifted somewhat once the sixth generation started kicking up its own dust. Like their American cousins, pony riders overseas also apparently liked to run a little wild now and again, inspiring the guys back in Dearborn to keep their spurs on.

"Mustang enthusiasts love their performance cars, and they showed that yet again," said Hau Thai-Tang, Ford Motor Company's chief product platform and operations office, in April 2021. "In a challenging year for the entire auto industry because of the global pandemic, Mustang performed very well, increasing its share in the global sports car segment."

Already frisky things, EcoBoosts could be hitched up to 20 more available horses beginning in 2020. And with born-again fun-mobiles like the Bullitt Mustang, GT350 and 350R, and record-shattering 760-horse GT500 leading the way that year, Ford's pony filled out 15.1 percent of the worldwide sporting market, up from 14.8 in 2019. Furthermore, Dearborn reported that Bullitt and Shelby sales combined went up 52.7 percent over that same span. Then along came another time machine, 2021's Mach 1, to additionally help turn up the heat.

And so the beat goes on. If you've always dreamed of a pony on your birthday, you're still in luck. Same goes for bucking broncos.

01

Off and Running

01

1964–1966

On Friday, April 17, 1964, Dearborn officials introduced America to an entirely new breed of automobile, a fun machine that brought buyers galloping into their friendly neighborhood Ford dealerships like there was no tomorrow. Demand instantly overwhelmed supply, with the few available showroom teases claimed even before they were unveiled. Tugs of war were common. In Garland, Texas, 15 customers wanted a local dealer's last Mustang. His solution was to give the car to the highest bidder, who then insisted on spending the night in his prize to ensure it wouldn't be sold out from under him before his check could clear the next day.

AVAILABILITY INSPIRED THE ONLY COMPLAINTS heard in 1964 concerning the new Mustang. A famous telegram sent to Henry Ford II probably said it best:

Henry Ford, I do declare
You have your Grandpa Henry's flair
He put a Ford in every home.
You put a Mustang there.
Congratulations.
The wait out here is somewhat sickly;
Could you fix me up more quickly?

Original forecasts claimed no more than 100,000 new ponies would hit the streets that first year, but Lee Iacocca knew better. His goal from the beginning was to break Detroit's new-model first-year sales record, set by Ford's own Falcon (at about 417,000) just four years prior. The battle cry around Dearborn early in 1964 became "417 by 4-17," meaning the plan was to sell at least 417,000 pony cars by April 17, 1965. Not a problem: the tally on 4-17-65 read 418,812, equaling 1,638 more Mustangs in 1965 than Falcons in 1960.

Of that record-breaking total, 121,538 were so-called 1964-½ Mustangs. Because it was introduced in the middle of a model year, Ford's first pony car rolled through an extended 18-month run that ended in August 1965. Most sources then identified all these Mustangs as 1965 models, but various running changes adopted in August 1964 made it relatively easy to differentiate those built before that date from those coming afterward. Listing those changes, most of them quite trivial, isn't easily done in 25 words or less. Fortunately, one major clue exists: '64-½ Mustangs used generators, '65s used alternators. Production for the true 12-month 1965 model run was 559,451 Mustangs.

Targeting emerging baby boomers was just one key to the Mustang's overnight success.

- Ford Division promotes Lee Iacocca to its general manager post in November 1960.
- Ford introduces the Mustang I two-seater to the press in October 1962.
- Plymouth rolls out its sporty Barracuda early in April 1964.
- The regular-production Mustang makes its grand public debut on April 17, 1964.
- A Mustang convertible paces the Indianapolis 500 in May 1964.
- The optional High Performance 289 V-8 is introduced in June 1964.
- A third body style, the 2+2 fastback, is introduced in September 1964.
- Mustang becomes Detroit's best-selling new model of all time in April 1965.
- The one-millionth Mustang rolls off the line on February 23, 1966.
- The Mustang's all-time production high, 607,568 cars, comes in 1966.

Above: In 1963, Ford tipped off much of the look of its upcoming pony car with the Mustang II show car, literally a modified pre-production model.

Opposite: In June 1964, Ford officials announced the availability of the optional High Performance 289 V-8, a hot small-block that backed up those sporty good looks with some decent muscle. Eagle eyes might notice the small "High Performance" lettering added behind the typical "289" fender badge on this 1964-½ Hi-Po convertible. *Mike Mueller*

Previous pages:
Left: Ford's new Falcon (at left with Donald Frey) established a first-year sales record in 1960. The Mustang (with Iacocca at right) then broke that record in April 1965.

Right: Various trim changes set the 1966 Mustang apart from its forerunners in 1964 and '65. Total production of 2+2 fastbacks in 1966 was 35,698. *Mike Mueller*

Pennsylvanian Ron Hermann (beaming here at the wheel with his granddaughter along for the ride) waited three months to take possession of his brand-new Mustang convertible in 1964. He never has let it go. Nor has he let it go downhill. Only 17,000 miles show on the odometer of this totally unrestored original, which still resides in Hermann's garage in 2007. *courtesy Ron Hermann*

Below: The tires on Ron Hermann's 1964-½ convertible are just as original as the car—the air inside must be nearly 45 years stale. *courtesy Ron Hermann*

According to Iacocca, another important facet involved "the three faces of Mustang." With a base six-cylinder engine, a Mustang coupe was a frugal economizer in 1964. Customers with fatter wallets could've created a relatively luxurious mini-T-bird. Last, but certainly not least, was a hot rod alter ego made possible by installing Ford's 271-horsepower High Performance 289 V-8, announced as an option in June 1964. All Mustangs, regardless of equipment, looked sporty—some simply played the part more convincingly.

Two body styles initially were offered, with a sexy convertible going for about $2,600 when fitted with the budget-conscious six. The more practical notchback coupe outsold its topless counterpart by nearly 3.5:1 that first year. A third variation, the fashionable 2+2 fastback, joined the original duo in September.

Six or V-8, top or not, the truly fresh 1964-½ Mustang became, like the Beatles that year, bigger than Jesus. Hot on the heels of an unprecedented marketing push came an equally overwhelming media response. Headlines transcended the automotive press, with Iacocca and his pride and joy even showing up concurrently on the covers of both *Time* and *Newsweek*.

Among those caught up in the promotional blitz 40-some years back was 18-year-old Ron Hermann. "Of course I saw all the ads," he recalls. "And I wanted to be the first on my block with a new Mustang." At the time, Hermann's father knew someone with clout at Ford, and this fellow made sure Ron's request took precedence over so many others. "Having friends in high places goes a long way," he says with a chuckle.

"A lot of people stared when I drove by; a lot of girls wanted to take rides."

Hermann put $100 down to secure the chance to buy the one Mustang then touring the Philadelphia area. "I followed the car around town to make sure no one messed with it. This was my car; I didn't want people touching it." He stayed on watch for three months, tightly clutching his promissory contract all along. "One guy offered me $500 for that piece of paper." But it was no sale.

When Hermann finally did take his Mustang home from Philadelphia's Barr Ford, he instantly became the talk of the town. "A lot of people stared when I drove by; a lot of girls wanted to take rides." Though he honored many of those requests, he

Mustang roots actually run all the way back to 1955, the year Ford unveiled another long-hood/short-deck wonder, the two-seat Thunderbird.

Right: A Falcon-based sports car was sketched up in September 1961.

Below: Gene Bordinat's designers began working on two-seat concepts in the summer of 1961.

never again used the car regularly after that. He still owns his untouched Mustang, claiming it has never seen rain or snow, nor taken on new tires. The odometer presently shows 17,000 miles. "To this day, I don't know why I did it, why I kept this car without driving it. My relatives kept saying, 'You should use it,' but I just couldn't."

Talk about devotion. Such legendary loyalty helps explain why the Mustang is still running 40-plus years after its birth, something no other pony car presently can claim.

Mustang roots actually run all the way back to 1955, the year Ford unveiled another long-hood/short-deck wonder, the two-seat Thunderbird, a modern classic that proved that small, fun packages could sell. Yet as much as loyalists loved the original T-bird, Dearborn officials just couldn't leave well enough alone; they widened the car's scope by adding a back seat in 1958. Purists could cry all they wanted, but all complaints were drowned out by the sound of bean counters laughing all the way to the bank as Thunderbird sales doubled that year.

Ford planners, meanwhile, kept their minds open to the possibilities of marketing another diminutive automobile. But when they tried the small-car thing again, they did so with the affordable, painfully mundane Falcon, introduced for 1960 along with two rivals, Chevrolet's Corvair and Plymouth's Valiant. Ford's first Falcon outsold Chevrolet's rear-engined compact by nearly a 2:1 margin on the way to shattering Detroit's record for instant success.

Such prosperity right out of the box certainly was nothing to sneeze at. Yet some Ford people still wondered what the results might have been had the Falcon not been such a plain-Jane vehicle. Among this group was the 36-year-old former marketing manager who had just been promoted to Ford Division's top office: Lee Iacocca. Unlike his conservative predecessor, Robert McNamara, Iacocca was ready and willing to rock the automotive world. As Iacocca later explained in his 1984 autobiography, McNamara "was a good businessman, but he had the mentality of a consumerist. He believed strongly in the idea of

Model names considered early on included "Cougar," which would resurface for Mercury's pony car in 1967. Apparently, a prancing feline didn't quite evoke the same emotional response as a galloping horse.

a utilitarian car, whose purpose was simply to meet people's basic needs."

Iacocca, on the other hand, had in mind what he called "a good-looking little youth car," and to get his ball rolling, he called together a group of creative players almost immediately after his November 1960 promotion. Included were product planners Donald Frey, Hal Sperlich, and Donald Petersen. Marketing man Bob Eggert, public relations manager Walt Murphy, and racing guru Jacques Passino were present, too. This group met every week for 14 weeks at Dearborn's Fairlane Motel and thus became known as the "Fairlane Committee." Putting ideas down on paper began in earnest late in 1961. Early parameters for Iacocca's youth car were quickly established: a wheelbase no longer than 108 inches, total weight of about 2,500 pounds, and a price tag equal to no more than a dollar a pound.

Iacocca also specified a back seat, even though Gene Bordinat's Advanced Styling studio had started drawing up various sporty two-seaters earlier that summer. Iacocca himself gave Bordinat

Above: The original Mustang looked and felt sporty regardless of which engine resided beneath that long hood. Bucket seats, a floor shifter, and a six-cylinder were all standard.

Right: The Mustang's unit-body platform shared much of its makeup with the compact Falcon.

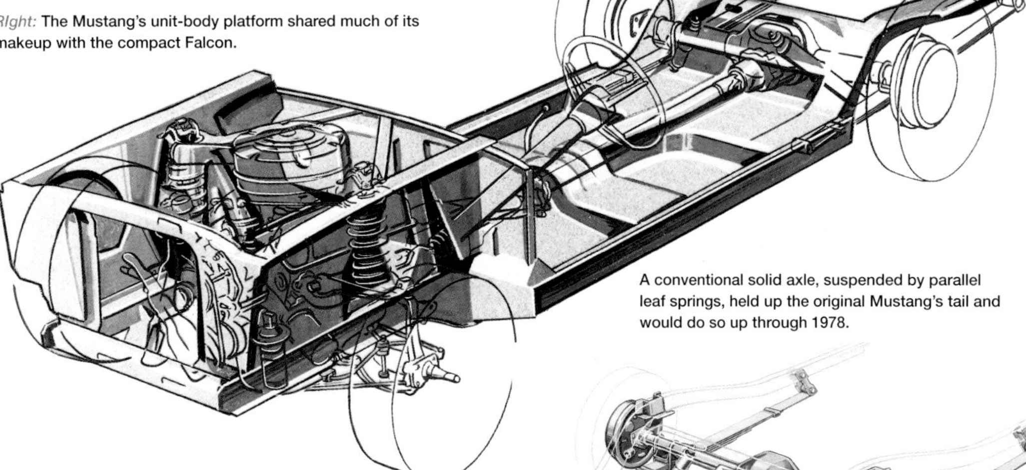

A conventional solid axle, suspended by parallel leaf springs, held up the original Mustang's tail and would do so up through 1978.

Front suspension consisted of a coil spring bolted atop an upper A-arm. A parallel control arm brought up the lower end.

the go-ahead for a full-fledged prototype project that would eventually mislead the ascot-wearing crowd into believing Ford was planning a true sports car. Unveiled in October 1962, this topless two-seater—soon known as the Mustang I—inspired more than one faulty prediction, including a *Motor Trend* report late in 1963 that claimed "Ford will produce a sports car to compete with the Corvette." Iacocca, Frey, and the rest knew the truth all along: the first car to wear the Mustang name was built solely to familiarize that moniker with the public in a definitely sporty fashion; the final product would be an entirely different animal.

Development of that new breed was well under way by early 1962, with six mockups presented to division management in August that year. In Bordinat's opinion, the best of this bunch was the "Cougar," created by Dave Ash, Joe Oros' assistant in the Ford studio. This design carried through with few major changes into production, though the name didn't. The project initially known by its in-house code, "T-5," took on various tags during development stages, including Henry Ford II's preference, "T-bird II." But in the end, one name fit like no other: Mustang it was.

It was Oros' Mustang that Iacocca took to Henry Ford II's office for approval on September 10, 1962. He then came away from what he called the toughest selling job of his career with a thumbs-up from the boss and a meager $40 million to develop and tool up the Mustang. In reality, he spent $65 million. Dearborn's top decision-makers also gave him a very tight deadline: "Job One," the first production Mustang, was slated to leave the assembly line on March 9, 1964.

Fortunately, engineers were given a head start on the project as the plan involved adapting as much of the Falcon's existing platform as possible, inspiring more than one slap from critics and jealous rivals alike. On top, Ford's groundbreaking vehicle looked brand new, thought arrow-slingers, but underneath it was as much a yawner as its compact forerunner. "Not so fast" was the retort from at least one of the men behind the machine. "The Mustang had a lot of Falcon parts in it," says Gail Halderman, "but it was not a glorified Falcon as many believe."

The first people outside of Ford to get the final word on the new Mustang were prominent magazine journalists invited to a confidential briefing in the fall of 1963. Press kits then went out to about 11,000 newspapers and magazines, followed by the official press introduction on Monday, April

13, 1964, at the New York World's Fair. Next, an unprecedented broadcast barrage began on Thursday evening, April 16, as Mustang television commercials ran on all three networks at the same time. Seemingly endless print ads popped up in essentially every major publication that weekend. But who had time to sit down with a paper? On Friday, the rush was on to see the little car America would be reading all about soon enough.

1962 Mustang I

Thoughts of a lighter, lower-priced variation on the 1955–1957 T-bird were still drawing consideration when Gene Bordinat's stylists began creating their two-seat concepts early in the summer of 1961. A clay model, enthusiastically approved by racer Dan Gurney, morphed into a running prototype in May 1962.

Bordinat had made Bob Maguire and Damon Woods chief stylists of this project earlier that year, with Maguire overseeing the exterior, Woods the interior. A team headed by John Najjar and Jim Sipple drew up plans for an innovative mid-engine machine, and it was Najjar who, legend has it, named the thing, borrowing the title from his favorite World War II fighter plane, North American Aviation's P-51 Mustang. Initially known simply as "Mustang," this sporty machine was renamed the Mustang I after the Mustang II show car appeared in 1963.

Fashioning the aluminum-bodied Mustang I's foundation was the job of Roy Lunn, the chassis engineer who later directed the design of Ford's world-beating race car, the GT-40. A tubular-steel birdcage space frame complete with roll bar was welded up as a home for a midship-mounted V-4 engine and four-speed transaxle, both borrowed from Ford of Germany's Taunus front-wheel-drive compact. Control arms at the corners were also tubular steel and were suspended by coil-over shocks. Wheels were cast magnesium measuring 13 by 5 inches.

The European 1,500-cc V-4 was boosted from its standard 89 horsepower to 109 by increasing compression to 11:1 and adding dual Weber carburetors and a more aggressive cam. The clutch was hydraulic, and the shifter worked via cables.

1962 Mustang I

Body Style	Two-seat roadster
Construction	Tubular-steel space frame beneath welded aluminum body
Wheelbase	90 inches
Length	154.3 inches
Height	39.4 inches at roll bar; 28.8 inches at cowl
Curb Weight	1,544 pounds
Wheels	13x5 cast magnesium
Tires	5.20x13
Suspension	In front, upper/lower tubular A-frames and coil springs; in back, upper tubular A-arms on top, trailing strut rods on bottom, and coil-over shock absorbers
Brakes	Front discs, rear drums
Engine	109-horsepower 1,500-cc (91.4-ci) 60-degree V-4, mounted amidships
Compression	11:1
Fuel Delivery	Dual Weber carburetors
Transmission	Four-speed manual with hydraulic clutch and cable-operated shifter

Ford teased sports car fans in 1962 with a two-seat Mustang prototype. The name became "Mustang I" in 1963 after the Mustang II show car was unveiled. Standing left to right are engineering vice president Herb Misch and design chief Gene Bordinat. Chassis engineer Roy Lunn is at the wheel.

Ford's original Mustang was up and running on October 2, 1962, and was then shipped to its public unveiling at Watkins Glen in New York, where it drew raves from the admiring press.

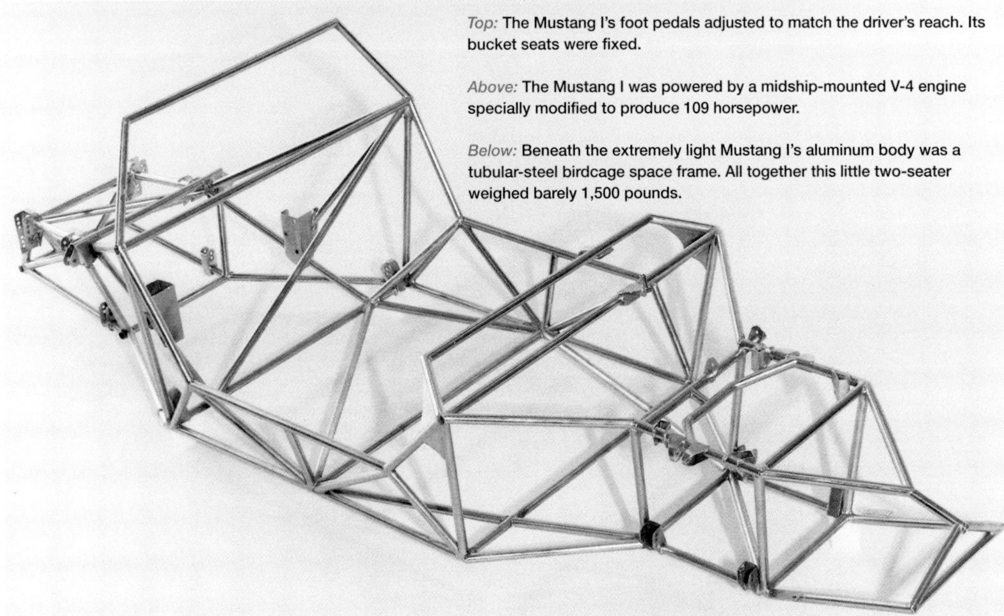

Top: The Mustang I's foot pedals adjusted to match the driver's reach. Its bucket seats were fixed.

Above: The Mustang I was powered by a midship-mounted V-4 engine specially modified to produce 109 horsepower.

Below: Beneath the extremely light Mustang I's aluminum body was a tubular-steel birdcage space frame. All together this little two-seater weighed barely 1,500 pounds.

Brakes were discs up front, drums in back. Inside, both the steering wheel and foot-pedal assembly could be adjusted to fit the driver; this was necessary because the leather-covered aluminum bucket seats were fixed in place.

Ford's original Mustang was up and running on October 2, 1962, and was then shipped to its public unveiling at Watkins Glen in New York, where it drew raves from the admiring press. Barrie Gill of the London *Daily Herald* claimed it was "one of the most exciting cars I have ever ridden in." *Car and Driver* called it "the first true sports car to come out of Dearborn." On the track, Dan Gurney reportedly reached 120 miles per hour at the wheel of the hot little two-seater—a vehicle that was all tease and no truth.

1963 Mustang II

Gene Bordinat decided to return to Watkins Glen in 1963 with another Mustang, an entirely different car that served as a link between his two-seat ideal and the actual pony car scheduled for release into the wild in 1964. This showboat was basically a standard preproduction model wearing customized nose and tail treatments and a lowered roof. Like the Mustang I, it was painted white with blue racing stripes, and it was named Mustang II to keep the heritage rolling.

According to Iacocca, showing off the Mustang II at "The Glen" in October 1963 was part of "a pretest of likely customer responses to styling and mechanical innovations we may be considering for future production models." According to some journalists, the Mustang II failed this test. *Motor Trend*'s psychics couldn't believe their eyes. In their words, the "Mustang II may herald the general lines of that division's upcoming sports car, but it likely isn't an actual prototype. It resembles the original Mustang not at all. It's rather a shame that the Mustang name had to be diluted this way."

Of course, by then, responses, negative or not, didn't matter. The deal was all but done. And within

1963 Mustang II

Construction	Unitized body/frame with detachable hardtop roof
Wheelbase	108 inches
Length	186.6 inches
Width	68.2 inches
Height	48.4 inches
Wheels	Custom mags
Suspension	Short-arm/long-arm with coil springs in front; solid axle with parallel leaf springs in back
Steering	Recirculating ball
Engine	289-ci V-8
Bore and Stroke	4.00x2.87 inches
Fuel Delivery	Single four-barrel carburetor
Transmission	Four-speed manual

six months, the final product would have all such critics dining on their words.

1964-½

More than 4,000 letters of praise from proud owners landed in Dearborn during the summer of 1964. Raves from the press too were plentiful.

"A market which has been looking for a car has it now," exclaimed a *Car Life* review. "It is a sports car, a gran turismo car, an economy car, a personal car, a rally car, a sprint car, a race car, a suburban car, and even a luxury car." According to *Road & Track*, "The Mustang is definitely a sports car, on par in most respects with such undisputed types as the MGB, Triumph TR-4 or Sunbeam Alpine." Back in *Car Life*'s words, "The car may well be, in fact, better than any domestically mass-produced automobile on the basis of handling and roadability and performance, per dollar invested." And all this about a machine that shared so much beneath the skin with its ho-hum Falcon cousin.

Steering components and suspension were modified Falcon hardware, as was the basic unit-body platform. Some dimensions did differ in the Mustang application, as the floor pan was dropped

Left: **The Mustang II featured a production model's body with customized nose and tail treatments and a chopped top.**

Below: **According to Lee Iacocca, the Mustang II show car constituted "a pre-test of likely customer responses to styling and mechanical innovations we may be considering for future production models."**

Right: Rather plain Falcon-based instrumentation was standard inside the 1964-½ Mustang. *Mike Mueller*

The quickest way to tell a 1964-½ Mustang apart from its similar 1965 successor involved a look under the hood, where the former relied on a generator (shown here on a Hi-Po 289 V-8). An alternator replaced that antiquated generator beginning with official 1965 production. *Mike Mueller*

Below: Two body styles were available in 1964: a notchback coupe and a sexy convertible. Convertible production that first year (1964 to 1965) was 73,112. *Mike Mueller*

down around the engine/trans to bring both the passengers and the roof closer to the ground. Cowl height in turn was cut in keeping with this lowering to help impart the sporty image Iacocca had in mind all along.

Power choices early on included a 170-ci six-cylinder or the Falcon's 260-cube small-block V-8. An enlarged V-8, the four-barrel-fed 289, was optional. A three-speed manual transmission was standard in all cases, with a four-speed stick and Cruise-O-Matic automatic available at extra cost behind all three. Among other delectable options were front disc brakes; power assists for the brakes, steering, and convertible top; air conditioning; and a Rally-Pac that added a clock and tachometer atop the steering column.

Easily the most expensive option, at $328, was announced in June 1964 and instantly lit the fires of buyers in the market for a truly wild horse. Rated at a tidy 271 horsepower, the High Performance 289 V-8 could wind out like a champ thanks to various modifications, beginning with a special cylinder block fitted with strengthened main bearing caps. Held in place by those two-bolt caps was a nodular-iron crankshaft that underwent random inspections during assembly for metallurgic content. Beefier rods were tied to that crank by large 3/8-inch bolts. Additional upgrades included stiffer dual valve springs, hardened pushrods, spring retainers and keepers, and screw-in rocker studs in place of the standard pressed-in units.

Feeding the Hi-Po 289 (also known by its option code: K) was a 600-cfm Autolite four-barrel on a typical cast-iron intake. A solid-lifter cam actuated standard 289 valves, and a dual-point distributor (with mechanical advance) fired the mixture. Also part of the K-code deal was the Special Handling Package (quicker steering and stiffer springs, shocks, and sway bar) and a set of 6.95x14 nylon "Red Band" tires. A three-speed manual was standard behind the Hi-Po, with a four-speed optional. An automatic wasn't available.

The K-code 289 remained the Mustang's hottest

1964 Indy 500 Pace Car

Body Style	Convertible
Wheelbase	108 inches
Length	181.6 inches
Tires	7.55x14 bias-ply Firestone Gold Line
Suspension	Short-arm/long-arm with cut-down coil springs in front; solid axle with de-arched leaf springs in back
Steering	Magic Circle recirculating ball
Brakes	Specially reinforced front discs, rear drums
Engine	Modified 271-horsepower 289-ci High Performance V-8
Bore and Stroke	4.00x2.87 inches
Compression	10.5:1
Fuel Delivery	Single four-barrel carburetor
Transmission	Four-speed manual
Production	2 or 3 actual pace cars (another 33 stock parade cars were built)

"The car may well be, in fact, better than any domestically mass-produced automobile on the basis of handling and roadability and performance, per dollar invested." —*Car Life*

engine option up through 1966. It was briefly listed in 1967 then was superseded by the 390 GT big-block. Hi-Po production for those three years was 7,273 in 1965, 5,469 in 1966, and only 472 in 1967.

1964 Indy 500 Pace Car

Iacocca's mass-market marvel was barely six weeks old when it paced the field for the 48th running of the greatest spectacle in motor racing on May 30, 1964. Though Ford's Fairlane was the original choice to lead the way at that year's Indianapolis 500, the Mustang had appeared just in time to serve as a much more sensational flagship for the annual Brickyard extravaganza.

Ford brought three specially prepared pony cars to Indy in 1964. Another 33 convertibles were required for the Festival Parade, plus one for use by the Festival Committee director and one more to carry the race queen around before the race. The only other Ford-prepared vehicles involved with the 1964 Indy 500 program were pace car replica coupes awarded as prizes in a company contest for the top 105 Ford salesmen. As many as 190 (perhaps more than 200) of these were built in April and early May. They featured the same lettering and racing stripes as their convertible counterparts but were painted Pace Car White instead of Wimbledon White. All were equipped identically: 260 two-barrel V-8, Cruise-O-Matic automatic, power steering, and white interior.

No pace car convertible replicas were released. But as many as 35 buyers did eventually own an "Indy Pace Car" Mustang droptop that year, after dealers got their hands on those hard-to-come-by Festival cars. These box-stock parade cars were variously equipped. Both four-speed and automatic-transmission versions were built, and interior colors numbered three: red, white, and blue.

The actual pace cars were fitted with all the race-day extras. Two flag stanchions were added in back, and three grab handles—two beside the

The sleek 2+2 fastback joined the Mustang lineup in September 1964. More than 77,000 were sold that first year. *Mike Mueller*

Benson Ford piloted the Mustang pace car around the track at Indianapolis during the start of the 48th running of the annual 500-mile spectacular on May 30, 1964.

Various minor differences helped differentiate the 1964-½ and 1965 Mustangs. Early cars featured a hood with beveled corners up front. *Mike Mueller*

> More than 4,000 letters of praise from proud owners landed in Dearborn during the summer of 1964. Raves from the press too were plentiful.

rear seat and one atop the windshield opposite the driver—were bolted in place to help keep pace-lap passengers in place.

Some mystery concerns the pace cars' mechanicals. Most reports claim they were fitted with hopped-up Hi-Po 289s. Some witnesses think the engines were actually experimental small-blocks tweaked with various hot components, including those used by the K-code V-8. In any case, these engines were balanced and blueprinted beyond typical Hi-Po specs, and their cylinder heads were ported and polished for better breathing. Extra attention also was paid to oiling to guarantee everything stayed together during that high-speed pace lap. A racing-style, wide-sump oil pan was added, as was an oversized radiator for ample cooling capability.

Underneath, cut-down front coil springs and de-arched rear leaves were used to lower the cars' center of gravity, while a superstiff anti-roll bar helped keep things on the level. Also assisting the cars in the slightly banked turns was a mismatched set of Koni shocks: 80/20s on the left, 50/50s on the right. Tires were 7.55x14 bias-ply Firestone Gold Lines. Front disc pads and rear shoes were beefed pieces. Heavier bracing was added from shock towers to cowl.

The fates of the actual pace cars remain a mystery. Some stories claim the Mustang driven by Benson Ford on race day in May 1964 was given to that year's winner, A. J. Foyt, and later wrecked. According to Indy officials, however, all three pace car convertibles were returned to Ford after the race. From there, the trio reportedly went to the Holman-Moody race shop in North Carolina. Holman-Moody then delivered one to Sebring, Florida, for pace car duty there; another perhaps went to Watkins Glen, New York, for the same job. It is believed the third may have been sent to California, possibly Riverside, to also serve as a pace car. Only one of the three, the Sebring car, has since resurfaced.

1964 & 1965

Model Availability	Two-door coupe, two-door convertible for 1964-½; 2+2 fastback added for 1965
Wheelbase	108 inches
Length	181.6 inches
Width	68.2 inches
Height	51.1 inches
Curb Weight	2,449 pounds, 1964-½ six-cylinder coupe; 2,615 pounds, 1964-½ six-cylinder convertible; 2,465 pounds, 1965 six-cylinder coupe; 2,650 pounds, six-cylinder convertible; 2,515 pounds, 1965 2+2 six-cylinder
Base Price	$2,320.96, six-cylinder coupe; $2,557.64, six-cylinder convertible; $2,533.19, six-cylinder 2+2 fastback; V-8 option added $105.63
Track (front/rear, in inches)	55.4/56, six-cylinder; 56/56, V-8
Wheels	13x4.5 four-lug, standard w/six-cylinder; 13x4.5 five-lug, standard w/V-8; 15x5 five-lug, optional w/Special Handling Package (discontinued in August 1964)
Tires	6.50x13, standard; 7.00x13, optional w/V-8; 6.50x14 optional (standard w/V-8 and Special Handling Package); 5.90x15, optional w/V-8 and Special Handling Package
Suspension	Independent upper A-arms, lower control arms w/coil springs in front; live axle with leaf springs in back
Steering	Recirculating ball (27:1 manual ratio, 22:1 power assist ratio)
Brakes	Four-wheel hydraulic drums
Engine	101-horsepower 170-ci six-cylinder, standard for 1964-½ model; 164-horsepower 260-ci V-8 optional for 1964-½ model; 210-horsepower 289-ci 4V V-8, optional for 1964-½ model; 120-horsepower 200-ci six-cylinder, standard for 1965 model; 200-horsepower 289-ci 2V V-8, optional for 1965 model; 225-horsepower 289-ci 4V V-8, optional for 1965 model; 271-horsepower High Performance 289 V-8, optional for 1964 and 1965 models
Bore and Stroke	3.50x2.94 inches (170 six), 3.68x3.13 inches (200 six), 3.80x2.87 inches (260 V-8), 4.00x2.87 inches (289 V-8)
Compression	8.7:1 (170 six), 9.2:1 (200 six), 8.8:1 (260 V-8), 9:1 (210-horsepower 289-4V V-8), 9.3:1 (200-horsepower 289-2V V-8), 10:1 (225-horsepower 289-4V V-8), 10.5:1 (High Performance 289 V-8)
Fuel Delivery	Autolite one-barrel carburetor (170 six), Autolite two-barrel (260 V-8), Autolite four-barrel (210-horsepower 289-4V V-8), 600-cfm Autolite four-barrel (High Performance 289 V-8), Autolite two-barrel (200-horsepower 289-2V V-8), Autolite four-barrel (225-horsepower 289-4V V-8)
Transmission	Three-speed manual, standard (not available w/High Performance 289 V-8); four-speed manual, optional (3.29:1 low, for six-cylinder; 3.16:1 low, for 260 V-8, 2.78:1 low, for 289 V-8, 2.32:1 low, for High Performance 289 V-8); Cruise-O-Matic automatic, optional (not available w/High Performance 289 V-8)
Axle Ratio	3.20:1, standard w/six-cylinder manual trans and four-speed manual; 2.83:1, standard w/six-cylinder automatic; 2.80:1, standard with 289 V-8 and automatic transmission; 3.50, standard w/High Performance 289 V-8
Production	121,538 1964-½ models; 559,451 1965 models

1965

As production rolled through August 1964, changes to the Mustang were most noticeable under the hood, where the standard six-cylinder was boosted to 200 cubic inches and the 260 V-8 was replaced by a 289 two-barrel small-block rated at 200 horsepower. Meanwhile, more compression boosted the 289 four-barrel V-8 to 225 horsepower for 1965, up from 210 horses in 1964.

An even more sporty flair entered the Mustang equation in September 1964, when the fastback version joined the original coupe and convertible. Designed by Gail Halderman, this sleek idea dated back to February 1963. A clay mockup was captured on film in May that year along with two inspirational machines, a Studebaker Avanti and an E-type Jaguar, seen in the background.

To set this new model apart, Ford people chose the 2+2 badge, a moniker borrowed from Pontiac, which had in turn borrowed it from Ferrari. In European terms, a 2+2 was a grand tourer—a relatively roomy, certainly sporty affair that added two rear passenger seats to the typical sports car package. Ford's more practical 2+2 Mustang incorporated a folding rear seat that, when down, opened up the entire area beneath that sweeping rear roofline for extra cargo or additional comfort, depending on your intentions. More than 77,000 2+2 Mustangs were sold the first year out.

In other news, two prominent option packages debuted in the spring of 1965, the first being the snazzy pony interior (officially known as the Interior Decor Group) with its galloping-horse seat inserts

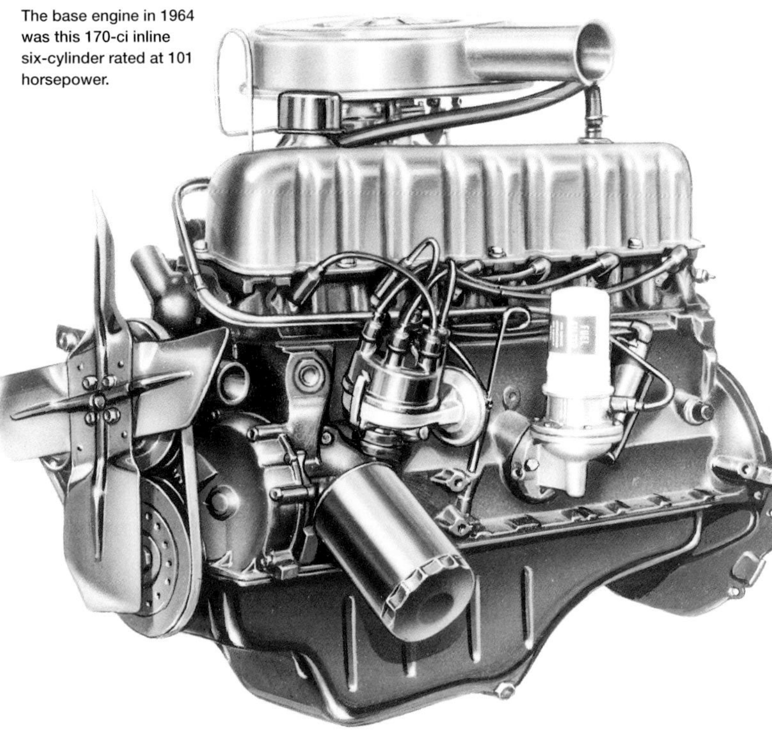

The base engine in 1964 was this 170-ci inline six-cylinder rated at 101 horsepower.

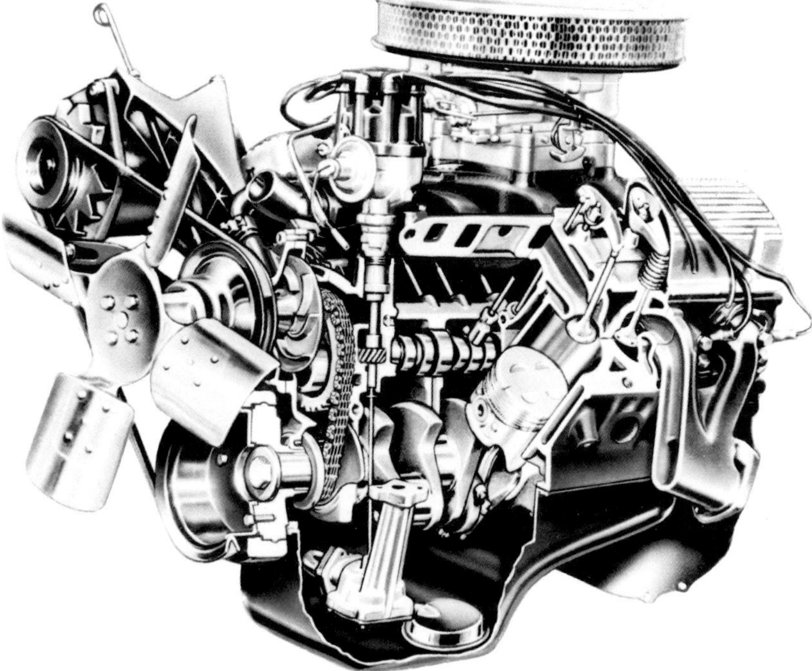

Fed by a 600-cfm Autolite four-barrel carburetor, the Hi-Po 289 produced 271 horsepower. Chrome dress-up was standard, and that bright air cleaner also let this hot small-block breathe easier.

Right: The American Machine and Foundry Company (AMF) introduced its own little pony just in time for the 1964 Christmas season. Priced at $12.95, this Midget Mustang rolled on a 23-inch wheelbase and stood a scant 14 inches high. AMF produced Mustang pedal cars for kids up through 1972. *Mike Mueller*

Below: Two Windsor V-8s were initially available in April 1964, a 210-horsepower 289 (with four-barrel carburetor) and this 260, rated at 164 horsepower.

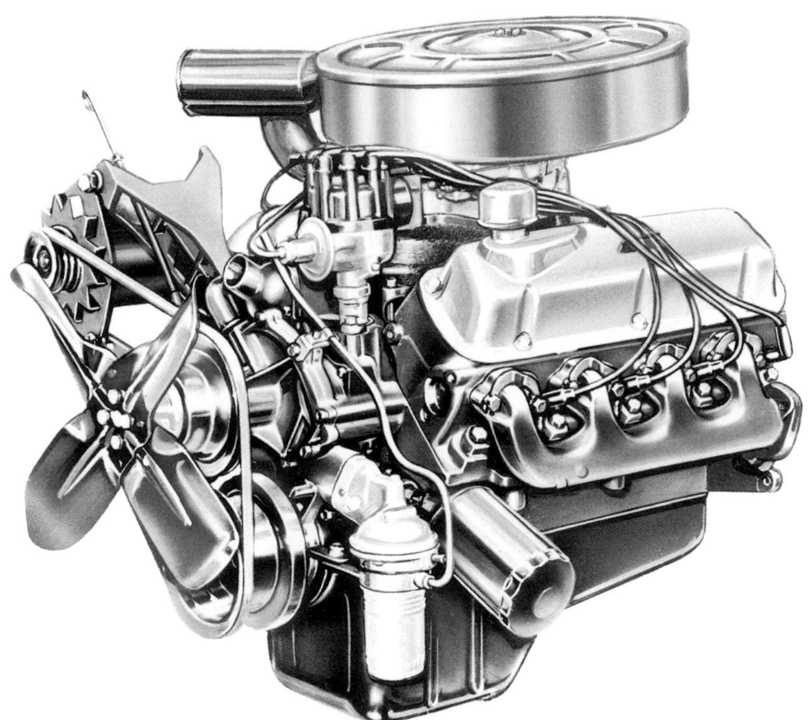

The 1965 hood edge featured a sharp crease in place of the beveling seen on 1964-½ models. *Mike Mueller*

An even more sporty flair entered the Mustang equation in September 1964, when the fastback version joined the original coupe and convertible.

and simulated walnut paneling. The other was the GT Equipment Group, introduced in April 1965 to help mark the Mustang's first birthday.

The GT package was available, in exchange for $165, on all three 1965 models but was only offered along with the Mustang's two optional four-barrel 289s, the 225-horsepower Challenger V-8 or the 271-horse Hi-Po. Included in the deal was the Special Handling Package, which featured stiffer springs, a thickened front stabilizer bar, and quicker (22:1) steering. All GT Mustangs also were fitted with 10-inch front disc brakes and dual exhausts.

Chrome trumpets protruding through brightly trimmed cutouts in a special rear valance panel ended those exhausts. Lower-body stripes, GT badges, and a unique grille bar framed by fog lamps at each end enhanced the image further.

Completing the GT package was a five-dial instrument panel in place of the standard, rather mundane, Falcon-style dashboard. Instead of the conventional left-to-right-sweeping 120-mile-per-hour speedometer braced by oversized fuel (left) and temperature (right) gauges, the five-dial GT instrumentation put a racy, round 140-mile-per-hour speedo directly in front of the driver. On each side were a pair of gauges: smaller round readouts for fuel and temperature remained to the far left and right, respectively, while between them and the speedometer were an oil pressure gauge (left) and an ammeter (right).

The pony interior included the same five-dial instrument panel with one difference—it was adorned with a simulated walnut appliqué. The GT five-dial panel was done in camera-case black. Both were trimmed out in chrome Mylar highlights.

1965 GT

Model Availability	Two-door coupe, two-door fastback, two-door convertible
Wheelbase	108 inches
Length	181.6 inches
Width	68.2 inches
Height	51.1 inches
Price (options)	GT Equipment Group, $165.03; 289-4V V-8, $52.92; High Performance 289 V-8, $327.92
Track	56 inches, front and rear
Wheels	14x5 stamped-steel
Tires	6.95x14 dual red band, standard
Suspension	Short/long control arms with heavy-duty coil springs and thicker front stabilizer bar in front; stiffer longitudinal leaf springs and solid axle in back
Steering	Recirculating ball with quicker 22:1 ratio
Brakes	Front discs, rear drums
Engine	225-horsepower 289-ci Windsor small-block V-8
Bore and Stroke	4.00x2.87 inches
Compression	10:1
Fuel Delivery	Single Autolite four-barrel carburetor
Transmission	Four-speed manual
Axle Ratio	3.00:1, standard; 3.89:1 and 4.11:1, optional
Production	15,106, total for all three body styles

Production rolled over in August 1964 after 121,538 1964½ models were built, but few noticed as the 1965 Mustang (shown here) featured few obvious changes. *Mike Mueller*

Above: The absence of any engine identification badge behind the headlight means this 1965 2+2 fastback is equipped with base six-cylinder power. *Mike Mueller*

Left: A larger 200-ci six-cylinder took over beneath base Mustang hoods when 1964-½ production rolled over into 1965. Output was 120 horsepower. *Mike Mueller*

Above: A snazzy wire wheel cover was a $44.83 option for the Mustang's 14-inch rim in 1964 and 1965. *Mike Mueller*

Right: The louvers in the 2+2 body's C-pillars were functional, and the rear seat folded down for storage. *Mike Mueller*

Below: With the rear seat down, the interior compartment back panel also could've been lowered to open up extra cargo-carrying capacity. *Mike Mueller*

Below right: A dapper shopper demonstrates the 1965 fastback's practical side.

Nearly all GT appearance features (save for the actual GT emblems) appeared as over-the-counter dealer options not long after the GT Equipment Group option was introduced. "Make your Mustang into a GT!" announced full-page 1965 magazine ads. "Your Ford dealer has the goods."

GT production that first year was 15,106. Another 25,517 and 24,078 followed in 1966 and 1967, respectively. Production fell to 17,458 in 1968, then down to 5,396 for the final GT in 1969.

1965 A/FX Drag Car

Henry Ford II loved racing, or at least he did during the early 1960s, when horsepower still translated into sales success. Henry II's desire to dominate the racing world led to many millions of dollars being invested both in an Indy 500 engine project that resulted in a win at the Brickyard in 1965 and a GT program that finally garnered Le Mans laurels in 1966.

More familiar full-sized Galaxies had dominated NASCAR events in 1963 and were no slouches in drag racing circles. To power these brutes, Ford engineers created a series of race-only 427 big-block V-8s, beginning with the "high-riser" rendition. This bruiser was joined by the exotic single-overhead-cam (SOHC) 427, the so-called "Cammer," in 1964. Banned from NASCAR that year, the Cammer soon became a major force in drag racing circles.

New on the 1965 drag circuit was the Factory Experimental (FX) class, a catch-all category created to keep up with the growing number of so-called factory super stocks then coming

1965 A/FX Factory Drag Car

Wheelbase	102 inches	**Bore and Stroke**	4.23x3.78 inches
Weight	3,200 pounds, estimated	**Compression**	12.0:1
Engine	427-ci SOHC V-8	**Fuel Delivery**	Dual four-barrel carburetors
Horsepower	616 at 7,000 rpm	**Transmission**	Four-speed manual
Torque	515 lb-ft at 3,800 rpm	**Production**	15

Above: Built by Holman-Moody in Charlotte, North Carolina, this special Mustang was created in 1965 for NHRA drag racing's new Factory Experimental (FX) class. Beneath that bubbled hood is a 427-ci SOHC V-8. *Mike Mueller*

Left: A floor shifter was standard (with either manual or automatic transmissions) from the start, though a console wasn't. A full-length console cost $50.41 in 1964 and 1965. *Mike Mueller*

The GT Equipment Group was introduced in April 1965, just in time to mark the Mustang's first birthday. Front disc brakes and the Special Handling Package were included in the GT deal, which was available for all three body styles in 1965. *Mike Mueller*

out of Detroit. Solid axles up front, acid-dipped superlightweight body shells, and altered wheelbases (for improved weight transfer during launches) were the norm in FX competition, and Chrysler was especially active early on when it came to such tricks.

Ford, of course, retaliated in 1965 with a run of Factory Experimental altered-wheelbase pony cars. After a prototype A/FX Mustang was built in Dearborn, the job was passed on to the legendary race shop run by John Holman and Ralph Moody in Charlotte, North Carolina.

Holman-Moody (H-M) built 15 A/FX Mustangs in 1965, starting with fastback models shipped to Charlotte without powertrains, hoods, fenders, or doors. The only glass installed was the sloping rear window. H-M men stripped the chassis of all stock suspension components, and specially fabricated jigs were then used to make the transformation a snap.

Among the most radical modifications were reworked rear wheelwells, quarter panels, and nearby floorboard—all redone to allow the rear axle to slide forward 3 inches. Additional body mods included the addition of Plexiglas windows and fiberglass fenders, hood, and doors, which helped cut weight down to about 3,200 pounds.

Suspension tweaks were equally extensive. A special crossmember was added in back to serve as a mounting point for traction bars that were welded onto the axle housing at their trailing ends. Extensions of these arms ran backward behind the axle to a point near the leaf spring shackles. There, these extensions served as mounting points for an extra set of shock absorbers. In front of the axle, mounting braces for the traction bars were drilled for five different locating points. Bolting the traction bars into the uppermost holes resulted in a no-load setting. Each hole down preloaded the rear suspension to a higher degree. This allowed the cars to be set up for the individual traction conditions of each track.

Suspension mods up front were even more radical. Shock towers were air-chiseled out (basically to make room for the 427 big-block to be installed), steel plates were welded into the upper third of each opening, and brackets were then welded onto these plates to supply mounting points for shortened upper A-arms. In place of the deleted stock coil springs went a pair of two-leaf flat springs that worked like torsion bars.

American mags went on at the corners, with the rear rims wearing 10-inch M+H slicks. Melting that M+H rubber in some cases was a 427 SOHC fed by twin four-barrels. Only seven A/FX Mustangs were initially fitted with the overhead-cam 427, as they were in short supply early in 1965. The other eight received high-risers, although most

Above left: Another sporty option in 1965 was the Rally-Pac, which mounted atop the steering column. A 24-hour clock was on the right, a tachometer on the left. The price for this instrumentation was $69.30. *Mike Mueller*

Above: Underdash air conditioning was optional from 1964 to 1966 and required a shorter console. Dashboard-integrated air conditioning didn't appear until 1967. *Mike Mueller*

Left: The optional Interior Decor Group was introduced in March 1965. Among its classy features were specially embossed seat inserts, which gave this coveted package the name "Pony Interior." *Mike Mueller*

Left: In 1965, famed Ford racer Gaspar "Gas" Ronda set an NHRA A/FX record in his SOHC Mustang, running the quarter-mile in 10.43 seconds.

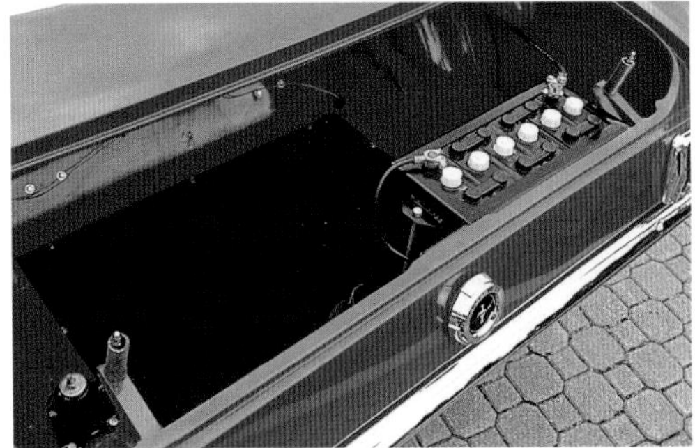

Top: Plans to put the high-winding 427 SOHC into limited production (only to make it legal for NASCAR stock car racing) never left the drawing board. *Mike Mueller*

Above: The battery was moved to the trunk in the A/FX Mustang's case to help put more weight on the rear wheels for better traction off the line. *Mike Mueller*

1966

Model Availability	Two-door coupe, two-door fastback, two-door convertible
Wheelbase	108 inches
Length	181.6 inches
Width	68.2 inches
Height	51.1 inches, coupe; 51.0 inches, convertible; 51.2 inches, 2+2 fastback
Curb Weight	2,488 pounds, six-cylinder coupe; 2,519 pounds, six-cylinder fastback; 2,650 pounds, six-cylinder convertible
Base Price	$2,416.18, six-cylinder coupe; $2,652.86, six-cylinder convertible; $2,607.07, six-cylinder 2+2 fastback; 200-horsepower V-8 added $105.63 to six-cylinder sticker; 225-horsepower V-8 added $52.85 to 200-horsepower V-8 model; High Performance 289 V-8, $276.34 with GT Equipment Group ($327.92 w/o GT package)
Track (front/rear, in inches)	55.4/56, six-cylinder; 56/56, V-8
Wheels	14x4.5 four-lug, standard w/six-cylinder; 14x5 five-lug, standard w/V-8
Tires	6.95x14 rayon, standard w/six and V-8; 6.95x14 nylon, optional; 6.95x14 premium nylon standard w/High Performance 289
Suspension	Independent upper A-arms, lower control arms w/coil springs in front; live axle with leaf springs in back
Steering	Recirculating ball
Brakes	Four-wheel hydraulic drums
Engine	120-horsepower 200-ci six-cylinder; 200-horsepower 289-ci 2V V-8;
	225-horsepower 289-ci 4V V-8; 271-horsepower High Performance 289 V-8
Bore and Stroke	3.68x3.13 inches (200 six), 4.00x2.87 inches (289 V-8)
Compression	9.2:1 (200 six), 9.3:1 (289-2V V-8), 9.8:1 (289-4V V-8), 10:1 (High Performance 289 V-8)
Fuel Delivery	Autolite one-barrel carburetor (200 six), Autolite two-barrel (289-2V V-8), Autolite four-barrel (289-4V V-8), 600-cfm Autolite four-barrel (High Performance 289 V-8)
Transmission	Three-speed manual, standard; four-speed manual, optional; Cruise-O-Matic automatic, optional
Axle Ratio	3.20:1, standard w/six-cylinder manual; 2.83:1, standard w/six-cylinder automatic; 2.80:1, standard w/289-2V V-8; 3.00:1, standard w/289-4V V-8; 3.50:1, standard w/High Performance V-8; 3.89:1, optional w/High Performance V-8
Production	607,568, all body styles (25,517 GT models)

were later refitted with Cammers once the engines became available.

Gaspar "Gas" Ronda set a National Hot Rod Association (NHRA) A/FX record in his altered Mustang in 1965, turning in a 10.43-second quarter-mile/134.73-mile-per-hour time slip. NHRA officials in 1966 modified their rules concerning altered-wheelbase cars, and most of the A/FX Mustangs were returned to Holman-Moody to have their rear suspensions relocated to the stock position.

1966

The Mustang broke another sales record previously held by the Falcon—on Wednesday, February 23, 1966, the one-millionth example built rolled off the assembly line, making Ford's pony car the fastest ever to reach seven digits. On March 2, the millionth model, a white 1966 convertible, posed along with various personalities at the end of the Dearborn line for a publicity photo. In the shot were Lee Iacocca, Donald Frey, Gene Bordinat, and an airline pilot from Newfoundland named Stanley Tucker.

Who was Captain Tucker? He was the lucky fellow who somehow managed to buy "Job One," the very first pony car built in March 1964. Two weeks before the Mustang's official introduction in April 1964, Tucker drove by his hometown Ford dealership in St. Johns and noticed a Wimbledon White Mustang convertible on display. This car had been touring Canada on special loan from Ford to promote sales north of the border. Dearborn officials intended to show it off in Canada and bring it back home for safekeeping. Forever. But such plans went awry when the dealer—unaware that the white convertible wore serial number 100001—sold it to Tucker. Attempts to buy Job One back from him were initially unsuccessful.

Two years and 10,000 miles later, Ford people tried again, this time with a trade: the number 1,000,001 Mustang, built to Tucker's specifications, in exchange for Job One. He agreed and went home with a fully loaded Silver Frost 1966 convertible, and he also joined the Ford elite for the one-millionth celebration. He was invited to tour the country with Job One but declined.

As for the millionth Mustang, it slipped into the dealer network and obscurity. Tucker's '66 convertible also rolled on into history. At least serial number 100001 remains proudly preserved today in the Henry Ford Museum in Dearborn.

All 1966 Mustangs received minimal updates. Eagle-eyed witnesses might've noticed a revised grille made up of small rectangular openings with long chromed horizontal lines, as opposed to the solid-gray honeycomb layout used in 1965. The revered "running horse" centerpiece also became fully floating in 1966, as the chrome crossbar from the previous year's grille was deleted.

Additional brightwork adjustments included making hood lip trim and rocker moldings standard for base models. In 1965, only GTs wore the former and fastbacks the latter. The fake rear quarter air

The most notable change for 1966 was a revised grille. Convertible production for 1966 was 72,119. *Mike Mueller*

As in 1965, all of the GT's appearance treatments were again available for non-GT models in 1966—witness the valance-exiting dual exhausts on this 2+2 fastback. *Mike Mueller*

GT production hit a high of 25,517 units in 1966. *Mike Mueller*

scoops tacked onto base coupes and convertibles in 1965 (GTs, fastbacks, and cars with the optional bodyside accent stripes didn't have these) were revised with a blacked-out opening and three horizontal strips to help enhance the simulation for 1966. Designers apparently felt the two simple trim pieces found on each flank of a 1965 Mustang didn't look enough like rear brake cooling vents. Rear brakes, however, never knew the difference.

Completing the exterior makeover were typically redesigned wheel covers, a restyled gas cap in back, and new standard backup lights. Inside, the 1965 Mustang's simple, Falcon-based instrument panel was replaced with the sportier five-dial layout offered the previous year as part of the GT Equipment and Interior Decor groups.

Making the five-dial dash (with slightly revised trim) standard in 1966 helped lower the price for the second-edition GT package, down from $165 to $152. Included for this price was a new GT gas cap. Not included were the bright rocker moldings that became standard 1966 features on other Mustangs. All remaining GT features carried over from 1966.

Most options carried over too, including the sexy Rally-Pac, originally introduced one month after the Mustang debuted. When ordered along with the Hi-Po 289, the Rally-Pac's standard 6,000-rpm tach was traded for an 8,000-rev unit. Another variation involved the unit's marriage to the five-dial dashboard in April 1965, because the original setup would've partially obstructed the driver's view of the 140-mile-per-hour speedo, as well as the oil pressure gauge and ammeter. A revised, low-profile Rally-Pac was then introduced for the GT cockpit and its pony interior counterpart. These were black crinkle, although some were painted to match the color of the steering column. Both original and low-profile Rally-Pacs were sold in 1965 depending on instrument panel installation. The latter type took over completely in 1966, when the five-dial dash became standard.

Of further note was the optional automatic transmission finally made available behind the Hi-Po 289 in 1966. And at the other end of the scale was the new Sprint 200 model, an affordable, budget-conscious six-cylinder Mustang with just a touch of quasi-elegant adornment.

Above: **The 1,000,001st Mustang built went to airline pilot Stanley Tucker of St. Johns, Newfoundland. Tucker bought the very first Mustang off the Dearborn line in 1964, and traded that historic machine for the millionth+1 model two years later.**

Above left: **The one-millionth Mustang left the Dearborn line on February 23, 1966. Here, Lee Iacocca opens the car's passenger door as Donald Frey takes a seat during a photo opportunity staged a week later on March 2.**

Above right: **A groovy 8-track player became a Mustang option in 1966. It cost $128.29.**

02

Wild Horses

02

SHELBY MUSTANGS

- Carroll Shelby is born January 11, 1923, in Leesburg, Texas.
- Shelby enters his first sports car race, driving a borrowed MG TC, and wins in 1952.
- *Sports Illustrated* names Carroll Shelby its Sports Car Driver of the Year in 1956.
- In 1959, driving for Aston Martin, Shelby becomes the second American (Phil Hill was the first) to win the 24 Hours of Le Mans.
- Shelby cops a United States Auto Club (USAC) roadracing championship in 1960; long-running heart problems force his retirement from racing that October.
- The first Shelby Cobra is built in February 1962 in Dean Moon's speed shop in Santa Fe Springs, California.
- Shelby American opens for business in Venice, California, in June 1962 in the former home of Lance Reventlow's Scarab racer.
- The big-block GT500 joins its small-block GT350 brother in 1967.
- Shelby Mustang production transfers from L.A. to Detroit in 1968.
- Shelby undergoes heart bypass operations in 1973 and 1978.
- Shelby passes away May 10, 2012.

Ford's wildly popular pony didn't exactly thrill everyone in 1964. Some witnesses who had hoped for a true sporting machine, a rival, perhaps, to Chevrolet's Corvette, felt jilted. Fortunately, their complaints didn't fall on deaf ears.

TAKING AIM AT AMERICA'S SPORTS CAR was as simple as putting the Mustang into the talented hands of Carroll Shelby, a snake-oil salesman if there ever was one. Since 1962, Shelby had been stuffing Ford V-8s into those teenie-weenie England-sourced AC Ace two-seaters, relying first on the 260-cube small-block, then its bigger 289 brother, and finally the ferocious 427-ci FE-series big-block. Shelby's venomous 427 S/C Cobras didn't just kick Corvettes' 'glass asses, they made 'em like it.

His Cobras struck as quickly as his Shelby American firm rose from the shadows into the international racing limelight. As *Car Life* explained in a May 1965 report, "Fast-moving Carroll Shelby does things at such a pace, by the time the news is in print, it's ancient history. And the news recently has been important enough to make him America's fifth largest auto producer. The Texan's successful midwifery to all sorts of Ford-powered performers since his original Cobra has resulted in elevation to almost division-within-a-division status at Ford, a sort of Bureau of Racing for Dearborn. [His] projects have multiplied to such an extent, [the] three-year-old Shelby American firm has had to move into the big hangars at Los Angeles International airport."

There, Shelby not only built his super snakes, he also took Ford's GT-40 race car in to raise up right after early racing results with this expensive, British-built beast left Henry Ford II disgusted. Dearborn officials in 1965 decided to "consolidate the construction and racing of all our GT-type vehicles within the same specialist organization," meaning Shelby's West Coast firm would add another Ford racer to its team, a move that soon had Henry II delighted. A year later, Ford's 427-powered GT racer became the first American entrant to win Le Mans, putting Enzo Ferrari in his place in the process.

Above: A chin spoiler was added to 1970 rollover models to help set them apart from their identical 1969 predecessors. *Mike Mueller*

Left: By 1966, Shelby American's Ford-powered lineup included some of the world's wildest machines, both for road and track. From left to right: 427 Cobra, GT-40, Daytona coupe, and Shelby GT350 Mustang.

Opposite: A definitely distinctive fiberglass nose added 3 more inches to the 1967 Shelby Mustang's overall length, and sequential taillights (borrowed from Mercury's Cougar) and a ducktail spoiler were added in back. *Mike Mueller*

Previous pages:
Left: Slightly revised tape striping appeared in 1966. White cars got blue stripes, while all other exterior finishes were complemented with white tape. *Mike Mueller*

Right: Output for the 1967 Super Snake reportedly was 520 horsepower. Modifications included Ford's 7,000-rpm competition kit and a big 780-cfm Holley four-barrel carburetor. *Mike Mueller*

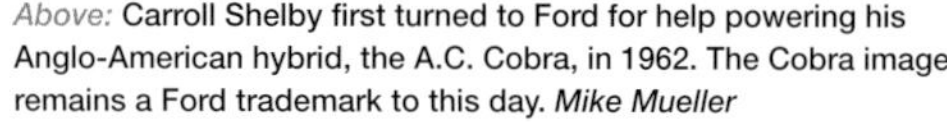
Above: Carroll Shelby first turned to Ford for help powering his Anglo-American hybrid, the A.C. Cobra, in 1962. The Cobra image remains a Ford trademark to this day. *Mike Mueller*

Above right: The heart of the original GT350 was a massaged High Performance 289 V-8 that produced 306 horsepower. *Mike Mueller*

Below: Helping boost the Hi-Po 289's output in Shelby applications was a 715-cfm Holley four-barrel carburetor. *Mike Mueller*

And as if Shelby didn't have enough on his plate in 1965, he also found himself in the Mustang business that year. Late in 1964, Lee Iacocca gave him yet another assignment: transform his newborn pony car into a real race horse, a hot-to-trot machine able, like the Corvette, to compete in SCCA racing. Shelby obliged even though, as he later admitted, he "wasn't real high on the project," basically because he preferred building true race cars to street-legal hot rods.

"That was the real idea—to go racing," said Shelby in a 1971 *Sports Cars of the World* interview. "I never wanted to build a lot of automobiles to make a lot of money. At the time my intention was to build 100 [Mustangs] a year, because that was what you had to build in order to race." But Iacocca wanted more than that, and what he wanted he usually got. Along with that, Iacocca was Shelby's best friend in Dearborn: turning him down was out of the question. "It was Lee Iacocca who really stayed behind us all the way, encouraged us and then he got us into the Mustang program," he added.

It was this new business that forced Shelby American to trade its original humble shop in Venice, California, for those roomier digs adjacent to LAX in March 1965. Introduced earlier that year, the first of Shelby's GT350 Mustangs was much more at home on a road course than on Main Street, U.S.A., explaining why it remains his favorite to this day. In his words, the 1965 GT350 was "a no-compromise car built to get the job done." From Ford's perspective, however, it was too mean a machine; its appeal was far too limited. Word immediately came west to civilize the GT350 for 1966, leaving Shelby himself a little disgusted.

"Big corporations tend to destroy the cars they create," he told *Mustang Monthly* in 1990. "All of the corporate vultures jumped on the thing and that's when it started going to hell," he explained earlier in 1971. "I was committed because Lee wanted me to build the GTs, which I helped out with, but it just went from bad to worse politically. I'm not knocking Ford, because when you get into bed with a big company they're all the same. I started trying to get out of the deal in 1967 and it took me until 1970 to get production shut down. I asked Lee all the time, you know, 'Let's knock this off.'"

Shelby's comments concerning his days playing with Ford's pony car have since softened, undoubtedly due to how high his Mustang variants have since been put up on pedestals by the true Blue Oval faithful. The big man behind those machines now resides on an even higher perch, so why would he want to take potshots at the cars his devoted fans love so dearly? All that aside, every Shelby Mustang built from 1965 to 1970 still impresses with its sensuality and strength. Who cares that they did grow progressively weaker over the years as far as sheer brute force was concerned? They still were among the coolest cruisers sold during their heyday, and 40 years later they remain highly valued collectibles.

Shelby's original plan back in 1965 involved building street-going GT350 Mustangs to legalize full-race alter egos for Sports Car Club of America (SCCA) B/Production competition, which specified the aforementioned minimum run of 100 cars. No problem. Ford supplied the bare-bones 2+2s from its San Jose plant, and Shelby American took care of the rest. GT350 production began in October 1964, with the official public unveiling coming January 27, 1965, to the overwhelming joy of those left disappointed the previous April.

"The GT350 is all that most of us wanted the original Mustang to be in the first place," exclaimed *Car Life* magazine's Jim Wright.

1965 GT350

"Fresh from considerable successes gained mating English chassis [and] hopped-up American V-8s, Carroll Shelby has decided to turn his talents in the field of hybrid husbandry loose on a product nearer and dearer to home: Ford's highly successful (in sales) but slightly disappointing (to the purist) Mustang," said Wright in *Car Life*'s April 1965 edition.

According to *Motor Trend*, what Shelby did was "take a 2+2, inject some Cobra venom, tone up the leg muscles [and] add lightness." Add lightness? Was the tall Texan a magician, too? Not exactly. He simply shaved off nearly 200 pounds by, among other things, deleting the back seat (a requirement anyway considering the SCCA B/Production class was for two-seaters) and exchanging Ford's standard steel hood for a scooped fiberglass unit.

"Venom" came from a Hi-Po 289 hopped up with a few Cobra-type additions: a 715-cfm Holley four-barrel on an aluminum intake, Tri-Y headers, and glass-pack bullet mufflers that bellowed through short, race-car-style cutout pipes exiting directly in front of each rear wheel. According to Shelby American dyno tests, these modifications translated into 306 horsepower.

1965 GT350

Model Availability	Two-door fastback
Wheelbase	108 inches
Length	181.6 inches
Width	68.2 inches
Height	51.2 inches
Curb weight	2,800 pounds
Base price	$4,311
Track	57 inches, front and rear
Wheels	15x5.5 Ford station wagon rims (15x6 Cragar five-spoke wheels, optional)
Tires	7.75x15 Goodyear Blue Dot
Suspension	Independent upper A-arms, lower control arms, w/coil springs in front; live axle with leaf springs in back
Steering	Recirculating ball (19:1 ratio)
Brakes	Front discs, rear drums
Engine	306-horsepower 289-ci High Performance 289 V-8
Bore and Stroke	4.00x2.87 inches
Compression	10.5:1
Fuel Delivery	715-cfm Holley four-barrel carburetor
Transmission	Borg-Warner T-10 close-ratio four-speed manual
Axle Ratio	3.89:1
Production	561, all painted white

Below left: Free-flowing Tri-Y headers brought up the exhaust end on the GT 350 V-8. *Mike Mueller*

Below right: Shelby V-8s also were fitted with a deep-sump oil pan. *Mike Mueller*

Right: Shelby American opened for business in 1962 in Venice, California. By 1965, the bustling firm had moved into bigger digs at Los Angeles International Airport, seen here behind this 1965 GT350 Mustang.

Below: Shelby's plan from the get-go was to build competition cars, and his first GT350 was more or less that: right out of the box, it was ready to race. GT350 production for 1965 was 561. All were painted white.

Toning "leg muscles" involved adding a 1-inch sway bar up front, override traction bars and suspension-travel-limiting cables in back, and Koni adjustable shocks at all four corners. Further handling enhancements included lowering the upper A-arms' mounting points by an inch, which then required special pitman and idler arms. A one-piece export brace was used in place of the stock Mustang's two-piece arrangement to tie the shock towers rigidly together for more precise suspension geometry. And a Monte Carlo bar tightened things up even more by spanning the gap between shock towers across the engine, thus triangulating underhood bracing.

All the cars delivered from San Jose to Shelby American showed up with full-sized Ford front disc brakes and Fairlane station wagon rear drums. All also featured aluminum-case Borg-Warner T-10 close-ratio four-speeds and big, burly 9-inch rear ends with Detroit Locker differentials. Remaining modifications were made at the LAX works, including the addition of blue "GT350" rocker panel stripes.

All 1965 GT350 Mustangs began life on the San Jose line wearing Wimbledon White paint on the outside with black appointments inside. Standard wheels were 15x5.5 station wagon rims shod in 7.75x15 Goodyear Blue Dot rubber. Attractive 15x6 five-spoke wheels, supplied by Cragar, were available at extra cost, as were Guardsman Blue Le Mans racing stripes that ran from nose to tail. Counting the first prototype, Shelby American built 561 GT350s in 1965.

1965 GT350R

The production tally for the 1965 GT350 was quoted as 562 for years, before research in 1994 determined that one of those cars was never built. This mystery machine originally was planned as part of a special run of R models, with the "R" predictably standing for racing. Two types of race-ready Shelby Mustangs were built that first year: road racers and drag cars. Nine of the latter rolled out of the Shelby hangar in 1965, followed by four more in 1966. Production of the roadracing GT350R in 1965 was 36, counting one prototype. R models were delivered from San Jose completely stripped: no headliners, carpeting, upholstery, sound deadener, or insulation. No side glass or rear windows, and no gas tank.

"The GT350 is all that most of us wanted the original Mustang to be in the first place," exclaimed *Car Life* magazine's Jim Wright.

As if the standard GT350 Mustangs weren't hot enough in 1965, Shelby also built 36 (counting one prototype) GT350R models that year. No compromises for daily use were included in this batch of mean Mustangs. Nonessential items like bumpers were removed in the R model's case. A special fiberglass apron filled the front bumper's space. Rear-quarter roof vents were covered with aluminum panels. *Mike Mueller*

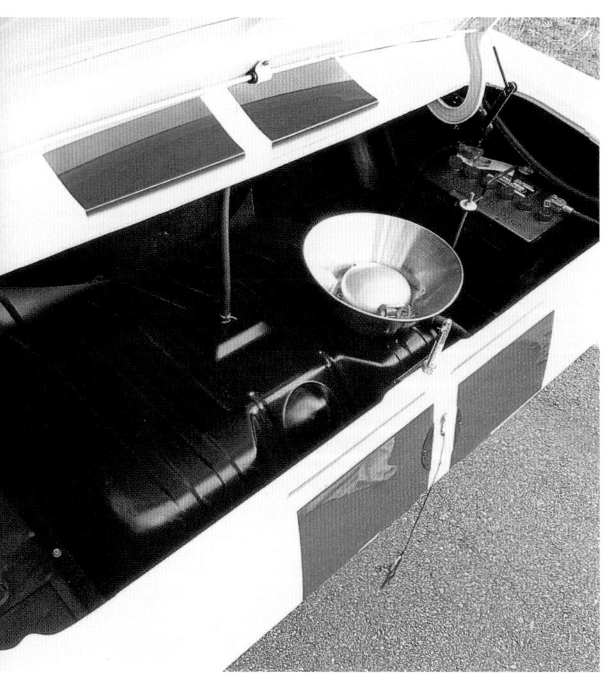

Above: A quick-fill 34-gallon fuel tank went into the R model's trunk, as did the battery and an electric fuel pump. *Mike Mueller*

Below: Nonessentials also disappeared inside the GT350R. Carpeting, stock seats and instrumentation, insulation, and the headliner were all deleted. A single bucket seat and four-point roll cage were added. *Mike Mueller*

1965 GT350R

Model Availability	Two-door fastback
Wheelbase	108 inches
Length	181.6 inches
Height	55 inches
Curb Weight	2,550 pounds
Base Price	$5,995
Track	57 inches, front and rear
Wheels	15x7 five-spoke American Racing rims
Tires	7.75x15 Goodyear Blue Dot
Suspension	Independent upper A-arms, lower control arms, w/coil springs in front; live axle with leaf springs in back
Steering	Recirculating ball
Brakes	Front discs, rear drums
Engine	Modified 289-ci High Performance 289 V-8 (output estimated between 325 and 360 horsepower)
Bore and Stroke	4.00x2.87 inches
Compression	10.5:1
Fuel Delivery	Single 715-cfm Holley four-barrel carburetor
Transmission	Borg-Warner T-10 four-speed manual
Axle Ratio	3.89:1
Production	36 (counting 1 prototype)

Above: The R model's weight-saving Plexiglas window shaved off some 20 pounds in back. *Mike Mueller*

Left: GT350R front brakes featured 11.3-inch rotors. Heavy-duty drums worked in back. *Mike Mueller*

Far left: Balanced and blueprinted, the specially prepared R-model V-8 was fitted with ported and polished cylinder heads, which helped this small-block produce up to 360 horsepower. *Mike Mueller*

On the track, the GT350R quickly proved its worth, with Shelby American driver Ken Miles piloting one to victory in its first SCCA outing in Texas on Valentine's Day, 1965.

A single bucket seat, four-point roll cage, sheet-aluminum inner door panels, and a fiberglass shelf in place of the back seat were installed at Shelby American. The stock Mustang dash pad was tossed aside, and a six-gauge instrument panel replaced original instrumentation. Plexiglas side windows in aluminum frames (without cranking mechanisms) went into the doors, helping cut some 25 pounds. Another 20 pounds were deleted by adding more Plexiglas in back.

Fuel for the GT350R was housed in a special 34-gallon container created by joining two bottom halves from standard 16-gallon Mustang tanks. Internal baffles went inside this tank, while a 3-inch snap-open filler cap went on top. Joining the tank in the trunk were the battery and an electric fuel pump.

Body modifications included covering the rear quarter roof vents and fuel filler in back with aluminum panels. Wheel openings were also re-radiused and flared to allow clearance for a set of wide 15x7 American Racing five-spoke mags wrapped in Goodyear racing rubber. Both bumpers were deleted, with the front replaced by a fiberglass apron incorporating a large center opening to aid airflow to both a large three-core Galaxie-based radiator and an external oil cooler. Two additional slots directed cooling air to the front brakes.

Beneath the hood, the R model's Hi-Po 289 was broken down, with all assemblies balanced, blueprinted, and reassembled to precise specs. Cylinder heads and manifolds were port matched, and the heads were ported and polished by Valley Head Service. Dyno tests produced readings of 325 to 360 horsepower.

On the track, the GT350R quickly proved its worth, with Shelby American driver Ken Miles piloting one to victory in its first SCCA outing in Texas on Valentine's Day, 1965. Shelby Mustangs won the B/Production championship that year, followed by two more SCCA titles in 1966 and 1967.

1966 GT350

A standard GT350 in 1965 was, in *Road & Track*'s words, "pretty much a brute of a car." According to *Hot Rod*, rest to 60 miles per hour required a scant 5.7 seconds. It had proven itself to be a real hot number, but was it too hot? Ford officials thought so; in their minds, cooling things down would surely widen the car's scope, meaning more customers would be willing to take one home. Retaining a racy image while softening some of the rough edges then became the goal.

First, the 1966 GT350 got a back seat so others could come along for the ride. An optional C4 automatic transmission was made available, as were paint choices: joining Wimbledon White in 1966 were blue, red, green, and black. Exterior changes included revised striping and the addition of rear quarter glass and functional, cooling side scoops.

Powertrain parts basically carried over, save for full tailpipes in place of those loud cutouts. Chassis changes, however, were plentiful in the best interests of cutting costs and lessening ride harshness. Lowering the upper A-arms in front was discontinued, and the rear override torque control arms were exchanged for simpler underride traction bars. Those stiff Koni shocks and gnarly Detroit Locker differentials remained but were now options.

Such changes were made in running fashion during the year, with the first 252 '66 GT350s sold as 1965 "leftovers," still fitted with many of the previous year's features. Plain-Jane 15-inch rims remained standard for those 252 cars, as did the Koni shocks before they became a dealer-installed option. Five-spoke Magnum 500 wheels became standard from then on. The Cragar-supplied 15-inch five-spokes remained available for the early leftovers, while new 14-inch aluminum-alloy 10-spoke wheels were optional for later cars.

Additionally, not all 1966 GT350s had back seats. Reportedly, about 82 of the leftovers arrived at Shelby American as two-seaters, and some of these cars apparently were fitted with a rear seat

Above: Various running changes made Shelby's second-edition GT350 a more civilized machine. The back seat was put back in, and an automatic transmission became available. Paint choices expanded to five for 1966: joining Wimbledon White were blue, red, green, and black. *Mike Mueller*

Below: Early 1966 Shelbys were fitted with these 15-inch five-spoke Cragar mag wheels. Later models that year got 14-inch Magnum 500 rims. *Mike Mueller*

1966 GT350

Model Availability	Two-door fastback (four convertibles also built specially by Shelby)
Wheelbase	108 inches
Length	181.6 inches
Width	68.2 inches
Height	51.2 inches
Curb Weight	2,884 pounds
Base Price	$4,428
Track	57 inches, front and rear
Wheels	15x6 stamped-steel rims or 15-inch Cragar five-spokes (14-inch, 10-spoke Shelby wheels optional)
Tires	7.75x 15 (6.95x14 with optional Shelby wheels)
Suspension	Independent upper A-arms, lower control arms, w/coil springs in front; live axle with leaf springs in back
Steering	Recirculating ball (19:1 ratio)
Brakes	Front discs, rear drums
Engine	306-horsepower 289-ci High Performance 289 V-8
Bore and Stroke	4.00x2.87 inches
Compression	10.5:1
Fuel Delivery	Single 715-cfm Holley four-barrel carburetor
Transmission	Borg-Warner T-10 close-ratio four-speed manual, standard; C4 automatic, optional
Axle Ratio	3.89:1
Production	2,378, including GT 350H

as a dealer option. Another 1965 standard touch—the override traction arms with their welded-on brackets—continued in place until their supply ran out, apparently after about 800 '66 GT350s were built. Traction-Master bolt-on traction bars were used from there.

A Paxton supercharger was a new option for 1966 and reportedly boosted output by 46 percent. According to *Motor Trend*, a blown GT350 could smoke the quarter-mile in 14.0 seconds at 102 miles per hour.

A GT350 convertible also appeared in 1966, although all four built were not initially offered to the public, instead either staying with Shelby or going as gifts to valued friends. As the last four GT350s off the line in 1966, each of these topless vehicles was painted a different color. All had underdash air conditioners, and all but one were automatics. They also featured nonfunctional side scoops because the top mechanism ruled out the installation of the internal ductwork.

1966 GT350H

Per Ford's plans, the more socially acceptable second-edition GT350 attracted nearly 2,400 buyers, including the Hertz Rent-A-Car company, which put 1,002 GT350s into its fleet. Late in 1965,

Above: Shelby supplied the Hertz rental car folks with 1,002 GT350H models in 1966, a practice that was repeated in 1969, 2006, and 2007. *Mike Mueller*

Left: New for 1966 were exclusive rear-quarter windows (for added distinctiveness) and functional bodyside scoops. The latter items supplied cooling air to the rear brakes. *Mike Mueller*

Below: Special hubs graced the GT350H's rims. While most Hertz models rolled on Magnum 500 wheels, some were fitted with Cragar mags. *Mike Mueller*

Right: A C4 automatic transmission was installed in most Hertz Shelbys in 1966, and these cars also featured a 595-cfm Autolite carburetor. The few manual-transmission GT350H models used the preferred Holley four-barrel. *Mike Mueller*

Opposite: New for 1967 was the big-block GT500, powered by Ford's 428-ci FE-series V-8. Fog lamp location on both GT350 and GT500 Shelby Mustangs in 1967 varied: some were close together in the center; others were mounted at opposite ends of the grille. *Mike Mueller*

1966 GT350H

Model Availability	Two-door fastback
Wheelbase	108 inches
Length	181.6 inches
Width	68.2 inches
Height	51.2 inches
Curb Weight	2,884 pounds
Rental Price	$17 per day or $70 per week, plus 17 cents per mile
Track	57 inches, front and rear
Wheels	Magnum 500 five-spokes or Cragar mags
Tires	Goodyear Blue Streaks
Suspension	Independent upper A-arms, lower control arms, w/coil springs in front; live axle with leaf springs in back
Steering	Recirculating ball
Brakes	Front disc, rear drums
Engine	306-horsepower 289-ci High Performance 289 V-8
Bore and Stroke	4.00x2.87 inches
Compression	10.5:1
Fuel Delivery	595-cfm Autolite four-barrel carburetor
Transmission	C4 automatic
Axle Ratio	3.98:1
Production	1,002, including 2 prototypes

Shelby American General Manager Peyton Cramer presented the idea to Hertz officials, who requested delivery of a prototype on October 26. A Wimbledon White GT350 was repainted black with gold striping and an appropriate "H" was added to the striping. A second prototype was requested in November, followed by an order for 100 GT350H Mustangs.

As much as 80 percent of the total run featured the gold-on-black treatment, but as many as 200 models came in typical Mustang colors. A few also were built using steel hoods in place of Shelby's fiberglass lids, and some wore Cragar mags instead of the more familiar Magnum 500 wheels. Most used C4 automatic transmissions and, like all 1966 GT350s with auto boxes, were fitted with a 595-cfm Autolite four-barrel carburetor. Four-speed GT350H models stuck with the 715-cfm Holley four-barrel.

Hertz's rates for the GT350H were $17 a day or $70 a week, plus 17 cents a mile in the New York area. According to Carroll Shelby, many GT350H rentals were wrecked that first winter in New York and others were returned to Hertz offices with mundane 289 V-8s installed in place of the hotter Hi-Po small-blocks. After all was said and done, Shelby bought the entire Hertz Shelby run back at a "reduced price."

1967 GT350 and GT500

Big news for 1967 involved the introduction of the GT500 with its 355-horsepower 428 big-block topped by twin Holley four-barrel carburetors. Both versions—GT350 and GT500—were treated to various distinctive body modifications. Included was an extended fiberglass nose piece that stretched overall length by 3 inches compared to a garden-variety 1967 Mustang. Recessed deep in this nose was a grille sporting twin driving lights that were mounted in differing positions, together in the middle or at opposite ends of the grille, depending on the state in which the car was originally delivered. Statutes in some states required minimum distances between headlights, explaining the variation.

G.T.500
EAGLE GT
GOODYEAR

Above: A wood-rimmed steering wheel, 140-mile-per-hour speedometer, and 8,000-rpm tachometer were standard inside the 1967 Shelby Mustang, as was a special underdash housing containing amp and oil pressure gauges. *Mike Mueller*

Below: GT500 production for 1967 was 2,048. Another 1,175 GT350s also were built by Shelby that year. *Mike Mueller*

1967 GT350 & GT500

Model Availability	Two-door fastback
Wheelbase	108 inches
Length	186.6 inches
Width	70.9 inches
Height	51.6 inches
Curb Weight	2,723 pounds, GT350; 3,286 pounds, GT500
Base Price	$4,195, GT350; $4,395, GT500
Track	58 inches, front and rear
Wheels	15x6.5 Shelby rims
Tires	E70x15
Suspension	Independent upper A-arms, lower control arms, w/coil springs in front; live axle with leaf springs in back
Steering	Recirculating ball (16:1 ratio)
Brakes	Front discs, rear drums
Engine	306-horsepower 289-ci High Performance V-8 (GT350), 355-horsepower 428-ci V-8 (GT500)
Bore and Stroke	4.00x2.87 inches (GT350), 4.13x3.98 inches (GT500)
Compression	10.5:1 (GT350), 10.5:1 (GT500)
Fuel Delivery	Single 715-cfm Holley four-barrel carburetor (GT350), two 600-cfm Holley four-barrel carburetors (GT500)
Transmission	Four-speed manual, standard; heavy-duty Cruise-O-Matic automatic, optional
Axle Ratio	3.89:1, standard for GT350 manual trans; 3.50:1, standard for GT350 automatic and GT500 manual; 3.25:1, standard for GT500 automatic
Production	1,175 GT350s; 2,048 GT500s

A fiberglass valance below the grille incorporated a large cutout that supplied more cooling air to the radiator. Above the grille, a fiberglass hood, stretched to meet the extended nose, incorporated a large, wide scoop with dual inlets. Functional louvers were added on each side of the hood scoop when optional air conditioning was ordered. Also functional were the new rear quarter side scoops, which came in two pairs: lower scoops for brake cooling, upper for extracting interior air.

Mercury Cougar sequential taillights and a fiberglass deck lid incorporating a large ducktail spoiler were added in back. Fiberglass quarter-panel extensions formed the spoiler's end caps, while a pop-open gas cap and a valance with cutouts for chrome exhaust tips completed the look.

The 1967 Shelby suspension was the standard Mustang's heavy-duty package, consisting of a thicker front stabilizer bar, adjustable Gabriel shock absorbers, and variable-rate front coil springs. Though the export brace again tied the shock towers together, the Monte Carlo bar no longer triangulated things beneath the hood. Standard rims were 15-inchers adorned by mag-style full wheel covers borrowed from the Thunderbird parts bin. Early options included 15x7 Kelsey-Hayes MagStar wheels, replaced later in the run by cast-aluminum 10-spoke wheels.

Big-block GT500s outsold their small-block GT350 running mates in 1967 on the way to a new Shelby Mustang production high. Two GT500 prototypes, one a notchback coupe, the other a ragtop, also were toyed with this year. These were the last California-built Shelbys, as production was transplanted from Los Angeles to the A. O. Smith works in Livonia, Michigan. Shelby's lease at the airport was up, and Dearborn officials needed no other excuse to bring the GT350/500 "home." Carroll Shelby was fed up with the deal by 1967, anyway.

1967 Super Snake

Before the Shelby Mustang moved east, Shelby American built one last great racehorse, the "Super Snake," an experimental GT500 powered by the king of Ford's FE-series big-block lineup: the fabled 427. The same V-8 had brought Dearborn much success during the mid-1960s on NASCAR tracks and at Le Mans. The reasoning behind this beast was simple enough: if the 428 FE fit between GT500 flanks, so too would the legendary, much more potent 427. Or so thought Don McCain.

Before the Shelby Mustang moved east, Shelby American built one last great racehorse, the "Super Snake."

McCain, Shelby American West Coast sales representative, was at the time also in charge of promoting performance-car sales at Mel Burns Ford in Long Beach, California. No stranger to making Mustangs go fast, he had been the man responsible for Shelby's GT350 drag car program, which eventually produced 13 race-ready rockets. The proposition was plain and simple: for $5,041, McCain would've put any weekend warrior behind the wheel of a factory-prepped quarter-mile killer. Fitted with various heavy-duty hardware and a

Distinctively different striping set the lone Super Snake Shelby apart from its 1967 GT500 brethren. *Mike Mueller*

1967 "Super Snake" GT500

Model Availability	Two-door fastback
Wheelbase	108 inches
Length	186.6 inches
Width	70.9 inches
Height	51.6 inches
Curb Weight	3,480 pounds
Base Price	$7,500
Track	58 inches, front and rear
Wheels	15x6.5 Shelby rims, originally installed
Tires	E70x15 Goodyear Speedway 350, originally installed
Suspension	Independent upper A-arms, lower control arms, w/coil springs in front; live axle with leaf springs in back
Steering	Recirculating ball
Brakes	Front discs, rear drums
Engine	520-horsepower 427-ci "medium-riser" Le Mans V-8 with Ford's 7,000-rpm racing kit
Bore and Stroke	4.23x3.78 inches
Compression	11.5:1
Fuel Delivery	Single 780-cfm Holley four-barrel carburetor
Transmission	Four-speed manual w/2.32:1 low gear
Axle Ratio	4.11:1
Production	1

Shelby American built one 427-powered GT500 prototype in 1967, and this machine was nicknamed "Super Snake." *Mike Mueller*

balanced 289 Cobra small-block, McCain's GT350 Drag Mustang package quickly proved itself worth the price—in 1965, one of them established an American Hot Rod Association (AHRA) quarter-mile standard of 12.40 seconds at 113 miles per hour.

Two years later, McCain approached Carroll Shelby with a plan to mate the new GT500 with the proven 427. Shelby nodded his approval, and a white '67 GT500, serial number 544, was chosen for the job. This prototype was adorned with distinctive racing stripes (triple instead of double) and a revised grille to aid cooling. But that was just icing on the cake. Behind that grille was a 427 medium-riser big-block specially prepared for the application. Its heads, single-carb intake, front cover, and water pump were made of weight-saving aluminum, as were the forged pistons. Valvetrain gear included a special 7,000-rpm kit featuring exceptionally light valves, a beefier crank, and bulletproof connecting rods. Additional high-rpm durability was guaranteed by a large-capacity oil pan with a remote oil filter and cooler.

Feeding this bully was a huge 780-cfm Holley four-barrel. Little was said about what exact cam grind was used, but results demonstrated it too was of the super variety. Completing the combustion process was a pair of racing-type bundle-of-snakes headers. On the dyno, this equipment totaled up to 520 horsepower. In the real world, that figure translated into 360 definitely usable horses.

Remaining pieces basically came right off Ford and Shelby shelves, save for the Traction-Master traction bars in back. Front discs, a Top Loader four-speed, a Detroit Locker differential with 4.11:1 gears—it was all in there. The only other nonstock installation came at the corners, where special Goodyear Thunderbolt rubber met the road.

Shelby Mustang production shifted from California to A. O. Smith in Livonia, Michigan, in 1968.

1968 GT350, GT500 & GT500KR

Model Availability	Two-door fastback, two-door convertible
Wheelbase	108 inches
Length	186.81 inches
Width	70.9 inches
Height	51.8 inches, fastback
Curb Weight	3,146 pounds, GT350 fastback (w/automatic transmission); 3,445 pounds, GT500 fastback (with automatic transmission)
Base price	$4,116, GT350 fastback; $4,238, GT350 convertible; $4,317, GT500 fastback; $4,438, GT500 convertible; $4,472, GT500KR fastback; $4,594, GT500KR convertible
Track	58 inches, front and rear
Wheels	15x6 stamped-steel rim with wheel cover, standard
Tires	E70x15 Goodyear Speedway 350
Suspension	Independent upper A-arms, lower control arms, w/coil springs in front; live axle with leaf springs in back
Steering	Recirculating ball
Brakes	Front discs, rear drums
Engine	250-horsepower 302-ci V-8 (GT 350), 360-horsepower 428-ci Police Interceptor V-8 (GT500), 335-horsepower 428 Cobra Jet V-8 (GT500KR)
Bore and Stroke	4.00x3.00 inches (GT350), 4.13x3.98 inches (GT500 and GT500KR)
Compression	10.5:1 (GT350), 10.5:1 (GT500), 10.6:1 (GT500KR)
Fuel Delivery	Single 600-cfm Holley four-barrel carburetor (GT350), single 715-cfm Holley four-barrel (GT500), single 735-cfm Holley four-barrel carburetor (GT500KR)
Transmission	Four-speed manual, three-speed automatic
Axle Ratio	3.89:1, standard for GT350 manual transmission; 3.50:1, standard for GT350 automatic and all GT500s; 3.25:1, standard for GT500KR convertible
Production	1,253 fastbacks, 404 convertibles, GT350; 1,140 fastbacks, 402 convertibles, GT500; 933 fastbacks, 318 convertibles, GT500KR

To try out these new tires, Shelby himself took the Super Snake to Goodyear's test track in San Angelo, Texas. On hand were various members of the press, including *Life* magazine staffers and CBS television reporters. Shelby showed up some four hours after the car landed in San Angelo but quickly made up for his tardiness by taking many of those left waiting for wild rides around the five-mile high-bank. Then he left almost as quickly as he had arrived. As Shelby American Chief Engineer Fred Goodell remembers, Carroll handed him his helmet and said, "Freddy, I've got to go to Washington. You'll have to finish this. Just wear my helmet, and nobody will know the difference." Goodell completed testing that day, averaging 142 miles per hour for 500 miles. Along the way, the car reportedly hit 170 miles per hour on the top end.

Yet even though on-track results were obviously impressive, the first 427 Shelby didn't exactly draw the attention McCain had hoped for. Initially, he had planned to offer 50 of his so-called Super Snakes through Mel Burns Ford. But that idea faded away after his prototype sat unsold on the lot for a year, its hefty $7,500 asking price scaring mere-mortal buyers away. Two airline pilots finally bought the car in 1968. End of story? Not exactly.

Although McCain's dream did not become reality, various 427 Shelby GT500s did make it into the wild in 1967. According to Goodell, perhaps as many as 10 others were built by Shelby. After letting his fingers do the walking through about half of Shelby American's 1967 invoices, Rick Kopec, head of the Shelby American Automobile Club, has managed to document two of these cars. Dozens more also ended up armed with 425-horsepower 427 dual-carb V-8s, either through dealer installations, warranty retrofits, or garage swaps.

1968 GT350 and GT500

The Michigan-built models were renamed Shelby Cobra GT350/500 for 1968, the year a convertible model was officially offered for public consumption. Changes were minor, with the most noticeable being the addition of safety-conscious side-marker lights and the substitution of larger '65 Thunderbird sequential taillights. The standard simulated-mag wheel cover also was restyled.

Above: GT500 fastback production for 1968 was 1,140. A louvered hood with leading-edge scoops was new this year for both the GT350 and GT500.

Left: After a handful of special GT350 convertibles were built in 1966, Ford officials opted to offer a mainstream topless model for 1968. GT500 convertible production that year was 402. A padded roll bar was standard.

Scoops abounded on the 1969 Shelby Mustang's new nose, while only one pair appeared in back, as opposed to the four rear-quarter scoops used on the GT350 and GT500 in 1967 and 1968. *Mike Mueller*

1969 & 1970 GT350 & GT500

Model Availability	Two-door fastback, two-door convertible
Wheelbase	108 inches
Length	190.62 inches
Height	50.6 inches, SportsRoof; 51.5 inches, convertible
Curb Weight	3,600 pounds, SportsRoof; 3,689 pounds, convertible
Base Price	$4,424, GT350 SportsRoof; $4,753, GT500 convertible;
	$4,709, GT500 SportsRoof; $5,027, GT500 convertible
Track	58.5 inches, front and rear
Wheels	15x7 five-spokes
Tires	E70x15 Goodyear Wide Oval; F60x15 Goodyear Polyglas belted, optional
Suspension	Independent upper A-arms, lower control arms, w/coil springs in front; live axle with leaf springs in back
Steering	Recirculating ball
Brakes	Front discs, rear drums
Engine	290-horsepower 351-ci V-8 (GT350), 335-horsepower 428-ci Cobra Jet V-8 (GT500)
Bore and Stroke	4.00x3.50 inches (GT350), 4.13x3.98 inches (GT500)
Compression	10.7:1 (GT350), 10.6:1 (GT500)
Fuel Delivery	Single 470-cfm Autolite four-barrel carburetor (GT350),
	single 735-cfm Holley four-barrel (GT500)
Transmission	Four-speed manual w/2.78:1 low, standard for GT350 (close-ratio four-speed w/2.32:1 low and Select-Shift Cruise-O-Matic automatic, optional); close-ratio four-speed w/2.32:1 low, standard for GT500 (Select-Shift Cruise-O-Matic automatic, optional)
Axle Ratio	3.25:1, standard for GT350 (3.00:1, optional); 3.50:1, standard for GT500; 3.00:1, mandatory with automatic trans and air conditioning; optional Traction-Lok ratios included 3.25:1 for GT350; 3.50:1, 3.91:1, and 4.30:1 for GT500
Production	3,153 total for 1969, including 3 prototypes; 789 total for 1970 updated models, GT350 and GT500
1969 GT350 Production	935 SportsRoofs, 150 Hertz SportsRoofs, 194 convertibles
1969 GT500 Production	1,536 SportsRoofs, 335 convertibles

A major upgrade came midyear as Ford's new 428 Cobra Jet V-8 became the new heart of the GT500. Sure, its advertised output (335 horses) was lower than the dual-carb 428's, but the shortfall was only on paper. "It's big and strong and very highly tuned," claimed a *Car Life* review of the Cobra Jet Shelby, called a GT500KR, the last two letters standing for "King of the Road." "At 6,000 rpm, the Cobra Jet will pull a semi-trailer up Pikes Peak." Quarter-mile performance registered in the mid-14-second bracket—great news considering that the 1968 GT350 was now offering only 250 standard horsepower supplied by the 302-ci small-block.

1969 GT350 and GT500

The KR reference was dropped in 1969, as all GT500s were now Cobra Jets, and the GT350 again got a new standard V-8, the 351-ci small-block, rated at 290 horsepower. New was a restyled fiberglass nose that featured various NACA (named for the National Advisory Committee for Aeronautics) ducts: two up front to supply cooling air into the engine compartment, two in back to let the hot air escape, and one in the middle for the engine's Ram-Air equipment. The fiberglass fenders incorporated brake-cooling ducts ahead of the front wheels, and another set of scoops allowed rear brake cooling. Rear scoops varied by body style: fastback scoops were inset up high, convertible scoops protruded and were lower to avoid a conflict with the top mechanism.

Rear styling remained familiar, save for revised aluminum exhaust outlets located side by side in the center of the valance panel. Although a five-spoke wheel was now standard, some early 1969 Shelbys apparently were fitted with Magnum 500s after defects showed up in the new rims. Standard rubber was an E70x15 Wide Oval, with a wider F60 tire offered at extra cost.

Above left: Standard power for the 1969 GT350 came from a 351 small-block V-8. Advertised output was 290 horsepower. *Mike Mueller*

Above right: The conventional Mustang's Deluxe Decor interior was standard inside the GT350 and GT500 in 1969. A simulated wood-grain dash and three-spoke rim-blow steering wheel were included in this package. *Mike Mueller*

Left: As in 1967 and 1968, the standard Shelby fastback interior featured a padded roll bar with inertia-reel shoulder harnesses. *Mike Mueller*

Right above: A new 15x7 five-spoke wheel became standard for Shelby Mustangs in 1969. Standard tires were E70 Wide Ovals. The F60 rubber seen here was optional. *Mike Mueller*

Right below: The 1969 Shelby console was identical to the conventional Mustang unit, save for a gauge housing and toggle switches for the driving lights and interior illumination. *Mike Mueller*

GT500 production for 1969 was 1,536 SportsRoofs and 335 convertibles. The GT350 breakdown was 935 SportsRoofs, 150 Hertz SportsRoofs, and 194 convertibles. *Mike Mueller*

As dynamic as the Shelby Mustang appeared in 1969, it wasn't long for this world with the original ideal all but gone.

1970 GT350 and GT500

As dynamic as the Shelby Mustang appeared in 1969, it wasn't long for this world with the original ideal all but gone. As *Car and Driver*'s Brock Yates explained, "The original Shelby GT350 was a fire-breather, it would accelerate, brake and corner with a nimbleness only a Corvette could match. The GT350, 1969-style, is little more than a tough-looking Mustang Grande—a Thunderbird for Hell's Angels. Certainly not the car of Carroll Shelby's dreams."

Shelby himself contacted Ford Vice President John Naughton in the fall of 1969, asking him to finally discontinue the GT350/500. Naughton complied, but cars remained in the pipeline. About 3,200 Shelbys were built for 1969, and nearly 790 of these were still around as the model year ended. The leftovers were then updated with 1970 serial numbers and were repackaged with chin spoilers and black hood stripes. And that was that.

Feature editor Joe Scalzo broke the bad news in *Car Life*'s October 1969 issue. "The Shelby, most enthusiasts agreed, had been dead, or close to death, for years. Each year since its 1965 inception [it] had become more of a compromised car: and even by Shelby's own admission it had lost its identity as a Supercar. As the stylists heaped on more chrome, they at the same time removed more and more of the car's performance features. At the time of its death it had entered a never-never land where it had neither the luxury of, say, the Mustang Mach 1, nor the performance and handling of the Boss Mustangs."

Case closed.

Above: Both fastbacks and convertible Shelby Mustangs in 1969 featured standard roll bars. As in 1968, the bars on convertibles were flatter and incorporated tie-down rings, reportedly for holding surfboards in place. *Mike Mueller*

Right: The KR designation was dropped after 1968, as all 1969 and 1970 GT500 models came standard with Cobra Jet power. *Mike Mueller*

Top: Total Shelby production for 1970 (coupe and convertible, GT350 and GT500) was 789. *Mike Mueller*

Above: Leftover 1969 Shelby Mustangs were simply redesignated 1970 models for the last GT350/500 run. *Mike Mueller*

Left: The 1969 and 1970 GT500's 428 Cobra Jet was again rated at a laughable 335 horsepower. All Shelby Mustangs from 1969 on, big- or small-block, featured functional Ram-Air hoods. *Mike Mueller*

03

Makin' Muscle

03

1967–1970

- A bigger, hopefully better Mustang first shows up on showroom floors on Friday, September 30, 1966.
- The first big-block Mustang debuts for 1967.
- Rival pony cars from Chevrolet and Pontiac appear for 1967 in the form of the Camaro and Firebird, respectively.
- Corporate cousin Mercury also rolls out a pony car, the Cougar, for 1967.
- Plymouth redesigns its Barracuda for 1967, making more room for a big-block V-8.
- Ford cancels the High Performance 289 V-8 option early in 1967.
- Henry Ford II makes Semon "Bunkie" Knudsen president of Ford Motor Company on February 6, 1968.
- Ford announces the Cobra Jet V-8 in April 1968 as a midyear option for Fairlanes, Torinos, Mustangs, Cougars, and midsized Mercurys.
- Ford introduces the Boss 302, Boss 429, Mach 1, and Grande Mustangs for 1969.
- Ford builds the last Mustang GT (until 1982) in 1969.
- Henry Ford II fires Bunkie Knudsen on September 11, 1969.
- Dodge's Challenger debuts for 1970 on Chrysler's all-new compact E-body platform.
- Lee Iacocca becomes Ford president on December 10, 1970.

Above: A rear spoiler and window slats were optional for the first Mach 1 in 1969. *Mike Mueller*

Opposite: The Grabber SportsRoof was introduced for 1970 wearing C-stripes reminiscent of the Boss 302's bodyside adornments. The hubcaps and trim rings also were part of the deal.

Previous pages:
Left: This fastback mockup, caught in a studio in January 1965, shows off much of the final 1967 look, save for its extended roofline and aggressive bodyside scoop.

Right: New C-stripes adorned the bodysides on the 1968 GT. Styled-steel wheels with "GT" hubcaps also were included in the deal.

Lee Iacocca and Bunkie Knudsen went together almost as well as the Hatfields and the McCoys. A disgruntled Iacocca had more than one bone to pick with Knudsen back then, beginning with complaints concerning the direction his baby took once Bunkie came on board in 1968. Already more massive, the Mustang almost overnight grew more muscular as well, to the growing disgust of the breed's founding father. Coupled with that was the plain fact that Knudsen dared to get in Iacocca's way.

SEMON E. KNUDSEN was the son of William S. Knudsen, the man who quit his production manager job at Ford in 1921, took the top spot at Chevrolet in 1924, and later became president of General Motors. A few decades down the road, the younger Knudsen's résumé took an opposite tack: Pontiac general manager in 1956, over the corporate fence to Chevrolet in 1961, then off the wall to Ford in February 1968, after he resigned in a fit following Ed Cole's appointment to GM president, a position he thought was his for the taking.

At the time, Iacocca was preparing for his own inaugural in Dearborn only to watch Henry Ford II elect Knudsen over him. "Henry was a great GM admirer," recalled Iacocca in his autobiography. "For him, Knudsen was a gift from heaven. Perhaps he believed Knudsen had all that famous GM wisdom locked in his genes. In any event, he wasted no time in making his approach. A week later, they had a deal. Knudsen would take over immediately as president at an annual salary of $600,000—the same as Henry's."

Fortunately, at least as far as Iacocca was concerned, Knudsen's stay in Dearborn lasted only a scant 19 months. Along with sponsoring the production of the hottest ponies yet during that short span, the former GM exec also managed to step on toes seemingly everywhere he tread around Ford Motor Company, leading Henry Ford II to more than once chastise him about his aggressive ways. Finally fed up, the boss gave Bunkie the boot on September 11, 1969.

Though some claimed Knudsen was trying to take over, Iacocca had a much simpler explanation for the short-term president's rapid fall from grace: "I wish I could say Bunkie got fired because he ruined the Mustang or because his ideas were all wrong. But the actual reason was because he used to walk into Henry's office without knocking. That's right—without knocking!"

With Knudsen knocked out, the door was left open for the rightful heir to the throne, who initially helped rule with two other executives in a triple play of sorts. Then on December 10, 1970, Iacocca was officially made president. Patience had paid off for

Mockups for an enlarged pony car body were going together even as the first Mustang was rolling off Ford dealer lots in record-breaking fashion in 1964.

Although dimensions grew, overall impressions remained familiar for the 1967 Mustang. A GT fastback (front) and GT coupe appear here. Total GT production for 1967 was 24,078. *Mike Mueller*

The mid-engine, two-seat Mach 2, which debuted at the 1967 Chicago auto show, relied on various stock Mustang components. Designed by Gene Bordinat and built by Roy Lunn's team, this sporty machine was created under order of Donald Frey as a possible replacement for Carroll Shelby's 427 Cobra.

the mover and shaker who opted to stay at Ford and watch Knudsen fail, an event not only he had rooted for. "The day Bunkie was fired there was great rejoicing and much drinking of champagne," he recalled. "Over in public relations, one of our people coined a phrase that soon became famous throughout the company: 'Henry Ford once said that history is bunk. But today, Bunkie is history.'"

As much as Knudsen was responsible for transforming the Mustang into a boulevard brute in 1971, blaming him solely for the breed losing its youthful figure isn't entirely fair. Putting on more pounds and more muscle had begun before Knudsen's arrival in direct response to competitive pressures coming primarily from GM. First to spur on Mustang growth was Pontiac's GTO, the famed factory hot rod that, in 1964, kicked off Detroit's original muscle car era. High-performance machines with loads of big-block V-8 power quickly became all the rage after the "Goat" began chewing up the road, leaving Ford planners little choice but to keep up or give up. Unfortunately, in the new Mustang's case, there was only room between its flanks for a small-block V-8.

Designs for a plumper pony were being considered even as the lithe original was galloping away with the attention of an entire nation in the summer of 1964. Clay mockups were sculpted as early as September that year, and the look that would evolve into the revised 1967 Mustang was taking serious shape by January 1965. All along, the idea was simple: change it but don't change it. As light car design exec Don Kopka explained before a Society of Automotive Engineers (SAE) gathering in October 1966, "Our mission was to refine and improve the breed without losing any of the Mustang's personality and without any sheetmetal changes that would destroy the strong identity established by the million-and-a-half Mustangs that were expected to be on the road before the 1967 model first saw the light of day."

The idea beneath that subtly reshaped skin involved, among other things, making more room for more engine, something General Motors' engineers were at the time planning for their upcoming copycat pony cars—Chevrolet's Camaro and Pontiac's Firebird—which both debuted for 1967. Funny thing, though: Ford people had no idea what their archrivals were up to when they began muscling up the Mustang. Much secrecy surrounded GM developments early on, leaving the Dearborn guys in the dark about the imminent arrival of the SS 396 Camaro and Firebird 400. That Ford had its own big-block horse in the starting gates ready to run for 1967 was almost as much blind luck as it was perfect planning.

1967

Critics were mostly in favor of the 1967 restyle, with *Hot Rod* magazine's Eric Dahlquist doing his best to help keep the pony car faithful. "Detroit has cobbled up so many fine designs in the last twenty years that when Ford decided to change the Mustang, everybody held their breath," he wrote. "But it's okay people, everythin's gonna' be all right."

"Anyone who likes the old Mustang ought to go nuts for the '67," added a *Car and Driver* review. "It's a much better looking car than the photographs show, and we think the styling is tougher than last year's."

Road & Track staffers, on the other hand, didn't quite agree. "The 1967 facelift has retained all the identifying characteristics of the first series but has fattened up the Mustang in all directions. It still has that chunky look about it and, frankly, looks a bit old-fashioned beside its new competitors."

A better looker or not on the outside, the 1967 Mustang definitely had a lot going for it beneath the skin, thanks to the hard work of chief engineer Tom Feaheny's team. The engineers did their best to improve ride and handling by revising front suspension geometry. In addition, steering effort was reduced while precision was increased.

Nearly all dimensions also increased, save for the wheelbase, which remained at 108 inches. Overall length (183.6 inches) and width (70.9 inches) grew 2 and 2.7 inches, respectively, while height went

As in 1966, the GT Equipment Group was offered only with a V-8 for all three 1967 body styles. Notice the ribbed cove panel here, a new appearance option for 1967 priced at $20. *Mike Mueller*

up nearly 1 inch to 51.8. Track too was stretched by 2 inches to 58 at both ends. Along with allowing a larger engine entrance beneath that long hood, these extra inches translated into more trunk space and a roomier interior, with the latter enhancement addressing earlier customer complaints concerning cramped rear seating. But such growth meant more weight, 140 extra pounds in the base six-cylinder coupe's case. At least the base price remained less than a dollar a pound.

Of course, that price grew too when the new optional big-block was dropped into the widened, reinforced engine bay. Rated at 320 horsepower, the 390-ci Thunderbird Special V-8 cost $263.71 in 1967. This venerable FE-series big-block was available with or without the GT Equipment Group, which jumped to $205.05 in 1967 after a set of warmly welcomed F70-14 Wide Oval tires became part of the deal. These fat Firestones cost $62.35 when ordered for non-GT models. Also available for all 1967 Mustangs were those classy five-spoke styled-steel wheels, which once again qualified as suitable icing for the GT cake.

Remaining GT features resembled those seen in 1966. Working in concert with those Wide Ovals was a heavy-duty suspension that included beefed shocks, a thick 0.84-inch front sway bar, and less-willing springs that were 30 percent stiffer up front, 26 percent in back. Front discs returned, this time with power assist. Fog lamps were again in the grille, a GT pop-open gas cap appeared at the tail, and GT stripes once more graced the lower bodysides.

New fender badges made news in 1967, as Ford people for this year only chose to set GT Mustangs apart depending on transmission choice. While manual-trans models wore familiar "GT" identification, automatic-equipped cars wore "GTA" badges, with the "A" adorned in red. Gas caps in both cases simply read "GT."

GT engine availability doubled in 1967 as the new 390 big-block was joined by the mundane 289 two-barrel small-block, sandwiching the 289 four-barrel and Hi-Po 289, both rollovers from 1966. As in 1965 and 1966, the four-barrel V-8s were fitted with dual exhausts capped off by chrome tips (quad outlets this time) when ordered for the GT/GTA package. The two-barrel 289 retained its single exhaust.

Also new for GT/GTA Mustangs in 1967 was a limited production option (LPO) available only with the Hi-Po small-block or 390 big-block. Called the Competition Handling Package, this group included a 0.94-inch-diameter front sway bar, Gabriel adjustable shocks, a superquick 16:1 steering gear, a 3.25:1 limited-slip differential, and big 15x6 wheels shod in either 6.50 or 6.70 Goodyear Blue Dot racing rubber. "Unique wheel covers" also

1967

Model Availability	Two-door coupe, two-door fastback, two-door convertible
Wheelbase	108 inches
Length	183.6 inches
Width	70.9 inches
Height	51.6 inches, hardtop and convertible; 51.8 inches, 2+2 fastback
Curb Weight	2,638 pounds, coupe; 2,659 pounds, fastback; 2,745 pounds, convertible
Base Price	$2,461.46, six-cylinder coupe; $2,592.17, six-cylinder fastback; $2,698.14, six-cylinder convertible; 200-horsepower 289 V-8 added $105.63; 225-horsepower 289 V-8 added $158.48; High Performance 289 V-8 added $433.55; 320-horsepower 390 V-8 added $263.71
Track	57.9 inches, front and rear (six-cylinder);
	58.1 inches, front and rear (V-8)
Wheels	14x4.5 four-lug, standard (six-cylinder); 14x5 five-lug,
	standard (289 V-8); 14x6 five-lug, standard (390 V-8)
Tires	6.95x14, standard (six-cylinder and 289 V-8—not available with GT and 390 V-8); 7.35x14, optional (not available with GT and 390 V-8); F70x14, standard with GT and 390 V-8, optional for 289 V-8s
Suspension	Independent upper A-arms and lower control arms w/coil springs in front; live axle with leaf springs in back
Steering	Recirculating ball (25.3:1, manual ratio; 20.3:1, power assist ratio)
Brakes	Four-wheel hydraulic drums
Engine	120-horsepower 200-ci six-cylinder, standard; 200-horsepower 289-ci Challenger V-8, optional; 225-horsepower 289-ci Premium Fuel V-8, optional; 271-horsepower 289-ci High Performance V-8, optional; 320-horsepower 390-ci FE-series V-8, optional
Bore and Stroke	3.68x3.13 inches (six-cylinder), 4.00x2.87 inches (289 V-8), 4.05x3.78 inches (390 V-8)
Compression	9.2:1 (200 six), 9.3:1 (289-2V V-8), 9.8:1 (289-4V V-8), 10:1 (High Performance 289 V-8), 10.5:1 (390 V-8)
Fuel Delivery	Single one-barrel carburetor (200 six), single two-barrel (289-2V V-8), single four-barrel (289-4V V-8), single four-barrel (High Performance 289 V-8), single four-barrel (390 V-8)
Transmission	Three-speed manual, standard; four-speed manual and automatic, optional
Axle Ratio	3.20:1, standard w/six-cylinder manual trans; 2.83:1, standard w/ six-cylinder automatic; 2.80:1, standard w/289-2V V-8 manual and automatic; 3.00:1, standard w/289-4V and 390 V-8s; 3.50:1, standard w/High Performance 289 V-8 manual and automatic
Production	472,121; all bodies, all models (24,087 GT models)

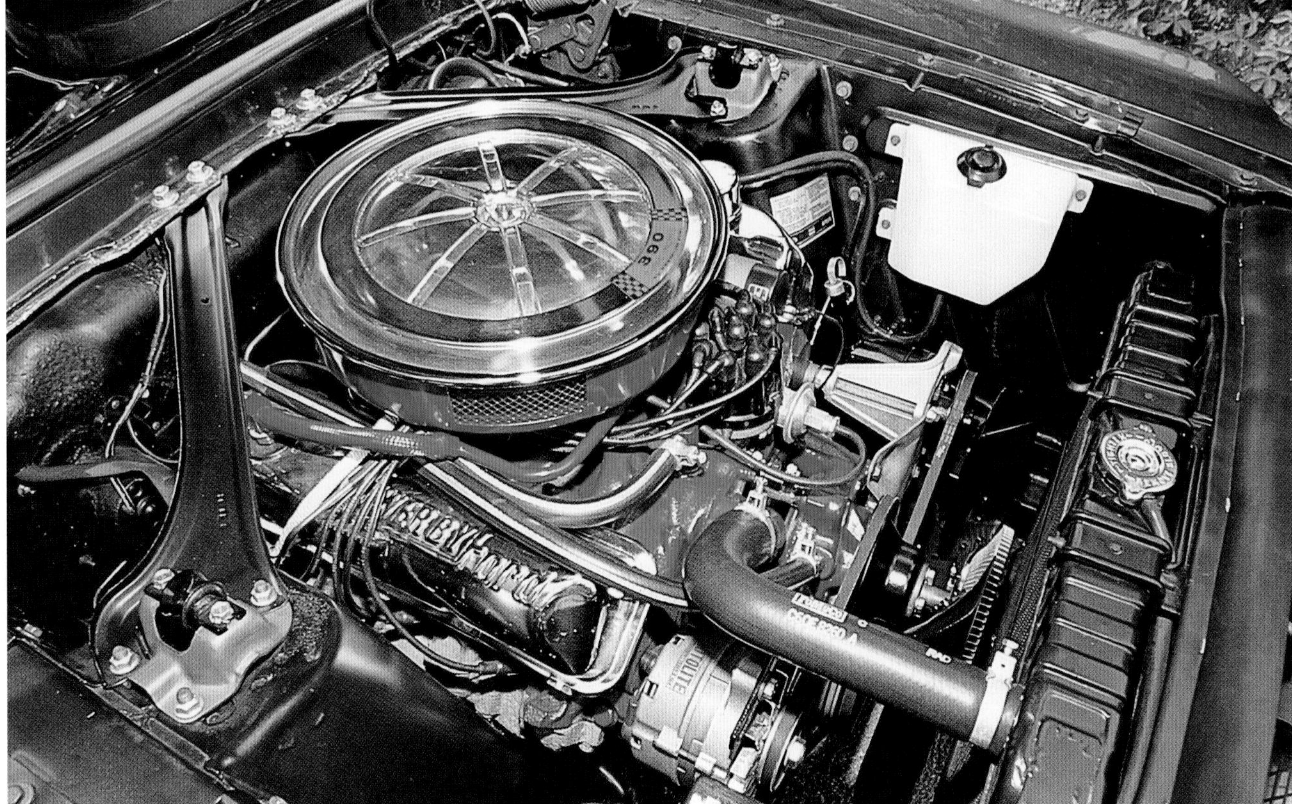

Above: New for 1967 was the way the GT Mustang was identified. A manual transmission model was simply a GT. Adding an automatic transmission changed the name to GTA. *Mike Mueller*

Left: The 1967 Mustang was beefed up, to Lee Iacocca's dismay, to make room for optional big-block power, in this case Ford's 320-horsepower 390-ci FE-series V-8. *Mike Mueller*

A better looker or not on the outside, the 1967 Mustang definitely had a lot going for it beneath the skin, thanks to the hard work of chief engineer Tom Feaheny's team.

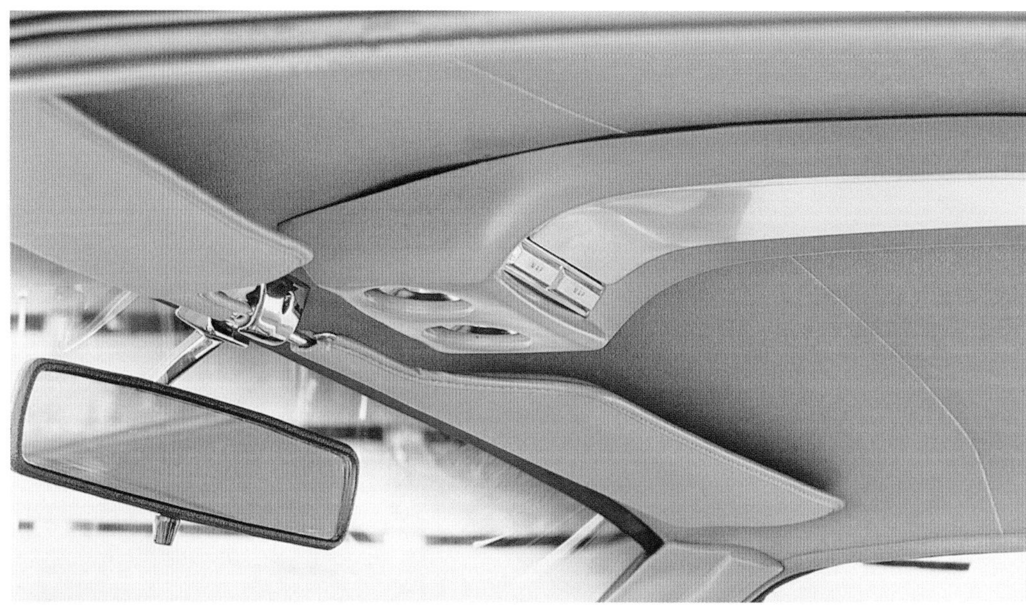

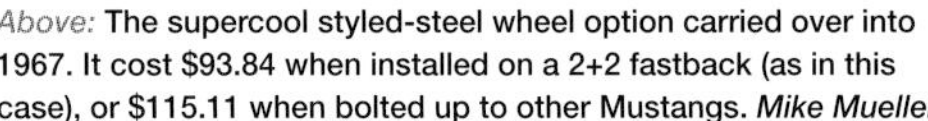

Above: The supercool styled-steel wheel option carried over into 1967. It cost $93.84 when installed on a 2+2 fastback (as in this case), or $115.11 when bolted up to other Mustangs. *Mike Mueller*

Top right: Another new bauble for 1967 was an overhead console, which was included in the Interior Decor package. Twin map lights were incorporated in this unit. *Mike Mueller*

Above right: The 1967 Mustang interior was restyled to impress buyers with a sportier cockpit feel. The optional console and deluxe three-spoke steering wheel enhanced the new image even further. *Mike Mueller*

were listed in the deal, and these simulated wires came from the Thunderbird parts bin, as no 15-inch covers were available in the Mustang realm in 1967. The Competition Handling option was as rare as it was expensive: $388.53.

GT popularity remained strong in 1967. Production for the model's first half-year run in 1965 was 15,106, followed by 25,517 in 1966. The figure for the third-edition GT (including its GTA alter ego) was 24,087.

Various other options debuted for the 1967 Mustang, including a conventional in-dash air conditioning system that replaced the underdash unit offered in 1965 and 1966. Totally new were fingertip speed control, a tilt-away steering column, an in-dash 6,000-rpm tachometer (located in the right-hand instrument pod), a convenience panel that added four warning lights above the radio, and an Exterior Decor Group that, among other things, included hood louvers that incorporated turn-signal indication lights. A revised Interior Decor Group also appeared, this time featuring a space-age overhead console and molded door panels with integral armrests.

A long list of safety features became standard in 1967, including a new brake system that relied on dual master cylinders—one for the front brakes, one for the rears. Four-way flashers, positive door locks (that couldn't be overridden by the interior door handle), a padded instrument panel, an impact-absorbing steering wheel with a heavily padded hub, and energy-absorbing armrests also were made part of the basic package.

Only four-barrel V-8s were available with the GT package prior to 1967. A two-barrel-fed 289 small-block then became available beneath 1967 GT/GTA hoods. *Mike Mueller*

A special run of 50 Super Stock Cobra Jet Mustangs (all painted Wimbledon White) was built first, beginning in December 1967. These track-ready ponies weighed a little less than regular-production examples, as their insulation and sound-deadener materials were deleted.

A redesigned styled-steel wheel, done in chrome or argent paint, appeared on 1968's options list. The center cap was plain when installed on non-GT models. *Mike Mueller*

1968

Changes for 1968 were subtle, to say the least. New were federally mandated bodyside-marker lights and "Mustang" fender script in place of the block letters used since 1964. Up front, the running-horse grille insert lost the long horizontal bars seen the previous year.

New options included a restyled styled-steel wheel with a vented look accented by a center cap and trim ring. This rim was available in chromed or argent-painted forms, and the center cap was appropriately adorned with "GT" lettering when included as part of the GT Equipment Group. Introduced too on the 1968 options lists were a collapsible spare tire and a rear window defogger that directed warm air to fogged glass on coupes and fastbacks.

The only other news of note involved the engine lineup, which again started with the standard 200-ci six-cylinder. New at the top, at least on paper, was the venerable 427-ci FE-series big-block V-8 topped by a single four-barrel carburetor. Apparently no 427 installations were made before this little-known option was discontinued in December 1967.

Far more familiar was the optional 390 GT big-block, which in 1968 was bumped up 5 horsepower to 325. In the small-block ranks, the old reliable 289 was stroked from 2.87 inches to 3.00, resulting in the new 302-cube V-8. Both the 289 and 302 found homes in 1968 Mustangs, with the former sold only with a two-barrel carburetor, the latter delivered in both two- and four-barrel forms.

The 230-horsepower 302 four-barrel was offered, along with the 390 big-block, to GT buyers in 1968, as two-barrel small-blocks were again barred from this application. The GT Equipment Group price dropped to its lowest to date ($146.71) that year after power front disc brakes were cut from the

1968

Model Availability	Two-door coupe, two-door fastback, two-door convertible
Wheelbase	108 inches
Length	183.6 inches
Width	70.9 inches
Height	51.6 inches, hardtop and fastback; 51.4 inches, convertible
Curb Weight	2,696 pounds, coupe; 2,723 pounds, fastback; 2,856 pounds, convertible
Base Price	$2,578.60, six-cylinder coupe; $2,689.26, six-cylinder fastback; $2,814.22, six-cylinder convertible; 195-horsepower 289 V-8 added $105.63; 230-horsepower 302 V-8 added $171.77; 325-horsepower 390 V-8 added $263.71
Track	58.5 inches, front and rear
Wheels	14x4.5 four-lug, standard (six-cylinder); 14x5 five-lug, standard (289 and 302 V-8s); 14x6 five-lug, standard (390 V-8)
Tires	6.95x14, standard (six-cylinder and small-block V-8s—not available with GT and 390 V-8); 7.35x14, standard for 390 V-8, optional for six and small-block V-8s (not available with GT); E70x14 Wide Oval, optional for all V-8s; F70x14, optional for all but six-cylinder models; radial tires optional for all engines but six-cylinder
Suspension	Independent upper A-arms and lower control arms w/coil springs in front; live axle with leaf springs in back
Steering	Recirculating ball (25.3:1, manual ratio; 20.3:1, power assist ratio)
Brakes	Four-wheel hydraulic drums
Engine	115-horsepower 200-ci six-cylinder, standard; 195-horsepower 289-ci Challenger V-8, optional; 230-horsepower 302-ci Challenger V-8, optional; 315-horsepower 390-ci FE-series V-8, optional
Bore and Stroke	3.68x3.13 inches (six-cylinder), 4.00x2.87 inches (289 V-8), 4.00x3.00 inches (302 V-8), 4.05x3.78 inches (390 V-8)
Compression	8.8:1 (200 six), 8.7:1 (289-2V V-8), 10:1 (302-4V V-8), 10.5:1 (390 V-8)
Fuel Delivery	Single one-barrel carburetor (200 six), single two-barrel (289-2V V-8), single four-barrel (302-4V V-8), single four-barrel (390 V-8)
Transmission	Three-speed manual, standard; four-speed manual and automatic, optional
Axle Ratio	3.20:1, standard w/six-cylinder manual trans; 2.83:1, standard w/six-cylinder automatic; 2.79:1, standard w/289-2V V-8 manual and automatic; 3.00:1, standard w/302-4V and 390 V-8s
Production	317,148; all bodies, all models (17,458 GT models)

package and made a separate option, at least when the 302 4V V-8 was ordered. Front discs, priced at $64.77, were mandatory whenever the 390 big-block was installed. Nearly all other GT components rolled over from 1967.

The aforementioned styled-steel wheels were the only rims available for the fourth-edition GT, and some appearance pieces differed in comparison to their 1967 forerunners. Fog lamps were back, but they no longer were tied together with a horizontal grille bar. GT badges rode higher up on each front fender as the rocker stripes were exchanged for flashy C-stripes running from the headlights to just behind the door. The 1967-style stripes could've been ordered in place of the large C-stripes. And customers who preferred a high profile at night could've shelled out for the Reflective Group, available only for GT Mustangs in 1968. The GT stripes and paint on the styled-steel wheels became highly reflective by way of this option.

GT production dipped to 17,458 in 1968. Included in this total was the 428 Cobra Jet Mustang, the mean machine that put the Mustang smack-dab in the middle of Detroit's muscle car race.

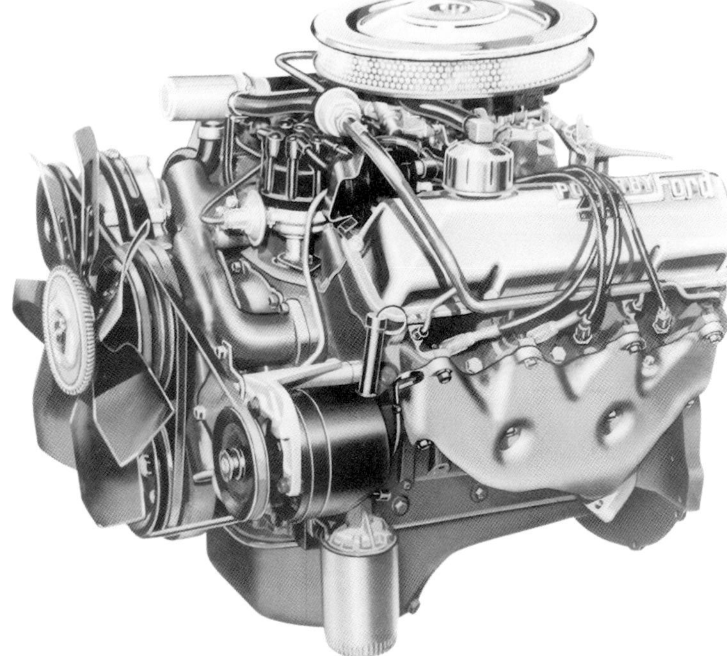

Above: Total fastback production for 1968 was 42,582. The easiest way to tell a 1967 and 1968 Mustang apart involved a peek at the front fender, where "Mustang" was done in script in 1968. Block letters were used the previous year. A redesigned styled-steel wheel appeared as a 1968 option. Done in either argent paint or chrome, this rim wore a small center cap and a trim ring. The cap was plain when installed on non-GT models. *Mike Mueller*

Left: While Ford's ferocious 427 V-8 was initially listed as a 1968 Mustang option, apparently none were built. This version featured a single four-barrel carburetor and was rated at 390 horsepower.

1968-½ 428 Cobra Jet

Discounting Carroll Shelby's variation on Ford's pony car theme, Mustangs didn't exactly qualify as muscle cars until the optional 428 Cobra Jet V-8 was introduced in April 1968. While the 390 GT variety looked tough on paper, it wasn't quite able to keep up with GM's hottest big-block Camaros and Firebirds. Ford's new 428 CJ, on the other hand, instantly transformed a 1968 Mustang into what *Hot Rod* magazine called "probably the fastest regular-production sedan ever built." And to think this particular better idea wasn't even Ford's . . .

The 428 Cobra Jet came about after Rhode Island Ford dealer Robert F. Tasca began building his own bigger, badder Mustangs late in 1967. Using existing 390, 427, and 428 FE-series V-8 parts, Tasca Ford's people created a stock pony car capable of roasting the quarter-mile in about 13 scintillating seconds. Bob Tasca carried a lot of weight around Dearborn, and when he proposed that Ford offer a regular-production counterpart, people listened.

"Bob likes to say he was the father of the Cobra Jet, and he's right," explained engineer Bill Barr. "When Tasca came to town, he was always immediately given an audience, and this time he flogged the company for what he wanted." Barr's team was then instructed to grant Tasca's wish.

Following Tasca's lead, they started with a 428 passenger-car block as a base, then added

Above: Being a GT model, the 1968-½ Cobra Jet Mustang came standard with styled-steel wheels wearing GT center caps. *Mike Mueller*

Top: A team of Cobra Jet Mustangs showed up in Pomona, California, for the 1968 NHRA Winternationals. From left to right are Gas Ronda, Jerry Harvey, Hubert Platt, and Don Nicholson. Not shown here is Al Joniec, whose CJ Mustang took top Super Stock (S/S) honors after burning up the quarter-mile in 12.12 seconds at 109.48 miles per hour.

1968½ 428 Cobra Jet

Model Availability	Two-door coupe, two-door fastback, two-door convertible
Wheelbase	108 inches
Length	183.6 inches
Width	70.9 inches
Height	51.6 inches, hardtop and fastback; 51.4 inches, convertible
Curb Weight	3,623 pounds
Price	$3,600, approximate
Track	58.5 inches, front and rear
Wheels	14-inch styled steel
Tires	F70 Wide Oval
Suspension	Independent upper A-arms and lower control arms w/coil springs in front; live axle with leaf springs and staggered rear shock absorbers (with manual trans only) in back
Steering	Recirculating ball
Brakes	Power front discs, rear drums
Engine	335-horsepower 428-ci Cobra Jet V-8
Bore and Stroke	4.13x3.98 inches
Compression	10.6:1
Fuel Delivery	Single 735-cfm Holley four-barrel carburetor
Transmission	Four-speed manual or heavy-duty Cruise-O-Matic automatic
Axle Ratio	3.50:1 gears in heavy-duty 9-inch differential; 3.91:1 and 4.30:1 ratios, optional
Production	2,827 (2,253 fastbacks, 564 hardtops, and 10 convertibles)

427 low-riser heads and a cast-iron version of Ford's aluminum Police Interceptor (PI) intake mounting a big 735-cfm Holley four-barrel carburetor. A 390 GT cam, PI rods, and 10.6:1 pistons went inside, while low-restriction dual exhausts completed the package. Advertised output was a token 335 horsepower.

No one is really sure who came up with the name, although it's obvious where the snake theme originated. According to Bob Tasca, Lee Iacocca had paid a high price for the rights to Carroll Shelby's established Cobra image and wasn't about to see all that cash go to waste.

"We already had the snake idea in our heads," added Bill Barr. "And we didn't do this like we normally did. We didn't just roll out the product with everyone standing around it scratching their asses trying to name it. Some artist in Styling had already created a drawing of the Cobra emblem—the snake with the wheels and exhausts coming out of its tail. We had the drawing; then the name came from there."

Offered in fastback, coupe, and convertible forms, the CJ Mustang featured a long list of standard performance pieces, including power front discs, braced shock towers, a beefy 9-inch rear end, staggered rear shocks (on four-speed models),

Above: **The Cobra Jet option was announced for the Mustang in April 1968. Total production that year was 2,827. Breakdown by body style was 2,253 fastbacks, 564 coupes, and 10 convertibles.** ***Mike Mueller***

Below: **The 428 CJ remained a Mustang option until 1970. The distinctive Shaker Ram-Air system became available atop the Cobra Jet in 1969.** ***Mike Mueller***

Right: Ford conservatively rated the 428 Cobra Jet V-8 at 335 horsepower. The Thermactor emissions control system is missing from this 1968-½ CJ Mustang. *Mike Mueller*

Above: The Mustang (and its corporate cousin Cougar) offered the 428 CJ option, while Ford's midsized Torino Cobra switched over to the new 429 Cobra Jet big-block up through that year. *Mike Mueller*

and a black-striped Ram-Air hood. An 8,000-rpm tach was standard with the four-speed, optional when a C6 automatic transmission was chosen. Part of the deal, too, was the GT Equipment Group, consisting of a heavy-duty suspension, F70 tires on styled-steel wheels, fog lamps, chromed quad exhaust tips, and GT identification.

Testing a specially prepared Cobra Jet prototype, *Hot Rod* magazine's Eric Dahlquist reported a sensational 13.56-second quarter-mile time. Thoroughly impressed, Dahlquist concluded that "the CJ will be the utter delight of every Ford lover and the bane of all the rest because, quite frankly, it is probably the fastest regular-production sedan ever built." Backing up this claim was a team of white Cobra Jet Mustangs that showed up in Pomona, California, for the 1968 NHRA Winternationals, where Al Joniec's CJ took top Super Stock honors after blistering the strip in 12.12 seconds at 109.48 miles per hour.

On the street, the CJ Mustang also left challengers sucking smoke. "Once you went down on the loud pedal, this baby could really fly," claimed Barr. "For stoplight Grand Prixes (sic) the 428 Cobra Jet was the bee's knees because nothing could stay with it."

"The Cobra Jet [Mustang] began the era of Ford's supremacy in performance," echoed Tasca. "It was the fastest, in my opinion, the fastest production car built in the world at that point."

Top: Southern California Ford dealers created the California Special, a Shelby Mustang knockoff, in 1968. A similarly adorned High Country Special was offered that year by Colorado dealers. *Mike Mueller*

Above: Shelby-style taillights and a rear spoiler brought up the rear of the 1968 California Special. *Mike Mueller*

1968 California Special

This special-edition Mustang looked a lot like one of Carroll Shelby's variants due to the plain fact that it shared various exterior components with the 1968 GT350 and GT500. Offered as part of a special promotional campaign staged by the Southern California Ford Dealer group, the 1968 GT California Special featured a ducktail spoiler, sequential Thunderbird taillights, and a functional bodyside scoop on each rear quarter panel, all taken from the Shelby convertible parts bin. Included as well was a blacked-out grille with Lucas fog lamps (some early cars used Marchal lamps), twin hood locks, exclusive striping, and "California Special" script at the tail. Additional GT/CS identification was added to the quarter-panel scoops.

Even though the GT nomenclature was used on all California Special Mustangs, individual examples were only true GTs if they were ordered with that specific options group. All California Specials were notchback coupes, and any engine could've been installed, even the base six-cylinder.

The economical Mustang E debuted for 1969 featuring six-cylinder power, a highway axle ratio, and an automatic transmission tweaked with a special torque converter. Only 96 were built, all fastbacks.

Most were powered by mundane two-barrel V-8s and thus weren't GTs. A few were sold with the 335-horsepower 428 Cobra Jet big-block.

A similarly equipped "High Country Special" also was offered in the Denver region in 1968. Production for both models was at least 4,325, of which 300 were High Country Specials.

1969

Things really got jumping around the Mustang corral in 1969. First, another restyle added even more heft to the body. Width and length again increased, as did weight. Meanwhile, the top dropped, contributing to a fresh look that came off effectively sleek. Especially sweet was the new "SportsRoof," Ford's latest name for its popular fastback models. SportsRoof accents included simulated rear-quarter air intakes and a ducktail spoiler in back.

Available Mustang engines also hit an all-time high in 1969. Joining the standard 200-ci six-cylinder was an optional six displacing 250 cubes, while the 302 small-block also was offered along with a bigger brother from Windsor that displaced 351 cubic inches. Two 351 Windsors were listed, one with a two-barrel carb, the other with a four-barrel. Both the 390 and 428 Cobra Jet big-blocks carried over from 1968; new for 1969 were the extreme Boss 302 and Boss 429 V-8s.

> According to *Car Life* magazine's road testers, the '69 CJ Mach 1 was "the quickest standard passenger car through the quarter-mile we've ever tested."

1969

Model Availability	Two-door coupe, two-door SportsRoof, two-door convertible
Wheelbase	108 inches
Length	187.4 inches
Width	71.3 inches, coupe and convertible; 71.8 inches, SportsRoof
Height	51.2 inches, coupe and convertible; 50.3 inches, SportsRoof
Curb Weight	2,835 pounds, coupe; 2,890 pounds, Grande coupe; 2,860 pounds, SportsRoof; 3,185 pounds, Mach 1; 2,945 pounds, convertible
Base Price	$2,618, six-cylinder hardtop; $2,618, six-cylinder SportsRoof; $2,832, six-cylinder convertible; $3,122, Mach 1; 250 six-cylinder added $25.91 (not available w/Mach 1); 302 V-8 added $105 (not available w/Mach 1); 351-2V V-8 added $58.34 to cost of 302 V-8; 351-4V V-8 added $84.25 to cost of 302 V-8 (351-4V cost $25.91 in Mach 1); 390 V-8 cost $158.08 ($99.74 in Mach 1); 428 Cobra Jet V-8 cost $287.53 ($224.12 in Mach 1); Ram-Air 428 Cobra Jet V-8 cost $420.96 ($257.46 in Mach 1)
Track	58.5 inches, front and rear
Wheels	14x4.5 four-lug, standard (200 six-cylinder); 14x5 five-lug, standard (250 six, 302, 351, and 390 V-8s); 14x6 five-lug, standard (428 Cobra Jet V-8)
Tires	C78x14, standard with six-cylinders and 302 V-8; E78x14, standard with 351 and 390 V-8; E70 Wide Oval, standard with GT; F70x14 Wide Oval, optional (not available with six-cylinders); FR70x14 Wide Oval radials, optional (not available with six-cylinders and 428 Cobra Jet V-8); F70x14 fiberglass-belted, standard w/482 Cobra Jet V-8
Suspension	Independent upper A-arms and lower control arms w/coil springs in front; live axle with leaf springs in back
Steering	Recirculating ball (25.4:1, manual ratio; 20.5:1, power assist ratio)
Brakes	Four-wheel hydraulic drums
Engine	115-horsepower 200-ci six-cylinder, standard; 155-horsepower 250-ci six-cylinder, optional (not available in Mach 1); 220-horsepower 302-ci V-8, optional (not available in Mach 1); 250-horsepower 351-ci V-8, optional (standard in Mach 1); 290-horsepower 351-ci V-8, optional; 320-horsepower 390-ci V-8, optional; 335-horsepower 428 Cobra Jet V-8, optional
Bore and Stroke	3.68x3.13 inches (200 six-cylinder), 3.68x3.91 inches (250 six), 4.00x3.00 inches (302 V-8), 4.00x3.50 inches (351 V-8), 4.05x3.78 inches (390 V-8), 4.13x3.98 inches (428 Cobra Jet V-8)
Compression	8.8:1 (200 six-cylinder), 9:1 (250 six), 9.5:1 (302 V-8), 9.5:1 (351-2V V-8), 10.7:1 (351-4V V-8), 10.5:1 (390 V-8), 10.6:1 (428 Cobra Jet V-8)
Fuel Delivery	Single one-barrel carburetor (200 and 250 six-cylinders), two-barrel carburetor (351-2V V-8), two-barrel carburetor (302 V-8), four-barrel carburetor (351-4V V-8), four-barrel carburetor (390 V-8), 735-cfm Holley four-barrel (428 Cobra Jet V-8)
Transmission	Three-speed manual, standard; four-speed manual and Cruise-O-Matic automatic, optional
Axle Ratio	Various choices, beginning with 2.75:1, up to 4.30:1
Production	299,824; all bodies, all models (5,396 GTs)

The 428 CJ no longer required the GT options group when ordered for a 1969 Mustang. Nor was Ram-Air equipment automatically included in the deal. But either way, with or without Ram-Air, the Cobra Jet's advertised output remained the same: 335 horsepower. What did change, and in a big way, was the Ram-Air CJ's image. In place of the conventional scooped hood used in 1968 was Ford's new "Shaker," which attached directly to the top of the air cleaner and protruded up through an opening in the hood. When the Cobra Jet started shaking side to side under torque load, so too did this fully functional, ribbed, black scoop—thus the formal name.

New too was the Super Cobra Jet, created by checking off the Drag Pack rear axle option, which consisted of either a 3.91:1 or 4.30:1 strip-ready axle ratio in a Traction-Lok limited-slip differential. Recognizing that these gears were best suited for on-track action, engineers further built up the CJ into the SCJ by adding tougher forged-aluminum pistons (in place of the CJ's cast slugs) and beefy

Top: **The last GT Mustang to appear until 1982 barely stood out in a crowd, save for its hood pins, nonfunctional scoop, and lower-body stripes. Total 1969 GT production (for all three body styles) was 5,396.**

Above: **Mustang convertible production for 1969 was 14,598. This drop-top is particularly rare—it features the 428 Super Cobra Jet V-8.** ***Mike Mueller***

Le Mans rods. Adding these heavier rods and pistons of course required rebalancing the engine. To do this, an external counter-balancer (among other things) was incorporated behind the crank's vibration damper. A racing-style external oil cooler, mounted on the front of the radiator core support on the driver side, completed the 428 SCJ package.

Along with the bodacious Boss 302 and Boss 429 Mustangs (both detailed in the following chapter), Ford rolled out another two new models for 1969. Introduced that year in hardtop form only, the quasi-luxurious Grande was created to emphasize the Mustang's softer side. Special exterior trim and a deluxe interior with simulated wood accents were among the list of classy standard features. Underneath, voided rubber bushings were installed into the leading mounts of each leaf spring in back, with the goal being to better absorb road shock. A special insulation package with 55 pounds of extra sound-deadener material was installed to help make the Grande, in Eric Dahlquist's words, "as quiet as Jack Benny when the check comes to the table."

Ford built 22,182 Grande Mustangs in 1969, followed by another 13,581 in 1970.

1969 Mach 1

The fourth new Mustang for 1969 was the fabulous Mach 1, a car that appealed to both drivers who loved to go fast and those who didn't mind simply looking like they were going fast. The road-hugging GT handling suspension (featuring typically stiffened springs and shocks and thicker front stabilizer bar) was standard underneath, and V-8 power represented the only way to fly. No wimpy sixes here. But standard too were loads of sporty imagery and classy surroundings. The Grande's "special sound package" was included, as were Comfortweave knitted-vinyl seat inserts. The base engine was a tame 250-horsepower 351-ci small-block topped by an economizing two-barrel carburetor. The idea was to make a more civilized machine compared to those gnarly, race-ready Boss Mustangs. With its wider scope, the first Mach 1 proved irresistible: sales soared to 72,458 that first year.

The Mach 1's visual attraction was impossible to miss. Nearly all of the hood and cowl were blacked out, and a trendy, nonfunctional scoop adorned the former. Racing-style hood pins with plastic-encased cable lanyards graced the hood's leading edge, and additional competition imagery included dual, color-keyed racing mirrors and a pop-open gas cap in back. Jazzy tape stripes with Mach 1 identification were added to the lower body and across the rear spoiler. Chromed styled-steel wheels brought up the corners.

Dual exhausts were standard behind all Mach 1 V-8s. Four four-barrel V-8s were optional: a 290-horse 351, 320-horse 390, and the two 428 Cobra Jets, with or without the Shaker hood. According to *Car Life* magazine's road testers, the '69 CJ Mach 1 was "the quickest standard passenger car through the quarter-mile we've ever tested." Their best run down the drag strip ended in only 13.86 seconds. "Are you ready for the first great Mustang?" they asked. "One with performance to match its looks, handling to send imported-car fans home mumbling to themselves, and an interior as elegant, and livable, as a gentleman's club?"

1969 Mach 1

Model Availability	Two-door SportsRoof
Wheelbase	108 inches
Length	187.4 inches
Width	71.8 inches
Height	50.3 inches
Curb Weight	3,185 pounds
Base Price	$3,122
Track	58.5 inches, front and rear
Wheels	14x5 five-lug, standard; 14x6 five-lug, standard (428 Cobra Jet V-8)
Tires	E70x14 fiberglass-belted
Suspension	Independent upper A-arms and lower control arms w/coil springs in front; live axle with leaf springs in back
Steering	Recirculating ball (25.4:1, manual ratio; 20.5:1, power assist ratio)
Brakes	Four-wheel hydraulic drums
Engine	250-horsepower 351-ci 2V V-8, standard; 290-horsepower 351-ci 4V V-8, optional; 325-horsepower 390-ci V-8, optional; 335-horsepower 428-ci Cobra Jet (with or without Ram-Air), optional
Bore and Stroke	4.00x3.50 inches (351 V-8), 4.05x3.78 inches (390 V-8), 4.13x3.98 inches (428 Cobra Jet V-8)
Compression	9.5:1 (351-2V V-8), 10.7:1 (351-4V V-8), 10.5:1 (390 V-8), 10.6:1 (428 Cobra Jet V-8)
Fuel Delivery	Two-barrel carburetor (351-2V V-8), four-barrel carburetor (351-4V V-8), four-barrel carburetor (390 V-8), 735-cfm Holley four-barrel (428 Cobra Jet V-8)
Transmission	Three-speed manual, standard; four-speed manual and Cruise-O-Matic automatic, optional
Axle Ratio	Various choices, from 2.75:1 up to 4.30:1
Production	72,458

While the Mach 1 was debuting to raves, the curtain was coming down on the aging Mustang GT.

Styled-steel wheels were included in the Mach 1 deal in 1969, as were a heavy-duty suspension and eye-catching striping. *Mike Mueller*

Above: An engine oil cooler was part of the Super Cobra Jet package in 1969 and represented the quickest way to pick one of these mean machines out in a crowd. *Mike Mueller*

Left: The 1969 Mach 1's base engine was a 351 small-block V-8. The Shaker-equipped 428 Cobra Jet big-block (shown here) was a $357.46 option. *Mike Mueller*

While the Mach 1 was debuting to raves, the curtain was coming down on the aging Mustang GT. Priced the same as in 1968, 1969's GT Equipment Group again featured a two-barrel V-8 in standard form, only it was the enlarged 351 Windsor small-block, rated at 250 horsepower. Additional GT power choices were the same four-barrel V-8s offered to Mach 1 buyers. As in 1967, dual exhausts with chrome quad outlets were included in the GT package but only behind the four-barrel V-8s.

The GT handling suspension was of course included, as were argent styled-steel wheels and that ever-present GT pop-open gas cap. GT rocker stripes returned for 1969 in four colors (black, white, red, or gold), depending on exterior paint and interior color choices. Racing-style hood pins were new, as was the Mach 1's nonfunctional hood scoop with integral turn-signal indicators. Missing was typical GT identification found on the fenders of earlier models. Only the gas cap in back and the styled-steel wheels' center caps carried GT identification in 1969.

Only 5,396 '69 GTs were built, all of them overshadowed by the two new Bosses and Mach 1. It would be 13 years before those two letters would again be used with Mustang in the same sentence.

1970

Mustang power sources grew even more plentiful in 1970, as the 1969 lineup carried over and was joined by a new small-block V-8, the 351 Cleveland. Both 351s, Windsor and Cleveland, were briefly listed together, creating more than a little confusion.

"Man, you've got to have a mind like a data processor to keep track of which engine is today's 'hot one,'" wrote *Sports Car Graphic*'s Paul Van Valkenburgh concerning Ford's 1970 engine roll call. "Call up E&F (Ford's Engine and Foundry) to ask how many different engine designs they've built recently and they'll say, 'You mean right now, or by quitting time?'"

Built at Ford's Cleveland, Ohio, engine plant—thus the name—the 351 Cleveland shared only its displacement with the old 351 manufactured in Windsor. Along with its 429-ci 385-series big-block cousin, the Cleveland small-block was the product of a plan to create lighter, cleaner-running, more efficient V-8s for a future where high economy and low emissions would be key. But that didn't mean the 351 Cleveland couldn't dish out its fair share of performance. Its free-breathing canted-valve heads—which also showed up atop the Boss 302 small-block—helped make this thoroughly modern V-8 a real screamer. Output for the two-barrel Cleveland was 250 horsepower, while its four-barrel running mate put out 300 horses in 1970.

Cleveland small-blocks were considered performance engines, yet they used two-bolt main bearing caps instead of the preferred, more durable, four-bolt caps normally designed into high-revving, high-horsepower engines. Cylinder heads also varied between the two- and four-barrel variations. Two-barrel heads had smaller valves and were of the open-chamber design. Four-barrel Cleveland heads featured wedge-shaped combustion chambers and larger valves.

Apparently engineers considered using the 385-series 429 Cobra Jet V-8 in the 1970 Mustang. It didn't actually appear between pony car flanks until 1971.

The 428 Cobra Jet remained a strong street performance option in 1970 but only for Ford Motor Company's pony cars, the Mustang and its Cougar cousin. Production of 428 Cobra Jet and Super Cobra Jet Mustangs for 1969 and 1970 was 13,193 and 2,671, respectively, bringing the three-year total to 18,691 before Ford finally ended the long-in-the-tooth FE-series big-block run. A notable SCJ change in 1970 involved the arrival of the gnarly, no-spin Detroit Locker differential, which became part of the Drag Pack option along with the 4.30:1 ratio. The Traction-Lok remained for the 3.91:1.

Of much lesser note in 1970 was a restyle that did away with two of the four headlights seen the previous year and replaced the outboard lamps with simulated air intakes. All 1969 models rolled

Above: A 351 two-barrel V-8 was again standard for the Mach 1 in 1970. Shown here is the optional four-barrel 351 Cleveland small-block, rated at 300 horsepower. *Mike Mueller*

Right: The most notable update for the 1970 Mach 1 involved the addition of finned-aluminum rocker panels. *Mike Mueller*

Total 1970 Mustang production was 191,522, including 96,151 coupes. A flat cove panel that year replaced the concave unit used in 1969.

1970

Model Availability	Two-door coupe, two-door fastback, two-door convertible
Wheelbase	108 inches
Length	187.4 inches
Width	71.7 inches
Height	50.3 inches
Curb Weight	2,875 pounds, coupe; 2,899 pounds, SportsRoof; 2,895 pounds, convertible; 3,406 pounds, Mach 1; 2,960 pounds, Grande coupe
Base Price	$2,721, six-cylinder coupe; $2,771, six-cylinder SportsRoof; $3,025, six-cylinder convertible; $2,926, six-cylinder Grande coupe; $3,271, Mach 1; 250 six-cylinder added $39 to cost of 200 six; 302 V-8 added $101 to cost of 200 six; 351-2V V-8 added $45 to cost of 302 V-8; 351-4V V-8 added $93 to cost of 302 V-8 ($48 in Mach 1); 428 Cobra Jet V-8 added $356 to cost of 302 V-8 ($311 in Mach 1); Ram-Air 428 Cobra Jet V-8 cost $421 ($376 in Mach 1)
Track	58.5 inches, front and rear
Wheels	14x4.5 four-lug, standard (200 six-cylinder); 14x6 five-lug, standard (250 six, 302 and 351 V-8s); 14x7 five-lug, standard (351-4V and 428 Cobra Jet V-8)
Tires	E78x14, standard w/six-cylinders and small-block V-8s; E78 white sidewalls, optional; E70, optional (standard w/351 V-8); F70, optional (standard w/428 Cobra Jet V-8)
Suspension	Independent upper A-arms and lower control arms w/coil springs in front; live axle with leaf springs in back
Steering	Recirculating ball (25.4:1, manual ratio; 20.5:1, power assist ratio)
Brakes	Four-wheel hydraulic drums
Engine	120-horsepower 200-ci six-cylinder, standard; 155-horsepower 250-ci six-cylinder, optional; 220-horsepower 302-ci V-8, optional; 250-horsepower 351-ci V-8, optional; 300-horsepower 351-ci V-8, optional; 335-horsepower 428 Cobra Jet V-8, optional
Bore and Stroke	3.68x3.13 inches (200 six-cylinder), 3.68x3.91 inches (250 six), 4.00x3.00 inches (302 V-8), 4.00x3.50 inches (351 V-8), 4.13x3.98 inches (428 Cobra Jet V-8)
Compression	8.7:1 (200 six-cylinder), 9:1 (250 six), 9.5:1 (302 V-8), 9.5:1 (351-2V V-8), 9.5:1 (351-2V V-8), 11:1 (351-4V V-8), 10.6:1 (428 Cobra Jet V-8)
Fuel Delivery	Single one-barrel carburetor (200 and 250 six-cylinders), two-barrel carburetor (351-2V V-8), two-barrel carburetor (302 V-8), four-barrel carburetor (351-4V V-8), 735-cfm Holley four-barrel (428 Cobra Jet V-8)
Transmission	Three-speed manual, standard; four-speed manual and Cruise-O-Matic automatic, optional
Axle Ratio	Various choices, from 2.75:1 up to 4.30:1
Production	190,272; all bodies, all models (13,591 Grande coupes, 40,970 Mach 1s)

over into 1970, with the still-cool Mach 1 powered by a two-barrel 351 small-block in standard form. Mach 1 sales dropped to 40,970 in 1970, but raves kept coming.

Next on the Mach 1 options list was the new 351 Cleveland four-barrel. The optional 390 FE-series big-block didn't return, but the 428 CJ did. Again, dual exhausts with chromed outlets—ovals this time—were included behind the four-barrel V-8s, and the Shaker Ram-Air option was available for all V-8s, not just the Cobra Jet. New for the 1970 Mach 1 was a rear stabilizer bar for the standard heavy-duty suspension. E70 rubber, dual color-keyed racing mirrors, and a competition-style pop-open gas cap were carryovers from 1969.

Mach 1 updates included a special plastic grille with unique driving lights and a black honeycomb rear panel appliqué. Large extruded aluminum moldings with dark accents and die-cast "Mach 1" letters also appeared along each rocker panel. In place of the hood pins and lanyards used in 1969 were simpler twist-type hood latches, and the styled-steel wheels were traded for simulated mag-type Sport wheel covers.

Revisions were made to the paint and tape accents as well. The blacked-out hood treatment was reduced to a paint stripe barely wider than the nonfunctional scoop. This paint was either low-gloss black or white depending on the exterior finish chosen. Thin tape stripes incorporating engine-displacement lettering bracketed that paint. A wide deck-lid tape stripe, also done in black or white, was interrupted in the middle to make room for large die-cast "Mach 1" letters.

Total Mustang production for 1970 was 191,522, down from 299,036 the previous year. But never fear; Lee Iacocca stood large and in charge as the year came to a close. Bunkie Knudsen was gone, though the pony he planned would stick around up through 1973. Then it was the founding father's turn to turn things around. Or so he thought.

04

Unbridled Performance

04

1969–1971 Boss Mustangs

- Along with Chevrolet's sexy 1963 Sting Ray, Larry Shinoda designs the images of the original Z/28 Camaro and Boss Mustang.
- According to Ford engineer Bill Barr, the Boss 302 manages 314 horsepower during dyno tests with all equipment in place and working. Stripped down, with no air cleaner and headers bolted on, the Boss 302 produces more than 390 horsepower.
- The Boss 429 V-8 is legalized for NASCAR racing beneath Mustang hoods; it worked under midsized Talladega lids on stock car tracks.
- David Pearson takes the 1969 NASCAR driver's championship in a Boss 429-powered Ford Torino Talladega. Former Mopar man Richard Petty is second in another Boss 429 Ford.
- Ford all but shuts down its racing program in November 1970.
- Ford's use in 1971 of the term "NASA hood" is actually a misnomer. The scoops on those hoods are technically known as "NACA" ducts around aviation circles. NACA, the National Advisory Committee for Aeronautics, was superseded by NASA, the National Aeronautics and Space Administration, in the late 1950s. Apparently Ford officials felt the American public in 1971 would recognize NASA but not NACA.

Above: All 1969 Boss 302 Mustangs and some 1970 models came with flat hoods, as Ram-Air equipment wasn't standard. Ford's new Shaker hood became available in 1970, but it wasn't installed on this Bright Yellow example. Color choices for 1970 expanded to 13, up from the four offered the previous year. *Mike Mueller*

Opposite: The functional hood scoop that came standard on the 1969 Boss 429 was the largest ever installed on a Mustang. The chin spoiler was standard too. It differed slightly from the Boss 302 unit due to the Boss 429 Mustang's lower stance.

Previous pages:
Left: Production of Boss 429 Mustangs was 857 in 1969 and 499 in 1970. *Mike Mueller*

Right: Low-gloss black paint on the hood and cowl was included in the Boss 302 deal in 1969, as were blacked-out headlight buckets and a front chin spoiler. The Magnum 500 wheels, rear window slats, and rear spoiler were optional.

Like Lee Iacocca, Bunkie Knudsen knew what a gold mine the youth market had become during the 1960s. In fact, Bunkie actually beat Iacocca to the punch where it came to targeting younger buyers (or those young at heart). Knudsen himself was only 43 in June 1956, when he became General Motors' youngest-ever general manager, and his prime goal then as Pontiac's new chief was to transform your grandpa's car company into a real exciter. "You can sell a young man's car to an old man," went his main motto at the time, "but you'll never sell an old man's car to a young man." With that said, he overnight put Pontiacs among the hottest things running around Detroit.

KNUDSEN LOVED YOUNG MEN'S CARS, and he also had a thing for racing his factory hot rods. Thanks to his high-powered planning, Pontiacs became drag racing dominators in 1960 and went on to thoroughly thrash all stock car rivals on the NASCAR circuit in 1962. By then, however, Knudsen had moved over to Chevrolet, where he continued promoting high performance, a pet practice he brought with him—much to the proud pony car papa's dismay—to Dearborn in February 1968. But disdain for his archrival aside, Iacocca couldn't argue one plain truth: muscle cars turned heads, at least for the moment. As long as young American car buyers had a need for speed, Ford's new boss was going to fill it.

"Knudsen likes performance and dabbles in it, some say, more than he should," remarked California Ford dealer Chuck Foulger. "But he knows what the market wants, and he knows how to accomplish his goals. I think Bunkie's dynamic thinking is just what Ford needs." *Motor Trend*'s Eric Dahlquist added, "When Mr. Knudsen came from GM, he brought along a strong belief in the power of performance."

Knudsen's beliefs were equally strong as far as the Mustang was concerned. In his mind, Ford's popular pony car was "a good-looking automobile, but there are a tremendous number of people out there who want good-looking automobiles with performance. If a car looks like it's going

Above: **Free-breathing canted-valve Cleveland cylinder heads were among the keys to the Boss 302 V-8's success. Valve sizes were 2.23 inches on intake, 1.71 on exhaust.**

Right: **A veritable race engine let loose on the street, the Boss 429 V-8 made hay at the drags as well as on NASCAR superspeedways. Renditions also appeared in Can-Am competition.**

Below: **The Boss 429 V-8 featured semi-hemi combustion chambers with centrally located spark plugs. Valve sizes were 2.28-inch intakes, 1.90-inch exhausts. A 735-cfm Holley four-barrel fed this beast.**

fast and doesn't go fast, people get turned off. If you have a performance car and it looks like a pretty sleek automobile, then you should give the sports-minded fellow the opportunity to buy a high-performance automobile."

Ford's street-performance savior, the 428 Cobra Jet Mustang, was already in the works when Knudsen accepted Henry II's offer. Able to run with GM's two big-block bullies—Chevrolet's SS 396 Camaro and Pontiac's Firebird 400 HO—the sizzling CJ certainly was a sensation, both on and off a drag strip. But Knudsen chose not to stop there. He wanted the Mustang to compete with all brands of pony car performance. In 1967, Chevy engineers had created another hot-to-trot Camaro, a nimble small-block screamer built with SCCA Trans-Am roadracing in mind. Named simply for its options code, the legendary Z/28 instantly became the pony car breed's best all-around performer—it could handle the curves as well as smoke the straight and narrow.

Knudsen wasn't above copping things from his former employer, be they ideas or the thinkers themselves. Thus was his plan to outdo the Z/28 Camaro: to produce, in his words, "absolutely the best-handling street car available on the American market." Helping meet this demand was another GM defector, designer Larry Shinoda, whom Knudsen brought over to Ford in May 1968. Included in Shinoda's prestigious résumé was the beautiful body for the 1963 Corvette Sting Ray and, coincidentally, the understated image for the 1967 Z/28.

At Ford, Shinoda became head of the Special Projects Design office, where he was tasked with fashioning a hot new look for the Z/28-beater then under hurried development for 1969. His contributions came two-fold: the trendy stripes, slats, and spoilers he designed caught the eye, while the moniker he campaigned for was soon on the lips of gearheads everywhere.

"They were going to call it 'SR-2,' which stood for 'Sports Racing' or 'Sports Racing—Group II,' which I thought was a dumb name," recalled Shinoda in a 1981 *Mustang Monthly* interview. His choice came from the too-cool-for-school lexicon of the day. "I suggested they call it 'Boss.'" Shinoda's square superiors at first couldn't relate to such hip nomenclature, but they soon were diggin' it.

Actually, two Boss Mustangs were born in 1969, both developed concurrently by Ford's performance contractor, Kar Kraft Engineering, in Brighton, Michigan. Kar Kraft began building the hot handler Knudsen called for in August 1968, completing the first prototype in only three weeks. This vehicle evolved into the Boss 302, Ford's answer to the Z/28. The other new Mustang, the bad-to-the-bone Boss 429, was an entirely different breed. Created to legalize the 429-ci "Blue Crescent" V-8 for NASCAR competition, this big-block beast, like the Cobra Jet Mustang, was best suited for straight-line speed runs.

After prototypes were up and running, these two polar opposites were tasked to separate

Above: The big Boss 429 V-8 was literally shoehorned between Mustang flanks at the Kar Kraft works in Brighton, Michigan.

Left: Ford began sending 1969 SportsRoof models to Kar Kraft's Brighton, Michigan, shop in December 1968. There they were stripped of their engines and stock shock towers in preparation for the Boss 429 V-8 installation.

Below: The first Boss 429 Mustang hit the streets in January 1969, nearly three months ahead of the first Boss 302.

development groups. The Boss 429 remained with a Kar Kraft team captained by Roy Lunn, while Ford Engineering took over full control of the Boss 302 project. Light Vehicle Powertrain Development Section leader Tom Feaheny had been on the receiving end of Knudsen's initial demand, and he passed the ball into the hands of chief light car engineer Howard Freers. Freers then turned to Matt Donner, principal ride and handling engineer for the Mustang and Cougar lines. Donner had been working with pony car suspensions from the get-go and also had done some tweaking for the Ford/ Mercury SCCA racing teams.

Even so, Donner and his comrades didn't quite have all the answers, at least according to Shinoda, who felt it was the transfusion of GM blood that made the difference. Ford "knew very little about vehicle dynamics when we [Knudsen and his GM defectors] came on board," said the outspoken Shinoda. "They never did any testing on a skid pad. Initially, they were saying that any kind of bolt-on aerodynamic stuff was bull, that you didn't need it. In fact, they even fought the rear wing because they were saying we've got a big enough spoiler already, which we didn't really have. And the front air dam? They argued about that, too. We finally had to show them how to use a skid pad and how you develop your vehicle dynamics on it to get optimum handling." Although Shinoda may have overstated things a bit, Ford's regular-production ways had been more conservative compared to Chevrolet's before 1969. Then along came the Boss 302 and Boss 429—radical machines to say the least.

1969 Boss 302

Ford's first Boss 302 rolled off the line on April 17, 1969, inspiring instant raves for the undeniable way in which it met Knudsen's demands. According to *Car and Driver*, the Boss 302 "is the best-handling Ford ever to come out of Dearborn and may just be the new standard by which everything from Detroit must be judged."

According to Donner, his Boss 302 suspension package involved "mostly adjustments." Geometry remained basically stock, with the most notable change involving the car's enlarged footprint. Donner chose superfat F60 Wide Oval tires mounted on 15x7 Magnum 500 wheels. Bolting on all that extra rubber required rerolling the front wheel arches to increase clearance. In addition,

Above: Richard Petty (at left), amazingly in a Ford, finished second to David Pearson in 1969 and both drove Boss-powered Talladegas that year. Pearson's 1969 championship was his second in a row.

Right: NASCAR only specified a minimum engine count to make a particular power source legal for stock car racing. So Ford put at least 500 Boss 429 V-8s on the street dressed in 1969 Mustang bodies. The Talladega models that ran in NASCAR competition with Boss 429 power that year came standard on the street with 428 Cobra Jet V-8s.

Opposite: Boss 302 Mustangs battled neck and neck with Chevy Z/28 Camaros on the SCCA Trans-Am circuit in 1969 and 1970.

beefed-up front spindles were developed to better handle increased cornering loads resulting from the Wide Ovals' stronger grip. Upper control arm mounting points also were initially taxed beyond their limits in prototype applications, so extra bracing was added to the shock towers. This bracing soon became a standard feature for any Mustang fitted with F60 rubber and the Competition Suspension option.

Remaining standard suspension pieces included expected stiffer springs and shocks, the latter supplied by Gabriel. Rear shocks were staggered (one mounted in front of the axle, the other behind) to help control axle wind-up. A thick 0.85-inch stabilizer bar was originally envisioned up front but was replaced by a 0.72-inch unit after a planned rear sway bar was dropped. Quick 16:1 manual steering was included in the Boss 302 deal, as were big 11.3-inch front disc brakes, followed by 10-inch drums in back. Power assist for both brakes and steering was optional.

Underhood power was supplied by an exclusive 302-ci small-block that actually was Ford's second choice for the Boss application. The first was the short-lived 302 tunnel-port V-8, introduced the following year strictly for Trans-Am competition. Though supremely powerful at about 450 horsepower, the cantankerous tunnel-port had problems keeping things together at high rpm. It also didn't qualify as a regular-production powerplant (few were built and none found their way into stock Mustangs), which Trans-Am rules began demanding explicitly after 1968. Up until then, SCCA officials had more or less looked the other way concerning existing homologation standards. But in 1969, the specification became plain and simple: Ford would have to make at least 1,000 Boss 302 Mustangs available for public purchase to qualify the model for Trans-Am competition.

Even if it had proved more durable, the tunnel-port 302 would've never worked for the new Boss Mustang. The exotic engine's huge ports (thus its nickname) precluded operation on the street, and high costs ruled out the relatively large production run required by the SCCA.

The solution?

Like the 428 Cobra Jet big-block the previous year, the Boss 302 small-block V-8 was created rather easily by cleverly mixing and matching existing hardware. Lead engineer Hank Lenox took the 302 tunnel-port's modified four-bolt Windsor-based block and mated it to new cylinder heads then being

1969 Boss 302

Model Availability	SportsRoof fastback
Wheelbase	108 inches
Length	187.4 inches
Height	50.4 inches
Weight	3,260 pounds
Base Price	$3,500
Track	59.5 inches, front and rear
Wheels	15x7 argent center sections with chrome trim rings
Tires	F60x15 Wide Oval
Suspension	Independent upper A-arms, lower control arms w/coil springs in front; live axle with leaf springs and staggered shocks in back, heavy-duty front sway bar
Steering	Recirculating ball (quick 16:1 ratio)
Brakes	Front discs, rear drums
Engine	290-horsepower 302-ci Boss 302 V-8 with Cleveland heads
Bore and Stroke	4.00x3.00 inches
Compression	10.5:1
Fuel Delivery	Single 780-cfm Holley four-barrel on aluminum high-rise intake
Transmission	Four-speed manual only
Axle Ratio	3.50:1
Production	1,628

readied for the 351 Cleveland V-8, the hot small-block scheduled for 1970. Ford's free-breathing Cleveland heads featured big ports and large, canted-angle valves. And in the Boss application, they also included hardened pushrods with guide plates, 1.73:1 rocker arms with screw-in studs, and single valve springs with dampers. A lumpy solid-lifter cam put the squeeze on those springs.

Into the Boss 302's block went a hardened, cross-drilled, forged-steel crank, forged connecting rods with heavy-duty 3/8-inch rod bolts, and 10.5:1 forged-aluminum TRW domed pistons. Although factory specifications claimed this assembly was good to 7,000 rpm, a rev limiter was included to keep a lid on things by shutting down the voltage from the vacuum advance dual-point distributor at 6,150 revolutions. Other rev-conscious pieces included an underdrive alternator pulley, a baffled 5-quart oil pan, a windage tray below the crank, a balanced water pump impeller, and a five-blade flex fan. Both the fuel and oil pumps were also high volume. Topping everything off was a thirsty 780-cfm Holley four-barrel on an aluminum high-rise intake manifold.

Advertised output was identical to the 302 V-8 that powered Chevy's Z/28: 290 horsepower. Most witnesses quickly recognized that this figure was conservative, to say the least. Quarter-mile numbers, according to Car and Driver, were 14.57 seconds at 97.57 miles per hour.

Backing up the Boss 302 V-8 was either a wide- or close ratio Top Loader four-speed. Automatics were not available. A heavy-duty nodular 9-inch rear end with 3.50:1 gears and indestructible 31-spline axles was standard. A Traction-Lok differential was optional, as were 3.91:1 and 4.30:1 gears. Choosing either of those last two ratios mandated the installation of an auxiliary oil cooler.

Finishing the package off topside was Shinoda's high-profile pizzazz. A front chin spoiler was standard, while a rear wing and boss-looking rear window slats were optional. Accentuating these were blacked-out paint treatments for the headlight buckets, hood and cowl, deck lid, and rear cove panel. Shinoda also deleted the typical SportsRoof's fake rear quarter scoops and roof pillar medallions. He then finished off his masterpiece by adding reflective C-stripes to the bodysides. Reminiscent of the stripes that graced the sides of Ford's dominating GT-40 race cars, these stick-on touches incorporated "Boss 302" identification at their leading edges.

Summed up, how did the Boss 302 compare to Chevy's Z/28?

"I really couldn't say the Boss 302 was dramatically better," concluded Shinoda. "I've driven both cars, and I don't think the Mustang handled that much better. In showroom trim, car for car, the Mustang was close, but I can't really say [it] was superior." The two basically tied on the track, with the Trans-Am Camaro taking SCCA laurels in 1969, the Boss 302 in 1970.

1969 Boss 429

Like its small-block little brother, the big, bad Boss 429 Mustang was hastily developed late in 1968 so that Bunkie could keep racing. "It was in the days just after Knudsen came on board," said Kar Kraft chief Roy Lunn concerning the Boss 429's rapid rise to power. "He was a real stock car enthusiast, and so stock car racing was being given a big thrust again. To remain competitive, we had to get that 429 hemi-head engine qualified, and the requirement was that you had to build a minimum of 500 in production vehicles."

Nowhere did those requirements specify that a model and engine in question be built together, so Ford made the Boss 429 V-8 an option for street-going Mustangs, cars that didn't qualify as NASCAR competitors. Once legalized between pony car flanks, the Boss 429 was transplanted behind the extended snout of Ford's Fairlane-based Torino Talladega, which came standard in regular-production trim with a 428 Cobra Jet big-block. Clearly, loopholes were made to be driven through.

Boss 429 Mustangs first hit the streets in January 1969, nearly three months ahead of the Boss 302. Kar Kraft was assigned production in this case because the humongous Boss 429 V-8 didn't drop easily into the pony car platform. Able to operate at a slower, steadier pace compared to Ford's own assembly lines, the Brighton works represented the best place to make the various time-consuming modifications required to bring the beast to life.

That process began once Ford started delivering garden-variety 1969 Mach 1s to Kar Kraft in December 1968. In Brighton, these cars lost their engines and stock shock towers, the latter replaced by specially reinforced pieces that increased engine compartment width by 2 inches to allow the behemoth Boss 429 V-8 entry between Mustang fenders. Those fenders too were modified, like the Boss 302's, to supply clearance for big F60 Wide Oval tires on wide 15x7 Magnum 500 wheels.

Clearance remained an issue beneath the hood, even with the reengineered shock towers installed. The power brake booster was thinned down to avoid contacting the huge valve cover on the driver side, and the battery was moved to the trunk, a relocation that also meant more weight would bear down on the rear wheels—just what a lead-footed driver wanted when he was trying to beat it off the line in great haste.

Additional front suspension tweaks included upper A-arm location points moved outward an inch and lowered another inch, beefed spindles, and a modified export brace on top to firmly tie the restructured shock towers to the cowl. Among further upgrades on the dirty side were superduty Gabriel shocks (again staggered in back) and thick sway bars measuring 0.94 inch front, 0.62 inch rear. Both power front discs and power steering were standard, as was a close-ratio four-speed (with a Ford shifter) that delivered torque to a Traction-Lok differential containing 3.91:1 gears.

Exterior modifications were minor compared to the Boss 302. The Boss 429 body retained the SportsRoof's rear roof pillar medallions and fake rear quarter scoops, and only simple "Boss 429" decals were added to the front fenders. The most notable add-on was the huge functional hood scoop, which was joined by dual color-keyed racing mirrors and a front chin spoiler, this one shaped

1969 Boss 429

Model Availability	SportsRoof fastback
Wheelbase	108 inches
Length	187.4 inches
Height	50.4 inches
Weight	3,530 pounds
Base Price	$4,900
Track	59.5 inches, front and rear
Wheels	15x7 Magnum 500 five-spoke
Tires	F60x15 Wide Oval
Suspension	Independent upper A-arms, lower control arms (suspension geometry modified to make room for big Boss 429 V-8) w/coil springs in front; live axle with leaf springs and staggered Gabriel shock absorbers in back
Steering	Recirculating ball with power assist (quick 16:1 ratio)
Brakes	Front discs, rear drums
Engine	375-horsepower Boss 429 V-8 with aluminum cylinder heads
Bore and Stroke	4.36x3.59 inches
Compression	10.5:1
Fuel Delivery	Single 735-cfm Holley four-barrel carburetor
Transmission	Four-speed manual only
Axle Ratio	3.90:1 Traction-Lok
Production	857

Like its small-block Boss brother in 1969, the Boss 429 featured specially flared fenders, customized pieces required to allow clearance for the F60x15 Wide Oval tires that came as standard equipment. *Mike Mueller*

Far left: Two different Boss 429 V-8s appeared in 1969. The first 279 models built featured S-code engines with beefy NASCAR-style connecting rods. Remaining 1969 models and most 1970 cars got T-code V-8s, which traded those rev-limiting rods for lighter pieces. A third variety, the A-code Boss, appeared in 1970 with revised smog controls. *Mike Mueller*

Left: All Boss 429 Mustangs for 1969 and 1970 rolled on 15x7 Magnum 500 five-spoke wheels. *Mike Mueller*

Below left: Standard wheels for the 1970 Boss 302 were 15-inch rims wearing flat hubcaps and trim rings. Notice the painted spokes (instead of chromed) on the Magnum 500 rims appearing in this factory photograph.

slightly shorter than the Boss 302's. A deck-lid spoiler and cool rear window slats were options.

The Boss 429's main attraction rested beneath that high-profile hood scoop. Exclusive to the Boss Mustang application, the impressive mill was basically born in 1968 when Ford introduced its 385-series thin-wall big-block family for its luxury lines. Competition implications were explored immediately, leading engineers to cast a reinforced iron block with four bolts holding down the bearing caps on four of the five mains. Huge, heavy cylinder heads with sewer-sized ports, massive inclined valves, and hemispherical combustion chambers were also cast out of iron but were recast in weight-saving aluminum once production was confirmed. Combustion chambers too were revised, leaving a shape that wasn't quite hemispherical, thus the commonly heard "semi-hemi" designation. Ford people preferred the "Blue Crescent" moniker, while racers made the "Shotgun motor" nickname popular.

Three semi-hemi V-8 variations appeared during the Boss 429 run. The first 279 models off the Kar Kraft line were fitted with S-code engines. These NASCAR-style big-blocks featured beefy connecting rods that clamped to a cross-drilled forged-steel crank using large, ½-inch bolts. Remaining Boss 429s for 1969 and most for 1970 got the T-code engine, which traded those heavy, rev-limiting rods for lighter pieces with ⅜-inch bolts. The first T engines featured the S-code's hydraulic cam and magnesium valve covers. But early in the T run, those magnesium covers were replaced with aluminum units and a slightly more aggressive solid-lifter cam superseded the hydraulic stick. The third Boss 429 rendition, found in very few 1970 models, was the A-code engine, which was basically a T motor with revised smog controls.

All Boss 429 V-8s, regardless of code, were topped by a 735-cfm Holley four-barrel carburetor on a dual-plane aluminum intake. All included a Drag Pack–style oil cooler. As for advertised output, Ford again applied a conservative rating: 375 horsepower. Actual power production undoubtedly was greater, although you'd never think so after listening to critics' comments.

More than one magazine called the Boss 429 "a stone" in 1969, and Larry Shinoda claimed the semi-hemi V-8 "was kind of a slug in the Mustang." Car Life's critics stood out as an exception after labeling the Boss 429 "the best enthusiast car Ford has ever produced." They published a quarter-mile pass of 14.09 seconds at 102.85 miles per hour.

These differing opinions were the result of great expectations. The Boss 429 was a full-fledged race engine unleashed on the street, leading some kibitzers to predict quarter-mile times well into the 13s, if not the 12s. But running a racer on Main Street, U.S.A. was not a simple task, leaving engineers no choice but to tame this monster to make it behave in everyday traffic. The Boss 429's big valves and ports were designed to make plenty of ponies at high revs. Yet the cam, although aggressive by most perspectives, was not capable of fully filling those ports with air/fuel mixture. The same went for that Holley four-barrel, which was big by most standards, but not by the Boss 429's. On top of all that, the factory-installed rev limiter turned off the juice just when the semi-hemi was starting to show some of its true potential.

Bunkie Knudsen, though, probably couldn't have cared less about the bad press. Remember, he loved to go racing, and that was the whole idea behind building the Boss 429.

1970 Boss 302

Following SCCA minimum-production guidelines, Ford built 1,628 Boss 302 Mustangs for 1969. Then came more Trans-Am racing rule changes. In 1970, the minimum requirement became 2,500

1970 Boss 302

Model Availability	SportsRoof fastback
Wheelbase	108 inches
Length	187.4 inches
Height	50.4 inches
Weight	3,260 pounds
Base Price	$3,720
Track	59.5 inches, front and rear
Wheels	15x7 stamped-steel rims, standard; Magnum 500 five-spokes, optional
Tires	F60x15 Wide Oval
Suspension	Independent upper A-arms, lower control arms w/coil springs in front; live axle with leaf springs and staggered shocks in back, heavy-duty front sway bar
Steering	Recirculating ball (quick 16:1 ratio)
Brakes	Front discs, rear drums
Engine	290-horsepower 302-ci Boss 302 V-8 with Cleveland heads
Bore and Stroke	4.00x3.00 inches
Compression	10.5:1
Fuel Delivery	Single 780-cfm Holley four-barrel on aluminum high-rise intake (Shaker Ram-Air hood scoop, optional)
Transmission	Four-speed manual only
Axle Ratio	3.50:1
Production	7,013

Above: The bright 15x7 Magnum 500 wheel was optional in 1970 Mustang ranks only for the Boss 302. *Mike Mueller*

Right: Non-Shaker Boss 302 V-8s in 1970 were topped by a chrome air cleaner lid. *Mike Mueller*

cars or a number equal to 1/250th of a given manufacturer's total production for the previous year, whichever was greater. In Ford terms, this translated into a run of at least 6,500 Boss 302s for 1970. The final tally that year was 7,013.

Updates were few. Mechanically, the '70 Boss 302 was identical underneath save for the addition of 1969's planned rear sway bar. With this bar in place, the front stabilizer was increased in size to 0.85 inch. Additional engineering revisions included a smaller intake valve and a crank that was no longer cross-drilled for extra lubrication. The former was added to help improve the Boss 302 V-8's low-rpm tractability. That latter replacement was made to save money.

On the outside, color choices expanded from the four offered in 1969 (Bright Yellow, Acapulco Blue, Calypso Coral, Wimbledon White) to 13, including the truly radioactive trio of "Grabber" colors: Grabber Blue, Grabber Green, and Grabber Orange. The black-out treatment was lessened on the hood, and the Boss bodyside stripes, again made of reflective 3M material, were revised to run up over the fender tops and down the hood. Magnum 500 five-spoke rims were optional in 1970, as they had been the previous year. A second option was a 15-inch version of the Mach 1's mag-style wheel cover. Conventional 15-inch steel rims with flat center caps and trim rings were standard.

A new contribution to the Boss 302 image, the optional Shaker hood scoop, was both fully functional and so damned cool. Unlike the standard air cleaner in 1969 and 1970, which incorporated a solenoid pop-off valve to allow underhood atmosphere a less-restrictive passage into the carburetor on demand, the Shaker rammed in denser outside air whenever the pedal hit the metal.

Apparently, some consideration was given to continuing the Boss 302 legacy into 1971—reportedly, appropriate decals were prepared. But both the original small-block Boss and its big-block running mate failed to return after 1970, victims of changing attitudes around Dearborn.

Left: A Hurst shifter became standard Boss 302 interior fare in 1970. *Mike Mueller*

Below: The Shaker scoop was a $65 option for the 1970 Boss 302. It also was available atop the 351 small-block and 428 Cobra Jet in other Mustang models. *Mike Mueller*

Below left: The Boss 302 V-8 produced 290 horsepower. Ford's too-cool-for-cool Shaker hood scoop became an option in 1970. *Mike Mueller*

1970 Boss 429

The Kar Kraft works rolled out 857 Boss 429 Mustangs for 1969, then followed that up with 499 more 1970 models before Knudsen's high-powered tale came to an abrupt close. Ford's reasons to race faded rapidly after Knudsen was sacked in September 1969, and the biggest Boss was among the first things to disappear as a result. Nineteen-seventy Mustangs first arrived in Brighton for conversion late in August 1969. Kar Kraft shipped its last Boss 429 on January 6, 1970. The shipper also quietly went away not long after Ford pulled the plug on its racing support in November 1970. Ironically, the Brighton works became home to Rectrans, Inc., Bunkie Knudsen's post-Ford venture. Rectrans built mobile homes designed by Knudsen's buddy, Larry Shinoda.

Like its small-block cousin, the second-edition Boss 429 was treated to a wider array of color

> Mechanically, the '70 Boss 302 was identical underneath save for the addition of 1969's planned rear sway bar.

Above: Only 499 Boss 429 Mustangs were built for 1970. A black-painted hood scoop replaced the body-colored unit used the previous year. *Mike Mueller*

Below: The Boss 429 Mustang was created to legalize its brutal big-block for NASCAR racing. On NASCAR tracks, the Boss 429 V-8 competed beneath the hoods of Ford's long-nose Talladegas. *Mike Mueller*

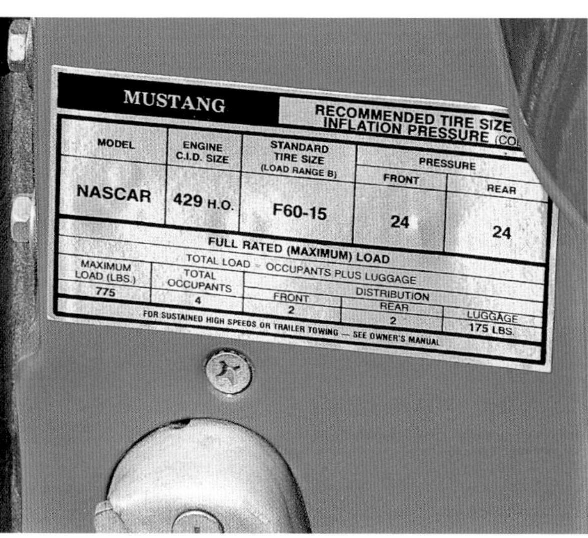

1970 Boss 429

Model Availability	SportsRoof fastback
Wheelbase	108 inches
Length	187.4 inches
Height	50.4 inches
Weight	3,530 pounds
Base Price	$4,900
Track	59.5 inches, front and rear
Wheels	15x7 Magnum 500 five-spoke
Tires	F60x15 Wide Oval
Suspension	Independent upper A-arms, lower control arms (suspension geometry modified to make room for big Boss 429 V-8) w/coil springs in front; live axle with leaf springs and staggered Gabriel shock absorbers in back
Steering	Recirculating ball with power assist (quick 16:1 ratio)
Brakes	Front discs, rear drums
Engine	375-horsepower Boss 429 V-8 with aluminum cylinder heads
Bore and Stroke	4.36x3.59 inches
Compression	10.5:1
Fuel Delivery	Single 735-cfm Holley four-barrel carburetor
Transmission	Four-speed manual only
Axle Ratio	3.90:1 Traction-Lok
Production	499

Left: A deluxe three-spoke rim-blow steering wheel was standard fare inside the 1970 Boss 429, as were Comfortweave high-back bucket seats. *Mike Mueller*

Below left: Known as a semi-hemi or Blue Crescent V-8, the Boss 429 was rated at a laughable 375 horsepower in 1969 and 1970.

Below right: Much of the Boss 351 V-8's makeup was identical to its Windsor-based cousin, the Boss 302. The Boss 351 featured four-bolt caps at all five main bearings, as opposed to three at the Boss 302's bottom end. *Mike Mueller*

> Both the original small-block Boss and its big-block running mate failed to return after 1970, victims of changing attitudes around Dearborn.

choices in 1970. Nearly all other cosmetic touches carried over, with the one notable exception involving the big hood scoop, which was painted low-gloss black. Mechanical upgrades included the addition of a Hurst shifter and the relocation of the rear sway bar from below the axle to above.

1971 Boss 351

Model Availability	SportsRoof fastback
Wheelbase	109 inches
Length	189.5 inches
Height	50.1 inches
Weight	3,560 pounds
Base Price	$4,420
Track	61.5 inches front, 61 inches rear
Wheels	15x7 Magnum 500 five-spoke
Tires	F60x15 Wide Oval
Suspension	Independent upper A-arms, lower control arms w/coil springs in front; live axle with leaf springs and staggered Gabriel shock absorbers in back
Steering	Recirculating ball with variable ratio
Brakes	Front discs, rear drums
Engine	330-horsepower Boss 351 HO V-8
Bore and Stroke	4.00x3.50 inches
Compression	11:1
Fuel Delivery	Single 750-cfm Autolite four-barrel carburetor
Transmission	Hurst-shifted four-speed manual only
Production	1,806

1971 Boss 351

Henry Ford II may have slammed the door shut on Ford's once-proud racing program in November 1970, but not all news was bad that month. The Boss 351 Mustang was introduced to at least keep things hot on the street.

The heart of the Boss 351 was the 351 High Output (HO) Cleveland V-8, an able small-block that could throw its weight around like most big-blocks. Rated at 330 horsepower, the HO featured superb free-flowing heads, which were nearly identical to those used by the Boss 302, save for revised cooling passages. Those excellent canted valves carried over from Boss 302 to HO right down to their diameter, as did much of the valvetrain. Both engines also shared screw-in rocker studs, hardened pushrods, and guide plates. The Boss 351's solid-lifter cam, however, was more aggressive than the Boss 302's.

The 351 HO's lower end was also beefier. As was the case inside the Boss 302's modified Windsor block, the HO's crank was held in place by four-bolt mains, but the latter had four-bolt caps at all five main bearings, not just three. The HO crank was cast (of high nodular iron) instead of forged, and it was specially tested for hardness. Forged connecting rods were shot peened and Magnafluxed and were clamped to the crank by superstrong ⅜-inch bolts. Pistons were forged-aluminum pop-up pieces. On top was a 750-cfm Autolite four-barrel on an aluminum dual-plane manifold. The dreaded Autolite rev limiter too was once more included to help keep a lid on things.

The Boss 351's standard supporting cast included a ram-induction hood, a special cooling package with a flex fan, and a Hurst-shifted wide-ratio four-speed—again, no automatics were offered. In back was a Traction-Lok 9-inch rear end with 31-spline axles and 3.91:1 gears. Underneath was the Competition Suspension package, which featured heavier springs, staggered rear shocks, and sway bars front and rear. Power front disc brakes were standard, too, as were F60 raised-white-letter rubber tires on 15x7 steel wheels adorned with the flat hubcaps and trim rings. Flashy Magnum 500 wheels were optional.

The Boss 351's standard appearance features were all but identical to those found on the 1971 Mach 1. Included up front were Ford's functional NASA hood, a chin spoiler, and a honeycomb grille with color-keyed surround. That Ram-Air hood incorporated twist locks and was done in either argent or blacked-out finish, depending on the body paint choice. Like the hood, Boss 351 standard lower-body paint accents and accent tape stripes were either black or argent, again depending on the chosen exterior finish. Black or argent treatment once more showed up at the rear. Among remaining features were dual racing mirrors and "Boss 351 Mustang" decals on the fenders and tail. A rear deck spoiler was optional. The

The Boss 351 was a 13-second screamer at the drag strip, making it an able competitor even up against big-block rivals.

Left: The Boss 351 Mustang was a one-hit wonder built for 1971 only. Production was 1,806. *Mike Mueller*

Opposite: Boss 351 interiors featured a Hurst shifter and the Instrumentation Group (oil pressure, alternator, and temperature gauges housed in the center of the instrument panel) as standard equipment. *Mike Mueller*

coveted Mach 1 sports interior was optional inside, while full instrumentation and high-back bucket seats were standard.

Inside or out, from nose to tail, the Boss 351 Mustang was a big winner in most critics' minds. Sure, some reviewers complained about visibility problems inherent to the 1971 SportsRoof restyle. But they couldn't deny the Boss 351's aggressive appearance and high-spirited nature. Few rivals could keep pace. As *Car and Driver* reported, the Boss 351 "offers drag strip performance [14.1 seconds at 100.6 miles per hour] that most cars with 100 cubic inches more displacement will envy." Enthusiastic *Motor Trend* testers pushed the envelope even further, producing a 13.8-second run, a figure that put the Boss 351 right up there with the hottest Fords ever built.

Many witnesses recognized too that the Boss 351 probably represented the end of the road for Blue Oval muscle. "This is probably the last chance you'll have to buy a machine of this kind," began a March 1971 *Sports Car Graphic* road test. "Ford is now diverting all its racing talent and dollars into solving safety and pollution problems and trying to satisfy government mandates. We have heard from reliable sources that for the '72 new-model release, all Ford products will be detuned to run on regular fuel. That means lower compression. Perhaps we'll just learn to live with the situation, like war and taxes, which we accept as facts of life. But we have few years left. We might as well take what we can get and live it up while we can."

A few years? Although the 351 HO did carry over into 1972—albeit in detuned form—the Boss 351 came and went as quickly as it ran. At least the Boss legacy went out with a bang.

05

Size Matters

05

1971–1973

- A Mustang base price (with V-8 power) tops $3,000 for the first time in 1971.
- Total production drops to 149,678 for 1971, down from 197,045 for 1970.
- Three body styles remain the norm during the 1971–1973 run: hardtop, SportsRoof, and convertible.
- Luxurious Grande and performance-minded Mach 1 models are offered from 1971 to 1973.
- Height is the only dimension that doesn't increase for the restyled SportsRoof Mustang in 1971. This body style measures 50.6 inches tall in 1970; its 1971 counterpart stands 50.1 inches from ground to top.
- The 429 Cobra Jet/Super Cobra Jet Mustang is offered only for 1971. Total CJ/SCJ production that year is only 1,250.
- The 1971 Boss 351 Mustang also is a one-hit wonder. Production is 1,806.
- The Boss 351 and Mach 1 Mustangs share numerous appearance features, but the 351 HO small-block V-8 is exclusive to the Boss in 1971.
- Power windows become optional for the first time in 1971.
- For the first time in its history, the Mustang's grille carries over unchanged from 1971 to 1972.
- Total production falls again in 1972 to 125,405.
- The Mustang convertible is the only topless model offered by Ford Division in 1973.
- Production rises in 1973 to 134,867.

Above: Plainly set up for the drag strip, this no-nonsense Cobra Jet coupe was delivered without a radio or any other frills in 1971. The Dual Ram Induction hood wasn't even included—to save both weight and cost perhaps? *Mike Mueller*

Opposite: The sleek Milano show car began making public appearances early in 1970 to preview the radical fastback form then being readied for the 1971 Mustang. The Milano's rear roof section was raised electrically to allow interior access.

Previous pages:
Left: Like the Boss 351 model, the 1971 Mach 1 featured a black honeycomb grille. A plain SportsRoof hood appeared on the base 302-powered Mach 1; the scooped NASA hood was a no-cost option with the 302. The NASA hood was included whenever a 351 or 429 Cobra Jet V-8 was ordered. *Mike Mueller*

Right: Two Sprint packages were offered for Mustang hardtops and SportsRoof models in 1972. Package A added blue-accented white paint with a USA shield on the rear quarters. Dual color-keyed mirrors and flat hubcaps with trim rings also were part of the deal. Package B traded those standard rims and hubcaps for sportier Magnum 500 wheels. *Mike Mueller*

Lee Iacocca thought Ford's pony car was fattened up enough in 1967; in 1971, he found his baby looking seriously obese. Anyone with eyes could see how much bigger the latest, hopefully greatest Mustang was compared to its predecessor. Both width and wheel track went up by a whopping 3 inches. Wheelbase was stretched 1 inch, and overall length went up by 2. Weight increased by about 400 pounds. And all these gains appeared especially evident in the form of the 1971 SportsRoof with its nearly flat rear roofline.

ACCORDING TO *SPORTS CAR GRAPHIC*, the newest fastback Mustang featured a "sheet metal shape that looks like it weighs its weight in better ideas. The new body gives one the feeling of being buried in a bunker. Gone is the light, airy feeling of lots of glass and a high seat with commanding view. We have returned to the bulbosity of the '49 Merc. The hood bulges into your line of sight from the force of thousands of pounds of pressure from styling, and the flat, minuscule rear backlite gives a beautiful view of the stars for two in the rear, but little else."

SportsRoof buyers in 1971 were quick to make note of the form's severely restricted rearward visibility thanks to those high, massive quarters and flattened glass. Those who didn't were sometimes quick to notice what happens when you back into poles, shopping carts, or other cars.

The main impetus for this growth was supplied by the new cleaner-running 385-series big-block V-8, introduced in 1968. Displacing 429 cubic inches in Thunderbird trim (Lincoln got a 460-cube version), the 385-series brute was lighter than its FE-series forerunner yet wider thanks to its free-breathing canted-valve heads. To replace the venerable 428 Cobra Jet (its days numbered due to ever-tightening federal emissions restrictions) on the Mustang options list, the socially acceptable 429 would require increased engine room between pony car flanks, a fact performance-conscious Bunkie Knudsen was keenly aware of. He needed just one look at Gail Halderman's mockup in February 1968 to give the go-ahead for a final expansion on the long-hood/short-deck theme. None of the other candidates mattered: the 1971 Mustang would be bigger and better (translated: faster) than ever.

Bunkie's idea of better, however, didn't mesh with Henry Ford II's opinion, nor with the new direction the market was taking as the 1970s dawned. What Knudsen didn't notice was the handwriting

Above: Some Thunderbird resemblances showed up in this early clay mockup (posed in May 1967) for the upcoming 1971 Mustang. Notice the 1968 Mustang in the background.

Right: Many of the final 1971 lines were being mocked up by September 1967. Not making it into production were the hideaway headlights shown here.

Left: Hidden headlights continued to be experimented with in October 1967, and this mockup also minimized the crisp bodyside character lines that eventually made their way into production.

Below: Bunkie Knudsen took one look at this mockup early in 1968 and gave the go-ahead for an even larger new Mustang.

on the wall, something Henry II and Iacocca were both watching intently. Heightened environmental consciousness and increased safety awareness among countless legislators bent on stuffing their caps full of feathers spelled the end for factory performance, as well as Bunkie Knudsen, at least at Ford Motor Company. Times had changed; he hadn't.

"He was a racing nut," remembered Iacocca, "but he failed to understand that the heyday of racing had passed." Henry II fired Knudsen in September 1969, Ford's once-grand motorsport program was all but shut down in November 1970, and the last truly muscular Mustangs were seen in 1971.

Fortunately, the breed carried on with much to offer drivers with a penchant for playfulness.

1971

Reviews among the automotive press were mixed concerning the 1971 Mustang, although all agreed the car was considerably tail heavy in appearance—in actuality, most of the weight rested on the front wheels. Just as it did back then, the restyled 1971 Mustang still represents a love/hate proposition; there never has been a middle ground. Purists then and now who prefer their pony cars to be of the polite, perky variety originally envisioned by Iacocca never have warmed up to Bunkie's big baby.

Subjective responses aside, the overall attraction still ran strong in 1971, as so much of what made the previous Mustang what it was carried over in

According to *Sports Car Graphic*, the newest fastback Mustang featured a "sheet metal shape that looks like it weighs its weight in better ideas."

proud fashion, with a few updates to spice things up. High-back bucket seats and a floor shifter were again included inside and were joined by a standard miniconsole. A radically restyled, much more dominant dash featured three instrument pods (instead of the four seen in 1970) and incorporated Ford's new Direct-Aire ventilation system to supply ample fresh air with all windows up. New too were steel Guard-Rail side-impact beams inside the doors to better protect occupants during T-bone collisions.

A full-sized console was typically optional but was understandably restyled to match the new dash. Full instrumentation was available at extra cost and also was redone appropriately, with the oil pressure, alternator, and temperature gauges located in a three-pod panel above the radio in the 1971 dashboard's enlarged center section. An 8,000-rpm tachometer, added to the left-hand pod in front of the driver, was included in the Instrumentation Group. This package was not available on six-cylinder models.

Power windows debuted on the Mustang options list in 1971, as did a partial vinyl top for SportsRoof models. An optional rear window defroster carried over from 1970 but was revised in a big way. Instead of the air-blow unit seen previously, the 1971 defroster relied on electronic circuitry silk-screened into the inside of the glass to warm things up on frosty mornings, at least on hardtops and SportsRoofs. These highly visible 1/32-inch-wide horizontal heater strips were not fitted to the glass window in the convertible top.

Standard power came from an enlarged six-cylinder displacing 250 cubic inches. The base V-8 was the familiar 302-cube small-block fed by a two-barrel carburetor. Nineteen-seventy's optional 351 Windsor V-8 was dropped in favor of the 351 Cleveland two-barrel, and a more powerful version of this small-block (with bigger valves and a four-barrel carb) was offered, too. A truly hot High Output version of the 351 Cleveland also appeared in 1971, but only for the Boss 351 Mustang, detailed in the previous chapter.

1971

Model Availability	Two-door SportsRoof, two-door coupe, two-door convertible
Wheelbase	109 inches
Length	189.5 inches
Width	74.1 inches
Height	50.8 inches, coupe; 50.5 inches, convertible; 50.1 inches, SportsRoof
Curb Weight	3,080 pounds, coupe; 3,200 pounds, convertible; 3,050 pounds, SportsRoof; 3,220 pounds, Mach 1
Base Price	$2,911, six-cylinder coupe; $3,006 V-8 coupe; $2,973, six-cylinder SportsRoof; $3,068 V-8 SportsRoof; $3,227, six-cylinder convertible; $3,322 V-8 convertible; $3,117, six-cylinder Grande coupe; $3,212, V-8 Grande coupe; $3,268, Mach 1 SportsRoof
Track	61.5 inches front, 61.0 inches rear
Wheels	14x6 stamped-steel, standard; 14x7 and 15x7 Magnum 500 five-spokes, optional
Tires	E78x14 black sidewall, standard w/six-cylinder and small-block V-8s; F70x14 required with 429-ci V-8; E70x14, standard for Mach 1; F70x14, optional for all models (except Boss 351); F60x15, standard for Boss 351, optional with all engines except six-cylinder
Suspension	Independent upper A-arms, lower control arms w/coil springs in front; live axle with leaf springs in back
Steering	Recirculating ball; 27.7:1 ratio, standard w/manual steering; 22.1:1 ratio, standard w/power assist; 15.7:1 ratio, standard w/Competition Suspension
Brakes	Four-wheel hydraulic drums, standard; power front discs, optional (standard w/Boss 351)
Engine	145-horsepower 250-ci inline six-cylinder, standard (not available for Mach 1 or Boss 351); 210-horsepower 302-ci V-8, optional (standard for Mach 1); 240-horsepower 351-ci 2V V-8, optional (available w/Ram-Air); 285-horsepower 351-ci 4V V-8, optional (available w/Ram-Air); 370-horsepower 429-ci Cobra Jet V-8, optional (available w/Ram-Air)
Bore and Stroke	3.68x3.91 inches (250 six), 4.00x3.00 (302 V-8), 4.00x3.50 (351 V-8), 4.36x3.59 (429 Cobra Jet V-8)
Compression	9:1 (250 six), 9:1 (302 V-8), 9:1 (351-2V V-8), 10.7:1 (351-4V V-8), 11.3:1 (429 Cobra Jet V-8)
Fuel Delivery	Motorcraft one-barrel carburetor (250 six), Motorcraft two-barrel carburetor (302 V-8), Motorcraft two-barrel (240-horsepower 351 V-8), Motorcraft four-barrel (285-horsepower 351 V-8)
Transmission	Three-speed manual, standard (not available with 351-4V, Boss 351, and 429 Cobra Jet V-8s); four-speed, optional (not available with 250 six, 302 V-8, and 351-2V V-8; standard w/Boss 351); Cruise-O-Matic automatic, optional (not available w/Boss 351)
Axle Ratio	3.00:1, standard w/six-cylinder manual trans; 2.79:1, standard w/302 V-8 manual trans; 2.75:1, standard w/351-2V V-8; 3.25:1, standard w/performance V-8s
Production	149,678; all bodies, all models (17,406 Grande coupes, 36,498 Mach 1 SportsRoofs, 1,806 Boss 351 SportsRoofs)

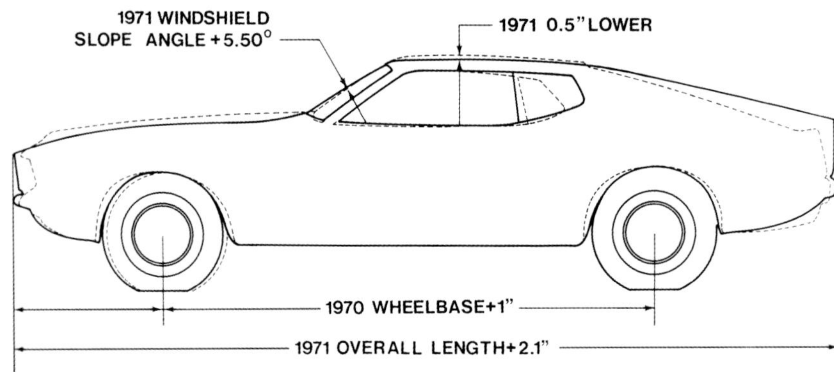

All dimensions, save for height, went up for the 1971 Mustang compared to its 1970 forerunner.

Left: Final front-end appearances for the 1971 Mustang took shape by June 1968.

Below: The Shelby Mustang was destined for retirement after 1970, but this 1968 mockup demonstrated a desire to keep the Cobra legacy alive for the 1971 body. Notice the 1969 Shelby in the background.

At the top of the performance pecking order was the aforementioned 429-ci V-8, a rather gentle giant when planted between T-bird fenders. But in Cobra Jet garb, this big-block instantly became a beast, as Torino Cobra buyers had discovered in 1970. The 370-horsepower 429 Cobra Jet replaced the 428 CJ in Mustang ranks for 1971 and, like its predecessor, could've been transformed into a Super Cobra Jet by checking off the Drag Pack option, which, among other things, included a choice between two race-ready rear axles: a 3.91:1 Traction-Lok or 4.11:1 Detroit Locker.

Included as well in the Drag Pack option for 1971 were various engine modifications. Heavy-duty forged-aluminum pistons were stuffed into the 429 SCJ's block, as was a more potent solid-lifter cam. On top, the Cobra Jet's Quadra-Jet carb was replaced by a larger 780-cfm Holley four-barrel bolted to a specially machined cast-iron intake. An external oil cooler was again included as part of the Super Cobra Jet deal, though not all 1971 SCJ Mustangs received this equipment.

The 429 CJ/SCJ was available on all 1971 Mustang models save, understandably, for the Boss 351.

Left: Only 6,121 Mustang convertibles were built for 1971. Base price (with a six-cylinder) was $3,227. Adding a V-8 upped the ante to $3,322.

Opposite top: A blacked-out rear cove panel also was standard for the 1971 Mach 1. The bright exhaust tips were standard when the 351 Cleveland small-block or 429 CJ big-block was installed. *Mike Mueller*

Opposite bottom: The upscale Grande returned for 1971 and again featured a standard vinyl roof. As previously, it was only offered in notchback coupe form. Grande production for 1971 was 25,274.

The 1971 Mach 1's base engine was a 302 two-barrel V-8 rated at 210 horsepower. Shown here is the optional 351 Cleveland four-barrel V-8, rated at 285 horsepower. *Mike Mueller*

The 429 CJ/SCJ was available on all 1971 Mustang models save, understandably, for the Boss 351. Part of the deal was a hood featuring twin nonfunctional scoops up front. Making those air inlets functional required adding the Ram-Air option, which once more didn't affect Cobra Jet output, nor did the change to Super Cobra Jet. A close-ratio, Top Loader, four-speed, or heavy-duty Cruise-O-Matic C6 automatic transmission went behind the 429 Cobra Jet. Mandatory options included power front discs, competition suspension, and F70 tires.

Like the luxury-conscious Grande (still with its upgraded interior and standard vinyl roof), the hot-to-trot Mach 1 carried over into 1971, and the latter machine again represented a suitably sexy resting place for the optional Cobra Jet big-block. As *Motor Trend*'s Bill Sanders saw it in 1971, the "Mach 1 is back in force, its sleek, exciting fastback creating the appearance of power in motion."

Image-conscious items included a black honeycomb grille mounting a pair of rectangular "sportslamps" just inboard of each headlight. A black honeycomb appliqué was also added at the tail. Taping was limited to a horizontal triple stripe across the tail. Bright lower-bodyside moldings were added to set off contrasting paint (black or argent depending on body color) applied below that trim.

While a conventional chromed bumper remained in back, the front unit was molded out of urethane and colored to match exterior paint. Color-keyed moldings replaced the bright fender caps and leading-edge hood trim found on garden-variety Mustangs in 1971. A popular option that helped contrast that monochromatic look up front was a

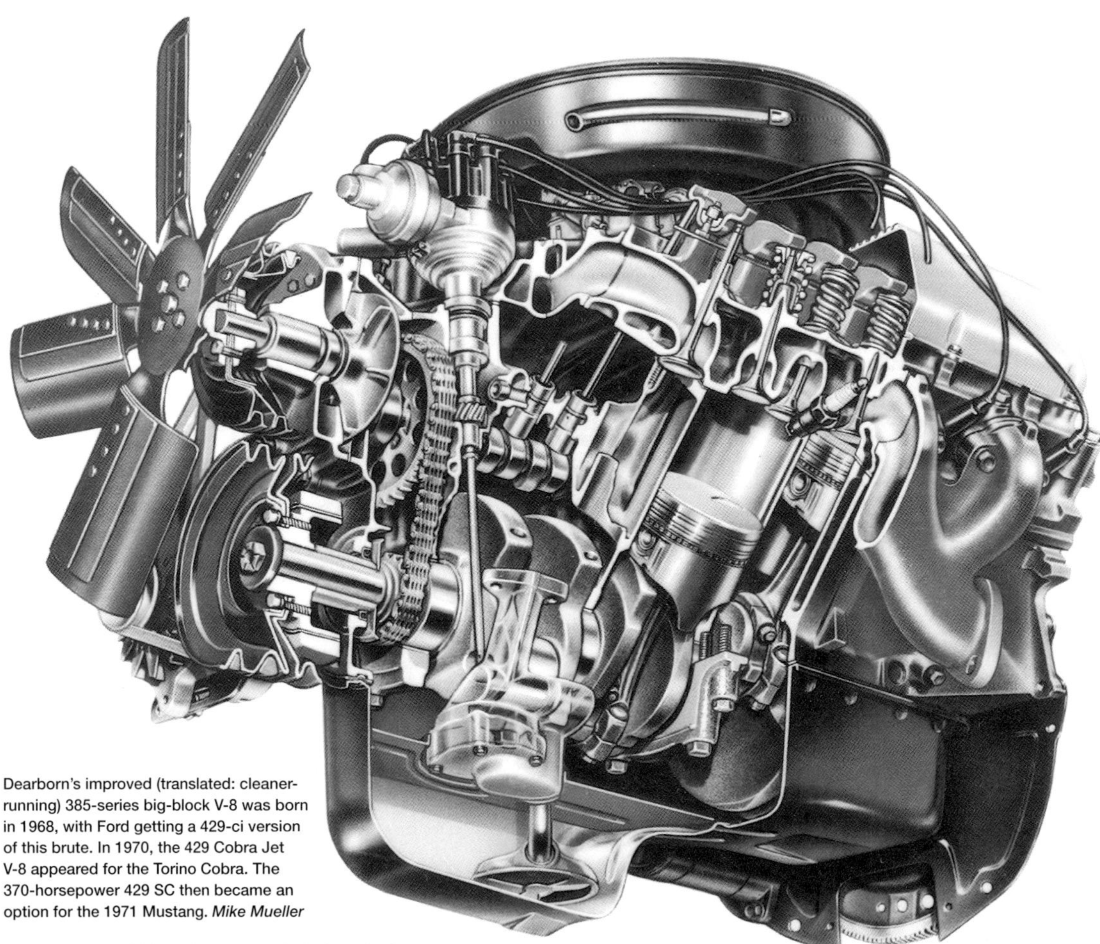

Dearborn's improved (translated: cleaner-running) 385-series big-block V-8 was born in 1968, with Ford getting a 429-ci version of this brute. In 1970, the 429 Cobra Jet V-8 appeared for the Torino Cobra. The 370-horsepower 429 SC then became an option for the 1971 Mustang. *Mike Mueller*

Left: A typical NASA hood in 1971 was for looks only: the scoops were nonfunctional. The Ram-Air plumbing shown here was added when the Dual Ram Induction option was ordered. *Mike Mueller*

Opposite and above: The supreme Mach 1 for 1971 was fitted with the optional 429 Cobra Jet V-8, which came with or without a functional Ram-Air hood. Mandatory options for the 1971 Cobra Jet Mach 1 included power front disc brakes, Competition Suspension, and fat F70 rubber. F60 Wide Oval tires were optional. *Mike Mueller*

> As *Motor Trend's* Bill Sanders saw it in 1971, the "Mach 1 is back in force, its sleek, exciting fastback creating the appearance of power in motion."

bodyside tape stripe that ran the length of the car, tapering off at the tail. These stripes were standard for the Boss 351 Mustang in 1971 and also were used on the little-known Sports Hardtop, a sales-promotional model introduced in the spring of 1971. This coupe was dressed up further with the Mach 1's honeycomb grille, lower-bodyside paint, and color-keyed urethane bumper. A nonfunctional NASA hood was included, too.

Completing the standard 1971 Mach 1 exterior were color-keyed racing mirrors and a racing-style pop-open gas cap in back. Twin round exhaust extensions were included whenever one of the optional four-barrel V-8s was ordered. Unlike previous Mach 1s, which came standard with a flashy hood, the base rendition in 1971 was fitted only with a typical Mustang lid—no scoops, no black-out stripes, no lettering, no competition-style hood pins.

Beneath that plain hood on a bare-bones Mach 1 in 1971 was the 210-horsepower 302 small-block. According to a Ford announcement, the meek little 302 replaced the base 351 used in 1969 and 1970 "to broaden the Mach 1's potential market appeal." If more sex appeal was desired, the standard 302 Mach 1 could've been fitted with the NASA hood at no extra cost. This attractive hood was included in the Mach 1 package whenever an optional V-8 was ordered in 1971. It featured twist-type locks, an accent stripe down the center done in either black or argent, and twin dummy scoops. The fully functional Dual Ram Induction hood was available atop all optional V-8s.

Right top: A typical Mustang interior was standard inside the 1971 Mach 1. The optional Mach 1 Sports Interior added knitted-vinyl high-back bucket seats with accent stripes, a deluxe two-spoke steering wheel, bright pedal trim, a deluxe dash with wood-tone center section, and molded door panels with integral armrests. *Mike Mueller*

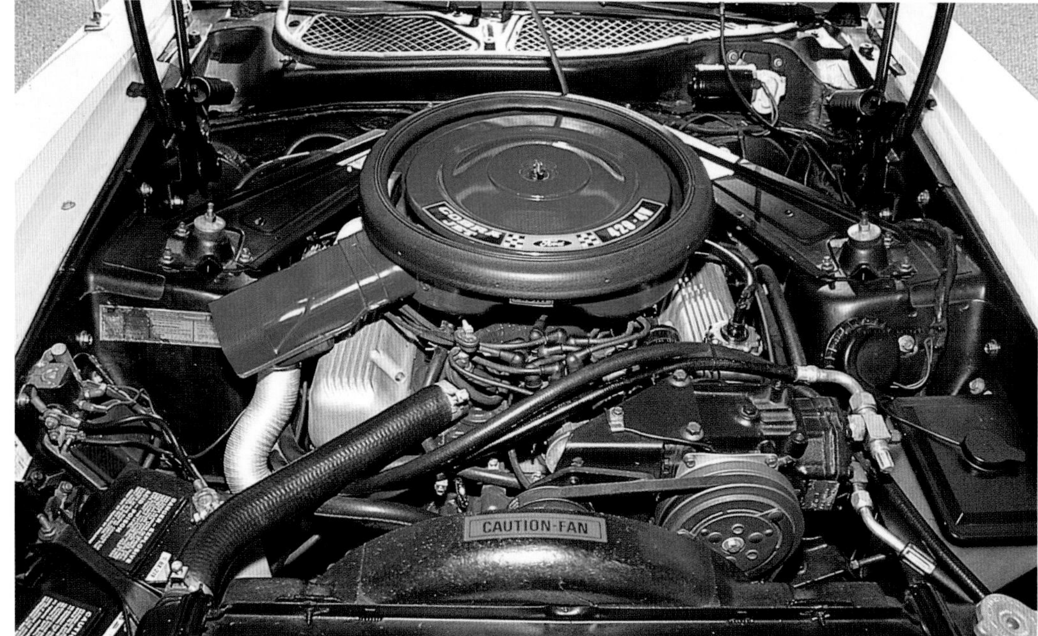

Right middle: Advertised output for the 429 Cobra Jet V-8 didn't change if the Dual Ram Induction hood was installed. That figure remained 370 horsepower. *Mike Mueller*

Right: Not all Cobra Jet Mustangs in 1971 were top-shelf Mach 1 models. Witness this rare CJ-powered bare-bones coupe. Notice the 15x7 wheels with plain hubcaps: these were required when the optional F60 tires were ordered this year. *Mike Mueller*

Above: Introduced in April 1971, this Sports Hardtop model offered some of the Mach 1's pizzazz at a lesser price.

Left: A bright air cleaner lid was used whenever a 429 CJ V-8 was installed without optional Ram-Air in 1971. This was the final year for the big-block Cobra Jet. *Mike Mueller*

1971

All 1971 Mach 1 Mustangs, big- or small-block, were fitted with the heavy-duty Competition Suspension, which featured beefed-up springs and shocks and sway bars front and rear. Base small-block Mach 1s that year rolled on E70x14 white-sidewall tires. F70 rubber was used with optional big-blocks, and truly fat F60x15 white-letter rubber (mounted on attractive 15x7 Magnum 500 wheels) was available at extra cost in all cases. Standard at the corners for the '71 Mach 1 were 14x7 rims dressed with flat center caps and deep-dish trim rings. Sport wheel covers like those used by the '70 Mach 1 were again optional in 1971.

A sporty Mach 1 interior, previously a standard feature, became an option too in 1971. Available for all SportsRoof models, this $130 package included bright pedal trim, special carpet with sewn-in rubber floor mats, simulated wood treatment (on door panel inserts and the dashboard's center instrument panel), and knitted-vinyl high-back buckets. An electric clock was also included in the left-hand instrument pod in front of the driver. Molded door panels, with integrated handles and armrests, completed the deal.

1972

As in 1971, Mustang sales dipped slightly in 1972 as rumors of a totally new pony car planned for 1974 grew. It took a sharp eye to pick out a 1972 Mustang, as next to nothing was done to differentiate it from its predecessor. Frontal styling carried over unchanged from 1971 (a first for the breed), and only a small "Mustang" script above the right taillight gave things away at a quick glance. In 1971, "Mustang" block letters were centrally located across the deck lid.

No big-block was available beneath the hood

Opposite: A small-block Cobra Jet V-8 was rolled out late in the 1971 run. This engine basically was a cross between the 351 Cleveland four-barrel engine and the Boss 351 Mustang's 351 HO. Output was 280 horsepower. *Below:* Revised tape stripes appeared for the 1972 Mach 1. Production was 27,675. Lower-body paint was either black or argent, depending on the exterior color choice, for the 1971–1973 Mach 1. *Mike Mueller*

1972

Model Availability	Two-door SportsRoof, two-door coupe, two-door convertible
Wheelbase	109 inches
Length	189.5 inches
Width	74.1 inches
Height	50.8 inches, coupe; 50.5 inches, convertible; 50.1 inches, SportsRoof
Curb Weight	3,090 pounds, coupe; 3,210 pounds, convertible; 3,060 pounds, SportsRoof; 3,046 pounds, Mach 1
Base Price	$2,729, six-cylinder coupe; $2,816, V-8 coupe; $2,786, six-cylinder SportsRoof; $2,783, V-8 SportsRoof; $3,015, six-cylinder convertible; $3,101, V-8 convertible; $2,915, six-cylinder Grande coupe; $3,002, V-8 Grand coupe; $3,053, Mach 1 SportsRoof
Track	61.5 inches front, 61.0 inches rear
Wheels	14x6 stamped-steel, standard; 14x7 and 15x7 Magnum 500 five-spoke, optional
Tires	E78x14 black sidewall, standard (not available w/351 HO V-8); E70x14, optional (standard for Mach 1); F70x14, optional; F60x15, optional (not available w/250 six, standard w/351 HO V-8)
Suspension	Independent upper A-arms, lower control arms w/coil springs in front; live axle with leaf springs in back
Steering	Recirculating ball; 27.7:1 ratio, standard w/manual steering; 22.1:1 ratio, standard w/power assist; 20.2:1 ratio, standard w/Competition **Suspension**
Brakes	Four-wheel hydraulic drums, standard; power front discs, optional
Engine	99-horsepower 250-ci inline six-cylinder, standard (not available for Mach 1); 141-horsepower 302-ci V-8, optional (standard for Mach 1); 177-horsepower 351-ci 2V V-8, optional (available w/Ram-Air); 266-horsepower 351-ci 4V V-8, 275-horsepower 351-ci HO V-8, optional
Bore and Stroke	3.68x3.91 inches (250 six), 4.00x3.00 (302 V-8), 4.00x3.50 (351 V-8)
Compression	8:1 (250 six), 8.5:1 (302 V-8), 8.6:1 (351-2V V-8), 8.8:1 (351-4V V-8), 8.8:1 (351 HO V-8)
Fuel Delivery	Motorcraft one-barrel carburetor (250 six), Motorcraft two-barrel carburetor (302 V-8), Motorcraft two-barrel (351-2V V-8), Holley four-barrel (351-4V V-8), Holley four-barrel (351 HO V-8)
Transmission	Three-speed manual, standard (not available with 351 V-8s or in California); four-speed, optional for 351-4V V-8 only (standard for 351 HO V-8); Cruise-O-Matic automatic, optional (not available w/351 HO V-8)
Axle Ratio	3.00:1, standard w/six-cylinder manual trans and 302 V-8 manual trans; 2.75:1, standard w/351-2V manual trans; 3.91:1, standard w/351 HO V-8
Production	125,093; all bodies, all models (18,045 Grande coupes, 27,675 Mach 1 SportsRoofs)

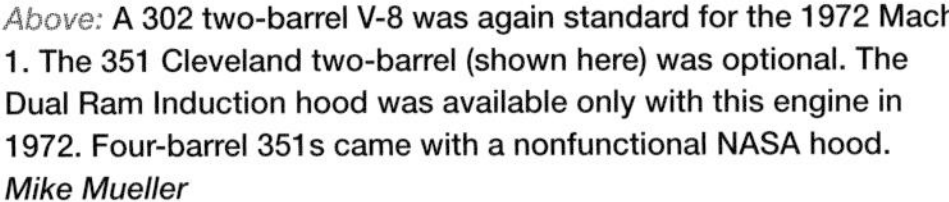

Above: A 302 two-barrel V-8 was again standard for the 1972 Mach 1. The 351 Cleveland two-barrel (shown here) was optional. The Dual Ram Induction hood was available only with this engine in 1972. Four-barrel 351s came with a nonfunctional NASA hood. *Mike Mueller*

Right above: Ford built 75,395 Mustang coupes for 1972. No changes were made up front this year, but at least a 1972 model could've been identified by the Mustang script above the right taillight. Block letters had spelled out the name across the tail the previous year.

Right middle: Grande coupe production for 1972 was 18,045. Base price (with a six-cylinder) was $2,915. A 1972 V-8 Grande started at $3,002.

Right below: Ford vice president and division general manager John Naughton (right) admires a new 1972 Sprint with *Popular Hot Rodding* magazine editor Lee Kelley. The Mustang was honored in *Popular Hot Rodding's* March issue that year as Car of the Decade.

as the 429 Cobra Jet retired at the end of 1971. Standard power once more came from the 250-ci six; optional were the 302 two-barrel V-8, 351 two-barrel, and 351 four-barrel. Two versions of the latter Cleveland small-block were offered: the 351 Cobra Jet and 351 HO.

The rare 351 HO was basically a toned-down version of the 1971 Boss 351 Mustang's exclusive power source. Led by John Bowers, Ford engineers had hoped to keep the Boss engine alive in a world fueled on unleaded gasoline even if the Boss Mustang itself was no longer around to benefit from their efforts. According to engineer Tom Morris of Ford's Special Engine Group, "the basic guts" of the two HO small-blocks were the same, with different cylinder heads, pistons, and camshafts incorporated in 1972. Perhaps the most prominent difference involved compression, which dropped from 11:1 to 8.8:1. The '72 HO's cam remained a mechanical unit, but it was tamed considerably to work with the lowered compression. Output was 275 horsepower.

Introduced late in the 1971 model run, the 351 Cobra Jet represented an attempt at crossbreeding the existing 351 four-barrel Cleveland with the 351 HO, with the goal being to offer at least some of the former Boss 351's performance at a fraction of the Boss 351's cost. Like the '72 HO, the 351 CJ borrowed the '71 Boss 351's burly cylinder block with its four-bolt main bearing caps—typical 351 Clevelands used two-bolt blocks. Again, different heads, pistons, and cam were used and compression was cut to 8.8:1.

Output for 1971's 351 Cobra Jet was 280 horsepower. A few minor emissions-conscious changes dropped that figure to 266 the following year. Curiously, neither the Cobra Jet nor HO could've been equipped with optional Ram-Air in 1972—the Dual Ram Induction hood was only offered for that year's 351 two-barrel. That the Ram-Air option was no longer available for the Mach 1's hottest V-8s was a matter of meeting Washington's toughened emissions standards. Apparently the wide-open Ram-Air 351 four-barrel couldn't be emissions certified, while the tamer two-barrel could when breathing in cooler, denser air. The same situation existed in 1973.

Like the basic Mustang itself, the 1972 Mach 1 looked an awful lot like its 1971 forerunner, with two noticeable exceptions. The easiest clue to the 1972 rendition's identity came in back, where a pop-open gas cap was no longer included; in its place was a standard Mustang cap. The other difference appeared on the window sticker, where the '72 Mach 1's base price bottomed out at a few hundred dollars less than 1971's.

Right above: Plain Mustang appointments (shown here) once more were standard inside the 1972 Mach 1. The flashier Mach 1 Sports Interior again was offered at extra cost. *Mike Mueller*

Right: Late in February 1972, Ford rolled out its latest Sprint Mustang, this time joined by similarly adorned Maverick and Pinto models.

Below: Convertible production stayed low in 1972; only 6,401 were built.

Ford put together 50 special Olympic Sprint convertibles for 1972 to help honor that year's Olympics. *Mike Mueller*

Patriotic red, white, and blue treatment carried over inside the 1972 Sprint and Olympic Sprint models. *Mike Mueller*

Left: All 50 Olympic Sprint convertibles were equipped with Ford's 302 two-barrel V-8, automatic transmission, power steering and brakes, and air conditioning. *Mike Mueller*

Below: A revised grille/headlight arrangement appeared for the 1973 Mustang, as did a standard impact-resistant urethane-covered front bumper. The blacked-out grille shown here was optional. *Mike Mueller*

All other standard equipment carried over from 1971, including the base 302 small-block. Again, the NASA hood wasn't included atop the 302 unless specified as a no-cost option. It was added automatically along with the three optional Cleveland small-blocks.

Although the Boss 351 didn't return for 1972, there was another special model offered that year, which also was a one-hit wonder. Introduced in late February 1972, Ford's third-edition Mustang Sprint—like its similarly dressed-up Pinto and Maverick cousins—wasn't easily missed with its exclusive patriotic finish: white with red-accented blue stripes on the hood, rockers, and rear cove panel. Equally patriotic was the U.S.A. shield applied to the rear quarters in honor of the country's 1972 Olympic team.

Originally offered only for 1972 hardtops and SportsRoofs, the Sprint option was listed in two forms, "package A" and "package B." Along with the aforementioned exterior touches, package A also included dual color-keyed racing mirrors and E70 white-sidewall rubber on 14-inch wheels with brushed-aluminum hubcaps and trim rings. Inside went unique upholstery featuring blue cloth inserts in white vinyl seats. On the outside was Ford's Exterior Decor Group, made up of a honeycomb grille and various color-keyed add-ons such as the front bumper, hood molding, and wheel lip moldings. Package B featured all that plus four F60 tires on 15-inch Magnum 500 wheels in place of the 14-inch wheel/tire combo.

This forged-aluminum wheel was a $142 option for standard Mustangs in 1973. It cost $110.92 when ordered along with the Mach 1 or Decor Group that year. The price was $118.77 when added to the 1973 Grande coupe. *Mike Mueller*

Mach 1 popularity reached an all-time high in 1973, as Mustang sales reversed themselves for one last fling before the first-generation pony car platform was retired.

1973

Model Availability	Two-door SportsRoof, two-door coupe, two-door convertible
Wheelbase	109 inches
Length	193.8 inches
Width	74.1 inches
Height	50.7 inches, coupe; 50.4 inches, convertible; 50.0 inches, SportsRoof
Curb Weight	3,239 pounds, coupe; 3,366 pounds, convertible; 3,240 pounds, SportsRoof; 3,090 pounds, Mach 1
Base Price	$2,760, six-cylinder coupe; $2,847, V-8 coupe; $2,820, six-cylinder SportsRoof; $2,907, V-8 SportsRoof; $3,102, six-cylinder convertible; $3,189, V-8 convertible; $2,946, six-cylinder Grande coupe; $3,033, V-8 Grande coupe; $3,088, Mach 1 SportsRoof
Track	61.0 inches front, 60.8 inches rear
Wheels	14x5.5 stamped-steel, standard; 14x6, optional w/E70 tires; 14x6 forged-aluminum rims, optional
Tires	E78x14 black sidewall, standard; F70x14 required with 429-ci V-8; E70x14, optional (standard for Mach 1); F70x14, optional; F78x14, optional (not available for Mach 1); GR78x14, optional (with or without white sidewall)
Suspension	Independent upper A-arms, lower control arms w/coil springs in front; live axle with leaf springs in back
Steering	Recirculating ball; 27.7:1 ratio, standard w/manual steering; 22.1:1 ratio, standard w/power assist; 15.7:1 ratio, standard w/Competition Suspension
Brakes	Four-wheel hydraulic drums, standard; power front discs, optional (standard w/Boss 351)
Engine	99-horsepower 250-ci inline six-cylinder, standard (not available for Mach 1); 141-horsepower 302-ci V-8, optional (standard for Mach 1); 177-horsepower 351-ci 2V V-8, optional (available w/Ram-Air); 248-horsepower 351-ci Cobra Jet V-8, optional
Bore and Stroke	3.68x3.91 inches (250 six), 4.00x3.00 (302 V-8), 4.00x3.50 (351 V-8)
Compression	8:1 (250 six), 8.5:1 (302 V-8), 8.6:1 (351-2V V-8), 8.8:1 351 Cobra Jet V-8
Fuel Delivery	Motorcraft one-barrel carburetor (250 six), Motorcraft two-barrel carburetor (302 V-8), Motorcraft two-barrel (351-2V V-8), Holley four-barrel (351 Cobra Jet V-8)
Transmission	Three-speed manual, standard (not available w/351 V-8s); four-speed manual, optional w/351 Cobra Jet V-8; Cruise-O-Matic automatic, optional (required w/351-2V V-8 and Ram-Air option)
Axle Ratio	3.00:1, standard (not available w/351 V-8s); 2.75:1, standard w/351-2V V-8; 3.50:1, standard w/351 Cobra Jet V-8 manual trans; 3.25:1, standard w/351 Cobra Jet automatic transmission
Production	134,817; all bodies, all models (25,274 Grande coupes, 35,439 Mach 1 SportsRoofs)

Although not initially offered, a handful of 1972 Sprint convertibles was also built. Fifty of these so-called "Olympic Sprint" ragtops were ordered in the spring of 1972 as part of a promotional plan put together by Ford's Washington, D.C., area district sales office. All 50 were created to take part in Washington's annual Cherry Blossom Parade, an April tradition in the nation's capitol.

Into these cars went 52 pretty princesses (one from each state, plus Guam and Puerto Rico) vying for the honor of 1972 Cherry Blossom Parade queen. But on parade day, temperatures hovered in the 20s and snow flurries collected on the capitol's icy streets along with all those pink-and-white cherry blossoms. The parade's grand marshal, Olympic track legend Jesse Owens, went running for cover early in the ceremony, followed shortly by D.C. mayor Walter Washington. At least one young Cherry Blossom queen candidate, Martha Schoonover, Miss Arkansas, finally demanded that the top go up on her ride immediately after she passed the viewing stand, following a bone-chilling 10-block crawl. We can only guess if Miss Alaska was left wondering what all the fuss was about.

After the other princesses were pried from their frosty perches, the 50 Olympic Sprint convertibles were sent off to various dealerships to be sold as high-profile reminders of an event most attendees would've just as soon forgotten.

1973

Another Mustang first occurred this year: a body carried over without a major restyle into a third model run. All previous shells had appeared for two years only and then were reshaped. But, with the much-anticipated Mustang II right around the

Production for the last convertible Mustang offered until 1983 jumped up to 11,853 in 1973. The exterior color shown here (Gold Glow) was one of three extra-cost metallic finishes offered for 1973. The Gold Glow finish was a $34.90 option. *Mike Mueller*

Deluxe molded door panels and knitted-vinyl seats were standard inside convertible Mustangs in 1973. The deluxe three-spoke steering wheel and full-sized console shown here were optional. *Mike Mueller*

Above: The Instrumentation Group was a $70.83 option for standard Mustangs in 1973. It included gauges for oil pressure, alternator, and coolant temperature. *Mike Mueller*

Right: Priced at $40.79, this optional 351 Cleveland two-barrel V-8 was rated at 177 horsepower in 1973. The Dual Ram Induction hood cost $76.33 that year. *Mike Mueller*

A trunk-mounted luggage rack was a dealer-installed option in 1973. *Mike Mueller*

corner, there was no justification for such fuss and muss for 1973.

At least designers made a few updates to set the latest Mustang apart: a honeycomb grille was added up front and bright taillight trim replaced the black bezels used previously. To meet Washington's new 5-mile-per-hour frontal impact standards, the 1973 Mustang was fitted with an impact-absorbing front bumper covered in body-colored urethane. Basically all mechanicals carried over unchanged, save for smaller valves and less compression in the optional 351 Cobra Jet.

The 1973 Mach 1 also rolled over nearly unchanged, with the most noticeable change involving new tape stripes that superseded the contrasting lower-bodyside paint used in 1972. Located down near where the bright delineation trim was found the previous year, the 1973 side stripes had "Mach 1" identification cut into them just ahead of each rear wheel. "Mach 1" lettering, offset to the passenger side, was also included in the rear deck stripe.

The Mach 1 engine lineup repeated, too. New for 1973 was an optional 14x6 forged-aluminum

slotted mag that replaced the 15-inch Magnum 500 wheel offered previously. The Sport wheel cover, with its simulated lug nuts, also remained a Mach 1 option.

Mach 1 popularity reached an all-time high in 1973, as Mustang sales reversed themselves for one last fling before the first-generation pony car platform was retired. The Mach 1's cut of Ford's pony car pie had been 24.2 percent in 1969. It hit 21.5 in 1970, 24.4 in 1971, and 22.1 in 1972. For 1973, the figure reached a hefty 26.3 percent, proving perhaps that Mustang buyers still preferred their rides to be on the wild side. That, however, was about to change, along with the entire American automobile industry. If only buyers knew it then.

Mach 1 production for 1973 was 35,439. The lower-bodyside tape stripes once again were new this year.

06

Back to Basics

06

1974–1978

- A new Ford compact, the Maverick, debuts midyear in 1969.
- Lee Iacocca calls for a downsized Mustang at management meeting in November 1969.
- Lincoln-Mercury begins importing its sporty V-6 Capri in April 1970.
- An even smaller compact, the Pinto, is unveiled (as a 1971 model) in September 1970.
- In August 1971, Lee Iacocca directs studio head Gene Bordinat to organize a design competition to determine the next new Mustang's form.
- Iacocca's "little jewel," the Mustang II, debuts in August 1973.
- The Arab oil embargo causes gas prices to skyrocket in October 1973.
- The Mustang II debuts for 1974 and is honored as *Motor Trend* magazine's Car of the Year.
- The first four-cylinder and V6 engines appear beneath Mustang hoods in 1974.
- Nineteen-seventy-four is the only year a V8 Mustang is not offered.
- Nineteen-seventy-four is the first year a convertible Mustang not offered.
- Ford's 5.0-liter (302 cubic inches) V8 becomes a Mustang II option in 1975.
- The King Cobra is offered for 1978 only.
- The Mach 1 is shelved after 1978.

Above: Mustang II production hit a low of 153,173 in 1977. Of these, 55,880 were three-door 2+2 hatchbacks (shown here) and 97,293 were two-door coupes.

Opposite: Mustang II sales for 1974 nearly reached 1964 standards. Popularity also was enhanced by a Car of the Year trophy awarded by *Motor Trend* magazine.

Previous pages:
Left: Black lower-body paint and color-keyed remote-control mirrors were standard for the 1975 Mach 1. *Mike Mueller*

Right: Cobra II production in 1977 was 11,948.

Necessity quite often is the mother of invention—or reinvention in the Mustang's case. Even if Lee Iacocca hadn't disapproved, even if customers hadn't complained, even if sales hadn't started lagging, Ford's ever-growing pony car still surely would have undergone a downsizing at some point during the 1970s due to competitive pressures applied from abroad.

INITIAL IMPETUS FOR JUST SUCH A SHIFT dated back to the 1950s, when foreign compact cars, primarily Volkswagen's "Bug," began taking tiny bites out of Detroit's pie. Ford's response—the 1960 Falcon—demonstrated in record-setting fashion that Americans did indeed want small, budget-conscious cars. But then Dearborn's first successful compact—like the Mustang it helped spawn—began to evolve into something bigger, something less efficient, something more costly. By 1966, the Falcon basically was a midsized machine, a car that dwarfed the various Japanese imports then taking their own seats at the American dessert table. With this new threat from the Far East in mind, Ford designers reinvented their compact, relying on the existing Falcon platform to roll out the new Maverick midyear in 1969.

Still not quite competitive (translated: small) enough, the Maverick was joined by the truly diminutive Pinto in September 1970. Called "the second part of a 1-2 punch against the imports" by Ford, this highly affordable (less than $2,000) subcompact became an overnight success, with 1971 sales topping 352,000. A whopping 480,000 more Pintos followed in 1972.

Meanwhile, Mustang sales for 1972 barely surpassed 125,000, down from nearly 300,000 for 1969. Explaining this fall from grace was simple enough. Every bit as disgruntled as Iacocca, loyal pony lovers had started making their complaints known to Ford as early as 1968, with one letter-writer later calling the Mustang a "luxury bus." Stockholders that year spoke up in protest concerning this growth, opening the door for the breed's founding father to make his move.

In November 1969—two months after Henry Ford II fired Bunkie Knudsen—Iacocca let Ford's top management know exactly how he felt about Mustang progress during a company conference held in West Virginia. Dearborn execs then immediately agreed to build a new sporty small car (code-named "Ohio") for 1974 using the Maverick platform as a base. A second proposal, tabbed "Arizona," also appeared, this one calling for an upscale Pinto for 1975. In the meantime, Iacocca and his band of loyalists had to stand by and watch as Bunkie's big baby bullied its way through 1971, 1972, and 1973.

Early on, it looked like the larger Ohio vehicle (rolling on a 103-inch wheelbase) would become the next new Mustang. But such thinking started to shift in April 1970 after Lincoln-Mercury began importing its sexy V-6 Capri into America. Nicknamed the "European Mustang," this sporty little (100.8-inch wheelbase) coupe had debuted in London in December 1968 and within a year was a rollicking success in Great Britain and West Germany. Buyers on this side of the Atlantic loved it, too, leading more than one Ford official to conclude that getting really small could be the next craze.

With the Capri (as well as subcompacts in general) selling like mad, the decision was made in July 1971 to forget the compact Ohio plan and proceed with the smaller Arizona (96.2-inch wheelbase). Nat Adamson, the advanced product planning manager who had led the Arizona design team from the beginning, was promoted to light car planning manager and put in charge of developing the next-generation pony car platform. Production was slated to begin in July 1973.

As for styling, early ideas (for both Arizona and Ohio) from Gene Bordinat's studio didn't exactly thrill anyone. So Iacocca turned to Alejandro de Tomaso and the famed Ghia studios in Turin, Italy, this after Ford bought controlling interest in Ghia in November 1970. Two Ghia prototypes (fastback and notchback coupe) were fashioned, and their look greatly influenced the form that then evolved at the hands of Ford designers.

One problem Bordinat's team encountered during its earliest downsizing design efforts involved an original specification calling for the installation of Ford's existing inline six-cylinder engine. Clearly too long for the proposed platform, the straight six was dropped in favor of a tiny 2.3-liter four-cylinder. Plans also called for an optional V-6, an enlarged version of the Capri's Euro-sourced bent-six.

Bordinat was an outspoken proponent for keeping only one body style for the next-generation Mustang. It was decided early on that dropping the convertible was only right, considering how fast topless sales were dwindling across the board in Detroit as the 1960s closed down. And many in management apparently sided with Bordinat; concentrating on a single body would be the plan. But no one would make a decision about which shape—fastback or notchback—would go from clay to steel.

Finally, in August 1971, Iacocca directed Bordinat to organize a design competition, much like the one staged during the first Mustang's creation process in 1962, to decide things once and for all. Four

Below: **Lee Iacocca's little jewel reversed the Mustang's course in 1974. Ford's pony car was once more a light, lively animal, as it had been 10 years before.**

groups took part, and it was a snazzy fastback that came from Al Mueller's Lincoln-Mercury studio that apparently won out in November. Not so fast. A nice notchback, inspired by the Ghia prototype and done by Don DeLaRossa's Advanced Design studio, reminded many witnesses of the Mustang's original image, which appeared first in notchback form in 1964 and was later morphed into a fastback. Iacocca, of course, wanted to revive as much of that image as possible. So in February 1972—a mere 16 months before production was scheduled to start—he surprised his designers with a direct order to put DeLaRossa's design back into the process with the fastback. Two bodies it would be. And in the fastback's case, the rear roof became a third door, making it a hatchback.

From the earliest planning stages, Iacocca also demanded that the new Mustang to come for 1974 be "a little jewel." He wanted an upscale small car, a lively, still-affordable machine that would put all rival four-cylinder models, foreign and domestic, to shame. Quality in all aspects—ride, comfort, fit, and finish—was key, and to that end engineers

Top: **A conceptual look into the Mustang's future, circa 1976.**

Above: **The original Mustang was based on Ford's groundbreaking compact, the Falcon. The second-generation pony car evolved from an even smaller compact, the Pinto, introduced for 1971. Production of the popular 1972 Pinto (shown here) soared to 480,000.**

Above: The convertible did not carry over into the Mustang II era. Only a hardtop coupe and 2+2 hatchback (shown here) were offered. Production was 257,148 for the coupe and 118,845 for the hatchback in 1974.

Right: Both the dressy Ghia and sporty Mach 1 (shown here) did roll over into the second-generation run. Production of 1974 Mustang II Mach 1 hatchbacks was 44,046.

Opposite top: The two-door Ghia coupe was base priced at $3,621 in 1974. A vinyl roof again came standard atop the Ghia Mustang.

Opposite bottom: A manually operated sunroof was a $149 option for two-door coupes only in 1974.

managed to curtail noise, vibration, and harshness (NVH) like no other compact creators before them.

Helping keep the NVH gremlins at bay was a U-shaped, isolated subframe up front, the work of engineers Bob Negstad and Jim Kennedy. Called the "toilet seat" around Ford's engineering offices, this unit absorbed engine vibrations and road shocks before they could be transmitted to the unit body's passenger compartment. Extra rubber insulation throughout the chassis and a special sound-deadener barrier, which melted to the floorboard during the paint baking process, additionally made for a reasonably quiet ride, certainly so for a compact.

Being a compact, being such a radical departure from previous models, the all-new pony car for 1974 needed an equally new name, or so thought Ford's promotional people. Reportedly, the North American Operations Public Relations office issued a written suggestion in August 1972: "Mustang II." The "II" would surely announce a rebirth, a new generation, not just the rollover of yet another model year. Henry Ford II was an easy sell—remember, he had wanted to call the original Mustang the "Thunderbird II"—and so the deal was done.

Iacocca later claimed in a 2004 *Mustang Monthly* interview that he pushed for the Roman numerals because the radically downsized 1974 model didn't deserve a direct tie to his original "Mustang"—this after he had had 30 years to second-guess the downturn that followed once the compact pony's newness wore off. Funny thing, though: he had been more than willing to bask in the limelight when Motor Trend magazine made the Mustang II its Car of the Year for 1974.

As it was, Ford's decision to remake the Mustang that year began looking like a stroke of genius just a few months after Iacocca's little jewel debuted in August 1973. In October, the Arab oil embargo overnight transformed gasoline into gold, which in turn made small, fuel-efficient cars a truly hot commodity on the American market. Clearly, had

Ford's decision to remake the Mustang that year began looking like a stroke of genius just a few months after Iacocca's little jewel debuted in August 1973.

Iacocca's bosses not listened to his claims that less actually could be more, they would have found their hands forced a few short years later. Either way, it would have been back to basics for the Mustang.

1974

"Small" wasn't a small enough word for the Mustang II, certainly so in comparison to its pony car predecessor from 1973. At 96.2 inches, the downsized Mustang's wheelbase dropped by 13 inches. The 1974 model also was 4 inches skinnier, 14 inches shorter, and some 300 pounds lighter. According to *Motor Trend*, this new breed stood as "a total departure from the fat old horse of the recent past."

Smallness was standard beneath the hood, too. By no means America's first modern four-cylinder, the Mustang II's base power source nonetheless qualified as this country's metric pioneer, as well as Dearborn's first (again from a thoroughly modern perspective) domestic-built four-banger. The 1971 Pinto had included a British-built 1.6-liter four as standard equipment and a German-built 2.0-liter four as an option. Both engines were of overhead-cam (OHC) design. When Ford engineers developed their own OHC four-holer for the Mustang II, they stuck with metrics to preserve parts interchangeability with the company's Euro-sourced engines. Manufactured at Ford's Lima, Ohio, plant, this 2.3-liter mill produced a tidy 88 horsepower and reportedly was good for as much as 23 miles per gallon. For those still allergic to metric wrenches, those 2.3 liters translated into 140 cubic inches.

The optional V-6 displaced 2.8 liters (171 cubic inches) and was rated at 105 horsepower. Like its four-cylinder running mate, it was fed by a Motorcraft two-barrel carburetor. Compression was 8.7:1 for the six, 8.4:1 for the four. Mechanical woes left many V-6 buyers wishing they'd stuck with the frugal four, while other drivers lamented the absence of optional V-8 power, a first for Ford's pony car lineage. But such complaints were overwhelmed by

1974

Model Availability	Two-door coupe, three-door hatchback
Wheelbase	96.2 inches
Length	175 inches
Width	70.2 inches
Height	50.0 inches, coupe; 49.7 inches, hatchback
Curb Weight	2,620 pounds, coupe; 2,699 pounds, hatchback; 2,866 pounds, Ghia coupe; 2,788 pounds, Mach 1
Base Price	$3,081, coupe; $3,275, hatchback; $3,427, Ghia coupe; $3,621, Mach 1
Track	55.6 inches front,
	55.8 inches rear
Wheels	13-inch, standard
Tires	B78 belted blackwall;
	BR78, standard for Ghia
Suspension	Independent upper A-arms, lower lateral arms w/coil springs in front; live axle with leaf springs in back
Steering	Rack and pinion
Brakes	Front discs (9.3-inch rotors), rear drums
Engine	88-horsepower 2.3-liter inline SOHC four-cylinder, standard; 105-horsepower 2.8-liter V-6, optional
Bore and Stroke	3.78x3.13 inches (four), 3.66x2.70 inches (V-6)
Compression	8.4:1 (four), 8.7:1 (V-6)
Fuel Delivery	Motorcraft two-barrel carburetor, both cases
Transmission	Four-speed manual, standard; Select-Shift Cruise-O-Matic automatic, optional
Axle Ratio	2.79:1, four-cylinder manual; 3.18:1, four-cylinder automatic; 3.00:1, V-6
Production	385,993; all bodies and models (89,477 Ghia coupes; 44,046 Mach 1 hatchbacks)

Right: The 1974 lineup rolled over unchanged into 1975. Production for the 1975 Ghia (shown here) was 52,320.

Below right: Mach 1 production for 1975 was 21,026. Base price was $4,188. *Mike Mueller*

the sounds of Mustang II owners pinching pennies at the pump. Plain and simply, it was soaring fuel costs that spurred on the new car's popularity in 1974. Production was nearly 386,000.

Additional standard features included a four-speed stick, rack-and-pinion steering, front disc brakes, and staggered rear shock absorbers. Ford's SelectShift Cruise-O-Matic automatic transmission was optional. While traditional parallel leaf springs brought up the Mustang II's tail, the front suspension was revised to put the coil springs between the upper and lower arms, as opposed to their previous location above the upper arms.

Four models were offered in 1974: two-door notchback coupe, three-door 2+2 hatchback, upscale Ghia coupe, and three-door Mach 1. The first three included the 2.3-liter four-cylinder as standard equipment, while the performance-oriented Mach 1 featured the V-6 with the four available as a credit option. As a replacement for the Grande, offered from 1969 to 1973, the Ghia came with a vinyl roof, wood-tone door panels, shag carpeting, deluxe seatbelts, remote-control mirrors, digital clock, and spoke-style wheel covers. Along with the V-6, the basic Mach 1 included dual color-keyed remote mirrors, Wide Oval tires on styled-steel wheels, and typical exterior striping.

Enhancing the Mach 1's appeal even further was the Rallye Package, also offered for other V-6-equipped models save for the Ghia. This option added a Traction-Lok differential, steel-belted white-letter tires on styled-steel wheels, extra cooling equipment, dual color-keyed remote mirrors, a Sport exhaust system, digital clock, leather-wrapped steering wheel, and a competition suspension. The latter consisted of stiffer springs, a rear stabilizer bar, and adjustable shocks.

Summed up, these performance parts may have looked good on paper, but they didn't get the job done in practice, a plain fact critics quickly pounced on. "While the Mach 1's general concept is enthusiast-oriented," claimed *Car and Driver*, "its poor acceleration, wide-ratio transmission and overweight chassis leave too much of its undeniably sporting flavor unsupported by nourishment." *Car Craft* called the latest Mach 1 "regrettably underpowered," then predicted that Ford would probably have to offer a V-8 version and soon.

1975

An optional V-8 fortunately did arrive in 1975, and stuffing this 5.0-liter (302-ci) small-block between Mustang II flanks resulted in a few noticeable changes. Underneath, a revised subframe crossmember and repositioned radiator were required, meaning a new, longer hood and remounted grille were needed on the outside. Topped too by a Motorcraft two-barrel, the 302 V-8 was net rated at 122 horsepower.

Nearly everything else—standard features, options, model lineup—rolled over from 1974. New standard items were steel-belted radial tires and solid-state electronic ignition. New on the options list was a manually controlled moonroof. And the 1975 Ghia coupe could have been adorned further with a Silver Luxury Group package that added silver metallic paint with Cranberry striping and silver bodyside moldings, a silver half-vinyl roof, a stand-up hood ornament,

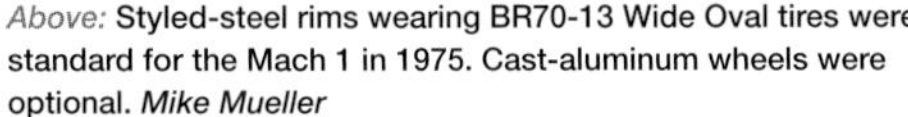

Above: Styled-steel rims wearing BR70-13 Wide Oval tires were standard for the Mach 1 in 1975. Cast-aluminum wheels were optional. *Mike Mueller*

Right: The Stallion package was introduced for 1976 to dress up the basic four-cylinder Mustang II MPG. The black-out treatment was also offered for the Pinto MPG and Maverick that same year.

1975

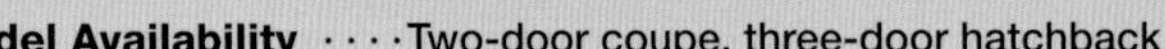

Model Availability	Two-door coupe, three-door hatchback
Wheelbase	96.2 inches
Length	175 inches
Width	70.2 inches
Height	50.0 inches, coupe;
	49.7 inches, hatchback
Curb Weight	2,660 pounds, four-cylinder coupe; 2,775 pounds, V-6 coupe; 2,697 pounds, four-cylinder hatchback; 2,812 pounds, V-6 hatchback; 2,704 pounds, four-cylinder Ghia; 2,819 pounds, V-6 Ghia; 2,879 pounds, Mach 1
Base Price	$3,529, four-cylinder coupe; $3,801, V-6 coupe; $3,818, four-cylinder hatchback; $4,090, V-6 hatchback; $3,938, four-cylinder Ghia; $4,210, V-6 Ghia; $4,188, Mach 1
Track	55.6 inches front, 55.8 inches rear
Wheels	13-inch, standard
Tires	B78 belted blackwall (B70 Wide Oval for Mach 1)
Suspension	Independent upper A-arms, lower lateral arms w/coil springs in front; live axle with leaf springs in back
Steering	Rack and pinion
Brakes	Front discs (9.3-inch rotors), rear drums
Engine	88-horsepower 2.3-liter inline SOHC four-cylinder, standard; 105-horsepower 2.8-liter V-6, optional; 122-horsepower 302-ci V-8, optional
Bore and Stroke	3.78x3.13 inches (four), 3.66x2.70 inches (V-6), 4.00x3.00 inches (V-8)
Compression	8.4:1 (four), 8.7:1 (V-6), 8.0:1 (V-8)
Fuel Delivery	Motorcraft two-barrel carburetor in all cases
Transmission	Four-speed manual, standard; Select-Shift Cruise-O-Matic automatic, optional
Axle Ratio	2.79:1, four-cylinder manual; 3.18:1, four-cylinder automatic; 3.00:1, V-6; 2.79:1, V-8
Production	188,575; all bodies, all models (52,320 Ghia coupes, 21,026 Mach 1 hatchbacks)

As much as saving on gas remained a priority across America, the attraction behind the downsized Mustang began to fade.

and a Cranberry interior in velour cloth with color-keyed sun visors and console.

An MPG package was offered midyear in 1975 that further depleted the Mustang II's performance image. Pairing the 2.3-liter four with a 3.18:1 highway axle made for snail-like acceleration but translated into more than 30 miles per gallon.

As much as saving on gas remained a priority across America, the attraction behind the downsized Mustang began to fade as, among other things, buyers became more and more dissatisfied with the Mustang II's tight confines. Sales dropped by more than 50 percent for 1975.

1976

With sales sticking around 187,000, the third-edition Mustang II was still the leader in the domestic subcompact field, even if that figure paled in

All base Mustang IIs fitted with the 2.3-liter OHC four-cylinders officially became MPG models in 1976, as Ford tried to preserve the fuel-saving notion as a major selling point.

1976

Model Availability	Two-door coupe, three-door hatchback
Wheelbase	96.2 inches
Length	175 inches
Width	70.2 inches
Height	50.0 inches, coupe; 49.7 inches, hatchback
Curb Weight	2,678 pounds, four-cylinder coupe; 2,756 pounds, V-6 coupe; 2,706 pounds, four-cylinder hatchback; 2,784 pounds, V-6 hatchback; 2,729 pounds, four-cylinder Ghia; 2,807 pounds, V-6 Ghia; 2,822 pounds, Mach 1
Base Price	$3,525, four-cylinder coupe; $3,791, V-6 coupe; $3,781, four-cylinder hatchback; $4,047, V-6 hatchback; $3,895, four-cylinder Ghia; $4,125, V-6 Ghia; $4,209, V-6 Mach 1; $4,154, V-8 Mach 1
Track	55.6 inches front, 55.8 inches rear
Wheels	13-inch, standard
Tires	B78; BR78, standard for Ghia; BR70, standard for Mach 1
Suspension	Independent upper A-arms, lower lateral arms w/coil springs in front; live axle with leaf springs in back
Steering	Rack and pinion
Brakes	Front discs (9.3-inch rotors), rear drums
Engine	92-horsepower 2.3-liter inline SOHC four-cylinder, standard; 105-horsepower 2.8-liter V-6, optional; 139-horsepower 302-ci V-8, optional
Bore and Stroke	3.78x3.13 inches (four), 3.66x2.70 inches (V-6), 4.00x3.00 inches (V-8)
Compression	9.0:1 (four), 8.7:1 (V-6), 8.0:1 (V-8)
Fuel Delivery	Motorcraft two-barrel carburetor in all cases
Transmission	Four-speed manual, standard; Select-Shift Cruise-O-Matic automatic, optional
Axle Ratio	2.79:1, four-cylinder manual; 3.18:1, four-cylinder automatic; 3.00:1, V-6; 2.79:1, V-8
Production	187,567; all bodies, all models (37,515 Ghia coupes, 9,232 Mach 1 hatchbacks, 25,259 Cobra II hatchbacks)

comparison to 1974's. Yet the little pony continued to struggle for an identity. All base Mustang IIs fitted with the 2.3-liter OHC four-cylinders officially became MPG models in 1976, as Ford tried to preserve the fuel-saving notion as a major selling point. Performance aspects, meanwhile, continued to wane as Mach 1 popularity dribbled away. After building 21,062 Mach 1s in 1975, Ford only managed 9,232 in 1976.

Of course, that drop can be explained by the appearance of the new Cobra II package, the work of Jim Wangers, who had helped get Pontiac's GTO up and running during the 1960s. Wangers'

Hardtop Mustang II production for 1976 was 116,023. Another 71,544 2+2 hatchbacks were built that year too.

firm, Motortown, did the Cobra II conversion, which included adding spoilers front and rear, a fake hood scoop, accent stripes, rear quarter window louvers, and various coiled-snake identification.

It was a supercool package, but it didn't necessarily mean the Mustang II behind those snakes was dangerous. The option was available with all three engines, meaning a budget-conscious MPG model could've been at the same time a killer-looking Cobra II. Crikey! Total Cobra II production that first year was 25,259.

A second new image package for 1976, the Stallion, was purely a looker only. Offered as well for the Pinto MPG and Maverick, this option dressed up a base four-cylinder Mustang II with a long list of black-out treatments. Black and silver paint apparently was the exterior of choice for the Stallion, although Ford reportedly offered as many as five black-accented combinations.

1977

While total Mustang II production fell to 153,000 in 1977, the percentage of 5.0-liter V-8 installations went up from 17.6 percent in 1976 to 25 percent, perhaps signaling that the pony car's performance appeal wasn't quite dead yet. Mach 1 sales, however, slowed again (to 6,719), while the Cobra II—now created in-house at Ford—also recoiled (to 11,948).

Dearborn even rolled out another hot option, the Sports Performance Package, available for all

Dearborn even rolled out another hot option, the Sports Performance Package, available for all models from Ghia to Cobra II.

Jim Wangers, one of the prime movers behind the Pontiac GTO's initial success in 1964, put his fingerprints on the Mustang II in 1976. Wangers' Motortown shop converted 2+2 hatchbacks that year into Cobra II models. Included in the conversion were spoilers front and rear, a nonfunctional hood scoop, rear-quarter window louvers, and abundant coiled-snake imagery.

1977

Model Availability	Two-door coupe, three-door hatchback
Wheelbase	96.2 inches
Length	175 inches
Width	70.2 inches
Height	50.3 inches, coupe; 50.0 inches, hatchback
Curb Weight	2,627 pounds, four-cylinder coupe; 2,750 pounds, V-6 coupe; 2,672 pounds, four-cylinder hatchback; 2,795 pounds, V-6 hatchback; 2,667 pounds, four-cylinder Ghia; 2,790 pounds, V-6 Ghia; 2,785 pounds, Mach 1
Base Price	\$3,702, four-cylinder coupe; \$3,984, V-6 coupe; \$3,901, four-cylinder hatchback; \$4,183, V-6 hatchback; \$4,119, four-cylinder Ghia; \$4,401, V-6 Ghia; \$4,332, V-6 Mach 1; \$4,284, V-8 Mach 1
Track	55.6 inches front,
	55.8 inches rear
Wheels	13-inch, standard
Tires	B78; BR78, standard for Ghia; BR70, standard for Mach 1
Suspension	Independent upper A-arms, lower lateral arms w/coil springs in front; live axle with leaf springs in back
Steering	Rack and pinion
Brakes	Front discs (9.3-inch rotors), rear drums
Engine	89-horsepower 2.3-liter inline SOHC four-cylinder, standard; 93-horsepower 2.8-liter V-6, optional; 139-horsepower 302-ci V-8, optional
Bore and Stroke	3.78x3.13 inches (four), 3.66x2.70 inches (V-6), 4.00x3.00 inches (V-8)
Compression	9.0:1 (four), 8.7:1 (V-6), 8.4:1 (V-8)
Fuel Delivery	Motorcraft two-barrel carburetor in all cases
Transmission	Four-speed manual, standard; Cruise-O-Matic automatic, optional
Axle Ratio	3.18:1, four-cylinder; 3.00:1, V-6 and V-8
Production	153,173; all bodies, all models (29,510 Ghia coupes, 6,719 Mach 1 hatchbacks, 11,948 Cobra II hatchbacks)

The vinyl-roofed Ghia hardtop once again rolled over into 1977. Production that year was 29,510. Base price was $4,119 with the standard four-cylinder. A 1977 V-6 Ghia cost $4,401.

Right: Mustang II production hit a low of 153,173 in 1977. Of these, 55,880 were three-door 2+2 hatchbacks (shown here) and 97,293 were two-door coupes.

Below: A trendy T-top roof became optional in 1977 for 2+2 hatchbacks only. It cost $629 for standard 2+2 models. The price was $587 when added atop the Cobra II.

models from Ghia to Cobra II. Included was the 5.0-liter V-8 backed by a heavy-duty four-speed manual transmission, power steering, power brakes, and 70-series radial tires. Among other new options were a four-way manually controlled driver's bucket seat and a trendy T-top roof, the latter available only on hatchbacks.

A Ghia coupe also could've been sexed up with the Sport Group option. Included in this deal was black or tan paint complemented with a blacked-out grille, a vinyl roof in Chamois Lugano or black Odense, bodyside moldings with matching vinyl inserts, a luggage rack, and cast-aluminum wheels. A leather-wrapped steering wheel and center console joined color-keyed appointments inside.

Later in the year, a 2+2 Rallye Appearance Package appeared to replace the Stallion option. It also featured various blacked-out touches, as well as gold accents atop either black or Polar White paint. Argent styled-steel wheels came in this package, while a black chin spoiler was a no-cost option.

1978

Mach 1 popularity actually surged in 1978, with production totaling 7,968. The Cobra II, on the other hand, dipped to 8,009—perhaps because of those garish tape stripes that now incorporated huge "Cobra" lettering on each door. The total tally for all 1978 Mustang II models rose to more than 192,400, a suitable send-off for the short-lived show pony.

Upgrades on the mechanical side included a plastic cooling fan for the V-6 and optional

Above: The Cobra II package was revised for 1978, this time including huge "Cobra" lettering on the doors. Production that year was 8,009.

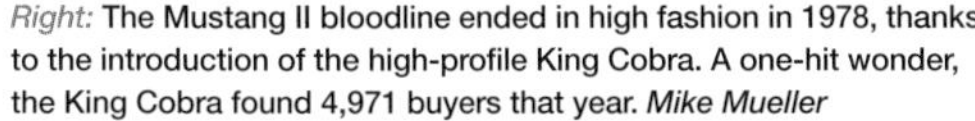

Right: The Mustang II bloodline ended in high fashion in 1978, thanks to the introduction of the high-profile King Cobra. A one-hit wonder, the King Cobra found 4,971 buyers that year. *Mike Mueller*

1978

Model Availability	Two-door coupe, three-door hatchback
Wheelbase	96.2 inches
Length	175 inches
Width	70.2 inches
Height	50.3 inches, coupe; 50.0 inches, hatchback
Curb Weight	2,608 pounds, four-cylinder coupe; 2,705 pounds, V-6 coupe; 2,654 pounds, four-cylinder hatchback; 2,751 pounds, V-6 hatchback; 2,646 pounds, four-cylinder Ghia; 2,743 pounds, V-6 Ghia; 2,733 pounds, Mach 1
Base Price	$3,555, four-cylinder coupe; $3,768, V-6 coupe; $3,798, four-cylinder hatchback; $4,011, V-6 hatchback; $3,972, four-cylinder Ghia; $4,185, V-6 Ghia; $4,253, V-6 Mach 1; $4,401, V-8 Mach 1
Track	55.6 inches front, 55.8 inches rear
Wheels	13-inch, standard
Tires	B78; BR78, standard for Ghia; BR70, standard for Mach 1
Suspension	Independent upper A-arms, lower lateral arms w/coil springs in front; live axle with leaf springs in back
Steering	Rack and pinion
Track	55.6 inches front, 55.8 inches rear
Wheels	13-inch, standard
Tires	B78; BR78, standard for Ghia; BR70, standard for Mach 1
Suspension	Independent upper A-arms, lower lateral arms w/coil springs in front; live axle with leaf springs in back
Steering	Rack and pinion
Brakes	Front discs (9.3-inch rotors), rear drums
Engine	88-horsepower 2.3-liter inline SOHC four-cylinder, standard; 90-horsepower 2.8-liter V-6, optional; 139-horsepower 302-ci V-8, optional
Bore and Stroke	3.78x3.13 inches (four), 3.66x2.70 inches (V-6), 4.00x3.00 inches (V-8)
Compression	9.0:1 (four), 8.7:1 (V-6), 8.4:1 (V-8)
Fuel Delivery	Motorcraft two-barrel carburetor in all cases
Transmission	Four-speed manual, standard; Cruise-O-Matic automatic, optional
Axle Ratio	3.18:1, four-cylinder; 3.00:1, V-6 manual; 3.40:1, V-6 automatic; 2.79:1, V-8
Production	192,410; all bodies, all models (34,730 Ghia coupes, 7,968 Mach 1 hatchbacks, 8,009 Cobra II hatchbacks)

Above: Total production for the last Mustang II was 192,410. The count for 1978 coupes was 116,034.

Below: Production of 1978 2+2 hatchbacks was 76,376.

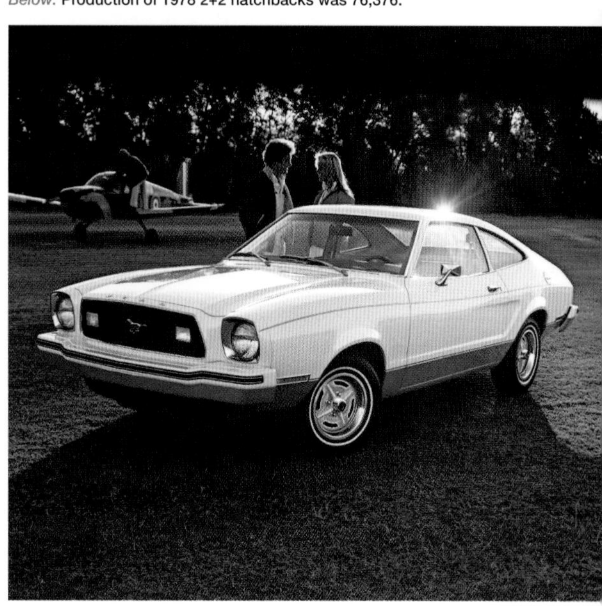

A leather-wrapped steering wheel and six-way manually operated drlver's bucket seat were options for the King Cobra in 1978. *Mike Mueller*

Output for the 1978 King Cobra's 5.0-liter V-8 was 139 horsepower. A two-barrel carburetor fed this meek small-block. *Mike Mueller*

According to John Asher, ". . . for the money, few American cars can match if for looks, handling, and overall performance."

1978 King Cobra

Model Availability	Three-door hatchback
Wheelbase	96.2 inches
Length	175 inches
Width	70.2 inches
Height	50.0 inches
Curb Weight	3,100 pounds
Price	$6,800
Track	55.6 inches front, 55.8 inches rear
Wheels	13-inch lattice-lace aluminum mag
Tires	Goodyear radial
Suspension	Independent upper A-arms, lower lateral arms w/coil springs in front; live axle with leaf springs in back
Steering	Rack and pinion
Brakes	Front discs (9.3-inch rotors), rear drums
Engine	139-horsepower 302-ci V-8
Bore and Stroke	4.00x3.00 inches
Compression	8.4:1
Fuel Delivery	Single Motorcraft two-barrel carburetor
Transmission	Close-ratio four-speed manual
Axle Ratio	2.79:1
Production	4,971

variable-ratio power steering. Another new option was the Fashion Accessory Group, which targeted female buyers with its lighted vanity mirror on the driver-side visor (hopefully only used when parked), illuminated entry, striped cloth seat inserts, and four-way adjustable driver's seat. Last, but certainly not least by any account, was the new King Cobra, an exclamation point of sorts for the Mustang II run.

1978 King Cobra

Definitely a child of the disco era, the 1978 King Cobra relied mostly on flamboyance to turn heads. As *Car Craft* magazine's John Asher explained, "With the real muscle car era now no more than a memory, cars like the Ford King Cobra are becoming the machismo machines of the late Seventies." Straight-line performance was nothing to scream about thanks to a standard 5.0-liter V-8 that was a mere shadow of its latter self. Sure, it would grow into a real screamer soon enough, but the "five-oh" Ford was only able to muster 139 horses in 1978.

"Ten years later and the Ford Mustang Cobra has not only lost its 'Jet,' it [has also] lost its venom," wrote *Cars* magazine's Don Chaikin. Chaikin's test crew managed only a 16.59-second quarter-mile pass, topping out at 82.41 miles per hour, in the King Cobra. Hell, even Dodge's Li'l Red Express pickup truck was faster that year. But did that make the last great Mustang II a loser?

Not at all, considering how well this mini-Mustang stacked up against other late-1970s image-conscious cruisers when parked outside of Studio 54. Priced at $1,277, the King Cobra option added distinctive accent striping, "King Cobra" identification, and an outrageous Cobra decal on the hood conveniently reminiscent of Pontiac's so-called "screaming chicken" Trans Am logo. Additional T/A reminders included a rear deck spoiler, wheel opening air deflectors, a front air dam, and a rearward-facing hood scoop.

While the scoop was nonfunctional, the openings in the air dam were real, feeding much-needed cooling air through ducts to the standard power-assisted front discs. Power steering was also

standard, as were four attractive lattice-lace 13-inch aluminum wheels wearing Goodyear radials. A polished dash insert and sport steering wheel spruced things up inside. Underneath were beefed springs, adjustable Gabriel shocks, and a rear stabilizer bar.

Despite its high price, not everyone was so willing to write off the King Cobra. According to John Asher, it was "far from an economy car, but for the money, few American cars can match it for looks, handling and overall performance."

"That's performance today," echoed Don Chaikin. "Going around corners quickly—and looking like you go around corners quickly—is where it's at. And this little King Cobra does just that."

As they say, image is everything.

07

Spurred On

07

1979–1993

- Henry Ford II fires Lee Iacocca in 1978.
- The 1979 Mustang is the first of the breed to use a MacPherson strut front suspension.
- Another Mustang first, optional turbo power, is offered in 1979.
- The new-for-1979 Fox-chassis model becomes the second Mustang to pace the Indianapolis 500.
- Donald Petersen becomes president of Ford Motor Company in March 1980.
- Ford officially announces its Special Vehicle Operations (SVO) in September 1980.
- The GT Mustang returns for 1982 after a 13-year hiatus.
- All Ford engines are painted light gray (instead of Ford Blue) beginning in 1982.
- The convertible Mustang, last seen in 1973, returns for 1983.
- Mustang celebrates its 25th birthday in 1984.
- An SVO Mustang is offered from 1984 to 1986.
- Henry Ford II dies of pneumonia in 1987.
- Ford's new Probe goes on sale in March 1988 as a 1989 model.
- The 6 millionth Mustang rolls off the line in 1989.
- Alex Trotman becomes Ford Motor Company chairman and CEO in 1993.

Above: Output for the 5.0-liter V-8 dropped to 205 horsepower in 1993 for no apparent reason. No mechanical modifications were made. Base price for a 1993 5.0-liter LX convertible was $20,293.

Opposite: Ford offered Indy 500 pace car replicas in 1979 to mark the Mustang's second appearance at the Brickyard. They were powered by either the 5.0-liter V-8 (front) or turbocharged four-cylinder (back). Turbo models featured only four-speed manual transmissions, while the V-8 cars could've been ordered with the four-speed or an automatic. Total production (all engines, all transmissions) was 10,478. Of these, 7,634 were built in Dearborn and 2,844 went together in San Jose, California. *Mike Mueller*

Previous pages:
Left: Base price for the 1983 V-8 GT hatchback was $9,328. The T-tops added another $1,055. *Mike Mueller*

Right: Base price for a 1987 GT convertible was $15,724. Tinted glass, a power top, and rear deck luggage rack were all standard.

Two eras came to an end at Ford in 1978, one memorable, the other not nearly so. As the model year closed, so too did the book on the short-lived Mustang II, a car that sold relatively well yet left so many customers unsatisfied. Few pony riders mourned its passing. Also leaving the Ford picture about the same time was Lido Anthony Iacocca, the Mustang's proud father. Apparently too proud—like his predecessor, Bunkie Knudsen, Ford's latest president had grown a bit big for his britches, or at least Henry Ford II thought so, and his opinion mattered most. Iacocca got a brusque boot to those pantaloons less than a month after the company's big 75th birthday party in June 1978. In Henry II's publicly stated words, he let Iacocca go "for insubordination." Privately, the big boss plain and simply had grown to dislike his aggressive marketing genius, who was then only 54 and still as much a prime mover as he was back in 1964.

HITTING THE GROUND RUNNING, Iacocca moved over to Chrysler Corporation in November 1978 and proceeded to work wonders there with a long-standing car company on the verge of oblivion. Among Chrysler's early saviors were its all-new minivans, Dodge Caravan and Plymouth Voyager, introduced in 1984. Not coincidentally, these two "garageable" utility vehicles clearly resembled a Ford concept (named Carousel) that had stood ready in 1973 to go into production two years later, had an energy crisis not emerged to kill it before it was born. Apparently Chrysler's new main man had taken more than his Rolodex with him after cleaning out his Dearborn office.

Though also rejected, this drawing more closely predicted the final Indy pace car graphics.

With a drag coefficient (Cd) of 0.44, the 1979 Mustang fastback represented one of Detroit's most aerodynamic offerings.

Ford's Special Vehicle Operations was officially announced in September 1980 with former Ford of Europe competition director Michael Kranefuss as its director. SVO's second in command, Glen Lyall (shown here), ran the Mustang SVO program.

At least he left a solid plan for the next new Mustang behind.

This pony car progress dated back to the summer of 1972, at a time when Ford people were finally getting serious about addressing the growing import threat. The compact Mustang II was being readied at the time, but fortunately the Dearborn brain trust was looking further ahead. Sporadic gasoline shortages around the country that year foretold hard times waiting right around the corner and made it even more imperative to improve fuel efficiency. Then the Arab oil embargo, instituted in October 1973, iced the deal—and gave foreign compacts additional momentum. Prior to 1970, the import share of the U.S. market had hovered around 10 percent. It was 15 percent within a few years and nearly 23 percent by 1979.

To combat this trend, Ford engineers and executives elected to take a wider approach to downsizing. First was a "luxury compact," the Granada, in 1975, followed by the new Fairmont in 1978. Even the prestigious Thunderbird—which had grown to enormous proportions by 1976—felt the axe, first in 1977 and again in 1980.

Along with its Mercury Zephyr counterpart, the Fairmont sprang from the Fox chassis project, first mentioned in Ford Motor Company paperwork in February 1973. In October 1974, the wheels officially began turning for a Fox-based Mustang II replacement, scheduled to appear a year after the Fairmont. The slimmed-down 1980 T-bird too was a Fox variant.

Design work on the Fox-chassis Mustang began in earnest early in 1975. Unlike the Mustang II, which was developed first as a fastback, the breed's third-generation rendition was sculpted up originally in notchback form, with a sloping roofline to be added later. Aerodynamics, then a new science around Detroit, became an important factor after engineers determined that a fuel-efficient car didn't necessarily have to be smaller: it could save on gas by cheating the wind.

Physical laws also came into play when it was time to choose materials. Much thought went into saving weight wherever possible in order to build a lesser pony car that featured more interior room than the cramped Mustang II. In the end, the Fox-chassis Mustang appeared to violate those laws in that it looked and felt bigger than the Mustang II, yet was actually lighter and thus easier on a gallon of fossil fuel. Though it was longer, taller, and easier on passengers' legs than its forerunner, the third-generation pony car weighed 200 pounds less. A soft front fascia, urethane bumpers, thinner doors and windows, and various lightening holes cut into the unit-body structure all contributed to those savings.

Once under way, the Fox body styling process was turned over to Jack Telnack, formerly the design vice president at Ford of Europe. Relocated back to Dearborn, Telnack became Ford's North American Light Car and Truck Design executive director in April 1975 and immediately made his presence felt. Though various studios (including Ghia in Italy) worked on initial designs, it was Telnack's own team that won over Iacocca and other execs.

Along with its splashy graphics, the Cobra package for 1979 included a tuned suspension with Michelin metric TRX tires on forged-aluminum wheels. The 2.3-liter turbocharged four-cylinder was standard; the 5.0-liter V-8 was a no-cost option.

Telnack's sleek, slippery work of art was so refined it rolled over with only minor changes right through final production approval in September 1976. And when it hit the streets in the fall of 1978 it amazed almost everyone with the way it cut through the atmosphere. With a drag coefficient (Cd) of 0.44, the 1979 Mustang fastback represented one of Detroit's most aerodynamic offerings. At 0.46, the new coupe's Cd amounted to a 25 percent improvement compared to the 1978 notchback.

Beneath that beautiful body were, per Fox chassis specs, revised suspension setups at both ends. Up front were MacPherson struts that featured coil springs wedged between the lower control arms and the subframe instead of wrapped around the strut towers. In back, the rear axle used coils in place of the traditional leaf springs and was held in place by a four-link system. A rear stabilizer bar was included, too. Rack-and-pinion steering and front disc brakes were again standard.

Standard power came from Ford's 2.3-liter four-cylinder topped by a single overhead camshaft. But an optional turbocharged four and 130-horsepower 5.0-liter V-8 hinted, however humbly, that just maybe pony car performance was back on the rise. Handling certainly improved during the Fox-chassis era, a welcome change not missed by press critics. In the opinion of *Motor Trend*'s John Ethridge, the 1979 Mustang could "now compete both in the marketplace and on the road with lots of cars that used to outclass it."

The first Fox-bodied pony also outclassed its predecessor as far as sales were concerned. By April, 1979 Mustangs were rolling off the lot twice as fast compared to Mustang IIs the year before.

1979

Model Availability	Two-door coupe, three-door hatchback
Wheelbase	100.4 inches
Length	179.1 inches
Width	69.1 inches
Height	51.8 inches
Curb Weight	2,431 pounds, four-cylinder coupe; 2,511 pounds, six-cylinder coupe; 2,451 pounds, four-cylinder hatchback; 2,531 pounds, six-cylinder hatchback; 2,539 pounds, four-cylinder Ghia coupe; 2,619 pounds, six-cylinder Ghia coupe; 2,548 pounds, four-cylinder Ghia hatchback; 2,628 pounds, six-cylinder Ghia hatchback
Base Price	$4,071, four-cylinder coupe; $4,344, six-cylinder coupe; $4,436, four-cylinder hatchback; $4,709, six-cylinder hatchback; $4,642, four-cylinder Ghia coupe; $4,915, six-cylinder Ghia coupe; $4,824, four-cylinder Ghia hatchback; $5,097, six-cylinder Ghia hatchback
Track	56.6 inches front, 57 inches rear
Wheels	13-inch, standard; 14-inch (Ghia)
Tires	B78x13, standard; BR78x14 (Ghia)
Suspension	Modified MacPherson hydraulic struts with coil springs and stabilizer bar in front; four-link solid axle with coil springs and stabilizer bar in rear (V-8)
Steering	Rack and pinion
Brakes	Front discs, rear drums
Engine	88-horsepower 2.3-liter SOHC four-cylinder, 140-horsepower turbocharged 2.3-liter SOHC four-cylinder, 109-horsepower 2.8-liter V-6, 85-horsepower 3.3-liter inline six-cylinder, 140-horsepower 5.0-liter V-8
Bore and Stroke	3.78x3.13 (four), 3.66x2.70 (V-6), 3.68x3.13 (3.3-liter six), 4.00x3.00 (V-8)
Compression	9:1 (four), 8.7:1 (V-6), 8.6:1 (3.3-liter six), 8.4:1 (V-8)
Fuel Delivery	Motorcraft two-barrel carburetor (88-horsepower four), Holley two-barrel and Garrett AiResearch turbocharge (131-horsepower four), two-barrel (V-6), Holley one-barrel (3.3-liter six), Motorcraft two-barrel (V-8)
Transmission	Four-speed manual, standard; automatic, optional
Axle Ratio	3.08:1, standard (88-horsepower four, V-6); 3.45:1 (turbo four); 2.47:1 (V-8 automatic)
Production	369,936 total (56,351 Ghia coupes, 36,384 Ghia hatchbacks)

1979

Revised dimensions for the Fox-chassis Mustang included more wheelbase (up 4.2 inches to 100.2) and more overall length (179.1 inches compared to 175) than the last Mustang II. Height went up an inch and a half (to 51.8 inches), while width shrunk from 70.2 inches to 69.1. Inside, the 1979 notchback contained 14 more cubic feet of usable space compared to its 1978 predecessor, 16 more for the fastback.

As was the case during the Mustang II era, no convertible was offered when the Fox platform debuted. The same two body styles (two-door coupe, three-door hatchback) rolled over into 1979, as did the optional Ghia package, available for both body styles. Ghia features included turbine-style wheel covers, BR78x14 radial tires, pinstripes, and various color-keyed body parts (rear quarter louvers, bodyside molding inserts, window frames, and dual remote-control mirrors). Low-back bucket seats

Right: Available models for 1979 again included a two-door coupe and three-door hatchback. As in 1978, no convertible was offered. Production for the coupe (shown here) was 156,666.

Below left: Output for the 5.0-liter V-8 in 1979 was 140 horsepower. Compression was 8.4:1. *Mike Mueller*

Below right: The 1979 Mustang's optional turbocharged 2.3-liter four-cylinder was only available with a four-speed manual transmission. Included in the deal were a sport-tuned exhaust system (with a bright tailpipe) and an 8,000-rpm tachometer inside. *Mike Mueller*

Bottom: Hatchback production for 1979 was 120,535.

and color-keyed door panels were standard inside.

The Cobra package carried over, too, and in base form included the force-fed 2.3-liter four, topped by its requisite hood scoop adorned with "Turbo" identification. The 5.0-liter V-8 fitted with a one-piece serpentine accessory drive belt was optional. Cobras got the new TRX sport suspension consisting of attractive aluminum wheels, Michelin metric rubber, and specially tuned springs and shocks. An 8,000-rpm tach and engine-turned instrument panel went inside.

In Ford's words, the new turbocharged four offered "V-8 performance without sacrificing fuel economy." But it unfortunately also brought along an oil leak problem (as well as other eventual gremlins) that rubbed buyers the wrong way. Factory recalls resulted, as did bad press. According to *Road & Track*, the turbo four was "marginally acceptable in its present state."

At least the optional 5.0-liter V-8 and TRX suspension were around. Next to no one could knock the latter, while the former offered just enough excitement to keep alive the dream of the great American muscle car. According to *Car and Driver*'s Don Sherman, the 1979 V-8 Mustang was "a piece of Detroit iron ready and able to over-rev your pulse rate."

Along with the V-8 and the two 2.3-liter fours, the 1979 options list also included the 2.8-liter V-6, yet another Mustang II leftover. Or at least it was offered early on. Supply problems forced Ford officials to shelve the V-6, replacing it instead with Ford's clunky, old 200-ci inline six, which would remain a Mustang option up through 1982.

1979 Indy 500 Pace Car Replica

Like its ancestor 15 years before, the new 1979 Mustang was chosen as the prestigious pace car for the annual running of the Indianapolis 500. This time, however, Dearborn officials chose to mark the occasion with quite a bit more flair. Ford established an all-time high for pace car replica production that year, rolling out 10,478 copies of the car that Jackie Stewart drove around the Brickyard on May 27, 1979, to start off the 63rd Indy 500. Of that total, 5,970 were fitted with

2.3-liter four-cylinders and four-speeds, 2,402 had the 5.0-liter V-8 backed by a four-gear, and 2,106 featured a 5.0-liter automatic combo.

All were painted silver metallic (with black accents and red/orange striping) and featured the coveted TRX suspension. Applying the pace car decals was up to either the dealer or owner. And unlike the actual Indy pacers, which were specially

Production for the 1979 Turbo pace car replica was 5,970. The breakdown for the V-8 version was 2,106 with automatic transmissions and 2,402 with four-speeds. *Mike Mueller*

The Cobra's engine-turned instrument panel was standard inside the 1979 Indy pace car replica. Also included were deluxe seatbelts, a leather-wrapped steering wheel, power steering and brakes, AM/FM stereo with cassette player and premium sound, and the Ghia sound insulation package. *Mike Mueller*

fitted with T-tops, the replicas came with the 1979 Mustang's optional flip-up, open-air roof. Additional standard items included a front air dam with foglamps, a nonfunctional rear-facing hood scoop, a rear spoiler, and uniquely patterned Recaro bucket seats.

1980

High-pressure P-metric radial tires and more effective halogen headlamps appeared on all Mustangs for 1980, and a maintenance-free battery was new beneath the hood. New on the options list were the Indy pace car's Recaro buckets, a roof-mounted luggage rack, and a Carriage roof that covered a notchback's top in diamond-grain vinyl to make it look like a convertible. Additional pace car parts (front air dam, hood scoop, rear spoiler) were added

1980

Model Availability	Two-door coupe, three-door hatchback
Wheelbase	100.4 inches
Length	179.1 inches
Width	69.1 inches
Height	51.8 inches
Curb Weight	2,497 pounds, four-cylinder coupe; 2,532 pounds, six-cylinder coupe; 2,531 pounds, four-cylinder hatchback; 2,566 pounds, six-cylinder hatchback; 2,565 pounds, four-cylinder Ghia coupe; 2,600 pounds, six-cylinder Ghia coupe; 2,588 pounds, four-cylinder Ghia hatchback; 2,623 pounds, six-cylinder Ghia hatchback
Base Price	$4,884, four-cylinder coupe; $5,103, six-cylinder coupe; $5,194, four-cylinder hatchback; $5,413, six-cylinder hatchback; $5,369, four-cylinder Ghia coupe; $5,588, six-cylinder Ghia coupe; $5,512, four-cylinder Ghia hatchback; $5,731, six-cylinder Ghia hatchback
Track	56.6 inches front, 57 inches rear
Wheels	13-inch, standard; 14-inch (Ghia)
Tires	P185/80R-12, standard; P17575Rx14 (Ghia)
Suspension	Modified MacPherson hydraulic struts with coil springs and stabilizer bar in front; four-link solid axle with coil springs and stabilizer bar in rear (V-8)
Steering	Rack and pinion
Brakes	Front discs, rear drums
Engine	88-horsepower 2.3-liter SOHC four-cylinder, 140-horsepower turbocharged 2.3-liter SOHC four-cylinder, 91-horsepower 3.3-liter inline six-cylinder, 119-horsepower 4.2-liter (255-ci) V-8
Bore and Stroke	3.78x3.13 inches (four), 3.68x3.13 (3.3-liter six), 3.68x3.00 (V-8)
Compression	9:1 (four), 8.6:1 (3.3-liter six), 8.8:1 (V-8)
Fuel Delivery	Motorcraft two-barrel carburetor (88-horsepower four), Holley two-barrel and Garrett AiResearch turbocharger (140-horsepower four), Holley one-barrel (3.3-liter six), Motorcraft two-barrel (V-8)
Transmission	Four-speed manual, standard; automatic, optional
Axle Ratio	3.08:1, standard (four, six); 3.45:1 (turbo four); 2.26:1 (V-8 automatic)
Production	271,322 total (23,647 Ghia coupes, 20,285 Ghia hatchbacks)

Above: Exterior changes were minor for 1980. Not so beneath the hood, where a truly meek 4.2-liter V-8 replaced the tried-and-true 5.0-liter. Total production for 1980 was 271,322, including 98,497 hatchbacks.

Right: The Cobra's tape treatment was revised in 1980, and it was dressed up further with the front air dam, hood scoop, and rear spoiler seen on the 1979 Indy 500 pace car replicas.

Above: A Carriage roof option appeared for 1980 to help make a notchback coupe look like a convertible. This appearance package cost $625.

Left: As in 1979, the 1980 Cobra was available with the turbocharged 2.3-liter or V-8. The Turbo Cobra appears here.

to the 1980 Cobra, which received yet another revised tape treatment. Ghia models, offered for both the two-door coupe and three-door hatchback, received a restyled steering wheel, and the Sport option carried over from 1979. Available for the hatchback, the latter package included styled-steel wheels with trim rings and various dress-up moldings for the rocker panels, windows, and bodysides.

The most notable change for 1980 came in the engine room, where most of 1979's performance promise essentially evaporated. The base 2.3-liter SOHC four-cylinder rolled over into 1980, as did its troublesome turbocharged alter ego. The old 3.3-liter inline six was again an option, but the rather peppy 302 V-8 was gone. In its place was a fuel-conscious 255-ci (4.2-liter) V-8 created by reducing the 302 block's bore from 4.00 inches to 3.68. Topped, like 1979's 302, by a two-barrel carburetor, the 4.2-liter small-block was rated at a measly 119 horsepower. Only 2.7 percent of the 1980 Mustang run featured this wimpy V-8, a direct result of yet another wave of spiking gas prices.

The 4.2-liter V-8 initially was only available with an automatic transmission in 1980. But a four-speed overdrive manual gearbox appeared midyear to spice things up at least a little.

1981

As in 1980, few noticeable changes were made to set the 1981 Mustang apart from what came before. This was the last year for the rather garish Cobra package, and the turbocharged four-cylinder was discontinued right off the bat after first being advertised in Ford literature. Reliability problems simply couldn't be licked. Notable new options

1981

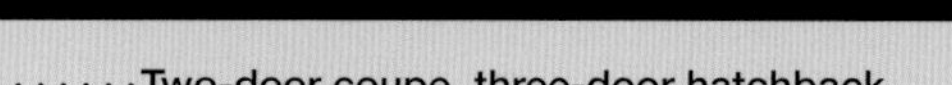

Model Availability	Two-door coupe, three-door hatchback
Wheelbase	100.4 inches
Length	179.1 inches
Width	69.1 inches
Height	51.8 inches
Curb Weight	2,524 pounds, four-cylinder coupe; 2,551 pounds, six-cylinder coupe; 2,544 pounds, four-cylinder hatchback; 2,571 pounds, six-cylinder hatchback; 2,558 pounds, four-cylinder Ghia coupe; 2,585 pounds, six-cylinder Ghia coupe; 2,593 pounds, four-cylinder Ghia hatchback; 2,620 pounds, six-cylinder Ghia hatchback
Base Price	$6,171, four-cylinder coupe; $6,384, six-cylinder coupe; $6,408, four-cylinder hatchback; $6,621, six-cylinder hatchback; $6,645, four-cylinder Ghia coupe; $6,858, six-cylinder Ghia coupe; $6,729, four-cylinder Ghia hatchback; $6,942, six-cylinder, Ghia hatchback
Track	56.6 inches front, 57 inches rear
Wheels	13-inch, standard; 14-inch, standard (Ghia)
Tires	P185/80R-13, standard; P175/75R-14, standard (Ghia)
Suspension	Modified MacPherson hydraulic struts with coil springs and stabilizer bar in front; four-link solid axle with coil springs and stabilizer bar in rear (V-8)
Steering	Rack and pinion
Brakes	Front discs, rear drums
Engine	88-horsepower 2.3-liter SOHC four-cylinder, 94-horsepower 3.3-liter inline six-cylinder, 115-horsepower 4.2-liter (255-ci) V-8
Bore and Stroke	3.78x3.13 inches (four), 3.68x3.13 (3.3-liter six), 3.68x3.00 (V-8)
Compression	9:1 (four), 8.6:1 (3.3-liter six), 8.2:1 (V-8)
Fuel Delivery	Motorcraft two-barrel carburetor (88-horsepower four), Holley one-barrel (3.3-liter six), Motorcraft two-barrel (V-8)
Transmission	Four-speed manual, standard; automatic, optional
Axle Ratio	3.08:1, standard (four, six); 3.45:1 (six, four-speed); 2.26:1 (V-8)
Production	182,552 total (13,422 Ghia coupes, 14,273 Ghia hatchbacks)

Most of the 1980 Mustang's makeup rolled over into 1981, save for the turbocharged four-cylinder, which was discontinued after being mentioned in early literature.

> Fortunately, help was on the way for Mustang buyers who preferred a little punch with their pony.

included a trendy T-top roof (now offered for both body styles), power windows, rear window louvers (for the hatchback), and a Traction-Lok differential.

Priced at $63, optional Traction-Lok went a long way toward easing another problem inherent to the Fox-chassis Mustang. Its four-link coil suspension in back proved highly susceptible to wheel hop during hard acceleration. Allowing both rear tires a chance to take a bite once the hammer went down inhibited this unwanted (and potentially dangerous) action.

Discounting the departed turbo four, 1981's engine lineup was a 1980 carryover, with the lame 4.2-liter V-8 still feebly leading the way. Fortunately, help was on the way for Mustang buyers who preferred a little punch with their pony.

1982

Ford engineers almost overnight found it fun to build cars again after Donald Petersen was promoted to the Ford Motor Company president's seat in March 1980. A newfound need to race was addressed immediately, with Ford's Special Vehicle Operations (SVO) formed later that year to further advance the company's motorsports involvement. Making real muscle for the Walter Mitty set too became a priority.

1982

Model Availability	Two-door coupe, three-door hatchback
Wheelbase	100.4 inches
Length	179.1 inches
Width	69.1 inches
Height	51.4 inches
Curb Weight	2,511 pounds, four-cylinder L coupe; 2,635 pounds, six-cylinder L coupe; 2,528 pounds, four-cylinder GL coupe; 2,652 pounds, six-cylinder GL coupe; 2,565 pounds, four-cylinder GL hatchback; 2,689 pounds, six-cylinder GL hatchback; 2,543 pounds, four-cylinder GLX coupe; 2,667 pounds, six-cylinder GLX coupe; 2,579 pounds, four-cylinder GLX hatchback; 2,703 pounds, six-cylinder GLX hatchback; 2,629 pounds, GT
Base Price	$6,345, four-cylinder L coupe; $7,062, six-cylinder L coupe; $6,844, four-cylinder GL coupe; $7,468, six-cylinder GL coupe; $6,979, four-cylinder GL hatchback; $7,390, six-cylinder GL hatchback; $6,980, four-cylinder GLX coupe; $7,604, six-cylinder GLX coupe; $7,101, four-cylinder GLX hatchback; $7,725, six-cylinder GLX hatchback; $8,308, GT
Track	56.6 inches front, 57 inches rear
Wheels	14-inch, standard
Tires	P175/75R-14, standard; P185/75R-14, standard (GT)
Suspension	Modified MacPherson hydraulic struts with coil springs and stabilizer bar in front; four-link solid axle with coil springs and stabilizer bar in rear (V-8)
Steering	Rack and pinion
Brakes	Front discs, rear drums
Engine	86-horsepower 2.3-liter SOHC four-cylinder, 87-horsepower 3.3-liter inline six-cylinder, 120-horsepower 4.2-liter (255-ci) V-8, 157-horsepower 5.0-liter HO V-8
Bore and Stroke	3.78x3.13 inches (four), 3.68x3.13 (3.3-liter six), 3.68x3.00 (4.2-liter V-8), 4.00x3.00 (HO V-8)
Compression	9:1 (four), 8.6:1 (3.3-liter six), 8.2:1 (4.2-liter V-8), 8.3:1 (HO V-8)
Fuel Delivery	Motorcraft two-barrel carburetor (86-horsepower four), Holley one-barrel (3.3-liter six), Motorcraft two-barrel (V-8)
Transmission	Four-speed manual, standard; automatic, optional
Axle Ratio	2.73:1, standard; 3.45:1 (four-cylinder manual); 3.08:1 (four-cylinder automatic); 3.08:1 (HO V-8)
Production	130,418

Truly big news for 1982 involved the return of both the Mustang GT, shelved since 1969, and the 5.0-liter V-8. Offered only for the three-door hatchback, the new GT came standard with power steering and brakes and a special handling package. Standard too was the new 5.0-liter High Output (HO) V-8, rated at 157 horsepower.

New model designations appeared for 1982. The two-door coupe was now available in basic L, dressier GL, or upscale GLX forms. Three-door hatchbacks were offered in GL, GLX, or GT renditions.

Two old fast friends returned for 1982: the 302 V-8 and the Mustang GT, the latter in hibernation since 1969. Offered only in three-door hatchback form, the 1982 GT came standard with a special handling suspension, power steering and brakes, P185/75 radial rubber on cast-aluminum wheels, and a Traction-Lok rear axle. The TRX wheels and tires were optional, as were Recaro buckets and the T-top roof. Additional standard features included a monochromatic exterior, exclusive front fascia with foglamps and air dam, special grille, nonfunctional hood scoop, and rear spoiler. Color choices were three: red, black, and metallic silver.

Available optionally for all 1982 Mustangs, the reborn 302 came standard beneath a GT hood. The tried-and-true small-block became known as the 5.0-liter HO V-8—"HO" for "high output." Internal improvements included a more aggressive cam and a double-roller timing chain in place of the standard link chain used in garden-variety 302s. Valve springs were stiffened to account for the lumpier cam, and a slightly larger two-barrel carburetor (356 cfm compared to 310) was bolted atop an aluminum intake. A dual-snorkel, low-restriction air cleaner with a bright lid allowed the HO to breathe easier, but a mundane single exhaust dealt with spent gases. Exhaust restrictions and tiny two-barrel notwithstanding, the HO V-8 produced 157 warmly welcomed horses, inspiring Ford promotional people to exclaim, "The Boss Is Back!"

Backing up the HO was the carryover four-speed single rail overdrive (SROD) manual transmission. And all 5.0-liter Mustangs, GT or not, received bright exhaust tips and welded-on traction bars, the latter pieces added to further limit wheel hop. Last but certainly not least was the chrome "5.0"

Exhaust restrictions and tiny two-barrel notwithstanding, the HO V-8 produced 157 warmly welcomed horses, inspiring Ford promotional people to exclaim, "The Boss Is Back!"

fender emblem that would soon constitute a badge of honor on the streets.

The 5.0 GT was an instant success in 1982. "It is a vastly improved automobile that goes, stops and handles well enough to outperform many of its more expensive competitors, both import and domestic," wrote *Motor Trend* magazine's Jim McCraw. "For our money, it's the best-balanced, most capable Mustang ever done." *Motor Trend*'s test of a 5.0-liter prototype produced a remarkable 0–60 pass in only 6.9 seconds, making this revived racer one of the quickest things running out of Detroit that year—certainly the quickest at the price. According to *Road & Track*, a 200-horsepower 1982 Corvette could only manage a 7.9-second run from rest to 60 miles per hour. Its base price was $18,290. The 1982 5.0 Mustang GT started at $8,397.

Remaining Mustang engines for 1982 carried over from 1981, with the aging inline six and woeful 4.2-liter V-8 working their final year. While overall appearances also carried over nearly unchanged, a revised model lineup appeared this year. At the top was the aforementioned GT; beginning at the bottom was the new L, followed by the GL and GLX. Like the GT, the base L was limited to one body style, in this case the two-door coupe. The GL and upscale GLX were offered in both coupe and hatchback forms.

1983

A new, more aerodynamic front fascia and restyled taillights appeared for 1983, while two optional engines reappeared: a V-6 and a turbocharged four-cylinder. The 3.8-liter Essex V-6 replaced the inline six and offered 105 horsepower, compared to 87 for its archaic predecessor. Also a marked improvement compared to its problem-plagued forerunner, the new turbo four featured electronic Bosch port fuel injection instead of an old-school two-barrel carburetor.

Electronic-controlled fuel injection had first appeared in Ford Motor Company ranks for the

1983

Model Availability	Two-door coupe, three-door hatchback, two-door convertible
Wheelbase	100.4 inches
Length	179.1 inches
Width	69.1 inches
Height	51.9 inches
Curb Weight	2,532 pounds, four-cylinder L coupe; 2,621 pounds, six-cylinder L coupe; 2,549 pounds, four-cylinder GL coupe; 2,638 pounds, six-cylinder GL coupe; 2,584 pounds, four-cylinder GL hatchback; 2,673 pounds, six-cylinder GL hatchback; 2,552 pounds, four-cylinder GLX coupe; 2,641 pounds, six-cylinder GLX coupe; 2,587 pounds, four-cylinder GLX hatchback; 2,676 pounds, six-cylinder GLX hatchback; 2,759 pounds, six-cylinder convertible; 2,891 pounds, V-8 GT hatchback
Base Price	$6,727, four-cylinder L coupe; $7,036, six-cylinder L coupe; $7,264, four-cylinder GL coupe; $7,573, six-cylinder GL coupe; $7,439, four-cylinder GL hatchback; $7,748, six-cylinder GL hatchback; $7,398, four-cylinder GLX coupe; $7,707, six-cylinder GLX coupe; $7,557, four-cylinder GLX hatchback; $7,866, six-cylinder GLX hatchback; $9,449, six-cylinder convertible; $9,328 pounds, GT hatchback; $13,479, V-8 GT convertible; $9,714, Turbo GT hatchback
Track	56.6 inches front, 57 inches rear
Wheels	14-inch, standard
Tires	P185/75R-14, standard; P205/70R-14 or P220/55R390 TRX (GT)
Suspension	Modified MacPherson hydraulic struts with coil springs and stabilizer bar in front; four-link solid axle with coil springs and stabilizer bar in rear (V-8)
Steering	Rack and pinion
Brakes	Front discs, rear drums
Engine	90-horsepower 2.3-liter SOHC four-cylinder, 140-horsepower turbocharged 2.3-liter SOHC four-cylinder, 105-horsepower 3.8-liter (232-ci) V-6, 175-horsepower 5.0-liter HO V-8
Bore and Stroke	3.78x3.13 inches (four), 3.80x3.40 (V-6), 4.00x3.00 (HO V-8)
Compression	9:1 (90-horsepower four), 8:1 (turbo four), 8.7:1 (V-6), 8.3:1 (HO V-8)
Fuel Delivery	Carter one-barrel carburetor (90-horsepower four), electronic fuel injection and Garrett AiResearch turbocharger (turbo four), Motorcraft two-barrel (V-6), 600-cfm Holley four-barrel (V-8)
Transmission	Four-speed manual, standard; T-5 five-speed manual and automatic, optional; T-5 five-speed, standard (GT)
Axle Ratio	3.08:1, standard (four-speed); 3.45:1, standard (five-speed); 3.08:1 or 2.73:1, standard (automatic)
Production	120,873

Above: A more aerodynamic front fascia appeared for 1983, as did restyled taillights in back. Black rocker panels and moldings were standard for the GL, shown here in coupe form. *Right:* Ford's 3.8-liter V-6 was standard for the GLX convertible in 1983. Base price was $9,449.

Left: GT Mustangs were available in 1983 with either the 5.0-liter HO or revived turbocharged four-cylinder. This T-top GT features the HO V-8, uprated to 175 horsepower for 1983. *Mike Mueller*

Below: Convertible Mustangs reappeared for 1983 after a 10-year hiatus. A GT convertible (available only with the HO V-8) was base priced at $13,479 that year. The rare 1983 Turbo GT hatchback cost $9,714.

A 90-horsepower carbureted 2.3-liter four remained the base engine for the 1983 Mustang, while the optional 5.0 HO remained top dog.

1980 Lincoln Versailles, this after the corporation introduced its electronic engine control (EEC) system for carbureted engines in 1978. An improved EEC II appeared in 1979, followed by the EEC III the following year. The latter was found on carbureted engines as well as Lincoln's 5.0-liter V-8 with centralized fuel injection. Next came Ford's superior EEC IV computer controls with an onboard self-diagnostic system in 1984.

The Mustang's first injected, turbocharged 2.3-liter four-cylinder also featured forged-aluminum pistons, special alloy valves, a lightened flywheel, and an oil cooler. Output was 145 horsepower. A 90-horsepower carbureted 2.3-liter four remained the base engine for the 1983 Mustang, while the optional 5.0 HO remained top dog. The HO now produced 175 horsepower, thanks mostly to a revised cam and new four-barrel carburetor, last seen atop a Mustang small-block in 1973.

Supplied by Holley, this four-holer flowed 600 cfm while further enhancing the 5.0's hot-to-trot reputation. "Power gains have not been made at the expense of driveability," claimed *Motor Trend*'s Tony Swan. "This is a wonderful engine to live with—smooth, responsive, civilized, yet always ready for the instant transition to snarling combat readiness."

Both the HO V-8 and turbo four were available in the 1983 GT, though the latter installations were quite rare: reportedly only 483 Turbo GTs were built. New for 1983 behind both performance powerplants was a Borg-Warner T-5 five-speed

Above: Cast-aluminum wheels cost an extra $354 for the GL and GLX Mustangs in 1983. They were priced at $404 for the L model. *Mike Mueller*

Right: The 5.0-liter HO V-8 was a $719 option for the 1983 GLX convertible. The HO option cost $1,476 on other Mustangs that year. *Mike Mueller*

Right: Power brakes and an automatic transmission were standard for the 1983 GLX convertible. *Mike Mueller*

Below: The 1984-½ 20th Anniversary Mustang was offered in both hatchback and convertible forms. Production of the former was 3,900. *Mike Mueller*

manual transmission, yet another major upgrade compared to the SROD four-speed it superseded.

Most GT mechanicals carried over from 1982, and some were even improved upon. Wider tires and a thicker rear stabilizer bar were added, and the second-edition GT received a revised hood scoop that faced backward. Black trim around the windshield and side glass completed the look. The TRX suspension was again optional.

A major midyear addition involved a new body style, as topless driving returned for the Mustang, but only after a little chisel work. All 1983 drop-tops began life as full-roofed notchbacks. Their steel roofs were cut off, and they were converted into convertibles with power tops and glass rear backlites. All were warmly received: convertible production made up 20 percent of the total Mustang run that year.

Both GT and GLX Mustangs were converted into convertibles for 1983, with the latter model making up the bulk of those ordered. Standard full-roofed GLX features included dual bright remote-control mirrors, bright rocker moldings, and a four-spoke steering wheel. GLX convertibles came standard with power brakes, tinted glass, dual black remote mirrors, and black rocker moldings.

1984

Another lineup change came in 1984. While the base L model remained, in both coupe and hatchback forms, next up in the pecking order was the LX, available as a coupe, hatchback, or convertible. At the top was the familiar GT hatchback and convertible. The 2.3-liter four-cylinder was standard for the L and LX, while the 3.8-liter V-6 was standard for the LX convertible. Again, the turbocharged four and 5.0 HO V-8 were both available for the GT.

Above: All 20th Anniversary Mustangs featured white exteriors and red interiors. *Mike Mueller*

Above left: Production of the 20th Anniversary hatchback was 3,900. Of these, 362 relied on the 2.3-liter Turbo drivetrain. This model features the 5.0-liter V-8. *Mike Mueller*

1984

Model Availability	Two-door coupe, three-door hatchback, two-door convertible
Wheelbase	100.5 inches
Length	179.1 inches, 181 inches (SVO
Width	69.1 inches
Height	51.9 inches
Curb Weight	2,538 pounds, four-cylinder L coupe; 2,646 pounds, V-6 L coupe; 2,584 pounds, four-cylinder L hatchback; 2,692 pounds, V-6 L hatchback; 2,559 pounds, four-cylinder LX coupe; 2,667 pounds, V-6 LX coupe; 2,605 pounds, four-cylinder LX hatchback; 2,713 pounds, V-6 LX hatchback; 2,873 pounds, V-6 LX convertible; 2,753 pounds, Turbo GT hatchback; 2,899 pounds, V-8 GT hatchback; 2,921 pounds, Turbo GT convertible; 3,043 pounds, V-8 GT convertible; 2,881 pounds, SVO
Base Price	$7,038, four-cylinder L coupe; $7,505, V-6 L coupe; $7,269, four-cylinder L hatchback; $7,678, V-6 L hatchback; $7,290, four-cylinder LX coupe; $7,699, V-6 LX coupe; $7,496, four-cylinder LX hatchback; $7,905, V-6 LX hatchback; $11,849, V-6 LX convertible; $9,762, Turbo GT hatchback; $9,578, V-8 GT hatchback; $13,245, Turbo GT convertible; $13,051, V-8 GT convertible; $15,596, SVO
Track (front/rear, in inches)	56.6/57, 57.8/58.3 (SVO)
Wheels	14-inch, standard; 16x7 aluminum wheels (SVO)
Tires	P185/75R-14, standard; P205/70R-14 (GT); P225/50VR-16 Goodyear NCT (SVO)
Suspension	Modified MacPherson hydraulic struts with coil springs and stabilizer bar in front; four-link solid axle with coil springs and stabilizer bar in rear (V-8)
Steering	Rack and pinion
Brakes	Front discs, rear drums; four-wheel discs (SVO)
Engine	88-horsepower 2.3-liter SOHC four-cylinder, 145-horsepower turbocharged 2.3-liter SOHC four-cylinder (Turbo GT), 175-horsepower turbocharged 2.3-liter SOHC four-cylinder (SVO), 120-horsepower 3.8-liter (232-ci) V-6, 165-horsepower 5.0-liter EFI V-8, 175-horsepower 5.0-liter HO V-8
Bore and Stroke	3.78x3.13 inches (four), 3.80x3.40 (V-6), 4.00x3.00 (HO V-8)
Compression	9:1 (90-horsepower four), 8:1 (turbo four), 8.7:1 (V-6), 8.3:1 (5.0-liter V-8)
Fuel Delivery	Carter one-barrel carburetor (88-horsepower four), electronic fuel injection and Garrett AiResearch turbochargers (turbo four), electronic fuel injection (V-6), electronic fuel injection (165-horsepower V-8), 600-cfm Holley four-barrel (HO V-8)
Transmission	Four-speed manual, standard; T-5 five-speed manual and automatic, optional; T-5 five-speed, standard (GT and SVO)
Axle Ratio	3.08:1, standard (four-speed); 3.27:1, standard (five-speed); 3.08:1 (V-6); 3.08:1 (V-8, five-speed); 2.73:1 (V-8, automatic); 3.27:1 (V-8, automatic); 3.45:1 (turbo four)
Production	141,480

Added to all 1984 engines was Ford's nicely efficient EEC IV system. Electronic fuel injection (EFI) also was adapted to the V-6 to help boost output to 120 horsepower. The GT's HO retained its four-barrel carburetor, but an EFI 5.0-liter V-8, rated at 165 horsepower, was introduced for automatic transmission applications. Ford's four-speed automatic overdrive (AOD) transmission was a new Mustang option for 1984. New too were quad shock absorbers in back.

GTs got V-rated tires, good for speeds above 130 miles per hour, in 1984, and the TRX option was offered for one final time. Gone at the end of this year too was the Turbo GT.

1984 20th Anniversary

Ford marked the Mustang's 20th birthday with a special anniversary GT model, and like its original ancestor, this pony emerged midyear and thus was adorned with an exclusive 1984-½ designation. All 5,260 20th Anniversary Mustangs shared the same appearance: Oxford White paint with Shelby-style "GT350" striping on each rocker panel. All

All 5,260 20th Anniversary Mustangs shared the same appearance: Oxford White paint with Shelby-style "GT350" striping on each rocker panel.

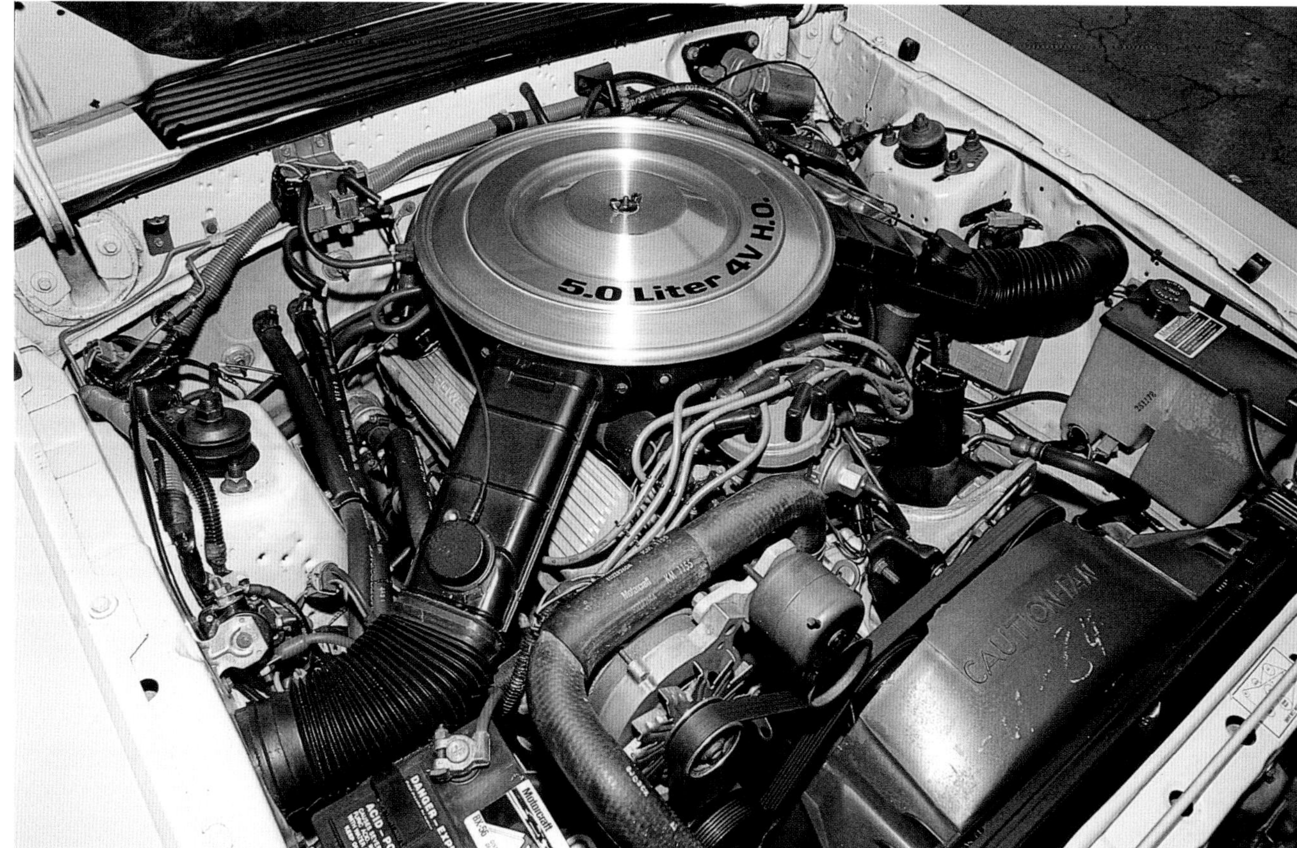

Right: V-8-powered 20th Anniversary Mustangs featured both automatic and manual transmissions, while their Turbo counterparts only came with sticks. Production breakdown for the 5.0-liter models was 2,604 manuals and 934 automatics. *Mike Mueller*

Below right: With its nontraditional offset hood scoop, the 1984 SVO Mustang was hard to miss on Main Street U.S.A. Published 0–60 performance was 7.5 seconds, certainly hot stuff for the day.

also came with Canyon Red interiors (featuring articulating sport seats) and special dashboard badges honoring their heritage.

Available as a convertible or a three-door hatchback, the 1984-½ Mustang could've been fitted with three different powertrains: the HO/five-speed, the EFI 302 with AOD transmission, or the 2.3-liter turbo four and five-speed manual. Body style breakdown for the 20th Anniversary run was 3,900 hatchbacks and 1,360 convertibles.

1984 SVO

The Turbo GT may have flopped, but that didn't stop Ford from trying another force-fed four-cylinder Mustang, this one created by SVO. Officially announced in September 1980, SVO was formed to create "a series of limited-production performance cars and develop their image through motorsport." Michael Kranefuss, previously competition director for Ford of Europe, was brought across the Atlantic to run SVO, and he wasted little time putting the third-generation pony car to work on International Motor Sports Association (IMSA) and SCCA road racing courses. A limited-production, high-performance street car followed four years later.

The definitely innovative 1984 SVO Mustang wowed critics with its truly hot performance, supplied by Ford's 2.3-liter four-cylinder. Beneath that nontraditional asymmetrical hood scoop were 175 standard horses developed from only 140 cubic inches. In comparison, the HO engine needed twice as many cylinders and 182 more cubes to make the same amount of power. How'd the SVO guys do it?

A Garrett AiResearch T3 turbocharger (producing a maximum boost of 14 psi at around 4,200 rpm) and fuel injection represented two keys to SVO's success. Ford's EEC IV system was included, too, and it not only made sure the port injectors delivered fuel as efficiently as possible, it worked the turbocharger's wastegate—this gate was mechanically controlled on Ford's other turbo fours. Also incorporated in the electronic control system was a switch on the dash that changed air/fuel metering calibrations depending on which grade of fuel was pumped in, regular or premium. This switch limited boost to 10 psi whenever regular unleaded was chosen.

Topping off the SVO four was another key: an air-to-air intercooler that lowered the temperature of the compressed atmosphere heading into the intake manifold. Cooler air is denser, and denser air

Left: Wearing an eye-catching biplane spoiler, the 1984 SVO Mustang was equally unconventional in back. Body cladding was also standard just ahead of the rear wheels.

Below: Mustang GTs got new wheels and tires in 1985: Goodyear Eagle P225/60VR Gatorbacks on 15x7 cast-aluminum rims. Output for the GT's HO V-8 that year hit 210 horsepower, a high for the carbureted 5.0-liter.

Officially announced in September 1980, SVO was formed to create "a series of limited-production performance cars and develop their image through motorsport."

is key to more efficient combustion, which in turn helped squeeze so many horses out of four little cylinders. But intercooling couldn't compensate for the one downside produced by all turbochargers: the lag time experienced as exhaust pressures build up to drive the impeller that spins up to compress the incoming air. Though turbo lag has been minimized in today's boosted engines, it still was an inherent hiccup that SVO Mustang drivers had to overlook back in 1984 to appreciate this particular brand of performance.

Make that a balanced brand. Estimated fuel economy was 21 miles per gallon in the city, an appealing 32 on the highway—this from a pony car that could outright run. According to *Car and Driver*, the 0–60 run went by in 7.5 seconds, the quarter-mile in 15.5 clicks.

Additional SVO Mustang standard features included a biplane spoiler in back and ground effects added just in front of the rear wheels. Throw in a Hurst-shifted five-speed manual transmission, Koni gas-charged shocks, quick-ratio steering, four-wheel disc brakes, and 16-inch aluminum wheels, and the sum of the parts equaled a street racer even European drivers could love.

Americans, however, couldn't quite warm up to what at the time amounted to one of the best all-around performers in pony car history. Only 9,844 SVO Mustangs were sold before the model was retired in 1986.

1985

The base L disappeared in 1985, leaving the LX, GT, and SVO models to take up the slack. Standard LX items included power brakes and steering, low-back bucket seats, and an AM/FM stereo. GTs got articulated sports seats and foglamps up front, and all models were treated to a new nose featuring an integral air dam and revised SVO-type grille opening. LX engine availability carried over from 1984.

The SVO was updated midyear and predictably

Another model lineup change came in 1984, as the LX appeared and the GL and GLX were dropped. The L then failed to carry over into 1985, when the pecking order became simply LX, GT, and SVO. As it had in 1984, the 1985 LX convertible (shown here) came standard with V-6 power.

1985

Model Availability	Two-door coupe, three-door hatchback, two-door convertible
Wheelbase	100.5 inches
Length	179.3 inches, 180.8 inches (SVO)
Width	69.1 inches
Height	52.1 inches
Curb Weight	2,559 pounds, four-cylinder LX coupe; 2,667 pounds, V-6 LX coupe; 2,605 pounds, four-cylinder LX hatchback; 2,713 pounds, V-6 LX hatchback; 2,873 pounds, V-6 LX convertible; 2,899 pounds, GT hatchback; 3,043 pounds, GT convertible; 2,881 pounds, SVO
Base Price	$6,885, four-cylinder LX coupe; $8,017, V-6 LX coupe; $7,345, four-cylinder LX hatchback; $8,477, V-6 LX hatchback; $11,985, V-6 LX convertible; $9,885, GT hatchback; $13,585, GT convertible; $14,521, SVO
Track (front/rear, in inches)	56.6/57, 57.8/58.3 (SVO)
Wheels	14-inch, standard; 15-inch, standard (GT); 16x7 aluminum wheels (SVO)
Tires	P195/75R-14, standard; P225/60R-15 (GT); P225/50VR-16 Goodyear NCT (SVO)
Suspension	Modified MacPherson hydraulic struts with coil springs and stabilizer bar in front; four-link solid axle with coil springs and stabilizer bar in rear (V-8)
Steering	Rack and pinion
Brakes	Front discs, rear drums; four-wheel discs, standard (SVO)
Engine	88-horsepower 2.3-liter SOHC four-cylinder, 205-horsepower turbocharged 2.3-liter SOHC four-cylinder (SVO), 120-horsepower 3.8-liter (232-ci) V-6, 165-horsepower 5.0-liter EFI V-8, 210-horsepower 5.0-liter HO V-8
Bore and Stroke	3.78x3.13 inches (four), 3.80x3.40 (V-6), 4.00x3.00 (HO V-8)
Compression	9:1 (90-horsepower four), 8:1 (turbo four), 8.7:1 (V-6), 8.3:1 (5.0-liter V-8)
Fuel Delivery	Carter one-barrel carburetor (88-horsepower four), electronic fuel injection and Garrett AiResearch turbocharger (turbo four), electronic fuel injection (V-6), electronic fuel injection (165-horsepower V-8), Holley four-barrel (HO V-8)
Transmission	Four-speed manual, standard; T-5 five-speed manual and automatic, optional; T-5 five-speed, standard (GT and SVO)
Axle Ratio	3.08:1, standard (four-speed); 3.27:1, standard (automatic); 2.73:1 (V-6); 3.08:1 (V-8, five-speed); 3.27:1 (V-8, automatic); 3.45:1 (turbo four)
Production	156,514

released as a 1985-½ model. Flush-mounted headlamps identified this turbocharged Mustang at a glance. But far more important were changes made beneath that hood scoop. SVO output increased to 205 thanks to a revised intake, improved turbo housing, a longer-duration cam, larger Bosch injectors, and less restrictive exhausts featuring twin tailpipes trailing the single catalytic converter.

That same Y-pipe exhaust system was introduced for the 1985 GT, as were new wheels and tires. The rims were 15x7 cast-aluminum units featuring 10 ornamental holes. The tires were Goodyear Eagle P225/60VR unidirectional Gatorbacks—superwide meats that greatly enhanced handling.

Additional GT performance enhancements came in the engine room, where maximum output was 210 horsepower, a record for the carbureted HO. Like the dual exhausts, tubular headers were new, as were friction-reducing roller lifters and yet another revised camshaft. Assisting this boost was a revamped accessory drive system that spun the air conditioning compressor, power steering pump, and alternator slower to reduce parasitic horsepower loss. The T-5 five-speed was upgraded with shorter throws between gears.

1986

The basic 1985 look rolled over essentially unchanged into 1986, as did the LX engine lineup save for one deletion: the automatic transmission 5.0-liter V-8 (with throttle body injection) was discontinued as its HO brother was offered for both automatic and manual gearbox applications this year. HO firsts for 1986 included true dual exhausts (with twin catalytic converters) and a sequential multiport EFI system in place of the traditional four-barrel carburetor. Output was revised to 200 horsepower, and additional upgrades included

1986

Model Availability	Two-door coupe, three-door hatchback, two-door convertible
Wheelbase	100.5 inches
Length	179.3 inches, 180.8 inches (SVO)
Width	69.1 inches
Height	52.1 inches; 51.9 inches, convertible
Curb Weight	2,601 pounds, four-cylinder LX coupe; 2,722 pounds, V-6 LX coupe; 2,661 pounds, four-cylinder LX hatchback; 2,782 pounds, V-6 LX hatchback; 2,908 pounds, V-6 LX convertible; 2,976 pounds, GT hatchback; 3,103 pounds, GT convertible; 3,028 pounds, SVO
Base Price	$7,189, four-cylinder LX coupe; $8,153, V-6 LX coupe; $7,744, four-cylinder LX hatchback; $8,708, V-6 LX hatchback; $12,821, V-6 LX convertible; $10,691, GT hatchback; $14,523, GT convertible; $15,272, SVO
Track (front/rear, in inches)	56.6/57, 57.8/58.3 (SVO)
Wheels	14-inch, standard; 15-inch, standard (GT); 16x7 aluminum wheels (SVO)
Tires	P195/75R-14, standard; P225/60R-15 (GT); P225/50VR-16 Goodyear NCT (SVO)
Suspension	Modified MacPherson hydraulic struts with coil springs and stabilizer bar in front; four-link solid axle with coil springs and stabilizer bar in rear (V-8)
Steering	Rack and pinion
Brakes	Front discs, rear drums; four-wheel discs, standard (SVO)
Engine	88-horsepower 2.3-liter SOHC four-cylinder, 200-horsepower turbocharged 2.3-liter SOHC four-cylinder (SVO), 120-horsepower EFI 3.8-liter (232-ci) V-6, 200-horsepower EFI 5.0-liter HO V-8
Bore and Stroke	3.78x3.13 inches (four), 3.80x3.40 (V-6), 4.00x3.00 (HO V-8)
Compression	9.5:1 (90-horsepower four), 8:1 (turbo four), 8.7:1 (V-6), 9.2:1 (HO V-8)
Fuel Delivery	Carter one-barrel carburetor (88-horsepower four), electronic fuel injection and Garrett AiResearch turbocharger (turbo four), electronic fuel injection (V-6), electronic fuel injection (165-horsepower V-8), electronic fuel injection (HO V-8)
Transmission	Four-speed manual, standard; T-5 five-speed manual and automatic, optional; T-5 five-speed, standard (GT and SVO)
Axle Ratio	3.08:1, standard (four-speed); 3.27:1, standard (automatic); 2.73:1 (V-6); 2.73:1 (V-8, five-speed); 3.27:1 (V-8, automatic); 3.73:1 (SVO)
Production	224,410

All SVO Mustangs featured a Hurst-shifted five-speed manual transmission. *Mike Mueller*

Total SVO Mustang production for the 1984–1986 run was 9,844. A 1986 model appears here. *Mike Mueller*

Below: True dual exhausts and a sequential multi-port electronic fuel injection system appeared for the GT's HO V-8 in 1986.

> The SVO Mustang, making its final appearance, was reined back to 200 horses.

high-swirl heads, a more efficient water pump, and a redesigned engine block featuring a thickened deck and cylinder walls.

New too in 1986 was a beefier 8.8-inch rear end, replacing the wimpy 7.5-inch unit used under earlier 5.0-liter models. The SVO Mustang, making its final appearance, was reined back to 200 horses.

1987

Model Availability	Two-door coupe, three-door hatchback, two-door convertible
Wheelbase	100.5 inches
Length	179.6 inches
Width	68.3 inches
Height	52.1 inches; 51.9 inches, convertible
Curb Weight	2,724 pounds, four-cylinder LX coupe; 3,000 pounds, V-8 LX coupe; 2,782 pounds, four-cylinder LX hatchback; 3,058 pounds, V-8 LX hatchback; 2,921 pounds, four-cylinder LX convertible; 3,197 pounds, V-8 LX convertible; 3,080 pounds, GT hatchback; 3,214 pounds, GT convertible
Base Price	$8,043, four-cylinder LX coupe; $9,928, V-8 LX coupe; $8,474, four-cylinder LX hatchback; $10,359, V-8 LX hatchback; $12,840, four-cylinder LX convertible; $14,725, V-8 LX convertible; $11,835, GT hatchback; $15,724, GT convertible
Track	56.6 inches front, 57 inches rear
Wheels	14-inch, standard; 15-inch, standard (GT)
Tires	P195/75R-14, standard; P225/60VR-15, standard (GT)
Suspension	Modified MacPherson hydraulic struts with coil springs and stabilizer bar in front; four-link solid axle with coil springs and stabilizer bar in rear (V-8)
Steering	Rack and pinion
Brakes	Front discs, rear drums
Engine	90-horsepower 2.3-liter SOHC four-cylinder, 225-horsepower EFI 5.0-liter HO V-8
Bore and Stroke	3.78x3.13 inches (four), 4.00x3.00 (HO V-8)
Compression	9.5:1 (90-horsepower four), 9.2:1 (HO V-8)
Fuel Delivery	Electronic fuel injection
Transmission	T-5 five-speed manual, standard; automatic, optional
Axle Ratio	3.45:1, standard (four); 3.73:1, optional (four); 2.73:1, standard (GT); 3.08:1, optional (GT)
Production	159,145

1987

Much of the Fox-chassis' engineering modernization had been completed by 1987, leaving only a somewhat tired body to attend to. Though trim tweaks and minor facelifts occurred over the years, much of the Mustang's look remained constant from 1979 to 1986. The next new Mustang retained the same basic shape and main sheet metal, but it nonetheless put on a definitely new face for 1987. Unmistakable in the rounded aero-nose of the base LX, this revamped look was even more startling in GT terms. Included was the LX's wraparound headlights, a complete ground effects skirt treatment, and an exclusive lattice taillight design. Unlike the LX, the new GT didn't have a grille opening between the headlights. Wind tunnel testing resulted in a 0.36 drag coefficient for the 1987 LX hatchback and 0.38 for its GT running mate.

Only two engines were listed, as the V-6 and SVO turbo four didn't return for 1987. New for the base 2.3-liter four was a multiport fuel injection system that helped boost output to 90 horsepower. Transmission choices also were simplified, as the four-cylinder and HO could've been bolted up to the AOD automatic or five-speed manual.

HO output peaked at 225 horsepower in 1987, thanks to the addition of better-flowing cylinder heads (borrowed from the Ford truck parts bin) and an improved EFI setup with larger throttle body bores, up from 58 millimeters to 60. A roller cam and tube headers carried over from 1986, and HO

> Either way, GT or LX, the '87 5.0-liter Mustang was a certified Camaro-killer. And it cost less, too.

A definitely new aero nose was unveiled for the GT Mustang in 1987, as was some extensive lower-body cladding. New too were the GT's standard 15-inch aluminum wheels in a turbine-style pattern.

Production of the affordable 5.0-liter LX Mustang jumped from 16,609 in 1987 to 30,877 the following year, including both hatchbacks and convertibles.

1988

Model Availability	Two-door coupe, three-door hatchback, two-door convertible
Wheelbase	100.5 inches
Length	179.6 inches
Width	68.3 inches
Height	52.1 inches; 51.9 inches, convertible
Curb Weight	2,751 pounds, four-cylinder LX coupe; 3,037 pounds, V-8 LX coupe; 2,818 pounds, four-cylinder LX hatchback; 3,105 pounds, V-8 LX hatchback; 2,953 pounds, four-cylinder LX convertible; 3,209 pounds, V-8 LX convertible; 3,193 pounds, GT hatchback; 3,341 pounds, GT convertible
Base Price	$8,726, four-cylinder LX coupe; $10,611, V-8 LX coupe; $9,221, four-cylinder LX hatchback; $11,106, V-8 LX hatchback; $13,702, four-cylinder LX convertible; $15,587, V-8 LX convertible; $12,745, GT hatchback; $16,610, GT convertible
Track	56.6 inches front, 57 inches rear
Wheels	14-inch, standard; 15-inch, standard (GT)
Tires	P195/75R-14, standard; P225/60VR-15, standard (GT)
Suspension	Modified MacPherson hydraulic struts with coil springs and stabilizer bar in front; four-link solid axle with coil springs and stabilizer bar in rear (V-8)
Steering	Rack and pinion
Brakes	Front discs, rear drums
Engine	90-horsepower 2.3-liter SOHC four-cylinder, 225-horsepower EFI 5.0-liter HO V-8
Bore and Stroke	3.78x3.13 inches (four), 4.00x3.00 (HO V-8)
Compression	9.5:1 (90-horsepower four), 9.2:1 (HO V-8)
Fuel Delivery	Electronic fuel injection
Transmission	T-5 five-speed manual, standard; automatic, optional
Axle Ratio	3.45:1, standard (four); 3.73:1, optional (four); 2.73:1, standard (GT); 3.08:1, optional (GT)
Production	211,225

availability was extended to include the LX line. In the lighter LX body, the 225-horse V-8 produced an impressive 14.17-second quarter-mile according to Hot Rod. In the same test, a 225-horse '87 GT tripped the lights in 14.60 seconds. Either way, GT or LX, the '87 5.0-liter Mustang was a certified Camaro-killer. And it cost less, too.

New turbine-style 15x7 wheels were exclusive to the 1987 GT. Standard for the 5.0-liter LX models were the 1986 GT's 15-inch alloy rims.

1988

HO LX production jumped from 16,609 in 1987 to 30,877 in 1988, further cementing the 5.0 Mustang as Detroit's "biggest bang for the buck." No further news was worthy to report this year as all features constituted 1987 carryovers, save for the LX's battery, which was a 540-amp unit. Previous models used 460-amp batteries.

The '88 GT convertible shown here was this author's ride from 1988 to 1999. It featured all options, including the no-cost 3.08:1 rear axle. *Mike Mueller*

1989

HO Mustangs delivered in environmentally conscious California in 1988 were fitted with a mass-airflow sensor in place of the speed-density fuel control system used in all other cases. In 1989, the superior mass-air system was installed

1989

Model Availability	Two-door coupe, three-door hatchback, two-door convertible
Wheelbase	100.5 inches
Length	179.6 inches
Width	68.3 inches
Height	52.1 inches; 51.9 inches, convertible
Curb Weight	2,754 pounds, four-cylinder LX coupe; 3,045 pounds, V-8 LX coupe; 2,819 pounds, four-cylinder LX hatchback; 3,110 pounds, V-8 LX hatchback; 2,966 pounds, four-cylinder LX convertible; 3,257 pounds, V-8 LX convertible; 3,194 pounds, GT hatchback; 3,333 pounds, GT convertible
Base Price	$9,050, four-cylinder LX coupe; $11,410, V-8 LX coupe; $9,556, four-cylinder LX hatchback; $12,265, V-8 LX hatchback; $14,140, four-cylinder LX convertible; $17,001, V-8 LX convertible; $13,272, GT hatchback; $17,512, GT convertible
Track	56.6 inches front, 57 inches rear
Wheels	14-inch, standard; 15-inch, standard (GT)
Tires	P195/75R-14, standard; P225/60VR-15, standard (GT)
Suspension	Modified MacPherson hydraulic struts with coil springs and stabilizer bar in front; four-link solid axle with coil springs and stabilizer bar in rear (V-8)
Steering	Rack and pinion
Brakes	Front discs, rear drums
Engine	90-horsepower 2.3-liter SOHC four-cylinder, 225-horsepower EFI 5.0-liter HO V-8
Bore and Stroke	3.78x3.13 inches (four), 4.00x3.00 (HO V-8)
Compression	9.5:1 (90-horsepower four), 9.2:1 (HO V-8)
Fuel Delivery	Electronic fuel injection
Transmission	T-5 five-speed manual, standard; automatic, optional
Axle Ratio	3.45:1, standard (four); 3.73:1, optional (four); 2.73:1, standard (GT); 3.08:1, optional (GT)
Production	209,769

While Ford press releases and factory photographs marked the Mustang's 25th birthday in 1989, no special treatment appeared for the cars themselves to the dismay of pony lovers across the country.

on all models in all states. The LX/HO combination was renamed "LX 5.0 Sport" this year, and a 140-mile-per-hour speedometer replaced the GT's 85-mile-per-hour unit midway through the 1989 run.

High hopes for a special 25th anniversary Mustang were dashed as Ford officials sat on their hands, probably because they had earlier planned to retire the Fox chassis in 1989 in favor of an all-new Mazda-sourced front-wheel-drive platform. Instead of replacing the Mustang, that front-driver became the Probe, introduced in 1988 as a 1989 model.

1990

Though they missed the big birthday in 1989, Ford people came back the following year with a run of Emerald Green LX convertibles adorned with small "25th Anniversary" badges, apparently because the Mustang was born as a 1965 model, not a 1964½.

Above: The GT Mustang for 1989 looked an awful lot like its 1988 predecessor, which looked just like its 1987 forerunner. The only notable change for the 1989 GT came beneath the hood, where a superior mass-air induction system was installed.

Right: Once more, no noticeable changes described the new Mustang, LX, and GT for 1990. Base price that year for a 5.0-liter LX convertible was $17,681.

An HO-powered coupe cost $12,107 in 1990. Base price for its 5.0-liter hatchback running mate was $12,950.

All featured white interiors. Reportedly 4,301 of these '90 LX anniversary convertibles were released.

Safety-conscious standard additions this year included rear-seat shoulder belts and a driver-side air bag. Adding the latter equipment meant a tilt steering column no longer could be installed. Deleted as well was the console's center armrest. And with that storage compartment gone, new map pockets were added to the door panels as compensation.

1991

New 16-inch wheels, requiring revised fenders for added clearance, replaced the smaller, difficult-to-clean GT rims used from 1987 to 1990. The 5.0-liter LX models used these bigger wheels too. A revised cylinder head (with two spark plugs per cylinder) helped the base four-cylinder jump up to 105 horsepower.

1992

Minor enhancements for 1992 included bumper strips, color-keyed bodyside moldings, and the introduction of an optional four-way power driver's seat. This year's GT convertible was the first Mustang base-priced beyond $20,000.

1993

Ford's intriguing SVT Cobra was new for 1993, but conventional Mustangs rolled over one more time before the Fox legacy finally wound down. A compact-disc player was new on the options list, and Ford officials chose to change the HO V-8's output rating to 205 horsepower despite the fact that no changes were made to the venerable small-block. Go figure.

1990

Model Availability	Two-door coupe, three-door hatchback, two-door convertible
Wheelbase	100.5 inches
Length	179.6 inches
Width	68.3 inches
Height	52.1 inches; 51.9 inches, convertible
Curb Weight	2,634 pounds, four-cylinder LX coupe; 2,715 pounds, V-8 LX coupe; 2,634 pounds, four-cylinder LX hatchback; 2,715 pounds, V-8 LX hatchback; 2,871 pounds, four-cylinder LX convertible; 2,952 pounds, V-8 LX convertible; 3,065 pounds, GT hatchback; 3,213 pounds, GT convertible
Base Price	$9,638, four-cylinder LX coupe; $12,107, V-8 LX coupe; $10,144, four-cylinder LX hatchback; $12,950, V-8 LX hatchback; $14,495, four-cylinder LX convertible; $17,681, V-8 LX convertible; $13,929, GT hatchback; $18,303, GT convertible
Track	56.6 inches front, 57 inches rear
Wheels	14-inch, standard; 15-inch, standard (GT)
Tires	P195/75R-14, standard; P225/60VR-15, standard (GT)
Suspension	Modified MacPherson hydraulic struts with coil springs and stabilizer bar in front; four-link solid axle with coil springs and stabilizer bar in rear (V-8)
Steering	Rack and pinion
Brakes	Front discs, rear drums
Engine	88-horsepower 2.3-liter SOHC four-cylinder, 225-horsepower EFI 5.0-liter HO V-8
Bore and Stroke	3.78x3.13 inches (four), 4.00x3.00 (HO V-8)
Compression	9:1 (four), 9:1 (HO V-8)
Fuel Delivery	Electronic fuel injection
Transmission	T-5 five-speed manual, standard; automatic, optional
Production	128,189

1991

Model Availability	Two-door coupe, three-door hatchback, two-door convertible
Wheelbase	100.5 inches
Length	179.6 inches
Width	68.3 inches
Height	52.1 inches; 51.9 inches, convertible
Curb Weight	2,759 pounds, four-cylinder LX coupe; 3,037 pounds, V-8 LX coupe; 2,824 pounds, four-cylinder LX hatchback; 3,102 pounds, V-8 LX hatchback; 2,960 pounds, four-cylinder LX convertible; 3,238 pounds, V-8 LX convertible; 3,191 pounds, GT hatchback; 3,327 pounds, GT convertible
Base Price	$10,157, four-cylinder LX coupe; $13,270, V-8 LX coupe; $10,663, four-cylinder LX hatchback; $14,055, V-8 LX hatchback; $16,222, four-cylinder LX convertible; $19,242, V-8 LX convertible; $15,034, GT hatchback; $19,864, GT convertible
Track	56.6 inches front, 57 inches rear
Wheels	14-inch, standard; 16-inch, standard (GT)
Tires	P195/75R-14, standard; P225/55ZR-16, standard (GT)
Suspension	Modified MacPherson hydraulic struts with coil springs and stabilizer bar in front; four-link solid axle with coil springs and stabilizer bar in rear (V-8)
Steering	Rack and pinion
Brakes	Front discs, rear drums
Engine	105-horsepower 2.3-liter SOHC four-cylinder, 225-horsepower EFI 5.0-liter HO V-8
Bore and Stroke	3.78x3.13 inches (four), 4.00x3.00 (HO V-8)
Compression	9:5 (four), 9:1 (HO V-8)
Fuel Delivery	Electronic fuel injection
Transmission	T-5 five-speed manual, standard; automatic, optional
Production	98,373

1992

Model Availability	Two-door coupe, three-door hatchback, two-door convertible
Wheelbase	100.5 inches
Length	179.6 inches
Width	68.3 inches
Height	52.1 inches; 51.9 inches, convertible
Curb Weight	2,775 pounds, four-cylinder LX coupe; 3,010 pounds, V-8 LX coupe; 2,834 pounds, four-cylinder LX hatchback; 3,069 pounds, V-8 LX hatchback; 2,996 pounds, four-cylinder LX convertible; 3,231 pounds, V-8 LX convertible; 3,144 pounds, GT hatchback; 3,365 pounds, GT convertible
Base Price	$10,215, four-cylinder LX coupe; $13,422, V-8 LX coupe; $10,721, four-cylinder LX hatchback; $14,207, V-8 LX hatchback; $16,899, four-cylinder LX convertible; $19,644, V-8 LX convertible; $15,243, GT hatchback; $20,199, GT convertible
Track	56.6 inches front, 57 inches rear
Wheels	14-inch, standard; 16-inch, standard (GT)
Tires	P195/75R-14, standard; P225/55ZR-16, standard (GT)
Suspension	Modified MacPherson hydraulic struts with coil springs and stabilizer bar in front; four-link solid axle with coil springs and stabilizer bar in rear (V-8)
Steering	Rack and pinion
Brakes	Front discs, rear drums
Engine	105-horsepower 2.3-liter SOHC four-cylinder, 225-horsepower EFI 5.0-liter HO V-8
Bore and Stroke	3.78x3.13 inches (four), 4.00x3.00 (HO V-8)
Compression	9:5 (four), 9:1 (HO V-8)
Fuel Delivery	Electronic fuel injection
Transmission	T-5 five-speed manual, standard; automatic, optional
Production	79,280

Above: All three LX body styles could be transformed into low-buck hot rods in 1991 thanks to the installation of the HO V-8, still rated at 225 horsepower. Base price for the 1991 four-cylinder LX coupe (shown here) was $10,157.

Below: Base price for the 1991 5.0-liter LX convertible was $19,242. A 1991 GT convertible cost $19,864.

The GT convertible became the first Mustang base priced beyond $20,000 in 1992. The sticker for the 5.0-liter LX coupe, shown here, began at $13,422.

The 225-horsepower HO V-8 made hay on the street scene from 1987 to 1992. Roller lifters and tubular headers helped this hot little small-block handle anything a Camaro driver could throw at it. *Mike Mueller*

1993

Model Availability	Two-door coupe, three-door hatchback, two-door convertible
Wheelbase	100.5 inches
Length	179.6 inches
Width	68.3 inches
Height	52.1 inches; 51.9 inches, convertible
Curb Weight	2,751 pounds, four-cylinder LX coupe; 3,035 pounds, V-8 LX coupe; 2,812 pounds, four-cylinder LX hatchback; 3,096 pounds, V-8 LX hatchback; 2,973 pounds, four-cylinder LX convertible; 3,259 pounds, V-8 LX convertible; 3,144 pounds, GT hatchback; 3,365 pounds, GT convertible
Base Price	$10,719, four-cylinder LX coupe; $13,926, V-8 LX coupe; $11,224, four-cylinder LX hatchback; $14,710, V-8 LX hatchback; $17,548, four-cylinder LX convertible; $20,293, V-8 LX convertible; $15,747, GT hatchback; $20,848, GT convertible
Track	56.6 inches front, 57 inches rear
Wheels	14-inch, standard; 16-inch, standard (GT)
Tires	P195/75R-14, standard; P225/55ZR-16, standard (GT)
Suspension	Modified MacPherson hydraulic struts with coil springs and stabilizer bar in front; four-link solid axle with coil springs and stabilizer bar in rear (V-8)
Steering	Rack and pinion
Brakes	Front discs, rear drums
Engine	105-horsepower 2.3-liter SOHC four-cylinder, 205-horsepower EFI 5.0-liter HO V-8
Bore and Stroke	3.78x3.13 inches (four), 4.00x3.00 (HO V-8)
Compression	9:5 (four), 9:1 (HO V-8)
Fuel Delivery	Electronic fuel injection
Transmission	T-5 five-speed manual, standard; automatic, optional
Production	114,228

Two special-edition 5.0-liter LX convertibles were released in 1993, one painted white, the other Canary Yellow.

08

Reborn Again

08

1994–2004

- Model choices revert back to two (coupe and convertible) in 1994, as the hatchback body doesn't carry over into the fourth generation.
- Four-wheel disc brakes become standard on all Mustang models for the first time in 1994.
- A V-6, last seen between pony car flanks in 1986, returns for the base Mustang in 1994.
- GT Mustang receives a new 4.6-liter overhead-cam V-8 in 1996.
- Racer Tommy Kendall wins a record 11 races in a row in his Mustang on the way to the 1997 SCCA Trans-Am championship.
- William Clay Ford Jr. is named Ford CEO in October 2001.
- General Motors builds its last Chevrolet Camaro and Pontiac Firebird in 2002.
- Ford celebrates its 100th anniversary on June 16, 2003.
- J Mays is named Ford Motor Company group vice president of design in 2003.
- The 2003 Mach 1 is the first Mustang to mate Ford's 4.6-liter DOHC V-8 with an automatic transmission.
- Ford's 300-millionth vehicle, a 2004 40th Anniversary Mustang GT convertible, leaves the Dearborn line on November 18, 2003.
- Dearborn assembly line rolls out its last Mustang, a red GT convertible, on May 10, 2004.

Above: First seen briefly in 2002, the Pony Package burst onto the national scene in 2003 to add a little GT flair to V-6 models. Bright wheels, a GT hood scoop, and leather-wrapped steering wheel were included in this deal.

Opposite: A V-6 convertible cost $20,150 in 1994. Production was 18,333. Power top, windows, and locks were standard.

Previous pages:
Left: Base price for the 1995 GT convertible was $22,595. The Canary Yellow clear-coat paint seen here was only available for GT and GTS Mustangs that year. *Mike Mueller*

Right: Total production for the 2001 Bullitt GT was 5,582: 3,041 in the appropriate Dark Highland Green; 1,818 in black; and 723 in True Blue. *Mike Mueller*

Talk about your close calls. If not for a fanatically loyal following, the Mustang as we know it might have faded into history along with the 1980s. As early as 1982, Ford planners had begun work on a replacement for the Fox-chassis model, then only three years old. This project, originally labeled "SN8," called for a frugal yet sporty front-wheel-drive compact priced a bit below the existing Mustang. To make the momentous switch from rear to front drive, Ford turned to Mazda, its joint-venture partner from Japan, and once this deal was done the proposal took on a new code name: "ST16." The two car companies from opposite sides of the world had a working prototype rolling by 1985, inspiring the rumor mill to claim that a "rice-burner" would supplant the old Fox in 1988 or 1989.

"HOLD YOUR HORSES!" came the collective cry from the Blue Oval faithful, who bombed Dearborn with more than 30,000 letters of protest during the summer of 1987. "Thousands of us will be forever grateful if the Mustang GT is granted a reprieve," wrote one veteran pony rider. Dealers too complained about the proposed Mazstang, as did critics in the automotive press. "The descendants of the '79 Mustang, namely the GTs, pulled the Mustang name out of the ditch that was dug by the Mustang II," wrote *Mustang Monthly* magazine's Donald Farr. "And now, after the Mustang has clawed its way to the top of the pony car heap once again, Ford plans to turn it into a front-wheel-drive copy of a Japanese car. Un-American, I say."

Dearborn officials couldn't help but hear the disapproving din. And after actually listening, they amazingly responded in favor of the folks who wouldn't stand by and watch their favorite car reoriented in Oriental fashion. In August 1987, Ford announced that its new front-driver would debut wearing a new name: Probe. Sharing most of its

Right: Ford planned to remake the Mustang on a front-wheel-drive platform early in the 1980s. But word got out, and the pony car faithful would have none of it. The traditional rear-drive Mustang remained in control, leaving the front-drive project to evolve into the Probe, introduced as a 1989 model. A 1996 Probe GT appears here.

Below: The white floorpan sections of the 1994 platform represent Fox-chassis carryovers. The red and yellow parts are new. The entire foundation was renamed "Fox-4."

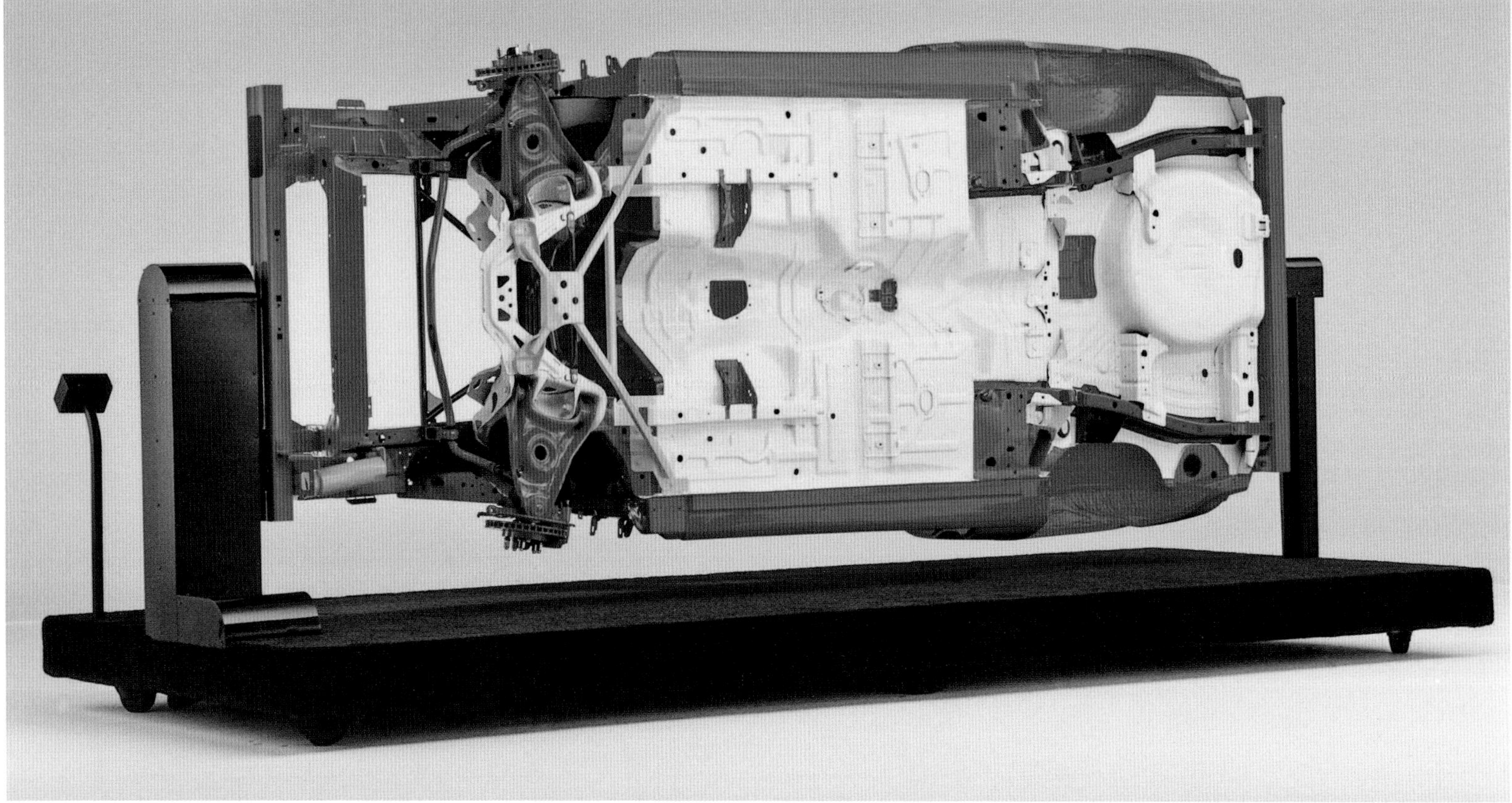

mechanicals with Mazda's MX-6 sport coupe, the Probe was launched in March 1988 as a 1989 model. As for the good ol' Fox-chassis Mustang, it would carry on up through 1993, with very few changes made from 1987 on. A repetitious horse, at the least, was better than a dead one.

Without a doubt, no one at Ford wanted to see the Fox legacy run on so long. But no serious work on a fourth-generation Mustang had begun until after the decision was made to go with the Probe. Even then, progress at first came painfully slow. Little was accomplished until Alex Trotman became executive vice president of Ford's North American Automotive Operations (NAAO) in 1989, after which time he asked two NAAO directors, Ken Nabroski and Steve Lyons, if they could get things rolling.

In August 1989, Nabroski turned to the Mustang's engineering design manager, John Coletti, and instructed him to pull together a special team of freethinkers to concentrate solely on the project. Coletti's so-called "skunk works" opened for business in September, with its nine members at first meeting rather informally every Thursday afternoon to develop a viable business plan and establish workable design parameters. Skunk works design man John Aiken, along with Dennis Reardon and Pat Schiavone, began sculpting an initial styling proposal in November, and both this clay and a basic plan were submitted for Trotman's approval in February 1990. By May, the program, code-named "SN95," was officially under way.

Coletti's gang was superseded by "Team Mustang," a dedicated group that would eventually peak at 450 members during SN95 development. In June 1990, Team Mustang took up residence in an old warehouse in Allen Park, Michigan, a location that was soon renovated into Ford's Danou Technical Center. Program manager Will Boddie first held the reins in Allen Park before becoming Ford's Small and Midsize Car Segment director. Mike Zevalkink then took Boddie's place atop Team Mustang in April 1991.

In 1990, a series of consumer clinics, or "gallop polls" as Ford people called them, were held across the country to help Team Mustang determine the pony car's future form. A long hood and short rear deck were givens, of course, but what of the rest of the new image? "The people we interviewed wanted galloping horses on the car," explained design manager Bud Magaldi. "But they also said that, even if you took the horses off, the car should still look like a Mustang." Important as well to these folks was an "American" feel. "Our research clinics proved to us that a car could be perceived as too European or too Japanese," added Magaldi.

Such was the case with an early design proposal, nicknamed "Bruce Jenner" in honor of the Olympic legend because, according to Magaldi, "it was a trim, athletic vehicle." But, again in his words, it also was "too smooth, too clean and friendly, too nice." Last but certainly not least, it looked a little too much like the Far East–flavored Probe.

Much more patriotic were two themes that resulted from a design competition kicked off in September 1990. Leading one team was John Aiken, the man behind the Bruce Jenner car. Leading the other was Dave Rees. Rees' group produced "Rambo," named for its rawboned, gutsy looks, which proved a bit too dramatic for the clinic critics. Aiken's latest proposal, on the other hand, was apparently just right: not too hard, not too soft. "It was called 'Arnold Schwarzenegger' because it looked like a Bruce Jenner that went down to the gym and put on some muscle and bulk," said Magaldi.

The middle-of-the-road Schwarzenegger design was approved for production in November 1990. From there, the project gained serious speed thanks to a new process at Ford called world class timing (WCT), which streamlined as many procedures as possible to cut costs and save time. The fourth-generation Mustang makeover represented Ford's first application of the WCT plan, and its heightened efficiency was plainly demonstrated. Going from clay model to regular production required a relatively scant 35 months, compared to the 48 months typically needed to bring previous new model lines to life. The project's bottom line too came in much lower than expected, down from the typical $1 billion developmental price tag to $700 million.

Bringing Team Mustang all together in the Allen Park facility was a major contributing factor to these savings. "A fundamental element of world class timing is to have the people who make the decisions housed together with the people who execute those decisions on a daily basis," explained Mike Zevalkink. According to Will Boddie, bringing all involved in the project beneath the same roof improved communications by trading traditional chimney-type channels with informal over-the-wall discussions. "Someone could ask me a question at the coffee pot, and I could make a

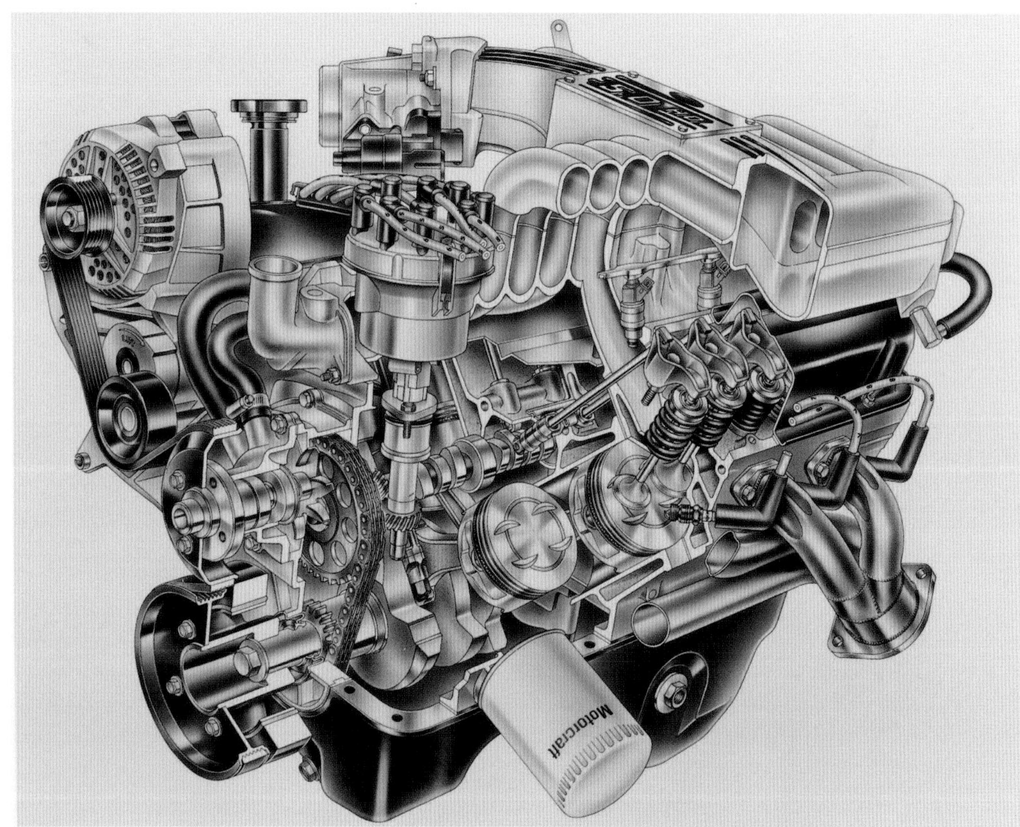

Top: **A Borg-Warner T-5 five-speed manual was standard behind the 1994 GT's HO V-8. Ford's four-speed AOD electronic automatic transmission was optional. A beefed suspension with quad shocks in back was once more standard GT fare.** ***David Kimble cutaway, courtesy Ford Motor Company***

Above: **The 5.0-liter pushrod V-8 also carried over into the next generation. Output for the 1994 HO was 215 horses, 10 more than the 1993 rendition.** ***David Kimble cutaway, courtesy Ford Motor Company***

Right: "It was, It is" was Ford's promotional battle cry for 1994. Designers worked overtime to remind Mustang buyers in 1994 of the original pony car (background) born in 1964. *Mike Mueller*

Below right: GT production for 1994 was 30,592 coupes and 25,381 convertibles. Foglamps in front and a spoiler in back were standard. Paint choices totaled 11, all vibrant in nature. *Mike Mueller*

decision in 10 seconds that might have taken three weeks if it had to go through some formal chain of command," added Boddie.

Job One, the first fourth-generation Mustang off the line, appeared in October 1993, two months ahead of schedule—the original projection had included 37 months of start-up time prior to full production. The WCT process aided this rush to market, yes. But Ford execs also were more than willing to credit Coletti's crew for getting so much early groundwork out of the way before full-fledged concept to creation (CTC) work began. Mentioned too was the plain fact that the latest, greatest pony car relied on existing powertrains and was based on a revamped version of the venerable Fox chassis, which in both cases translated into some serious savings in time and money for the engineers.

Little else carried over, however. Reportedly, 1,350 of the car's 1,850 components made their debut when the 1994 Mustang went on sale December 9, 1993. As for the sum of those parts, it certainly equaled "new" in most minds.

1994

"It was, it is," or so claimed Ford advertisements in 1994. While comparatively few nuts and bolts rolled over from 1993, much of what made America fall in love with earlier Mustangs showed up in the fourth-generation model's makeup, beginning with that old familiar galloping horse in the grille. Inviting further reminiscence were the C-shaped

1994

Model Availability	Two-door coupe, two-door convertible
Wheelbase	101.3 inches
Length	181.5 inches
Width	71.8 inches
Height	52.9 inches, coupe; 52.8 inches, convertible
Curb Weight	3,055 pounds, V-6 coupe; 3,193 pounds, V-6 convertible; 3,258 pounds, GT coupe; 3,414 pounds, GT convertible
Base Price	$13,355, V-6 coupe; $20,150, V-6 convertible; $17,270, GT coupe; $21,960, GT convertible
Track	60.6 inches front, 59.1 inches rear
Wheels	15x6.5, standard (V-6); 16x7.5, standard (GT); 15x7, optional (V-6); 17x8, optional (GT)
Tires	P205/65R-15, standard (V-6); P225/55ZR-16, standard (GT)
Suspension	Modified MacPherson struts with gas-charged shocks, coil springs, and stabilizer bar in front; four-link solid axle with coil springs in back
Steering	Power-assisted rack and pinion (14.7:1 ratio)
Brakes	Four-wheel discs (ABS optional)
Engine	145-horsepower 3.8-liter (232-ci) V-6, 215-horsepower 5.0-liter (302-ci) V-8
Bore and Stroke	3.80x3.40 inches (V-6), 4.00x3.00 inches (V-8)
Compression	9.0:1 for both engines
Fuel Delivery	Sequential electronic fuel injection
Transmission	Five-speed manual, standard; four-speed automatic, optional
Axle Ratio	2.73:1, standard; 3.08:1 and 3.27:1 axles optional for GT
Production	123,198 total (30,592 GT coupes, 25,381 GT convertibles)

Above: The familiar running-horse logo returned to the Mustang grille in 1994 as part of a nostalgic plan to revive pony car memories. *Mike Mueller*

Top: Base price for the 1994 GT coupe was $17,270. A Traction-Lok rear axle was included in the GT deal. *Mike Mueller*

scoops just ahead of the rear wheels and the three-element taillights in back. The latter units were now horizontal, as opposed to the original Mustang's vertical layout, but Ford people still insisted on making this family tie. Nostalgic connections continued inside, where a flashy dual-cockpit arrangement also harked back to warm and fuzzy days gone by. "By having a rich history, the Mustang provided us with dozens of styling accents from the past that we could draw on and enhance," said interior designer Emeline King.

"We brought back a lot of the Mustang heritage in a very contemporary way," added Bud Magaldi. "That seemed to be what people wanted us to do."

"There's a latent passion that wells up in people when they see this car," said Mike Zevalkink. "It's a car for today, but it touches their past in a personal way. The wonderful changes that have been made

Above: Electronic fuel injection again shot the juice to the GT's HO V-8 in 1994. Compression was 9.0:1. *Mike Mueller*

Right: The standard GT wheel in 1994 was a 16x7.5 cast-aluminum piece. This optional rim measured 17x8. Four of them cost $380. *Mike Mueller*

An optional removable hardtop option was considered for the 1994 convertible but didn't make it into production. This feature reappeared in 1995 for the SVT Cobra convertible.

in this automobile will, we feel, bring back this country's love affair with the Mustang."

Hiding within all those warm memories was the revised Fox-4 foundation, which retained the basic floorpan from the third-generation Mustang but was thoroughly new elsewhere. "This is not a carryover platform," claimed Boddie. "The '94 car behaves very well, even at its limits. It's a more developed, friendly car than its competitors. It's more refined." More unit-body stiffness was the root of this refinement, with the coupe measuring 44 percent more torsionally rigid than its predecessor, the convertible a whopping 80 percent stiffer. Attaining such structural strength meant dropping the familiar hatchback body for fairly obvious reasons. "It is very difficult, if not impossible, to build a torsionally stiff three-door hatchback," said Boddie.

Topless buyers in 1994 were especially pleased with these gains. The tighter body, reshaped more aerodynamically, helped make the new convertible much easier to live with. "You can cruise along at freeway speeds and hold a normal conversation with your passenger without raising your voice," explained Boddie. An easy-to-handle, one-piece convertible boot also fit nicely behind the rear seat back, that is, if an owner chose to use it. "The convertible top is level with the deck," continued Boddie. "The car looks good, even if the convertible boot isn't put on."

Along with doing away with most of the twists and shakes common to the previous platform, the much more rigid Fox-4 chassis offered improved steering and handling characteristics, thanks to revised suspension geometry up front and a standard anti-roll bar in back for base models, a first for non-GT Mustangs. A slightly longer wheelbase and wider track also contributed to the car's newfound surefootedness, something press critics couldn't help but notice. "Where the old [GT] got by on its kick-butt, straight-line performance, the new car provides a much more entertaining, better rounded package," claimed *Road & Track*'s Jim Miller.

Enhancing the attraction further were standard power-assisted four-wheel discs for both the base Mustang and GT. Rotor diameters, in each case, were 10.9 inches for the vented front units, 10.5 for the solid rears. A Bosch anti-lock brake system (ABS) was optional.

Standard power for the base model came from Ford's proven 3.8-liter pushrod V-6, which made 40 more horses than the 2.3-liter four-cylinder used by the 1993 LX. The ever-popular 5.0-liter HO small-block V-8, now rated at 215 horsepower, carried over for the GT and the GT alone—there would be no more budget-conscious 5.0-liter base Mustangs. Borg-Warner's T-5 five-speed stick was standard behind the 3.8 and 5.0, with the familiar AOD-E four-speed electronic automatic transmission again an option for both.

GT customers once more got a beefed-up suspension (consisting of variable-rate front coils and the Quadra-Shock setup in back) and a Traction-Lok rear axle. Fog lamps returned up front, as did a spoiler (a wing this time) at the tail. New was an underhood brace that tied the shock towers to each other and to the cowl to help preserve steering precision during hard cornering.

1995

Model Availability	Two-door coupe, two-door convertible
Wheelbase	101.3 inches
Length	181.5 inches
Width	71.8 inches
Height	53.0 inches, coupe; 52.8 inches, convertible
Curb Weight	3,055 pounds, V-6 coupe; 3,257 pounds, V-6 convertible; 3,280 pounds, GT coupe; 3,451 pounds, GT convertible
Base Price	$13,355, V-6 coupe; $20,795, V-6 convertible; $17,905, GT coupe; $22,595, GT convertible
Track	60.6 inches front, 59.1 inches rear
Wheels	15x6.5, standard (V-6); 16x7.5, standard (GT); 15x7, optional (V-6); 17x8, optional (GT)
Tires	P205/65R-15, standard (V-6); P225/55ZR-16, standard (GT)
Suspension	Modified MacPherson struts with gas-charged shocks, coil springs, and stabilizer bar in front; four-link solid axle with coil springs in back
Steering	Power-assisted rack and pinion (14.7:1 ratio)
Brakes	Four-wheel discs (ABS optional)
Engine	145-horsepower 3.8-liter (232-ci) V-6, 215-horsepower 5.0-liter (302-ci) V-8
Bore and Stroke	3.80x3.40 inches (V-6), 4.00x3.00 inches (V-8)
Compression	9.0:1 (V-6 and V-8)
Fuel Delivery	Sequential electronic fuel injection
Transmission	Five-speed manual, standard; four-speed automatic, optional
Axle Ratio	2.73:1, standard; 3.08:1 and 3.27:1 axles optional for GT
Production	186,986

Top: No noticeable changes announced the 1995 Mustang's arrival. Base price for the V-6 convertible was $20,795. Total convertible production (V-6 and GT) was 48,264 that year.

Above: The 1995 GT coupe was base priced at $16,910.

If it ain't broke, don't fix it.

Along with ABS, new options for 1994 included remote keyless entry, an antitheft system, a compact-disc player, and the Mach 460 sound system, the latter named for its 460 watts of peak power delivered through eight speakers. Also listed early on was a removable hardtop for the 1994 convertible, but supply troubles delayed delivery of this high-priced convenience until 1995, and then only for the SVT Cobra.

1995

If it ain't broke, don't fix it. Such was the case as the Mustang rolled over into 1995. No changes of note were made, save for the introduction of an optional combination AM/FM stereo/CD player. The only major breaking story involved the introduction of the stripped-down GTS coupe, a send-off of sorts for the revered 5.0-liter pushrod V-8 in its last year beneath Mustang hoods.

1995 GTS

Ford officials at first claimed that the popular HO-powered base Mustang would not carry over into the fourth generation. Then along came an official listing in Ford's fleet-ordering guide late in the summer of 1994 for the new "GTS" coupe. Like the 5.0-liter LX, the promised GTS was to possess GT performance at a lower price thanks to the deletion of various bits of excess baggage from the standard package. Just like that there was joy once more in Mudville, as Mustang buyers again would be able to spend fewer bucks for the biggest bang.

But it was not to be, at least not in the fall of 1994. Word soon got around that the deal was off: no GTS Mustangs were mentioned in factory brochures, no GTS Mustangs were advertised, no GTS Mustangs were available. Initially listed under Preferred Equipment Package (PEP) 248A, the option was nowhere to be found when showrooms began showing off the 1995 models, and some early press reports claimed it had been cancelled. A few Ford people in high places even claimed PEP 248A never existed in the first place despite its appearance in fleet order paperwork.

Then GTS Mustangs began popping up in April 1995, this after production had indeed started rolling that January. According to Motor Trend's Detroit-watchers, factory sources told them Ford finally made the GTS a reality to help whittle down its supply of 5.0-liter pushrod V-8s, clearing the way for the upcoming 4.6-liter modular motor, scheduled for a 1996 introduction.

"Not true," said Mustang market plans manager Joe Castelli. "We in the field were expecting the GTS all along. And there is no need to get rid of

Cost-cutting measures inside the GTS coupe included deleting the GT's sport seats and leather-wrapped steering wheel. *Mike Mueller*

There was no skimping beneath the 1995 GTS coupe's hood. The GT's 215-horse HO V-8 carried over untouched. *Mike Mueller*

1995 GTS

Model Availability · · · Two-door coupe only
Wheelbase · · · · · · · · · 101.3 inches
Length · · · · · · · · · · · · · 181.5 inches
Width · · · · · · · · · · · · · · 71.8 inches
Height · · · · · · · · · · · · · 53.0 inches
Curb Weight · · · · · · · · 3,246 pounds
Base Price · · · · · · · · · $16,910
Track · · · · · · · · · · · · · · 60.6 inches front, 59.1 inches rear
Wheels · · · · · · · · · · · · 16x7.5
Tires · · · · · · · · · · · · · · P225/55ZR-16
Suspension · · · · · · · · · Modified MacPherson struts with gas-charged shocks, coil springs, and stabilizer bar in front; four-link solid axle with coil springs in back
Steering · · · · · · · · · · · Power-assisted rack and pinion (14.7:1 ratio)
Brakes · · · · · · · · · · · · · Four-wheel discs (ABS optional)
Engine · · · · · · · · · · · · · 215-horsepower 5.0-liter (302-ci) V-8
Bore and Stroke · · · · 4.00x3.00 inches (V-8)
Compression · · · · · · · 9.0:1
Fuel Delivery · · · · · · · Sequential electronic fuel injection
Transmission · · · · · · · Five-speed manual, standard; four-speed automatic, optional
Axle Ratio · · · · · · · · · · 2.73:1, standard; 3.08:1 and 3.27:1 axles optional for GT
Production · · · · · · · · · 6,370 (4,848 with automatic transmissions, 1,522 with manuals)

Joining the GT (right) in 1995 was the GTS coupe (left), a stripped-down V-8 model that reminded Mustangers of the 5.0-liter LX. *Mike Mueller*

the [5.0-liter V-8], it remains a usable engine and will still be going into the Explorer." On top of that, Dearborn projected the GTS would only make up a mere 7 percent of the total Mustang mix for 1995, not much of a whittle in anyone's book. Reportedly, the GTS's production in January amounted to only 2 or 3 percent, then ramped up to 9 percent in April.

According to Castelli, the GTS came about "basically by request from the dealer body. Dealers are the voice of the customer, and customers were asking for a value-laden product, a 'cheaper V-8' if you will." Castelli could only guess why the GTS took so long to arrive.

Apparently, existing demand was judged strong enough to allow Ford to skip all promotion puffery, adding to the perceived mystery. "We left it up to the dealers to do the marketing," said Castelli. And they also left it up to buyers to find the car. Nowhere, save for on the original window sticker, did a GTS Mustang officially announce its presence. Standard GT badges appeared on the fenders, and that was it as far as external imagery was concerned.

On the other hand, a 1995 GTS coupe could've been identified by those in the know thanks to its missing fog lamps and rear wing, items cut to keep costs at bay. Gone as well were the GT's sports sets, leather-wrapped steering wheel, and illuminated vanity mirror inside. All other standard GT features—5.0-liter power, 16-inch wheels, and sport suspension—carried over untouched. Summed up, the GTS cost some $1,200 less than its GT cousin.

Available optional equipment for the GTS included all GT goodies—17-inch wheels, Power Group, etc.—save for the sport buckets and interior leather treatment, which couldn't be added at any cost. Nor could the fog lamps and rear wing, because they weren't offered as options for any 1995 Mustang.

Although the 248A package returned for 1996, the shadowy GTS name didn't. Production for 1995 was 6,370: 4,848 with automatic transmissions, 1,522 with five-speed manuals.

1996

Picking a 1996 Mustang out of a crowd required a peek in back, where the segmented taillights were laid out in a vertical fashion, as they had been in 1964. Eagle-eyed pony watchers might have noticed the screen added to the grille up front to hide the radiator. Restyled 17-inch wheels (featuring five spokes) appeared as well as a new GT option, while the cheap GT 248A package came back for an encore, finding another 5,479 buyers.

The latest main attraction was found beneath the GT's hood, where the fourth-generation Mustang finally was treated to a next-generation V-8. Though the beloved 5.0-liter certainly was no slouch, it was still considered a leftover of sorts when the SN95 era began. "For at least six years now, Mustang was a terrific engine in search of a better car," wrote *AutoWeek*'s John Clor in 1994. "Now it's a better car in search of even more power."

That search gained some serious speed in 1996 as the venerable pushrod small-block was traded for Ford's thoroughly modern 4.6-liter modular V-8. Mod motor roots ran back to 1987, with the idea being to create an adaptable engine family that could evolve into various forms, sharing many parts in the process. Early examples were of single-overhead-cam (SOHC) design and featured aluminum heads with two typical valves per cylinder. The first of these, rated at 190 horsepower (210 with optional dual exhausts), debuted for the Lincoln Town Car in 1991. Two years later, the Mk VIII Lincoln appeared with an all-aluminum, dual-overhead-cam (DOHC), 32-valve, 4.6-liter V-8 rated at 280 horsepower. The use of four cams and four valves per cylinder each represented Ford Motor Company regular-production firsts.

As the 1996 Mustang GT's new heart, the 4.6-liter SOHC V-8 was rated at the same 215 horsepower produced by the last 5.0-liter HO. Nonetheless, it represented a marked improvement: it ran smoother and cleaner, was more efficient, and promised even more performance potential for future Mustangs. Ford's Special Vehicle Team demonstrated just some of that promise by adding DOHC to the 4.6-liter V-8, resulting in a 305-horsepower screamer that came standard in the 1996 SVT Cobra.

According to Mustang vehicle line director Janine Bay, Ford's mod motor transformed the GT "from a good to a great car. We've opened up the usable rpm range, providing a whole lot more fun and power through the entire rpm band," said Bay.

"What the 4.6-liter engines bring to customers is a new sense of performance and excitement," added John Hasse, supervisor of Mustang V-8 engine systems. "Buyers of the 1996 Mustangs will feel the old excitement of the original mid-sixties pony cars, but they'll also appreciate the benefits of the mid-nineties technology."

Fitting the slightly taller SOHC V-8 beneath the 1996 Mustang's hood required various modifications, including reshaping the main crossmember up front and lowering steering and suspension components. A thicker front stabilizer bar was added to compensate for the revised suspension geometry, and additional underhood clearance was created by using a clever, compact brake booster that borrowed its hydraulic pressure from the power steering pump.

New transmissions also appeared for the 1996 Mustang as the T-5 manual was traded for a stronger, quieter T-45 five-speed. Taking the old automatic overdrive (AOD) transmission's place

1996

Model Availability	Two-door coupe, two-door convertible
Wheelbase	101.3 inches
Length	181.5 inches
Width	71.8 inches
Height	53.2 inches, coupe; 53.4 inches, convertible
Curb Weight	3,057 pounds, V-6 coupe; 3,269 pounds, V-6 convertible; 3,279 pounds, GT coupe; 3,468 pounds, GT convertible
Base Price	$15,180, V-6 coupe; $21,060, V-6 convertible; $17,610, GT coupe; $23,495, GT convertible
Track	60.6 inches front, 59.1 inches rear
Wheels	15x6.5, standard (V-6); 16x7.5, standard (GT); 15x7, optional (V-6); 17x8, optional (GT)
Tires	P205/65R-15, standard (V-6); P225/55ZR-16, standard (GT)
Suspension	Modified MacPherson struts with gas-charged shocks, coil springs, and stabilizer bar in front; four-link solid axle with coil springs in back
Steering	Power-assisted rack and pinion (14.7:1 ratio)
Brakes	Four-wheel discs (ABS optional)
Engine	150-horsepower 3.8-liter (232-ci) V-6, 215-horsepower 4.6-liter (281-ci) SOHC V-8
Bore and Stroke	3.80x3.40 inches (V-6), 3.60x3.60 inches (V-8)
Compression	9.0:1 (V-6 and V-8)
Fuel Delivery	Sequential electronic fuel injection
Transmission	Five-speed manual, standard; four-speed automatic, optional
Production	135,620 total (31,624 GT coupes, 17,917 GT convertibles)

Base price for a 1996 V-6 convertible (shown here) was $21,060. Production was 15,246. *Mike Mueller*

Standard items inside the base Mustang for 1996 included cloth reclining bucket seats, dual remote mirrors, dual air bags, a digital clock, and a tilt steering wheel. A power top was again the norm for convertibles. *Mike Mueller*

The biggest news for 1996 involved the GT's standard power source. In place of the venerable 5.0-liter pushrod V-8 was the new 4.6-liter mod motor with a single overhead cam in each cylinder head. Base price for the 4.6-liter SOHC GT coupe was $17,610 in 1996. Production was 31,624.

A GT convertible cost $23,495 in 1996. Production was 17,917.

was the smoother, more efficient 4R70W electronic automatic.

The base Mustang's 3.8-liter V-6 too was treated to a few enhancements, beginning with a power boost. "With 150 horsepower at 4,000 rpm and 215 foot-pounds of torque at 3,000 rpm, the V-6 Mustang offers one of America's best power-to-affordability ratios," said Janine Bay.

Additional V-6 improvements included a stiffer, more structurally rigid cylinder block, which helped reduce NVH. The 3.8-liter also was fitted with lighter valvetrain components and a revised cam that offered a smoother, quieter idle. A new high-flow oil pump and a refined oil pan helped out in the NVH department too. Long-life platinum-tipped spark plugs appeared in all 1996 Mustang engines, V-6 and V-8, as did a durable stainless-steel exhaust system.

Along with their Cobra counterparts, all 1996 GTs were equipped with a passive anti-theft system (PATS) that used a specially encoded key and ignition switch to resist hot-wiring.

1997

As in 1995, the new Mustang for 1997 made next to no headlines. Easily the most important change involved making the PATS system standard on all models, V-6 and V-8. New too was a mildly revised grille opening that allowed more cooling air access

1997

Model Availability	Two-door coupe, two-door convertible
Wheelbase	101.3 inches
Length	181.5 inches
Width	71.8 inches
Height	53.2 inches, coupe; 53.4 inches, convertible
Curb Weight	3,084 pounds, V-6 coupe; 3,264 pounds, GT; 3,288 pounds, V-6 coupe; 3,422 pounds, GT convertible
Base Price	$15,880, V-6 coupe; $21,280, V-6 convertible; $18,525, GT coupe; $24,510, GT convertible
Track	60.6 inches front, 59.2 inches rear
Wheels	15x6.5, standard (V-6); 16x7.5, standard (GT); 17x8, optional (GT)
Tires	P205/65TR-15, standard (V-6); P225/55ZR-16, standard (GT)
Suspension	Modified MacPherson struts with gas-charged shocks, coil springs, and stabilizer bar in front; four-link solid axle with coil springs in back
Steering	Power-assisted rack and pinion (14.7:1 ratio)
Brakes	Four-wheel discs (ABS optional, standard w/GT convertible)
Engine	150-horsepower 3.8-liter (232-ci) V-6, 215-horsepower 4.6-liter (281-ci) SOHC V-8
Bore and Stroke	3.80x3.40 inches (V-6), 3.60x3.60 inches (V-8)
Compression	9.0:1 (V-6 and V-8)
Fuel Delivery	Sequential electronic fuel injection
Transmission	Five-speed manual, standard; four-speed automatic, optional
Production	108,344 total (18,464 GT coupes, 11,413 GT convertibles)

The GT coupe's base sticker was $18,525 in 1997. Production was 18,464.

Above: **The vertical three-element taillights introduced for 1996 carried over into 1997. A GT convertible cost $24,510 that year. Production was 11,413.**

Again, no noticeable updates were made for 1998. Base price for the 1998 GT coupe was $19,970. Production was 28,789. ***Mike Mueller***

to an improved cooling package for the GT. GT seats received a new flecked pattern, and the V-6 convertible featured an optional gray leather interior in place of the white previously offered. The exterior paint card was slightly reshuffled (Aztec Gold and Autumn Orange appeared, while Bright Tangerine and Opal Frost were dropped), and another set of restyled 17-inch wheels (diamond-cut, brightly machined with dark-gray metallic centers) became optional for the GT. Automatic models got a more ergonomic shifter that was thicker and incorporated an overdrive button on the knob.

1998

Newly polished aluminum wheels became standard in 1998, as did a premium sound system (with both cassette and CD capabilities) for the base coupe and convertible. Added to the basic package that year were air conditioning, power windows, power locks, power deck lid release, and remote keyless illuminated entry, all without an extra cent being charged compared to 1997's V-6 models. GT buyers, meanwhile, were treated to 10 more horses from their 4.6-liter V-8s, meaning the

Top: GT convertible production for 1998 was 17,014. Base price was $23,970. Above: Revised cylinder heads helped the 1998 4.6-liter V-8 reach the same output peak realized by the 5.0-liter HO engine. *Mike Mueller*

Right: The clock pod formerly mounted on the dash was eliminated in 1998; the time readout was incorporated into the radio.

Newly polished aluminum wheels became standard in 1998, as did a premium sound system (with both cassette and CD capabilities) for the base coupe and convertible.

1998

Model Availability	Two-door coupe, two-door convertible
Wheelbase	101.3 inches
Length	181.5 inches
Width	71.8 inches
Height	53.2 inches, coupe; 53.4 inches, convertible
Curb Weight	3,065 pounds, V-6 coupe; 3,210 pounds, GT; 3,227 pounds, V-6 coupe; 3,400 pounds, GT convertible
Base Price	$15,970, V-6 coupe; $20,470, V-6 convertible; $19,970, GT coupe; $23,970, GT convertible
Track	60.6 inches front, 59.2 inches rear
Wheels	15x6.5, standard (V-6); 16x7.5, standard (GT); 17x8, optional (GT)
Tires	P205/65TR-15, standard (V-6); P225/55HR-16, standard (GT)
Suspension	Modified MacPherson struts with gas-charged shocks, coil springs, and stabilizer bar in front; four-link solid axle with coil springs in back
Steering	Power-assisted rack and pinion (14.7:1 ratio)
Brakes	Four-wheel discs (ABS optional, standard w/GT convertible)
Engine	150-horsepower 3.8-liter (232-ci) V-6, 225-horsepower 4.6-liter (281-ci) SOHC V-8
Bore and Stroke	3.80x3.40 inches (V-6), 3.60x3.60 inches (V-8)
Compression	9.0:1 (V-6 and V-8)
Fuel Delivery	Sequential electronic fuel injection
Transmission	Five-speed manual, standard; four-speed automatic, optional
Production	175,522 total (28,789 GT coupes, 17,024 GT convertibles)

Seventeen-inch cast-aluminum wheels were a $500 option for the 1998 GT. Mounted on these rims were P245/45ZR17 Goodyear Eagle tires. *Mike Mueller*

mod motor now matched the 5.0-liter HO's peak 225-horsepower rating.

New options for 1998 included a Convenience Group (floor mats, rear window defroster, cruise control, and a power driver seat) and two Sport packages. The GT Sport Group included 17-inch wheels, special striping for the hood and fenders, a leather-wrapped shift knob, and an oil cooler. The V-6 Sport Appearance Group included alloy rims, a rear spoiler, a leather-wrapped steering wheel, and lower-body accent striping.

Ford's "New Edge" design philosophy helped sharpen the 1999 Mustang's focus. A crisp, more aggressive image resulted. Production of V-6 coupes for 1999 was 73,180.

1999

Unlike their rivals at General Motors, Ford people were nowhere near as big on birthday parties during the 1990s. Special-edition Corvettes, Camaros, and Firebirds commemorating various mileposts were seemingly everywhere then. But similar momentous occasions came and went in Dearborn with nary a balloon popped. Rumors of a super-duper 25th anniversary Mustang in 1989 led to nothing more than a limited run of green-painted convertibles quietly released early in 1990. The badges used on that one even stated "25 Years," which didn't quite add up—remember, the Mustang was born in 1964, not 1965. Then the breed's 30th anniversary arrived at the same time a glorious rebirth was occurring in 1994. Again no candles were extinguished.

That Ford officials more than once chose not to celebrate so many years of success can be explained simply enough. Why rub it in? While Detroit's longest-running pony car continued galloping along, its much-ballyhooed rivals from GM were stumbling toward a finish line that wasn't far off. Mustangs outsold Camaros from 1993 on, with the former outnumbering the latter by nearly a 2:1 margin by 1997. Mustang production topped 175,000 in 1998, a healthy figure to say the least. Chevy's Camaro and Pontiac's Firebird, meanwhile, were on their last legs facing a painful cancellation that finally came four years later.

1999

Model Availability	Two-door coupe, two-door convertible
Wheelbase	101.3 inches
Length	181.5 inches
Width	73.1 inches
Height	53.2 inches, coupe; 53.4 inches, convertible
Curb Weight	3,069 pounds, V-6 coupe; 3,211 pounds, V-6 convertible; 3,273 pounds, GT coupe; 3,429 pounds, GT convertible
Base Price	$16,470, V-6 coupe; $21,070, V-6 convertible; $20,870, GT coupe; $24,870, GT convertible
Track	60.6 inches front, 59.2 inches rear
Wheels	15x6.5, standard (V-6); 16x7.5 forged aluminum, standard; 17x8 forged aluminum, optional
Tires	P205/65TR-15, standard (V-6); P225/55HR16 BFGoodrich, standard (GT); P245/45ZR-17 Goodyear Eagle, optional (GT)
Suspension	Modified MacPherson struts with gas-charged shocks, coil springs, and stabilizer bar in front; four-link solid axle with coil springs in back
Steering	Power-assisted rack and pinion (14.7:1 ratio)
Brakes	Four-wheel discs (ABS optional)
Engine	190-horsepower 3.8-liter (232-ci) V-6, 260-horsepower 4.6-liter (281-ci) SOHC V-8
Bore and Stroke	3.80x3.40 inches (V-6), 3.60x3.60 inches (V-8)
Compression	9.36:1 (V-6), 9.0:1 (V-8)
Fuel Delivery	Sequential electronic fuel injection
Transmission	Five-speed manual, standard; four-speed automatic, optional
Production	133,637 total (19,634 GT coupes, 13,699 GT convertibles)

An extra inch was added to the driver's seat track for 1999 to accommodate taller drivers.

Above: The Mustang's revered running horse was corralled in 1999 with an extra bit of surrounding trim. *Mike Mueller*

Left: V-6 output for 1999 was boosted up to 190 horsepower, only 15 less than the GT's HO V-8 was making in 1993. *Mike Mueller*

Opposite: Enlarged 3-inch-diameter dual tailpipes were installed on the 1999 GT to help announce the improvements made beneath the hood.

Finally, for 1999, more than a little fanfare marked a Mustang birthday. All models received tasteful 35th Anniversary fender badges and special pony seat embroidery. And that wasn't all. A 35th Anniversary Limited Edition Package also was offered for GTs only.

Priced at $2,695, this option group (coded 54Y) added a raised hood scoop, large rear quarter scoops, revised rocker moldings, and a unique rear spoiler. A black tape appliqué adorned the hood, and a black honeycomb panel was inserted between the taillights. Brightly machined 17x8 five-spoke aluminum wheels with unique galloping pony center caps went on at the corners. Inside was a Midnight Black GT leather interior with silver insert panels for the seats and doors, anniversary logo floor mats, a silver instrument panel (also marked with 35th Anniversary script), and an aluminum shift knob for manual-transmission models. Production of 1999 35th Anniversary Mustangs was 4,628.

But wait, there was more. Total Mustang production for 1999 was 133,637, all of which were noticeably updated inside and out. On top was a revitalized shell, a product of Ford's New Edge

Above: Midnight Black leather/vinyl seats with silver leather inserts were standard inside a 35th Anniversary Limited Edition GT in 1999. Silver leather door trim inserts and a specially masked instrument cluster also were part of the deal. *Mike Mueller*

Above right: Offered for 1999 GT models only, the 35th Anniversary Limited Edition Package added a raised hood scoop, large rear-quarter scoops, revised rocker moldings, a unique rear spoiler, and 17x8 five-spoke aluminum wheels. *Mike Mueller*

Right: Larger valves, reground camshafts (with higher lift and longer duration), and straightened intake runners helped the GT's 4.6-liter SOHC V-8 make 260 horsepower in 1999. *Mike Mueller*

design school. Following in the taut tire tracks of the angular, aggressive GT90 concept car shown off a few years before, the restyled 1999 Mustang featured chiseled lines and sharp creases in place of the soft contours and compound curves that, according to some critics, allowed early SN95 models to look a little "Japanese," an impression Ford people reportedly had tried to avoid at all costs.

The New Edge pony car sliced out a fresh image all its own while still preserving many nostalgic impressions prized by its creators. It didn't copy existing trends; it wasn't a jellybean, it wasn't a cube, yet it certainly was still a Mustang. "Our visual theme is based on the most stable geometric form—the pyramid," said chief designer Doug Gaffka. "We've also enhanced or revived some classic Mustang styling cues." Among these was the familiar chrome corral surrounding the traditional galloping horse now housed in a honeycomb grille. Sculptured side scoops behind the doors and tri-bar taillights also stirred memories, as did the muscular hood fitted with a recessed scoop.

Improvements beneath those sharpened edges included a revamped chassis to further improve ride, handling, and steering. Rear track was increased by 1.4 inches and rear suspension travel expanded about an inch. Upgraded floorpan sealing and rocker panel insulation reduced road noise, and convertibles were additionally reinforced to get a better handle on inherent body shakes. Optional traction control, a Mustang first, appeared in 1999 and required the installation of ABS, which was standard on the GT.

Standard GT power increased, too, to 260 horsepower after the 4.6-liter SOHC V-8 was fitted with bigger valves, reground cams with higher lift and longer duration, and straighter intake runners. The base V-6 also was pumped up to 190 horsepower.

"We've made improvements that are much more than skin-deep," said Janine Bay, then chief program engineer, in October 1998. "It all adds up to the fact that the 1999 Mustang really has a lot to offer. Its design is strong, contemporary, and true to Mustang's original concept. Performance improvements make the 1999 models very exciting and satisfying to drive. Make no mistake about it, everything we've done—and will continue to do—makes Mustang better and better, building on its heritage of free-spirited fun in a rear-wheel-drive, all-American sports car."

2000

- **Model Availability** · · · Two-door coupe, two-door convertible
- **Wheelbase** · · · 101.3 inches
- **Length** · · · 181.5 inches
- **Width** · · · 73.1 inches
- **Height** · · · 53.1 inches, coupe; 53.2 inches, convertible
- **Curb Weight** · · · 3,064 pounds, V-6 coupe; 3,203 pounds, V-6 convertible; 3,227 pounds, GT coupe; 3,375 pounds, GT convertible
- **Base Price** · · · $16,520, V-6 coupe; $21,370, V-6 convertible; $21,015, GT coupe; $25,270, GT convertible
- **Track** · · · 60.6 inches front, 59.2 inches rear
- **Wheels** · · · 15x6.5, standard (V-6); 16x7.5 forged aluminum, standard; 17x8 forged aluminum, optional
- **Tires** · · · P205/65TR-15, standard (V-6); P225/55HR16 BFGoodrich, standard (GT); P245/45ZR-17 Goodyear Eagle, optional (GT)
- **Suspension** · · · Modified MacPherson struts with gas-charged shocks, coil springs, and stabilizer bar in front; four-link solid axle with coil springs in back
- **Steering** · · · Power-assisted rack and pinion (14.7:1 ratio)
- **Brakes** · · · Four-wheel discs (ABS optional)
- **Engine** · · · 190-horsepower 3.8-liter (232-ci) V-6, 260-horsepower 4.6-liter (281-ci) SOHC V-8
- **Bore and Stroke** · · · 3.80x3.40 inches (V-6), 3.60x3.60 inches (V-8)
- **Compression** · · · 9.36:1 (V-6), 9.0:1 (V-8)
- **Fuel Delivery** · · · Sequential electronic fuel injection
- **Transmission** · · · Five-speed manual, standard; four-speed automatic, optional
- **Production** · · · 215,383

2000

The new, edgy Mustang rolled over into 2000 all but unchanged, save for the addition of two standard safety features: child seat tether anchors went behind the rear seating area, and an interior deck lid release (with glow-in-the-dark illumination) was installed inside the trunk. A restyled six-spoke wheel appeared for base models. ABS was again standard for the GT, optional for the V-6.

A Spring Feature Package was released midyear for the GT only. Included in this deal, priced at $995, were the scoops used in 1999 on the hood and quarter panels of the 35th Anniversary

The new, edgy Mustang rolled over into 2000 all but unchanged, save for the addition of two standard safety features.

A new safety feature became standard inside the 2000 Mustang as child-seat tether anchors were added behind the rear seats. An interior deck-lid release also was added inside the trunk. Base price for a 2000 GT coupe was $21,015.

Above: Production of V-6 convertibles in 2000 was 41,368. Base price was $21,370.

Right: An automatic overdrive transmission was an $815 option in 2000. The Mach 460 stereo also appearing here cost $395. *Mike Mueller*

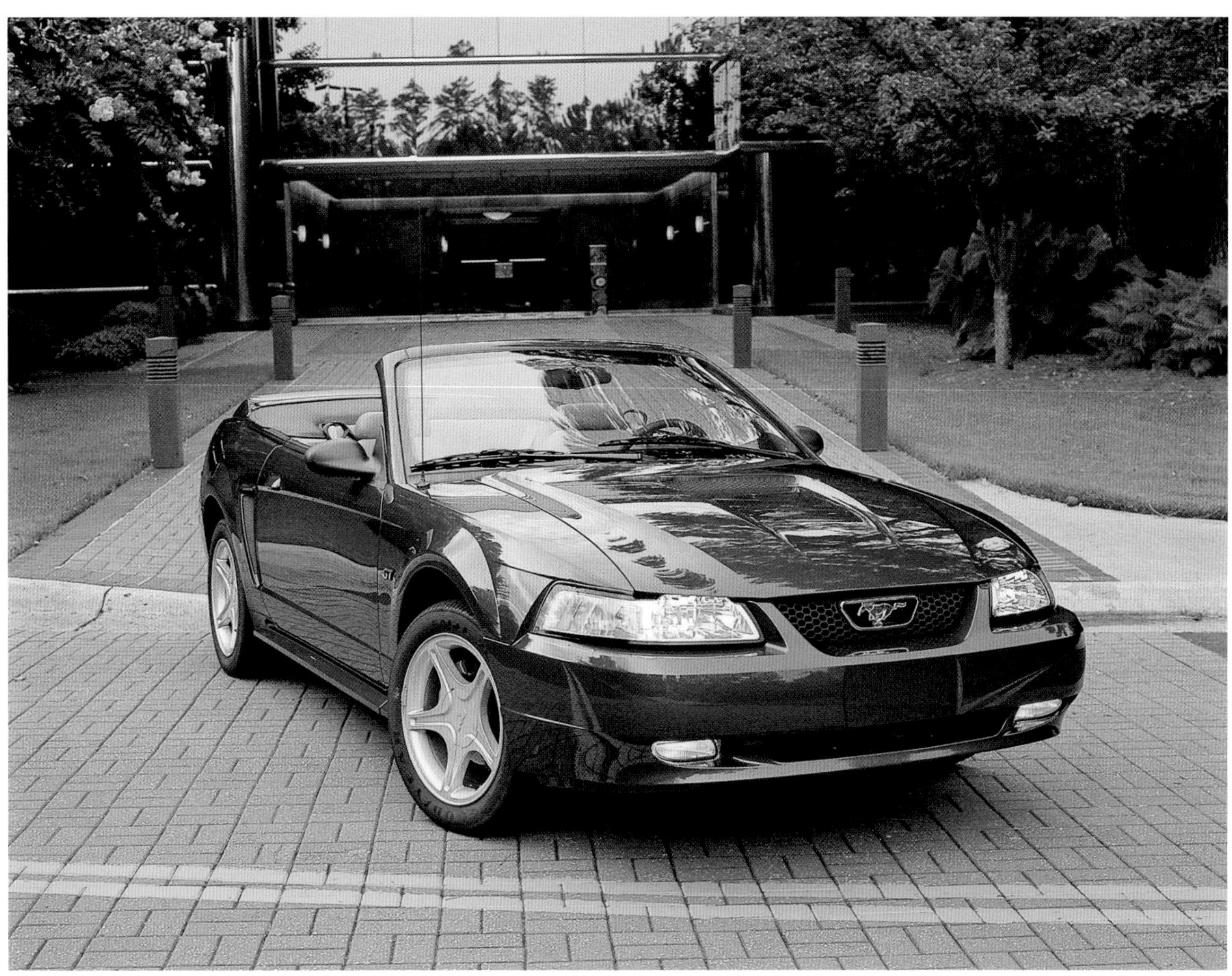

GT convertible production in 2000 was 20,224. Base price was $25,270. The 17-inch aluminum wheels appearing here were a $500 option. *Mike Mueller*

Below: A new lineup for 2001 separated both the V-6 and V-8 Mustangs into Standard, Deluxe, and Premium variations. Pricing began at $16,995 for a Standard V-6 coupe.

Mustang. The hood scoop was adorned with black decals sporting color-keyed GT lettering and additional black lettering spelled out "MUSTANG" across the rear fascia. Completing the package were brightly machined 17x8 five-spoke wheels in place of the standard GT's 16-inch rims.

2001

All GTs received standard 17-inch wheels and the 35th Anniversary scoops for 2001. And, as in 2000, the V-6's optional Sport Appearance Group included larger 16-inch wheels and tires. A redesigned center console (with revised cup holders, a tissue holder, and a power outlet) went inside, and an electric rear window defroster, formerly an option, became standard on all models.

The truly nostalgic Bullitt Mustang appeared for 2001, as did an entirely new submodel structure that separated both the V-6 and V-8 lineups into Standard, Deluxe, and Premium variations. Only the V-6 coupe came in bare-bones Standard trim. All V-6 convertibles and GTs (with or without tops) were equipped with either Deluxe or Premium equipment, with some of the items in these packages already included in the GT deal. Convertible applications of the Deluxe and Premium packages differed slightly too compared to their coupe counterparts.

Above: All GTs came standard with 17-inch wheels in 2001. This particular 17-inch nostalgic mag was the standard rim for the Premium GT. *Mike Mueller*

Right: The most expensive Mustang in 2001 was the Premium GT convertible, priced at $28,035.

First on the order sheet was the Standard coupe, which featured the 3.8-liter V-6, a five-speed stick, 15-inch painted wheels, four-wheel disc brakes, air conditioning, dual front air bags, AM/FM stereo with CD player, and a fold-down rear seat. Next up was the Deluxe package, which added cruise control, a six-way power driver seat, floor mats, and a rear spoiler to the Standard collection. At the top was the Premium deal, consisting of the following extras: traction control and ABS, AM/FM radio with six-disc CD player and Mach 460 sound system, a leather-wrapped steering wheel, and polished alloy wheels.

In the Premium V-6's case, those bright wheels measured 16 inches across—but, as mentioned, all GTs, Deluxe or Premium, automatically hit the ground rolling on 17-inch rims. Additionally, an automatic transmission was standard on all Premium convertibles, optional on their Deluxe running mates. And a Premium drop-top, like Premium GT coupes and convertibles, featured standard leather upholstery—leather-trimmed bucket seats were optional for the Premium V-6 coupe. Most of the items added as standard pieces at each rung of this pecking order were available at extra cost for the submodel or models below. Predictably, the Sport Appearance Group, which was included as part of the Premium package,

2001

Model Availability	Two-door coupe, two-door convertible
Wheelbase	101.3 inches
Length	181.5 inches
Width	73.1 inches
Height	53.1 inches, coupe; 53.2 inches, convertible
Curb Weight	Ranged from 3,064 pounds for base coupe to 3,379 pounds for GT convertible
Base Price	Ranged from $16,995 for base coupe to $28,035 for Premium GT convertible
Track	60.6 inches front, 60.2 inches rear
Wheels	15x6.5, standard (V-6); 16x7.5 forged aluminum, standard; 17x8 forged aluminum, optional
Tires	P205/65TR-15, standard (V-6); P225/55HR16 BFGoodrich, standard (GT); P245/45ZR-17 Goodyear Eagle, optional (GT)
Suspension	Modified MacPherson struts with gas-charged shocks, coil springs, and stabilizer bar in front; four-link solid axle with coil springs in bac
Steering	Power-assisted rack and pinion (14.7:1 ratio)
Brakes	Four-wheel discs (ABS optional)
Engine	190-horsepower 3.8-liter (232-ci) V-6, 260-horsepower 4.6-liter (281-ci) SOHC V-8
Bore and Stroke	3.80x3.40 inches (V-6), 3.60x3.60 inches (V-8)
Compression	9.36:1 (V-6), 9.0:1 (V-8)
Fuel Delivery	Sequential electronic fuel injection
Transmission	Five-speed manual, standard; four-speed automatic, optional
Production	163,818

The scoops included in the 35th Anniversary option in 1999 became standard for the GT in 2001. *Mike Mueller*

was not offered for the value-conscious Standard coupe. And traction control was standard for all GTs regardless of the trim package installed.

2001 Bullitt GT

Moviegoers and Mustang fans alike still can't get enough of this famed car chase, arguably one of the best in Hollywood history: the late Steve McQueen in his dark-green fastback pony car, hot on the heels of a sinister Dodge Charger, running up, over, and around the steep streets of San Francisco. McQueen's 1968 crime drama, *Bullitt*, is best remembered for this scene, and indeed many channel surfers nowadays ride in just in time for those 12-odd minutes of squealing tires and gnarly exhaust notes, then sail off for another golden oldie—*Vanishing Point* perhaps? Some car nuts have nothing but those 12 minutes on tape.

Why not? The sounds, the fury, the fiery explosion at the end—could it get any better? Ford people certainly thought not when they opted to revive such images some 30 years later. Nostalgia played a major role throughout the SN95 era, so no one was all that surprised when project manager Scott Hoag's team rolled out its Bullitt Mustang concept car for the Los Angeles auto show in January 2000. And wouldn't you know it? A regular-production follow-up then went on sale in April 2001.

Like the two 1968 fastbacks specially prepared for McQueen 35 years ago, the 2001 Bullitt Mustang was tweaked underneath, this time with stiffer springs and shocks, thicker anti-roll bars, and reinforced subframe connectors. Overall height was dropped by 0.75 inch. Bigger brakes were added, too, but with ABS and traction control included to

The truly nostalgic Bullitt Mustang appeared for 2001, as did an entirely new submodel structure that separated both the V-6 and V-8 lineups into Standard, Deluxe, and Premium variations.

Red brake calipers were part of the Bullitt image, as were the five-spoke aluminum wheels reminiscent of American Racing's popular Torq Thrust mags. *Mike Mueller*

2001 Bullitt

Model Availability	Two-door coupe only
Wheelbase	101.3 inches
Length	181.5 inches
Width	73.1 inches
Height	52.35 inches
Curb Weight	3,273 pounds
Price	$26,830
Track	60.6 inches front, 60.2 inches rear
Wheels	17-inch aluminum mags
Tires	P245/45ZR-17
Suspension	Independent MacPherson struts with coil springs, front; independent with control arms, toe-control links, and coil springs, rear
Steering	Power-assisted rack and pinion
Brakes	Four-wheel discs with power assist
Engine	265-horsepower 4.6-liter SOHC V-8
Bore and Stroke	3.60x3.60 inches
Compression	9.0:1
Fuel Delivery	Sequential electronic fuel injection
Transmission	Five-speed manual
Production	5,582 (3,041 in Dark Highland Green, 1,818 in black, 723 in True Blue)

help avoid ditches like the one McQueen piled up in near the end of his celluloid pursuit.

The Bullitt Mustang's 4.6-liter mod motor produced as many as 5 horses more than a typical GT V-8, thanks primarily to a specially tuned exhaust system that emitted a gutsy growl reminiscent of the rumblings that helped *Bullitt* draw an Academy Award nomination for sound. Also mimicking McQueen's ride were the wheels (available optionally on other GTs): five spokes done in identical style to American Racing's old Torq-Thrusts.

Among other special touches were red brake calipers, a racing-type brushed-aluminum gas filler door, and "BULLITT" block letters on the tail. Retro-style instrumentation and upholstery, extra brightwork for the shifter and floor pedals, and exclusive doorsills further enhanced the image inside.

All that remained was for a driver to prove that he or she could solve those switchbacks better than McQueen. Total Bullitt Mustang production for 2001 was 5,582 in three colors: the appropriate Dark Highland Green (3,041), black (1,818), and True Blue (723).

Old-style instrumentation further enhanced the Bullitt image. *Mike Mueller*

Bright "Bullitt" badging was added at the tail. Base price for the 2001 Bullitt Mustang GT was $26,230. *Mike Mueller*

Specially tuned exhausts helped the Bullitt Mustang's 4.6-liter V-8 produce 5 more ponies than its GT counterpart. A five-speed manual transmission was included in the deal. *Mike Mueller*

2002

Standard 16-inch alloy wheels were introduced for base Mustangs in 2002, and a hip MP3/CD player became available for all models. The Standard/Deluxe/Premium order structure rolled over from 2001, as did the same basic pony car. News of note involved the limited offering of a V-6 option group initially called the "Regional Appearance Package." Available only in Florida and only with certain paint choices, this deal included bright wheels, a GT hood scoop, a leather-wrapped steering wheel, special door graphics, and a rear fascia adorned with "Mustang" black lettering. Brochures called this group the "Pony Package." Only 1,577 V-6 Pony Mustangs were built for 2002.

2003

Major news for 2003 involved the appearance of both a special package to help mark Ford Motor Company's 100th anniversary and a new model, the reborn Mach 1. Minor refinements included various safety enhancements for all models. The SN95's A-pillar, headliner, sun visors, and D-ring seatbelt attachments were revised to inhibit impact-related head injuries. Both driver and passenger air bags were revised, as were seatbelt pretensioners, all in the best interests of improved crash

2002

Model Availability	Two-door coupe, two-door convertible
Wheelbase	101.3 inches
Length	181.5 inches
Width	73.1 inches
Height	53.1 inches, coupe; 53.2 inches, convertible
Curb Weight	3,066 pounds, coupe; 3,208 pounds, convertible
Base Price	Ranged from $17,475 for base coupe to $28,645 for Premium GT convertible
Track	60.6 inches front, 60.2 inches rear
Wheels	16-inch, standard (V-6); 17-inch, standard (GT)
Tires	P225/55R-16, standard (V-6); P245/45ZR-17, standard (GT)
Suspension	Modified MacPherson struts with gas-charged shocks, coil springs, and stabilizer bar in front; four-link solid axle with coil springs in back
Steering	Power-assisted rack and pinion (14.7:1 ratio)
Brakes	Four-wheel discs (ABS, optional)
Engine	190-horsepower 3.8-liter (232-ci) V-6, 260-horsepower 4.6-liter (281-ci) SOHC V-8
Bore and Stroke	3.80x3.40 inches (V-6), 3.60x3.60 inches (V-8)
Compression	9.36:1 (V-6), 9.0:1 (V-8)
Fuel Delivery	Sequential electronic fuel injection
Transmission	Five-speed manual, standard; four-speed automatic, optional
Production	145,518

Sixteen-inch alloy wheels became standard for base V-6 Mustangs in 2002. Base pricing began at $17,475 that year.

The same basic Mustang and pecking order (GT/V-6 in Standard, Deluxe, or Premium trim) carried over into 2002.

2003

Model Availability	Two-door coupe, two-door convertible
Wheelbase	101.3 inches
Length	181.5 inches
Width	73.1 inches
Height	53.1 inches, coupe; 53.2 inches, convertible
Curb Weight	3,066 pounds, coupe; 3,208 pounds, convertible
Base Price	Ranged from $17,720 for base coupe to $28,706 for Premium GT convertible
Track	60.6 inches front, 60.2 inches rear
Wheels	16-inch, standard (V-6); 17-inch, standard (GT)
Tires	P225/55R-16, standard (V-6); P245/45ZR-17, standard (GT)
Suspension	Modified MacPherson struts with gas-charged shocks, coil springs, and stabilizer bar in front; four-link solid axle with coil springs in back
Steering	Power-assisted rack and pinion (14.7:1 ratio)
Brakes	Four-wheel discs (ABS optional)
Engine	190-horsepower 3.8-liter (232-ci) V-6, 260-horsepower 4.6-liter (281-ci) SOHC V-8
Bore and Stroke	3.80x3.40 inches (V-6), 3.60x3.60 inches (V-8)
Compression	9.36:1 (V-6), 9.0:1 (V-8)
Fuel Delivery	Sequential electronic fuel injection
Transmission	Five-speed manual, standard; four-speed automatic, optional
Production	150,895

Above: Sixteen-inch wheels became standard for V-6 Mustangs in 2002. This painted 16-inch aluminum rim was used on Standard and Deluxe coupes in 2003. *Mike Mueller*

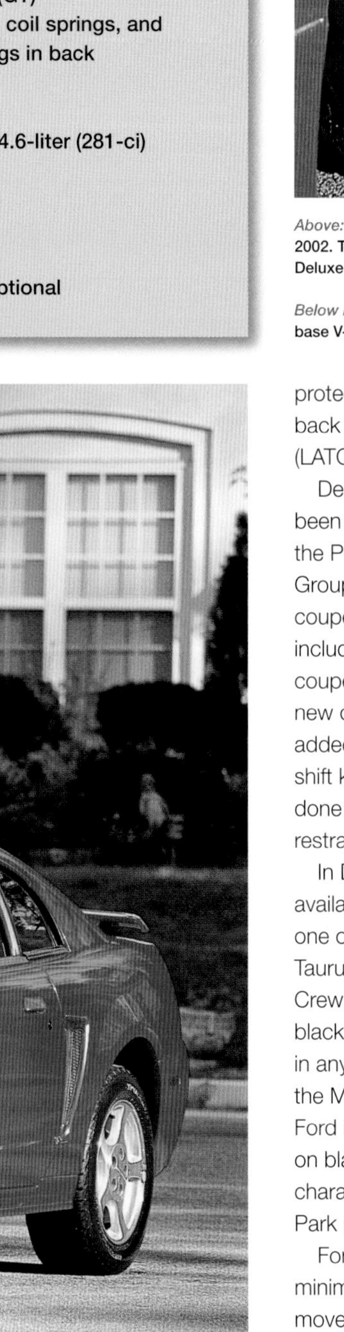

Below left: Pricing for the 2003 Mustang began at $17,720 for the base V-6 coupe. *Mike Mueller*

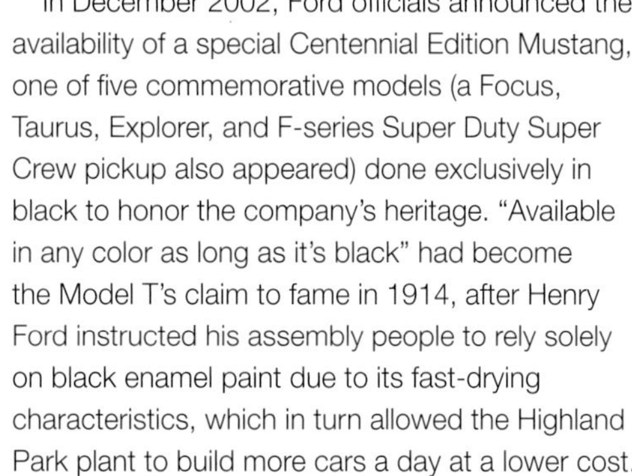

protection. And fastening hardware was added in back for the lower anchors and tethers for children (LATCH) child safety seat system.

Deluxe and Premium base models could've been treated to a little GT feel with the addition of the Pony Package, while the Sport Appearance Group remained available for the Deluxe V-6 coupe. All (V-6, GT, Mach 1, and SVT Cobra included) but the budget-conscious Standard coupe could've been dressed up further with a new option, the Interior Upgrade Package, which added stainless-steel pedal trim, a leather-wrapped shift knob, door lock posts and a shift boot ring done in an aluminum finish, and a four-way head-restraint system.

In December 2002, Ford officials announced the availability of a special Centennial Edition Mustang, one of five commemorative models (a Focus, Taurus, Explorer, and F-series Super Duty Super Crew pickup also appeared) done exclusively in black to honor the company's heritage. "Available in any color as long as it's black" had become the Model T's claim to fame in 1914, after Henry Ford instructed his assembly people to rely solely on black enamel paint due to its fast-drying characteristics, which in turn allowed the Highland Park plant to build more cars a day at a lower cost.

Ford also introduced the five-dollar-a-day minimum wage at Highland Park that year, and that move too was commemorated, beginning April 1, 2003, with a five-dollar-a-day "Centennial Lease" offer. Reportedly, Ford sold 93 Mustangs the day before this 48-month deal was announced. Another 850 found drivers during the first week of the Centennial Lease's availability.

"Henry Ford helped create the American middle class when he introduced the five-dollar-[a] day age, and our effort to share this heritage with consumers has been a huge success," said Ford President Steve Lyons. "We've tapped an incredible reserve of goodwill for Ford and a deep well of Mustang excitement."

Like the four other Centennial models, the special-edition 2003 Mustang featured 100th Anniversary badges on the fenders and deck lid and Premium Verona-grain Imola leather seats in two-tone parchment inside. Also included in the deal were a Centennial Gift Pack (including a watch, key chain, and black leather owner portfolio) and a copy of the book, The Ford Century. As mentioned, black clear-coat paint was mandatory, and only GT premium coupes and convertibles could be ordered with this package. Scheduled production for the Centennial Edition Mustang was 3,000 units. Reportedly, the final tally read 1,323 convertibles, 717 coupes.

2003 Mach 1

In the 260-horsepower Mustang GT, Ford already had arguably the biggest bang for the buck on the market in 2003. But if price was less of a concern, there also was the SVT Cobra, back in America after a one-year hiatus, this time with 390 seriously

2003 Mach 1

Model Availability	Two-door coupe only
Wheelbase	101.3 inches
Length	181.5 inches
Width	71.8 inches
Height	52.9 inches
Curb Weight	3,465 pounds
Base Price	$28,805
Track	60.6 inches front, 60.2 inches rear
Wheels	17x8 Heritage five-spoke aluminum
Tires	Goodyear P245/45ZR-17
Suspension	Modified MacPherson struts with gas-charged shocks, coil springs, and stabilizer bar in front; four-link solid axle with coil springs in back
Steering	Power-assisted rack and pinion (15.3:1 ratio)
Brakes	Power-assisted four-wheel discs (13-inch Brembo units, front; 11.6-inch rotors, rear) w/ABS
Engine	305-horsepower 4.6-liter DOHC V-8 with four valves per cylinder
Bore and Stroke	3.60x3.60 inches
Compression	10.1:1
Fuel Delivery	Sequential electronic fuel injection with 57-millimeter throttle body and functional Shaker hood scoop
Transmission	Tremec 3650 five-speed manual (automatic, optional)
Axle Ratio	3.55:1 Traction-Lok
Production	9,652

Left and opposite: Mach 1 production for 2003 was 9,652. Another 7,182 followed for 2004. Base price for this 2003 model was $28,705. A lowered suspension was standard for the 2003 Mach 1, as were 17x8 Heritage wheels wearing ZR45 Goodyear Eagle tires. *Mike Mueller*

The 2003 Mach 1 was offered in six colors: red, blue, black, grey, yellow, and white.

A *Popular Hot Rodding* road test of a Cobra Jet Mach 1 in 1969 resulted in a 13.69-second quarter-mile pass topping out at 103.4 miles per hour. A *Mustang Monthly* test of a 2003 Mach 1 produced a 12.97/105.1 time slip.

supercharged horses. In between was an obvious gap, in both performance and pricing. No problem. In November 2002, the Dearborn assembly line began rolling out a third hot-to-trot pony car, the 2003 Mach 1 coupe, a Mustang that looked a lot like a time machine.

Base price for a Deluxe GT coupe in 2003 was $23,705, while that year's Cobra coupe started at $33,460. Armed with 305 horsepower, the born-again Mach 1 was priced at $28,705. For that amount, a Mustang buyer received more than enough retro touches to help make it feel like it was 1969 all over again. First and foremost was the familiar Shaker scoop poking up through the '03 Mach 1's striped hood.

"Let your mind go and it's the Sixties all over the place," wrote *Hot Rod*'s Ro McGonegal about this black breather, which, like its fully functional ancestor, could rock like Mick Jagger, once torque started twisting things underneath. Supplying that torque was a 2003 redo of the 2001 Cobra's 32-valve, DOHC V-8, a certified screamer that made the later, greater Mach 1 even speedier than its big-block forerunner. It also made the new Mach 1 the first non-SVT Mustang to offer DOHC V-8 power.

A *Popular Hot Rodding* road test of a Cobra Jet Mach 1 in 1969 resulted in a 13.69-second quarter-mile pass topping out at 103.4 miles per hour. A *Mustang Monthly* test of a 2003 Mach 1 produced a 12.97/105.1 time slip.

The 2003 Mach 1 could outhandle its predecessor, too, thanks to a lowered suspension that featured stiffer springs, Tokico struts, and 17x8 wheels shod in Goodyear Eagle ZR45 rubber. Those aluminum five-spoke Heritage wheels were unique to the 2003 Mach 1 and fit the nostalgic image to a T, as did those blacked-out front and rear spoilers and the old-fashioned rocker panel stripes. Fog lamps too were standard up front, per GT specs.

Additional standard equipment included a Tremec five-speed manual transmission, power rack-and-pinion steering, power four-wheel Brembo disc brakes, stainless-steel dual exhausts, and a Traction-Lok 8.8-inch differential with 3.55:1 gears. A beefed-up 4R70W automatic transmission was optional.

Ordering the automatic required a few changes within the DOHC V-8. Crankshafts in auto-box engines were cast pieces, while their counterparts in manually shifted Mach 1s were forged steel. Output ratings remained the same, but redlines differed—5,800 revs in automatic cars versus a grand more in the manuals. Additional 4.6-liter DOHC updates in 2003 (in both cases) included revised cylinder heads with rerouted water passages, new cams (the intake valves were controlled by a bumpstick borrowed from Ford's 5.4-liter truck engine), and revamped exhaust manifolds that were port-matched to the heads.

Standard interior treatments also brought back memories as the Mach 1 was fitted with a bright aluminum shifter ball and a nostalgic instrument cluster, both features that had appeared previously on Bullitt Mustangs. Summed up, the Mach 1 was, in Ford's words, a "modern interpretation of an American icon."

Total 2003 Mach 1 production was 9,652: 7,709 with five-speed manuals, 1,943 with automatics. Breakdown by color was 2,513 in Torch Red, 2,250 in Azure Blue, 1,611 in black, 1,595 in Dark Shadow Grey, 869 in Zinc Yellow, and 814 in Oxford White.

2004

Ford's venerable Dearborn assembly plant opened in 1918 and was at first home to Eagle boats, sub-chasers meant for World War I duty. Fordson tractors started rolling out its doors after the war, as did the new Model A later in 1928. Various trucks, Mercurys, and other war machines (for a second World War) followed over the decades: then came the exciting new Mustang in 1964. Job One, the very first pony car built, was driven off the Dearborn line on March 9 that year by Ford employee Oscar Horespian.

Top: **The Mach 1 interior brought back imagery seen inside the Bullitt Mustang in 2001. Both manual and automatic transmissions were installed.** ***Mike Mueller***

Above: **This 16-inch bright machined-aluminum wheel was standard on V-6 Deluxe and Premium models in 2004.** ***Mike Mueller***

The 2003 Mach 1 was powered by a Cobra-sourced 32-valve DOHC 4.6-liter V-8 topped by yet another retro touch—a Ram-Air Shaker hood scoop. Output for this road rocket was 305 horsepower. *Mike Mueller*

Horespian, who worked at Ford from 1942 to 1980, returned to Dearborn 40 years later to ride another pony off into the sunset. On May 10, 2004, he took a seat next to another Ford veteran, 32-year man Fred Galicki, as Galicki drove a red GT convertible beneath a banner announcing the "Final Stampede." This was the last Mustang built at the aging Dearborn facility, which was finally being torn down after serving as the home to some 6.7 million pony cars. Another 2 million or so were built in San Jose, California, and Metuchen, New Jersey, but Dearborn will always be remembered as the place where the Mustang was born.

All Mustangs built that final year in Dearborn wore special anniversary fender badges marking 40 legendary years. Save for a slight power boost (to 193 horsepower) for the base V-6, everything else rolled over essentially unchanged from 2003, an understandable move considering Ford's next all-new pony car was waiting in the wings for 2005. Waiting to build the fifth-generation pony were workers at the AAI plant in Flat Rock, Michigan, home to Mazda products since 1988. Reportedly, $644 million was spent on the AAI facility to allow the 2005 Mustang to be produced alongside the Mazda 6.

2004

Model Availability	Two-door coupe, two-door convertible
Wheelbase	101.3 inches
Length	183.2 inches
Width	73.1 inches
Height	53.1 inches, coupe; 53.2 inches, convertible
Track (front/rear, in inches)	60.02/60.06 (V-6), 59.8/59.3 (GT)
Wheels	16-inch painted rims, standard (base coupe); 17-inch painted rims, standard (GT); 17-inch five-spokes, optional
Tires	P225/55R-16, standard (V-6); P245/45ZR-17, standard (GT)
Suspension	Modified MacPherson struts with gas-charged shocks, coil springs, and stabilizer bar in front; four-link solid axle with coil springs in back
Steering	Power-assisted rack and pinion
Brakes	Power-assisted four-wheel discs
Engine	193-horsepower 3.8-liter (232-ci) V-6, 260-horsepower 4.6-liter (281-ci) SOHC V-8
Bore and Stroke	3.80x3.40 inches (V-6),
	3.60x3.60 inches (V-8)
Compression	9.36:1 (V-6), 9.0:1 (V-8)
Fuel Delivery	Sequential electronic fuel injection
Transmission	Five-speed manual, standard; four-speed automatic, optional
Production	159,587

A 2004 V-6 Deluxe coupe came standard with a five-speed manual transmission, six-way power driver's seat, and cruise control. *Mike Mueller*

Available for 2004 Premium coupes and convertibles only, the 40th Anniversary Package added specially painted wheels and the Interior Upgrade Package. The exterior finish was Crimson Red unless Oxford White or black was specified.

For the last run of fourth-generation Mustangs, both the SVT Cobra and Mach 1 returned, and both retired as 2004 production closed. New paint represented the only news of note for the 2004 Mach 1, as Competition Orange was introduced and 2003's Zinc Yellow was traded for Screaming Yellow. Total production this time was 7,137, with color breakdowns of 763 for Screaming Yellow, 1,019 for Competition Orange, 1,038 for Dark Shadow Grey, 1,059 for black, 697 for Oxford White, 1,309 for Azure Blue, and 1,252 for Torch Red.

The Pony Appearance Package and Sport Appearance Group remained available in V-6 ranks (optional for the Deluxe coupe, standard with the Premium coupe and convertible), and again couldn't be ordered in tandem. New for both V-6 and GT was a special 40th Anniversary Package that also couldn't be combined with either of the base line's appearance options.

Included in the 40th Anniversary deal were 17-inch five-spoke wheels painted exclusively in Arizona Beige Metallic (with bright rims); additional Arizona Beige stripes on the hood, doors, and deck lid; color-keyed foldaway mirrors; a Medium Parchment interior with matching floor mats wearing anniversary logos; and an anniversary plaque next to the shifter. The Interior Upgrade Package also came in the Anniversary Package, which was offered for Premium coupes and convertibles only. Convertibles were adorned further with a Deluxe Parchment cloth top. Exclusive Crimson Red paint was mixed up for the 40th Anniversary Mustang, but two additional choices, Oxford White and black, were available, too.

Ford built its 300 millionth car—a 40th Anniversary GT convertible—in 2004.

09

Hissing Horses

09

SVT 1993–2007

- The first Cobra is offered as a coupe only in 1993.
- The 1993 Cobra is the first Mustang to feature 17-inch rims and directional tires.
- All Cobras feature manual transmissions.
- The first SVT Cobra convertible is offered in 1994, and it becomes the third Mustang to pace the Indianapolis 500.
- Three race-ready Cobra R models are offered, in 1993, 1995, and 2000.
- SVT temporarily shelves its Lightning pickup after 1995.
- Chameleon-like Mystic paint is introduced as a Cobra option in 1996.
- The SVT Contour debuts in 1997 as a 1998 model.
- The Lightning truck reappears, this time with a supercharged V-8, for 1999.
- The SVT Focus debuts for 2002.
- Ford announces a new deal with Carroll Shelby to develop performance products, August 15, 2003.
- Chief engineer John Coletti resigns at the end of 2004, taking with him the driving force behind the Cobra.

The battle between Mustang and Camaro for street credibility was a close call during the 1980s. Both the GT and Z28 camps laid claim to the title of biggest bang for the buck in those years, and neither was necessarily wrong. Maximum power outputs were comparable, as were published acceleration figures. Then Chevrolet just had to go and stuff the 5.7-liter LT1 V-8, introduced for the 1992 Corvette, into the 1993 Camaro. At 275 horsepower, the Z28's reenergized small-block easily overshadowed its 5.0-liter HO rival from Ford, down from its peak of 225 horses to 205 for 1993. What was a performance-conscious pony rider to do?

FORTUNATELY, FORD'S RECENTLY FORMED SPECIAL VEHICLE TEAM (SVT) provided an immediate answer. New for 1993 were two SVT machines, the F-150 Lightning truck and Mustang-based Cobra. The Lightning, built from 1993 to 1995 and again from 1999 to 2004, at one time held the official title of world's fastest production pickup, before being bested early in 2004 by Dodge's insane 500-horsepower, Viper-powered SRT-10. The Cobra quickly evolved into a truly venomous species—not just one of the best performance buys in America but the entire planet. By 1996, SVT Cobras were making 305 horsepower, followed by a zenith of 390 horses in 2003. Cobra production ceased after 2004, but the SVT tag carried on, reappearing on the 2007 Shelby GT500. Absolutely the meanest Mustang ever, the reborn Shelby makes 500 horsepower, putting it in a domestic league with the Viper and Chevy's Z06 Corvette—at considerably less cost.

Founded in 1991, SVT was created to pick up where Ford's Special Vehicles Operations left off in the 1980s. No, SVO didn't wither away after its turbocharged Mustang retired in 1986; it continued overseeing Dearborn's competition ventures and marketing the company's high-performance goodies into the 1990s. But in 1999 the SVO shingle too was retired as the group was renamed Ford Racing Technology. Mustang modifiers and racers now have the Ford Racing Performance Parts people supplying them with hot-from-the-factory hardware.

Above: Coupe production by color in 1999 was 1,619 in black; 1,219 in red; 794 in white; and 408 in green. "Mustang"-embossed lettering on the rear bodywork returned for the 1999 Cobra coupe and convertible.

Opposite: Janine Bay, the so-called "mother of the Cobra Mustang," was the first head of Ford's U.S.-based Special Vehicle Engineering group. John Plant oversaw the Special Vehicle Team when it opened for business in 1991. Here the duo poses proudly with the first 1993 Cobra off the line.

Previous pages:
Left: Total production for 1994 Cobra coupes was 5,009. Breakdown by exterior color was 1,795 (black clear coat); 1,908 (Rio Red clear coat); and 1,306 (Crystal White clear coat). Interior choices were cloth or leather, done in black or saddle. *Mike Mueller*

Right: A 1995 R model weighed in at 3,226 pounds, compared to 3,365 for that year's standard Cobra coupe. A competition-ready fuel cell was standard. *Mike Mueller*

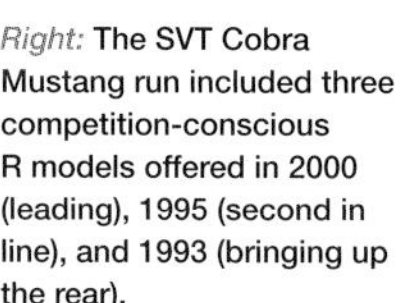

Right: The SVT Cobra Mustang run included three competition-conscious R models offered in 2000 (leading), 1995 (second in line), and 1993 (bringing up the rear).

Below: Total Cobra Mustang production for 1993 was 4,993. Breakdown by color was 1,854 in black clear coat; 1,784 in Vibrant Red clear coat; and 1,355 in Teal Metallic clear coat. Interior choices included black cloth, gray cloth, or gray leather.

That the SVO Mustang came and went so quickly, and rather quietly, wasn't necessarily the car's fault. Even Ford people were willing to admit later that making muscle, not marketing it, was Special Vehicles Operations' strongpoint during the SVO Mustang's brief run from 1984 to 1986. Offering world-class performance based on a meat-and-potatoes Mustang platform wasn't such a bad idea; the plan just needed a bit more support on the business end. Enter SVT.

"SVT's mission is to apply the best available resources, both from inside and outside Ford, to explore new ways of creating and marketing high-performance vehicles," went the group's creed. "This cross-functional team is charged with delivering limited-edition, high-performance, niche-segment cars and trucks designed to delight serious drivers over a variety of road conditions and surfaces."

Creating such vehicles wasn't all that tough; SVO had demonstrated that. What set SVT apart from its forerunner was a sharpened promotional focus. SVT didn't actually build any niche-segment cars and trucks; that was left up to another entity also started up in 1991: Special Vehicle Engineering (SVE). From the get-go, it was SVT's responsibility to familiarize buyers with these machines, to make sure the products kept improving, to keep a proud legacy running on for more than just a couple of years. SVT's second task was to ensure that these low-volume products didn't flounder in the marketplace (like the SVO Mustang): a tightly organized network of specially trained and certified SVT dealers was put in place to keep the customer both satisfied and interested, year after exciting year.

Responsible for getting SVT off the ground were Robert L. Rewey and Neil W. Ressler. Rewey was Ford's executive vice president for sales and marketing, Ressler was executive director of vehicle engineering, and both were big fans of high performance. Ressler started the ball rolling in the early 1990s, asking engineer Janine Bay to build a hopped-up Mustang using existing Ford mechanicals. Relying on SVO parts, Bay created a 5.0 HO engine capable of about 40 horsepower more than the standard issue. She then took her one-off concept car to Ford's marketing people, who in turn looked to Rewey for approval. Rewey complied, as did Ford chairman Harold "Red" Polling.

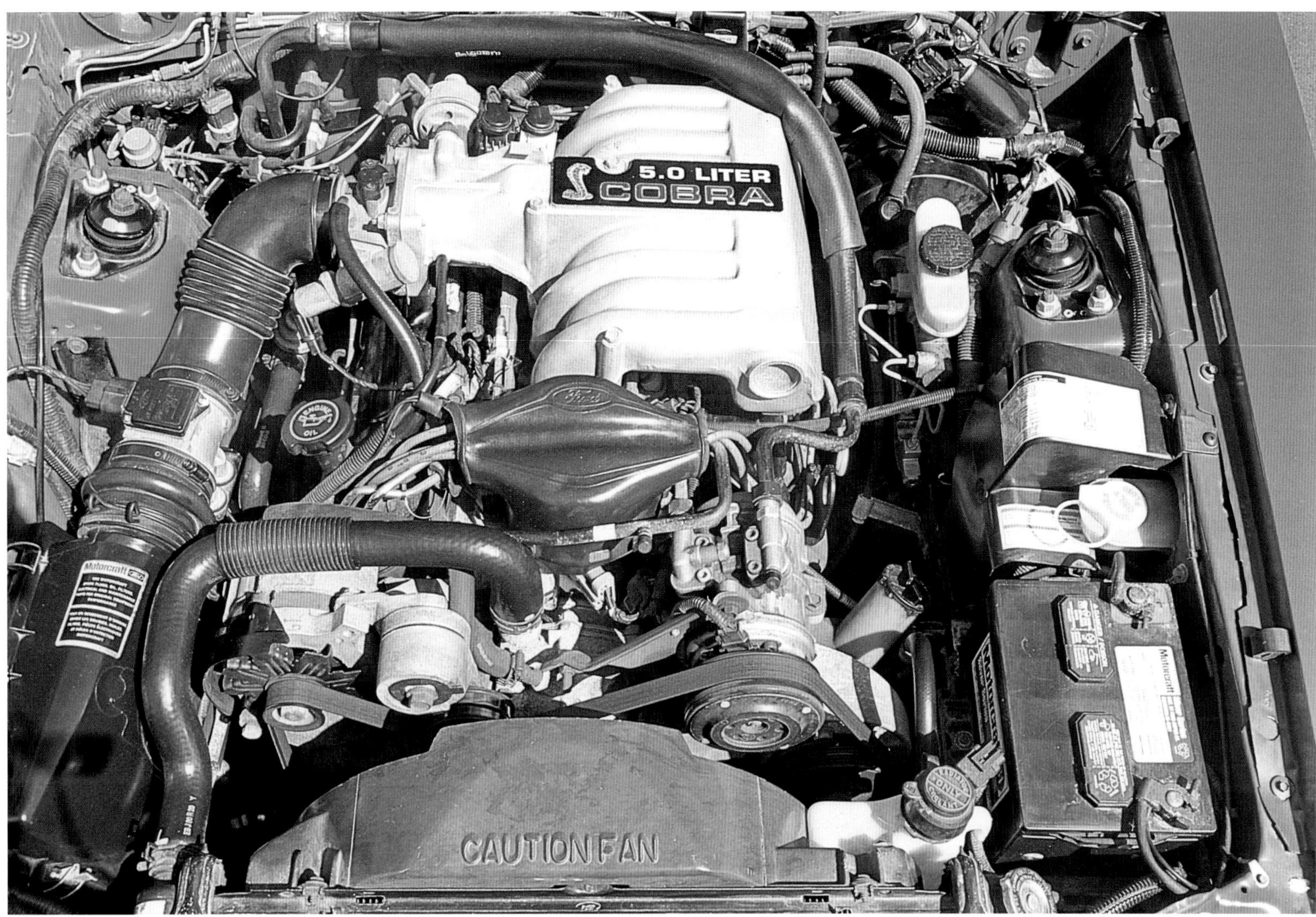

Various GT-40 components from the Ford Motorsport parts bin helped the 1993 Cobra's 5.0-liter V-8 produce 235 horsepower, an advertised figure some witnesses felt was a conservative rating.

Ressler then pulled together a development team modeled after Ford's European Special Vehicle Engineering group, which was already building limited-production specialty cars across the Atlantic. The U.S.-based SVE was first managed in 1991 by Bay, then Rod Mansfield, who had run SVE in Europe. John Coletti took over at SVE in 1994 and remained the driving force behind the Cobra until his retirement in 2004.

When SVT opened for business in 1991, it was led by John Plant, whose former tour of duty at BMW (before joining Ford in the late 1970s) helped make him the right man for the job. After all, it was SVT's goal to produce a Mustang that offered a better-balanced, Euro-style brand of performance—a car that handled as well as hauled ass. As Plant told *Automobile* magazine in 1994: "SVT is not in the business to build hot rods. We build cars that feel exciting on real-world roads."

SVT's first car, the Cobra, made its debut at the Chicago Auto Show in February 1992, as did its first truck, the Lightning. Unlike the SVE-built Cobra, the Lightning was the work of Ford Truck Operations, which had been working independently on its own performance product while the SVT/SVE organization was getting under way. Once Ressler got wind of this project, he decided it just had to join the Cobra in the SVT lineup. The tandem then went on sale early in 1993.

1993 Cobra

SVT's first Mustang appeared just in time to help send the aging Fox-chassis pony car out with a bang. Offered in coupe form only, the 1993 Cobra was dressed up tastefully on the outside with a distinctive rear spoiler, unique rear bumper cover and rocker moldings, and, of course, those soon-to-be-traditional coiled-snake fender badges. Up front was the 1993 GT's air dam (with foglamps), complemented by a small grille opening (this area was closed on a '93 GT) containing an existing tradition—a running-horse logo. Not since 1978 had this familiar pony been seen galloping across a Mustang's nose.

Inside was a GT interior augmented with floor mats featuring "Cobra" embroidery. Articulating GT sport seats, done in black or gray cloth, were standard, with gray leather appointments available at extra cost. A premium AM/FM/cassette stereo with six speakers was standard too. A CD player was optional. Three clear-coat exterior finishes were offered: black, Vibrant Red, and Teal Metallic.

Standard were four-wheel disc brakes, the first to appear in Mustang ranks since the SVO model disappeared in 1986. Ventilated rotors measured 10.84 inches across in front, 10.07 in back. Wheels were attractive 17x7.5 units, the Mustang's first 17-inchers. Tires were P245/45ZR17 Goodyear Eagle Gatorbacks.

Suspension tweaks ran opposite of the norm as they softened the ride instead of stiffening it. While variable spring rates for the front struts carried over from the GT, relaxed linear rear springs were used. Shock valving too was revised for decreased stiffness, and the front stabilizer bar shrank from 1.30 inches (for the GT unit) to 1.125 inches. The GT's rear stabilizer bar carried over.

Working in concert, these components created what SVT people liked to call "controlled compliance." The idea was to let the wheels travel up and down more easily for a better ride (compared to the rather harsh GT) while still keeping a steady grip on the road for excellent handling. Those big, hairy Gatorbacks helped the '93 Cobra stick to the pavement despite increased roll characteristics.

1993

Model Availability	Three-door hatchback
Wheelbase	100.5 inches
Length	179.6 inches
Width	69.1 inches
Height	52.1 inches
Curb Weight	3,255 pounds
Base Price	$18,805
Track	57.9 inches front, 57 inches rear
Wheels	17x7.5 cast aluminum
Tires	Goodyear P245/45ZR-17
Suspension	Modified MacPherson hydraulic struts with coil springs and stabilizer bar in front; four-link solid axle with coil springs and stabilizer bar in rear
Steering	Power-assisted rack and pinion
Brakes	Four-wheel vented discs (10.81-inch front rotors, 10.07-inch rears)
Engine	235-horsepower 5.0-liter V-8
Bore and Stroke	4.00x3.00 inches
Compression	9.0:1
Fuel Delivery	Sequential electronic fuel injection, tuned-length intake manifold
Transmission	Borg-Warner T-5 five-speed manual
Axle Ratio	3.08:1 Traction-Lok
Production	4,993

Power came from a 5.0-liter HO V-8 fitted with various race-ready GT-40 components from the Ford Motorsports' catalog. Atop the block were GT-40 heads featuring larger valves and ports compared to standard HO units. These heads also used stiffer valve springs and friction-reducing roller-tipped rocker arms made of lightweight aluminum. A two-piece GT-40 intake was used but incorporated a cast-aluminum lower runner section in place of the more complex tubular bottom offered through Ford Motorsports. Though the tubular runners breathed easier, the cast piece was cheaper. Backing things up was one transmission only, a Borg-Warner T-5 five-speed manual.

According to SVT paperwork, the '93 Cobra V-8 produced 235 horsepower, a mere 30 more than the '93 GT's 5.0-liter. Many witnesses claimed fudging, and some sources put actual output at more like 270 horses. Road tests seemed to support this claim, with *Muscle Mustangs & Fast Fords* magazine publishing a sizzling 13.75-second (at 98.27 miles per hour) time slip for the quarter-mile.

According to SVT paperwork, the '93 Cobra V-8 produced 235 horsepower, a mere 30 more than the '93 GT's 5.0-liter.

1993 Cobra R

When Dearborn officials wanted to see their newborn Mustang win at the track in 1965, they turned to Carroll Shelby, who proceeded to transform Ford's polite pony car into the race-ready GT 350R. Nearly 30 years later, another special R-model Mustang appeared, this one by way of SVT.

The Cobra R came about after SVO people asked SVE supervisor Steve Anderson in the fall of 1992 about building a lightweight SVT Mustang for competition purposes. Following some quick testing, the R Competition Package was put together and approved by Neil Ressler. Dealer announcements were made on April 7, 1993, and SVT began taking orders first thing on April 15. All were spoken for by midday. Initial plans called for a 100-car production run; the final tally was 107. All featured Vibrant Red paint and Opal Gray interiors.

While cost considerations prevented Anderson's group from making any improvements to the engine internally, the R model's 235-horse 5.0-liter V-8 was enhanced with extra cooling capabilities. A larger radiator (used previously on the 1984 Lincoln's turbo diesel six-cylinder) was bolted in along with a

Right: Only 107 R-model Cobras were built in 1993, all done in Vibrant Red clear-coat paint. Interiors too were identically appointed in LX Mustang gray cloth.

Opposite: Joining the 235-horse 5.0-liter V-8 beneath a 1993 R-model Cobra's hood were a heavy-duty two-row aluminum radiator and special cooling hardware for both engine oil and power steering fluid.

Like the conventional 1993 Cobra, the Cobra R was offered only in hatchback form. And like Carroll Shelby's first GT 350 in 1965, the first SVT R model was delivered without a back seat.

de-gas surge tank. Engine oil and power steering fluid also got special cooling systems.

Additional race-ready upgrades included a foundation beefed up with Fox-chassis convertible bracing underneath, a shock tower brace beneath the hood, Koni struts and shocks, and a 31-millimeter front stabilizer bar. The suspension was lowered an inch, and variable spring rates were increased to 750–850 lb-in in front, 240–360 in back. Brakes were huge 13-inch Kelsey-Hayes

1993 Cobra R

Model Availability	Three-door hatchback
Wheelbase	100.5 inches
Length	179.6 inches
Width	69.1 inches
Height	51.1 inches
Weight	3,125 pounds
Price	$25,217
Track	57.9 inches front, 57 inches rear
Wheels	17x8 aluminum
Tires	Goodyear P245/45ZR-17
Suspension	MacPherson-type struts (from Koni) with coil springs and stabilizer bar in front; four-link solid axle with coil springs and stabilizer bar in back (spring rates stiffened at both ends)
Steering	Rack and pinion with power assist (and heavy-duty cooler)
Brakes	Four-wheel discs (13-inch in front, 10.5-inch in back)
Engine	235-horsepower 5.0-liter V-8
Bore and Stroke	4.00x3.00 inches
Compression	9.0:1
Fuel Delivery	Sequential electronic fuel injection, tuned-length intake manifold
Transmission	Borg-Warner T-5 five-speed manual
Axle Ratio	3.08:1 Traction-Lok
Production	107

discs with PBR twin-piston calipers in front, 10.5-inch Lincoln Mk VII discs in back. The standard Cobra's four-lug wheels were traded for the five-lug units then being readied as an option for the upcoming 1994 Mustang GT. These 17x8 rims were painted black, fitted with a chrome center cap, and shod in P245/45ZR17 Goodyear Gatorback tires.

Various nonessential items were deleted to save weight: foglamps, radio, air conditioner, power windows and locks, the back seat, all sound deadener, most body sealer, etc. Total weight savings equaled about 130 pounds. The R model's bottom line, on the other hand, went up by roughly $7,200 compared to the 1993 Cobra coupe's base sticker. That hike, however, clearly was no hindrance.

1994 Cobra

The Cobra coupe rolled over into the SN95 era and was joined by a topless running mate. Like the 1993 coupe, the 1994 convertible was available only in red. Three clear-coat colors again were available for the 1994 Cobra coupe: Rio Red, Crystal White, and black. Production breakdowns for the three shades were 1,908 for red, 1,795 for black, and 1,306 for white.

Controlled compliance was again the order of the day underneath, with the 1994 GT's stiff variable-rate springs (400–505-lb-in fronts, 165–265 rears) traded for softer, linear coils (400 lb-in at the nose, 160 out back). A thicker tubular rear stabilizer bar (27 millimeters instead of 25) was added, as were P255/45ZR17 Goodyear Eagle tires on big, bright five-lug wheels measuring 8 inches wide.

Bigger brakes also were part of the package, with 13-inch vented discs and twin-piston PBR calipers (instead of the single-piston '94 GT units) leading the way up front. Rear rotors were 11.65 inches across with single-piston calipers. Optional for the 1994 GT, ABS was standard for its Cobra counterpart.

Standard 1994 Cobra venom came from the ever-present 5.0-liter V-8 fitted with a more aggressive cam, GT-40 cast-iron heads with bigger valves, specially tuned intake with a larger throttle body, and less restrictive exhausts. This time the output rating was 240 horsepower, 25 more than the nearly all-new GT's small-block. That enlarged intake equipment was so tall it left no room for the shock-tower-to-cowl brace found on 1994 GTs. Remaining drivetrain components were 1993 Cobra carryovers.

This time the output rating was 240 horsepower, 25 more than the nearly all-new GT's small-block.

1994

Model Availability	Two-door coupe and two-door convertible
Wheelbase	101.3 inches
Length	181.5 inches
Width	71.8 inches
Height	53.4 inches
Curb Weight	3,365 pounds, coupe;
	3,567 pounds, convertible
Base Price	$20,765, coupe;
	$23,535, convertible
Track	60 inches front, 58.7 inches rear
Wheels	17x8 aluminum five-spoke
Tires	P255/45ZR-17 Goodyear
	Eagle GS-C
Suspension	Modified MacPherson hydraulic struts with coil springs and stabilizer bar in front; four-link solid axle with coil springs and stabilizer bar in back
Steering	Power-assisted rack and pinion (14.7:1 ratio)
Brakes	Power-assisted four-wheel vented discs w/ABS (13-inch front rotors, 11.65-inch rears)
Engine	240-horsepower 5.0-liter V-8
Bore and Stroke	4.00x3.00 inches
Compression	9.0:1
Fuel Delivery	Sequential electronic fuel injection and tuned-length intake manifold
Transmission	Borg-Warner T-5 five-speed manual
Axle Ratio	3.08:1 Traction-Lok
Production	5,009 coupes, 1,000 Indy 500 pace car replica convertibles

Left: At 240 horsepower, the 1994 Cobra V-8 made 25 more ponies than its 1994 GT counterpart. GT-40 heads with bigger valves helped create that difference. *Mike Mueller*

Below left: All 1994 Cobra convertibles featured saddle leather interiors. A leather-wrapped shift knob and "Cobra"-labeled floor mats were standard for coupes and convertibles. *Mike Mueller*

Opposite: A convertible joined the Cobra Mustang coupe in the SVT lineup in 1994, and color choices expanded to three (black, red, or white) for the full-roofed models. All topless Cobras that year were red Indy 500 pace car replicas, though not all featured the commemorative decals. *Mike Mueller*

On the outside, 1994 SVT Mustangs were fitted with a special front fascia (incorporating round foglamps) and a unique rear spoiler, not to mention those coiled-snake fender emblems. Exclusive treatments inside included logo floor mats; a "Cobra" embossed steering wheel; leather wrapping for the shift knob, boot, and parking brake handle; and a reversed black-on-white instrument panel with 160-mile-per-hour speedometer. A four-way power driver's seat with power lumbar support; power windows, locks, and mirrors; an interior deck lid release; a rear window defroster; cruise control; and air conditioning were all standard.

1994 Cobra Indy 500 Pace Car Convertible

A topless Cobra appeared just in time to become the third Mustang to pace the Indianapolis 500. All 1,000 Rio Red SVT Mustang convertibles built for 1994 were Indy 500 pace car replicas, although not all wore the appropriate exterior identification. Adding those commemorative decals was purely up to the customer—they were delivered in the trunk. A special pace car dash plaque was included whether the customer wanted it or not.

All also featured saddle interiors (coupes used both saddle and black), tan tops, and special black accents on their wheels. Included in the deal were all power features, leather appointments, Ford's Mach 460 AM/FM/CD stereo, and air conditioning. Fully loaded was an understatement.

1995 Cobra

Changes were minor for the second-edition SVT Mustang. Like its Lightning running mate, the 1995 Cobra received an SVT badge on its tail. And, to prevent rock damage to the lower body, a vertical spat was added to the leading edge of each rocker panel extension. All 1995 Cobra convertibles were painted black, wore black tops, and featured a saddle leather interior.

New that year for roofless Cobras was the removable hardtop option first announced along with the new SN95 Mustang in 1994. Held back due to supply problems and quality-control concerns in 1994, the plastic lid finally made it into the wild atop 499 of the 1,003 black Cobra convertibles released for 1995. Both its price and weight were hefty: $1,825 for the former, 90 pounds for the latter. A fat wallet was needed to own one, and an extra pair of helping hands was required for removal, after which a lift-off top could nestle down into a convenient carrier that rolled on four casters, making storage, at least, a little simpler.

In other news, the SVT Lightning was temporarily shelved at the end of the year.

1995 Cobra R

The "R" may have stood for racing, but many of the 107 competition-ready Cobras built for 1993 ended up in collectors' garages awaiting a later sale to the highest bidder. So much for good intentions.

When SVT people announced a second Cobra R in December 1994, they also mentioned a different approach that would, it was hoped, ensure more action and less auctioning. The 1995 Cobra R would be sold by any one of the 720 certified SVT dealers only to individuals "who could show evidence of current membership in a recognized sanctioning body, as well as additional proof of his intent to campaign the car."

All 250 second-edition R models were spoken for almost overnight after SVT started taking orders on January 5, 1995. It was then only a matter of a few months before 1995 Cobra R Mustangs started showing up for resale in classified ads. The sticker price was $35,499. Some ads were asking as much as $50,000. So much for best-laid plans.

1995

Model Availability	Two-door coupe and two-door convertible
Wheelbase	101.3 inches
Length	181.5 inches
Width	71.8 inches
Height	53.4 inches
Curb weight	3,365 pounds, coupe; 3,567 pounds, convertible
Base price	$21,300, coupe; $25,605, convertible
Track	60 inches front, 58.7 inches rear
Wheels	17x8 aluminum five-spoke
Tires	P255/45ZR-17 Goodyear Eagle GS-C
Suspension	Modified MacPherson hydraulic struts with coil springs and stabilizer bar in front; four-link solid axle with coil springs and stabilizer bar in back
Steering	Power-assisted rack and pinion (14.7:1 ratio)
Brakes	Power-assisted four-wheel vented discs w/ABS (13-inch front rotors, 11.65-inch rears)
Engine	240-horsepower 5.0-liter V-8
Bore and Stroke	4.00x3.00 inches
Compression	9.0:1
Fuel Delivery	Sequential electronic fuel injection and tuned-length intake manifold
Transmission	Borg-Warner T-5 five-speed manual
Axle Ratio	3.08:1 Traction-Lok
Production	4,255 coupes, 1,003 convertibles (includes 499 with removable hardtop option)

Like its Lightning running mate, the 1995 Cobra received an SVT badge on its tail.

A second Cobra R appeared for 1995, this one painted only in Crystal White clear coat. Production was a mere 250, all with the base Cobra's saddle cloth interior. *Mike Mueller*

An extra spat was added to the Cobra-specific lower-body cladding's leading edge (directly behind the front wheel) to help limit road-hazard damage to the 1995 Cobra Mustang's bodywork. All 1,003 convertibles built that year were painted black and featured black soft tops. Production of coupes (done in the same three colors as in 1994) was 4,005. Breakdown by color for the coupes was 1,433 in black; 1,447 in red; and 1,125 in white.

The fortunate few who got their mitts on a 1995 Cobra R were treated to the Mustang's Mustang, the potentate that pony horsepower hounds had been begging for since the late 1980s. Power came from the 5.0-liter HO small-block's bigger brother, the 351-ci Windsor V-8, the same engine then serving as the heart of the Lightning F-150 pickup. In the SVT Lightning, the 5.8-liter V-8, with its GT-40 heads and matching induction setup, was rated at 240 horsepower. A larger-diameter air meter body, more compression (9:1, compared to 8.8:1), and some additional cam timing upped that output ante to 300 horses.

Behind the 351 went a heavy-duty Tremec five-speed manual transmission, a piece of torture-proof equipment better suited than Ford's typical T-5 trans to handle all that extra torque. Bringing up the rear were 3.27:1 gears in a limited-slip 8.8-inch differential. Additional exclusive Cobra R equipment included an air-to-oil engine oil cooler (the 1995 Cobra used a water-to-oil unit), a water-to-oil power steering cooler (the standard Cobra's was of air-to-oil design), and a track-wise 20-gallon fuel cell instead of the standard Mustang's 16-gallon tank.

Cobra Rs also differed greatly from their conventional Cobra counterparts in the handling department. Along with bringing the car about ¾ inch closer to the ground, R-model suspension tweaks also added beefier springs front and rear. Make that much beefier—the 1995 Cobra's linear-rate springs measured 400 lb-in in front, 160 in back. The Cobra R's progressive spring rates were

1995 Cobra R

Model Availability	Two-door coupe
Wheelbase	101.3 inches
Length	181.5 inches
Width	71.8 inches
Height	52.7 inches
Curb Weight	3,326 pounds
Base Price	$35,499 (plus $2,100 gas-guzzler tax)
Track	60.5 inches front, 59.2 inches rear
Wheels	17x9 aluminum five-spoke
Tires	BFGoodrich Comp T/A P255/45ZR-17
Suspension	Modified MacPherson hydraulic struts with coil springs and stabilizer bar in front; four-link solid axle with coil springs and stabilizer bar in back
Steering	Power-assisted rack and pinion
Brakes	Power-assisted four-wheel vented discs w/ABS (13-inch front rotors, 11.65-inch rears)
Engine	300-horsepower 5.8-liter (351-ci) V-8
Bore and Stroke	4.00x3.50 inches
Compression	9.0:1
Fuel Delivery	Sequential electronic fuel injection with 65-millimeter throttle body and tuned-length GT-40 intake manifold
Transmission	Tremec TR3550 five-speed manual
Axle Ratio	3.08:1 Traction-Lok
Production	250; all painted white with no radio, air conditioner, or back seat and a 20-gallon fuel cell instead of conventional gas tank

Like its 1993 forerunner, the 1995 R model came without a back seat. No nonsense was again a fair description. *Mike Mueller*

700–850 lb-in up front, 200–260 out back. Struts and shocks were adjustable Koni units, and the front stabilizer bar was 30 millimeters in diameter, 5 millimeters thicker than the Cobra piece. Both the 1995 Cobra and Cobra R used a 27-millimeter rear stabilizer bar and the same brakes.

Wheels were exclusive, aggressive-looking aluminum 17x9 five-spokes shod in P255/45ZR17 BF Goodrich Comp T/A rubber. These rims also supplied the only official exterior identification in the form of distinctive center caps featuring the familiar coiled-snake motif surrounded by a bold, red "R."

Helping further set the Cobra R apart from a garden-variety Mustang was its bulging fiberglass hood, added to clear both the taller GT-40 induction equipment and a shock tower crossbrace. The latter piece wasn't included on standard Cobras. The standard Cobra's round foglamps, on the other hand, weren't included in the R-model package. And all 250 1995 Cobra Rs featured Crystal White paint on the outside, saddle appointments inside.

All also were delivered without radios, air conditioners, or back seats. Other than the electrically controlled mirrors standard on all Mustangs, no power conveniences were available. Sound deadener and insulation were deleted. No nonsense clearly was the intention.

1996

The SVT Mustang moved up into a higher-performance league in 1996 thanks to the introduction of Ford's new modular motor. This 4.6-liter V-8 was sensation enough between '96 GT fenders with its single overhead cam in each cylinder head. But the Cobra rendition was even hotter with twice as many cams, twice as many valves, and nearly 50 percent more horsepower. Output for the GT's cast-iron SOHC V-8 was 215 horsepower, while its all-aluminum DOHC Cobra cousin produced 305 horses, enough to blast the SVT Mustang through the quarter-mile in less than

Standard 1995 R-model power came from a 351-ci Windsor V-8 modified with GT-40 induction components. Output was 300 horsepower. Also notice the shock tower crossbrace. A bulging fiberglass hood was required to clear this extra hardware, as well as the taller GT-40 parts. *Mike Mueller*

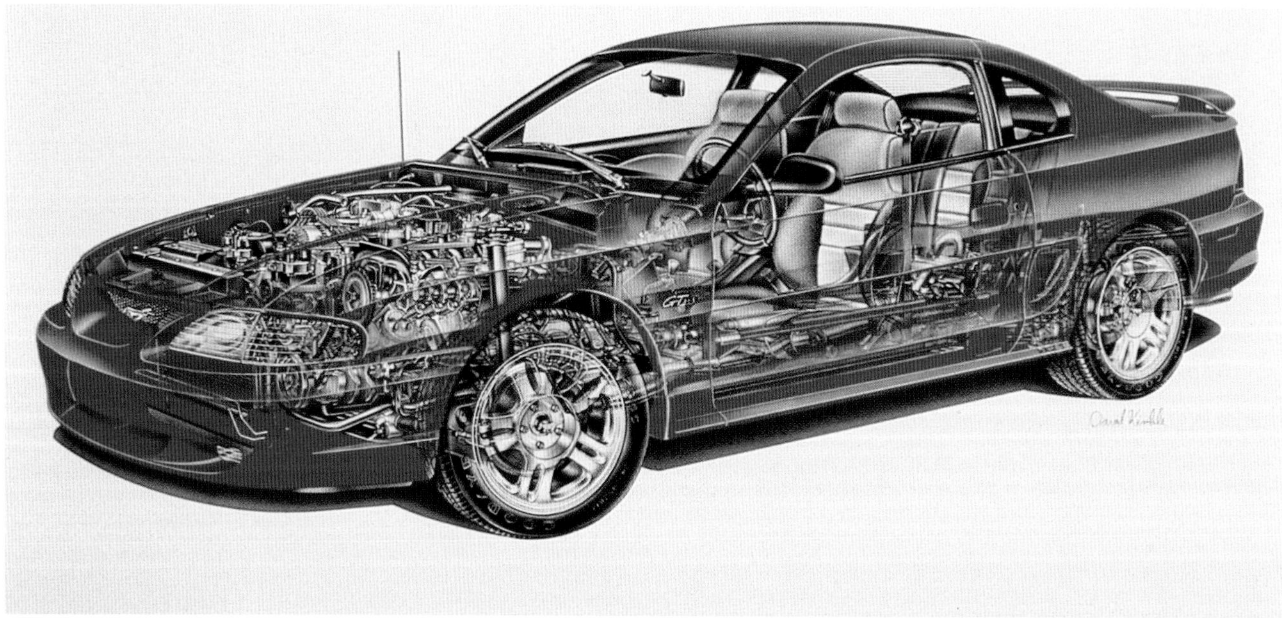

New for the 1996 Cobra was a twin-scooped hood. But the really big news came beneath that lid, as the old 5.0-liter V-8 was replaced by Ford's new mod motor, a 4.6-liter DOHC V-8 featuring four valves per cylinder. Coupe production breakdown by color for 1996 was 2,124 in black; 1,429 in white; and 1,940 in red. *David Kimble cutaway, courtesy Ford Motor Company*

Manufacturing the 4.6-liter Cobra V-8 required a $3.4 million outlay to create a special assembly line at Ford's Romeo, Michigan, engine works.

1996

Model Availability	Two-door coupe and two-door convertible
Wheelbase	101.3 inches
Length	181.5 inches
Width	71.8 inches
Height	53.4 inches
Curb Weight	3,391 pounds, coupe; 3,531 pounds, convertible
Base Price	$24,810, coupe; $27,580, convertible
Track	60 inches front, 58.7 inches rear
Wheels	17x8 aluminum five-spoke
Tires	P255/45ZR-17 Goodyear Eagle GS-C
Suspension	Modified MacPherson hydraulic struts with coil springs and stabilizer bar in front; four-link solid axle with coil springs and stabilizer bar in back
Steering	Power-assisted rack and pinion (14.7:1 ratio)
Brakes	Power-assisted four-wheel vented discs w/ABS (13-inch front rotors, 11.65-inch rears)
Engine	305-horsepower 4.6-liter (281-ci) DOHC V-8
Bore and Stroke	3.60x3.60 inches
Compression	9.85:1
Fuel Delivery	Sequential electronic fuel injection and tuned-length intake manifold
Transmission	Borg-Warner T-45 five-speed manual
Axle Ratio	3.27:1 Traction-Lok
Production	7,492 coupes (includes 1,999 with Mystic paint), 2,510 convertibles

14 seconds. The 1996 Cobra was a dozen miles per hour faster (152 miles per hour) on the top end than its 5.0-liter pushrod predecessor and a good half-second quicker (5.9 clicks) running 0–60.

Talk about biggest bang for the buck. Discounting foreign exotics, there were only three other convertibles on American roads in 1996 fitted with DOHC engines producing more than 300 horsepower, and all three cost more than $65,000. At $28,080, the topless '96 Cobra looked like a steal in comparison.

Manufacturing the 4.6-liter Cobra V-8 required a $3.4 million outlay to create a special assembly line at Ford's Romeo, Michigan, engine works. The first of its kind in the mass-production world, this hands-on line, in the words of Romeo plant manager Harvey Byrne, allowed Ford "the opportunity to build specialty engines at low volumes, cost effectively, and at high quality." Each engine was hand-built by two technicians who moved through 10 workstations where the parts and tools for the various assembly processes were waiting. An autographed plaque was affixed to each engine at the end of the line to let everyone know who the proud parents were.

"This is the only place in the Ford group, apart from Aston Martin, where employees put their signature on an engine," explained Byrne. "This is a mark of pride in the product and a commitment to the quality with which it is built." Hand-built, hand-signed Romeo V-8s remain a proud tradition beneath the hood of today's Shelby GT500 Mustang.

New too for 1996 was a Borg-Warner T-45 five-speed manual transmission, created specially for V-8 Mustangs to work smoother and quieter than the T-5 gearbox used in previous years. The T-45 was also much stronger than the T-5, and that was a good thing considering the increased output it had to endure beneath the '96 SVT Cobra's hood.

That hood was restyled for 1996, with two aggressive scoops moved up into the domed section required to clear the taller DOHC mod motor. Far less noticeable on the car's underside was an improved suspension and stronger, more precise steering gear. Most other Cobra features carried over from 1995, including the wheels and color choices. The former were now accented in gray metallic like the '94 Indy pace car convertible's rims, while the latter (applied to

Left: A "Cobra"-embossed rear bumper cover was new out back for the 1996 SVT Mustang. Previous models used the GT's "Mustang"-tagged cover. Black, white, and red were again offered, but the latter shade for 1996 was called Laser Red. Convertible production breakdown by color was 1,054 in black; 494 in white; and 962 in red. Cobra wheels for 1996 were also updated with dark gray metallic accent paint within their spokes. *Mike Mueller*

Below: The 1996 Cobra's 4.6-liter DOHC V-8 was rated at 305 horsepower. Notice the strut-tower/firewall bracing, another new Cobra feature that year. *Mike Mueller*

Cobra interiors carried over unchanged into 1996, with the same upholstery choices appearing for coupes. Convertibles, on the other hand, were no longer limited to saddle leather appointments. Cloth or leather done in black or saddle was available, as were tops colored black, white, or saddle. *Mike Mueller*

both coupes and convertibles) again consisted of red (now Laser Red), black, or white. Totally new for 1996 was a fourth finish, the so-called Mystic paint.

Some three years in the making, Ford's Mystic clear-coat metallic finish was an $815 option in 1996 and was applied only to Cobra coupes. As an SVT release explained, the Mystic option featured "a light-refracting finish that exhibits four major metallic colors—green, amber, gold and purple—and changes hue based on the light intensity and angle from which it is viewed." In truth, the effect was far more fluid than that, as numerous other colors flashed in and out, including emerald green, violet blue, magenta, burgundy, amber/gold, root-beer brown, golden black, etc. Sometimes the car would appear all one color, while often it would radiate many shades at once—all depending on light angles and the viewer's changing perspective. No matter how you looked at it, the prismatic effect truly was eye-popping.

Prismatic paints were nothing new when Ford teamed up with Flex Products Inc. and the BASF Corporation to produce the Mystic Cobra. But this dazzling, certainly daring finish from a Detroit automaker represented a first, as did the extent of its light- and mind-bending abilities. "The degree to which you can obtain a color shift effect in a paint has never been this great," claimed BASF's Patrick Mormile. "This unique pigment should be viewed as a breakthrough technology," added BASF chief color designer Jon Hall.

Total Mystic Cobra production in 1996 was 1,999, with 1,990 of those featuring black leather interiors, the other 9 fitted with black cloth appointments inside.

1997

The quickest clue to a '97 Cobra's identity came up front, where the previously used honeycomb grille was dropped to allow more cooling air into the larger radiator included on all Mustangs that year. A spoiler was optional in back; it had been standard for all previous Cobras. Rio Red returned for 1997, joining black, white, and a new color, Pacific Green.

1998

That next to nothing changed in 1998 wasn't necessarily a bad thing considering what a great ride awaited anyone with about 30 grand to spend. "The Ford SVT Mustang Cobra continues to showcase the commitment of the Ford Special Vehicle Team to driving enjoyment for 1998," explained press releases. "Visual and mechanical refinements enhance SVT's cardinal [priorities] of performance, substance, exclusivity and

1997

Model Availability	Two-door coupe and two-door convertible
Wheelbase	101.3 inches
Length	181.5 inches
Width	71.8 inches
Height	53.4 inches
Curb Weight	3,391 pounds, coupe; 3,531 pounds, convertible
Base Price	$25,535, coupe; $28,135, convertible
Track	60 inches front, 58.7 inches rear
Wheels	17x8 aluminum five-spoke
Tires	P255/45ZR-17 Goodyear Eagle GS-C
Suspension	Modified MacPherson hydraulic struts with coil springs and stabilizer bar in front; four-link solid axle with coil springs and stabilizer bar in back
Steering	Power-assisted rack and pinion (14.7:1 ratio)
Brakes	Power-assisted four-wheel vented discs w/ABS (13-inch front rotors, 11.65-inch rears)
Engine	305-horsepower 4.6-liter (281-ci) DOHC V-8
Bore and Stroke	3.60x3.60 inches
Compression	9.85:1
Fuel Delivery	Sequential electronic fuel injection and tuned-length intake manifold
Transmission	Borg-Warner T-45 five-speed manual
Axle Ratio	3.27:1 Traction-Lok
Production	6,961 coupes, 3,088 convertibles

Another new color appeared on the SVT palette in 1997: Pacific Green, a shade offered that year only. Rio Red was the name for the color on the left. Notice the missing rear spoilers. Standard on previous Cobra Mustangs, this wing became optional in 1997. Coupe production by color was 2,369 in black; 1,543 in white; 1,944 in red; and 1,055 in green. *Mike Mueller*

What had worked so well in 1994 was still operating at full throttle four years later.

value." What had worked so well in 1994 was still operating at full throttle four years later, so why mince words, especially when there was so little else to say?

Save for a cupholder here, a little more stereophonic prestige there, there was not all that much new about the 1998 SVT Cobra. Most notable were redone wheels modeled after the 1995 Cobra R's five-spokes. Metallic Laser Red again replaced Rio Red, and two new colors—Bright Atlantic Blue and Chrome Yellow—were introduced. Introduced too for 1998 was another SVT model, this one based on Ford's four-door Contour.

Below: Two new clear-coat colors appeared in 1998: Atlantic Blue and Chrome Yellow. New R-model-style wheels also debuted. Coupe production breakdown by color was 1,708 in black; 958 in white; 1,236 in red (now Metallic Laser Red); 563 in blue; and 709 in yellow.

1998

Model Availability	Two-door coupe and two-door convertible
Wheelbase	101.3 inches
Length	181.5 inches
Width	71.8 inches
Height	53.4 inches
Curb Weight	3,391 pounds, coupe; 3,531 pounds, convertible
Base Price	$25,710, coupe; $28,510, convertible
Track	60 inches front, 58.7 inches rear
Wheels	17x8 aluminum five-spoke
Tires	P255/45ZR-17 Goodyear Eagle GS-C
Suspension	Modified MacPherson hydraulic struts with coil springs and stabilizer bar in front; four-link solid axle with coil springs and stabilizer bar in back
Steering	Power-assisted rack and pinion (14.7:1 ratio)
Brakes	Power-assisted four-wheel vented discs w/ABS (13-inch front rotors, 11.65-inch rears)
Engine	305-horsepower 4.6-liter (281-ci) DOHC V-8
Bore and Stroke	3.60x3.60 inches
Compression	9.85:1
Fuel Delivery	Sequential electronic fuel injection and tuned-length intake manifold
Transmission	Borg-Warner T-45 five-speed manual
Axle Ratio	3.27:1 Traction-Lok
Production	5,174 coupes, 3,480 convertibles

Above: Like Atlantic Blue, Chrome Yellow paint appeared for the SVT Mustang in 1998 only. Convertible production by color that year was 1,256 in black; 578 in white; 842 in red; 249 in blue; and 555 in yellow. *Mike Mueller*

Right: The bracing between the strut towers and firewall seen beneath Cobra Mustang hoods in 1996 and 1997 was deleted for the 1998 model. *Mike Mueller*

Below: Beneath Ford's restyled "New Edge" body in 1999 was an independent suspension, an SVT Mustang exclusive that year. The 1999 Cobra also was enhanced with a boost to 320 horsepower. *David Kimble cutaway, courtesy Ford Motor Company*

Bottom: A second-generation Lightning F-150 pickup (upper left) joined the SVT lineup for 1999. To the left of the 1999 Cobra coupe and convertible is that year's SVT Contour, which featured a 200-horsepower V-6. Notice the 1999 SVT Mustang's revised five-spoke wheels.

1999

The SVT Lightning pickup returned for 1999 and was joined by a truly new Cobra based on the nicely restyled New Edge Mustang. Ford unveiled the '99 Cobra in Las Vegas at the annual Specialty Equipment Manufacturers Association (SEMA) show in November 1998. Coupe production began in February 1999.

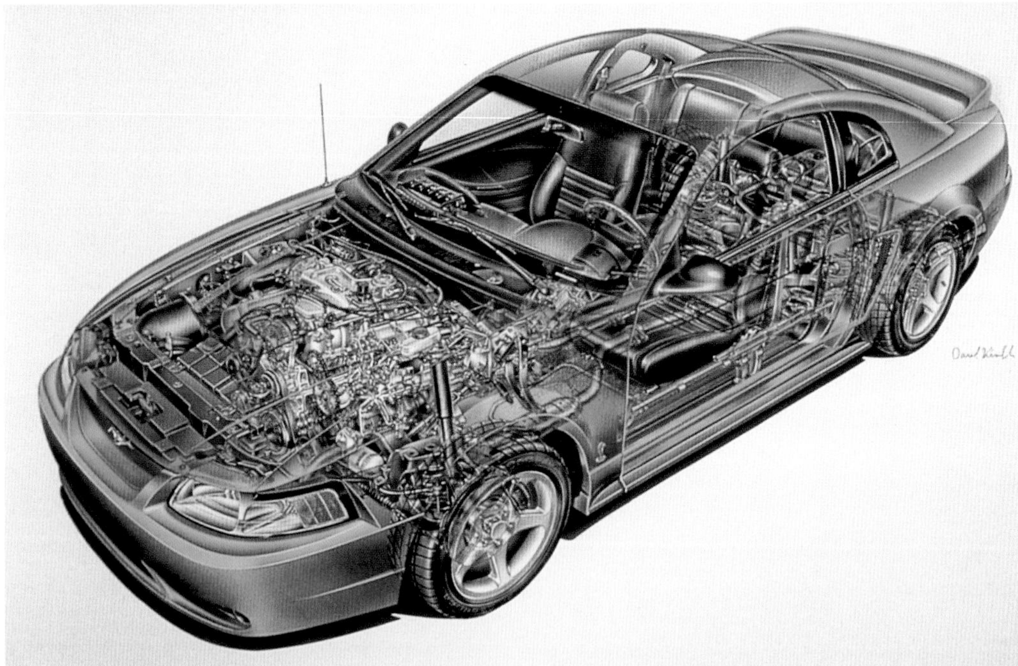

Fifteen more ponies were new beneath the hood. Improved intake port geometry, revised combustion chambers (that created a "tumbling" air/fuel charge), and a new coil-on-plug ignition system contributed to this boost to 320 horsepower. Traction control was now standard, as was a rather sophisticated independent rear suspension (IRS).

"With its new [IRS], the SVT Cobra breaks away from other 'pony cars' in this segment," said chief engineer Janine Bay. "The ride and handling characteristics Cobra offers are world-class in every respect." This IRS setup was completely self-contained, meaning it could simply bolt up to the unit body in place of the conventional solid axle.

"What we had to do [was] package a new independent rear suspension in not only the same space as the old solid-axle design, but we had to use the same mounting points," explained development engineer Eric Zinkosky. "We virtually 'reverse-engineered' the IRS from known suspension hardpoints, and we had to keep everything inside the same box."

All parts were exclusive to the Cobra, save for the aluminum differential housing and wheel bearings, which came from the Lincoln Mk VIII. Inside that housing were 3.27:1 gears. The IRS also incorporated a 26-millimeter tubular stabilizer bar as opposed to the 25-millimeter unit used in 1998. Up front, a 28-millimeter bar replaced the '98 Cobra's 29-millimeter piece.

With its IRS and extra power, the 1999 Cobra promised even more performance. But magazine road tests demonstrated otherwise. The latest SVT Mustangs were slower than their predecessors, a result some blamed on extra pounds put on by the new rear suspension. Upon further review, SVT people discovered that the revised V-8 was not making the horsepower advertised. To fix this, they halted Cobra sales on August 6, 1999, and recalled

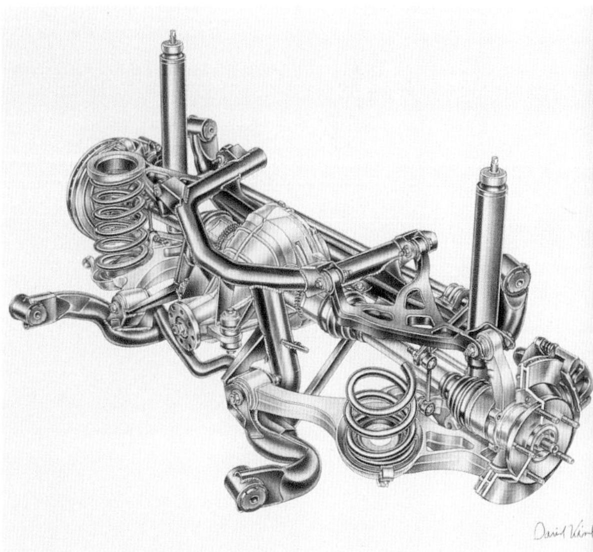

The 1999 Cobra's independent rear suspension (IRS) setup was completely self-contained; it simply bolted up to the pony car unit body in place of the conventional solid axle used that year by the Mustang GT. *David Kimble cutaway, courtesy Ford Motor Company*

1999

Model Availability	Two-door coupe and two-door convertible
Wheelbase	101.3 inches
Length	183.5 inches
Width	73.1 inches
Height	53.2 inches
Curb Weight	3,430 pounds, coupe; 3,560 pounds, convertible
Base Price	$27,470, coupe; $31,470, convertible
Track	59.9 inches, front and rear
Wheels	17x8 aluminum five-spoke
Tires	P255/45ZR-17 Goodyear Eagle GS-C
Suspension	Modified MacPherson hydraulic struts with coil springs and stabilizer bar in front; independent multi-link with upper/lower control arms, half-shafts, coil springs, and stabilizer bar in back
Steering	Power-assisted rack and pinion (15.0:1 ratio)
Brakes	Power-assisted four-wheel vented discs w/ABS (13-inch front rotors, 11.65-inch rears)
Engine	320-horsepower 4.6-liter (281-ci) DOHC V-8
Bore and Stroke	3.60x3.60 inches
Compression	9.85:1
Fuel Delivery	Sequential electronic fuel injection and tuned-length intake manifold
Transmission	Borg-Warner T-45 five-speed manual
Axle Ratio	3.27:1 Traction-Lok
Production	4,040 coupes, 4,055 convertibles

all cars. Intake manifolds and engine management hardware were replaced, as was the exhaust plumbing from the catalytic converters back.

As much as customers appreciated this commitment to quality, there was a downside: doing all the recall work meant canceling the 2000 Cobra production run. Darn.

2000 Cobra R

Although no civilian Cobras were built for 2000, the SVT gang did roll out its third R-model coupe, a really red beast that looked hotter than hell even while sitting still. Once on the prowl, there were simply no questions asked.

"This is the fastest, the best-handling Mustang ever," said SVE manager John Coletti. "It will set a performance benchmark for competition. Cobra R combines high-performance hardware and engineering that go a long way toward making it the best of the breed."

Tops on that hardware shelf was a supreme 5.4-liter mod motor featuring dual overhead cams in aluminum heads, a forged-steel crank, billet-steel connecting rods, forged-aluminum pistons, and a McLeod aluminum flywheel. Output was a whopping 385 horsepower. Tube headers followed up by Borla mufflers and side-exiting exhausts

Below: Better-breathing cylinder heads and a new coil-on-plug ignition system helped the 1999 Cobra's 4.6-liter DOHC V-8 make 320 horsepower. Standard traction control also appeared that year.

handled spent gases, while a bulletproof Tremec six-speed manual gearbox delivered 385 lb-ft of torque to an 8.8-inch rear axle containing 3.55:1 Gerodisc gears.

Helping counter all that brute force were Brembo four-piston aluminum front brake calipers that put the clamps on 13-inch rotors. Cooling ducts were also built in up front to help keep those big discs from melting down. Rear discs measured 11.65 inches across, per typical Cobra specs.

Wheels were huge 18x9.5 units wearing suitably large 265/40ZR-18 BFGoodrich tires specially constructed for the Cobra R application. Eibach racing springs (that lowered the car's height by 1.5 inches in front, 1 inch out back) were at all four corners, as were Bilstein shock absorbers. In the rear was a 21-gallon Fuel Safe fuel cell and a big rear wing for added aerodynamic stability at high speeds—a good thing considering the 2000 Cobra R's 170-mile-per-hour top end. Additional standard features included IRS, ABS, Recaro bucket seats inside, and a power-dome hood complemented by aerodynamic front-splitter bodywork.

Only 300 of these uncivilized animals were built for 2000. And, as Specialty Vehicle Marketing Manager Tom Scarpello explained it, "Three hundred

The tally for the 2000 R model was still small: only 300 were built, all painted Performance Red. Distinctive body modifications included a 7-inch-high rear wing and a front splitter fascia, both wind tunnel tested for supreme aerodynamics.

2000 Cobra R

Model Availability	Two-door coupe
Wheelbase	101.3 inches
Length	183.5 inches
Width	73.1 inches
Height	52.2 inches
Curb Weight	3,590 pounds
Price	$54,995
Track	59.7 inches, front and rear
Wheels	18x9.5 aluminum five-spoke
Tires	P265/40ZR-18 BFGoodrich g-Force
Suspension	Modified MacPherson struts with Eibach coil springs and Bilstein shock absorbers in front; independent dual A-arms with GKN 31-spline half-shafts, Eibach coil springs, and Bilstein shock absorbers in back
Steering	Rack and pinion with power assist (15.0:1 ratio) and fluid cooler
Brakes	Four-wheel vented discs w/ABS (13.0-inch Brembo front rotors, 11.65-inch rears)
Engine	385-horsepower 5.4-liter (330-ci) DOHC V-8 (aluminum heads, cast-iron block)
Bore and Stroke	3.552x4.165 inches
Compression	9.60:1
Fuel Delivery	Sequential electronic fuel injection and tuned-length intake manifold
Exhausts	Stainless-steel headers, Bassani X-pipe, 1998 Cobra catalytic converters, Borla mufflers, side-exit tailpipes
Transmission	Tremec T-56 six-speed manual
Axle Ratio	3.55:1 Gerodisc hydro-mechanical differential in 8.8-inch axle
Production	300; all painted Performance Red with Dark Charcoal interiors (all also featured a Fuel Safe bladder-type fuel cell, Recaro bucket seats, 180-mile-per-hour speedometer, and B&M Ripper shifter with leather-wrapped knob)

Right: Recaro bucket seats, a B&M Ripper Shifter (with leather-wrapped knob), and a 180-mile-per-hour speedometer were among standard interior features for the 2000 Cobra R.

Below: Powering the 2000 R model was a 5.4-liter DOHC V-8 featuring four valves per cylinder. Output was 385 horsepower.

> "This is the fastest, the best-handling Mustang ever," said SVE manager John Coletti.

people will be able to have a lot of fun in this car, and be very competitive racing it. This car elevates the whole idea of Mustang—without changing what it's been about for more than 35 years."

2001

The conventional Cobra Mustang coupe and convertible returned for 2001, this time offered in eight colors. New in back was "Cobra" identification in place of the standard "Mustang" indentation seen on the 1999 SVT models. More supportive seating also appeared, as did plusher leather/suede surfaces for those seats. Polished wheels were optional, and everything else carried over from 1999. Those 320 horses were on the job this time around, and they ably demonstrated their strength when asked by the press. According to *Muscle Mustangs & Fast Fords*, quarter-mile performance was 13.34 seconds at 104.23 miles per hour.

SVT officials again opted to interrupt Cobra Mustang production in 2002, concentrating instead on development of their gnarliest snake yet, which debuted at the Chicago Auto Show (as a 2003 model) in February that year. Reportedly, 100 2002

2001

Model Availability	Two-door coupe and two-door convertible
Wheelbase	101.3 inches
Length	183.5 inches
Width	73.1 inches
Height	53.2 inches, coupe; 53.5 inches, convertible
Curb Weight	3,430 pounds, coupe; 3,560 pounds, convertible
Base Price	$28,605, coupe; $32,605, convertible
Track	59.9 inches, front and rear
Wheels	17x8 aluminum five-spoke
Tires	P255/45ZR-17 BFGoodrich Comp T/A
Suspension	Modified MacPherson hydraulic struts with coil springs and stabilizer bar in front; independent multi-link with upper/lower control arms, half-shafts, coil springs, and stabilizer bar in back
Steering	Power-assisted rack and pinion (15.0:1 ratio)
Brakes	Power-assisted four-wheel vented discs w/ABS (13-inch front rotors, 11.65-inch rears)
Engine	320-horsepower 4.6-liter (281-ci) DOHC V-8
Bore and Stroke	3.60x3.60 inches
Compression	9.85:1
Fuel Delivery	Sequential electronic fuel injection and tuned-length intake manifold
Transmission	Borg-Warner T-45 five-speed manual
Axle Ratio	3.27:1 Traction-Lok
Production	3,867 coupes, 3,384 convertibles

"Cobra"-embossed lettering returned to the SVT Mustang's tail in 2001, and polished wheels became an option. Eight colors appeared that year, with the coupe production breakdown reading 979 in black; 556 in Laser Red; 373 in white; 556 in silver; 514 in gray; 226 in Performance Red; 316 in blue; and 347 in yellow.

Cobras were built with right-hand drive for delivery to Australia.

2003

Ten years after it first began marketing niche-market machines, Ford's Special Vehicle Team celebrated a decade in business in 2003 with an appropriate anniversary model based on its superb Cobra Mustang. "Our SVT Mustang Cobra owners are some of the most loyal customers anywhere, and we are proud to share this anniversary milestone with them," said Tom Scarpello. "The Cobra name has been synonymous with Ford performance for 40 years—and with SVT for the last 10 years. We are proud to carry the torch for this performance icon."

Available for both Cobra coupes and convertibles in 2003, SVT's 10th Anniversary package consisted of appropriate logos on the deck lid and floor mats, leather interior appointments done in black with red inserts, and a carbon fiber look added to the steering wheel, shifter boot, and brake handle. But the main attraction came beneath the hood.

All SVT Mustangs for 2003, anniversary model or not, were powered by a sensationally supercharged (and intercooled) 4.6-liter DOHC V-8 that pumped out 390 seriously mean horses, making it a "true performance value," according to Scarpello. "The next closest competitor to meet or exceed the SVT Cobra's 390 horsepower costs more than $50,000." Base prices for the 2003 Cobra coupe and convertible were $34,750 and $38,995, respectively.

Code-named the "Terminator" in-house at SVT, the supercharged Cobra owed its existence to developments first made beneath the Lightning pickup's hood in 1999. Residing there was a 5.4-liter aluminum-head SOHC mod motor topped by a Roots-type Eaton supercharger. Output was 360 horsepower. That figure was boosted to 380 horses in 2001. A few enlarged pieces (mass airflow meter and air intake opening) and a higher-flow intake manifold helped produce those extra ponies. On a test track in 2003, a stock supercharged Lightning hit 147 miles per hour, inspiring the Guinness World Records people to officially acknowledge it as the world's fastest production pickup. But the Lightning wasn't the only SVT vehicle to make its mark that year.

"Every once in a while, a car comes along that really shakes up the status quo," added Scarpello. "Since the '64-½ Mustang, there have been a number of Mustangs that set the standard for performance when they were introduced. The 2003 SVT Cobra is the new benchmark, and proudly carries on the tradition of Mustang performance leadership."

Along with its superb chassis (carried over from 2001), the 2003 Cobra contained that awesome Terminator V-8, a product of SVT chief engineer John Coletti's ongoing pursuit of ultimate performance. According to Cobra program manager Tom Bochenek, Coletti had decided that the existing 4.6-liter V-8 had gone about as far as it could go with natural aspiration. Bolting on the force-fed Lightning's blower simply represented the next logical choice.

"We had some pretty successful SVT Mustangs [before 2003]," said Coletti, "but the whole idea is to improve. That's what we're committed to, and the number-one thing our customers want is enhanced performance. The supercharged engine allowed us to go where we needed to go—to give our customers a whole lot more car than ever before."

Initial plans called for an Eaton M-90 supercharger, but it was too small for the 32-valve engine's demands. The Lightning's larger M-112 blower proved to be just the ticket for the 4.6, with the latter installation requiring a relocated air inlet (moved from the top in the truck to the back for the Cobra) to clear the Mustang's much lower hood. Key to the Eaton unit's efficient operation was an air-to-water intercooler, which relied on its own independent coolant reservoir instead of borrowing fluid from the engine.

Additional upgrades included revised aluminum cylinder heads, a longer-duration cam, and an expected drop in compression (from 9.85:1 to 8.5:1) to compensate for the supercharger's extra boost (7.5 to 8 psi). Coletti's people also didn't trust the aluminum cylinder block to handle the demands made by all that newfound blown performance, so they switched to a conventional cast-iron block. Special forged pistons with dished tops went inside those iron bores, and they were tied to the existing Cobra V-8's forged-steel crank by eight super-heavy-duty Manley H-beam forged connecting rods.

An increased-capacity fuel pump was added to ensure ample flow to larger, freer-flowing injectors. The mass air meter predictably grew, from 80 millimeters to 90. A revised two-piece intake manifold also was required for the supercharger application, while the throttle body (with twin 57-millimeter bores) was a carryover.

The sum of these parts equaled the wildest ride ever delivered by Ford's long-running pony car. "It has power that gives gratification on demand," bragged Coletti. "When you open the throttle, it just goes!" SVT tests resulted in a top end of 155 miles per hour for the Terminator Mustang. Only 4.5 seconds were needed to go from rest to 60 miles per hour, according to *Car and Driver*. And *Muscle Mustangs & Fast Fords* magazine claimed a 12.67-second burst through the quarter-mile, topping out at 110.11 miles per hour.

2003 & 2004

Model Availability	Two-door coupe and two-door convertible
Wheelbase	101.3 inches
Length	183.5 inches
Width	73.1 inches
Height	52.5 inches, coupe; 52.9 inches, convertible
Curb Weight	3,665 pounds, coupe; 3,780 pounds, convertible
Base Price	$34,750, 2003 coupe; $37,730, 2003 convertible; $39,275, 2003 10th Anniversary convertible; $35,370, 2004 coupe; $39,750 2004 convertible
Track	60.3 inches, front and rear
Wheels	17x9 aluminum five-spoke
Tires	P275/40ZR-17 Goodyear Eagle F1
Suspension	Modified MacPherson struts with heavy-duty coil springs, stabilizer bar, and Bilstein shocks in front; independent multi-link layout with heavy-duty coil springs, stabilizer bar, and Bilstein shocks in back
Steering	Power-assisted rack and pinion (15.0:1 ratio)
Brakes	Power-assisted four-wheel vented discs w/ABS (13-inch front rotors, 11.65-inch rears)
Engine	390-horsepower 4.6-liter DOHC V-8
Bore and Stroke	3.60x3.60 inches
Compression	8.5:1
Fuel Delivery	Sequential electronic fuel injection with supercharger
Transmission	T-56 six-speed manual
Axle Ratio	3.55:1
Production	8,394 coupes and 5,082 convertibles in 2003; 3,768 coupes and 1,896 convertibles in 2004

As in 2000, no standard SVT Mustangs were built for U.S. consumption in 2002. Fortunately, the breed returned for 2003 in coupe and convertible forms. Coupe production, by paint choice, was 2,251 in black; 638 in Torch Red; 621 in white; 242 in Satin Silver; 992 in Silver Metallic; 955 in RedFire; 1,052 in Sonic Blue; 490 in Zinc Yellow; 851 in Dark Shadow Gray; and 302 in Mineral Gray. The convertible breakdown was 1,679 in black; 582 in Torch Red; 308 in white; 81 in Satin Silver; 548 in Silver Metallic; 610 in RedFire; 355 in Sonic Blue; 319 in Zinc Yellow; 446 in Dark Shadow Gray; and 154 in Mineral Gray.

Drawing the most attention in 2003 was the latest Cobra's new heart: a supercharged 4.6-liter DOHC V-8 that produced 390 horsepower. Some owners claimed as many as 430 horses for this blown mod motor. This engine helped the 2003 Cobra earn the nickname the "Terminator" in-house at SVT.

Right: Among the 10th Anniversary Cobra's interior features was red leather upholstery trimmed in black.

Below: A second magical paint package, called "Mystichrome," appeared for the 2004 SVT Cobra. That time, the color-changing finish was offered for coupes and convertibles. Production was 515 for the former and 495 for the latter.

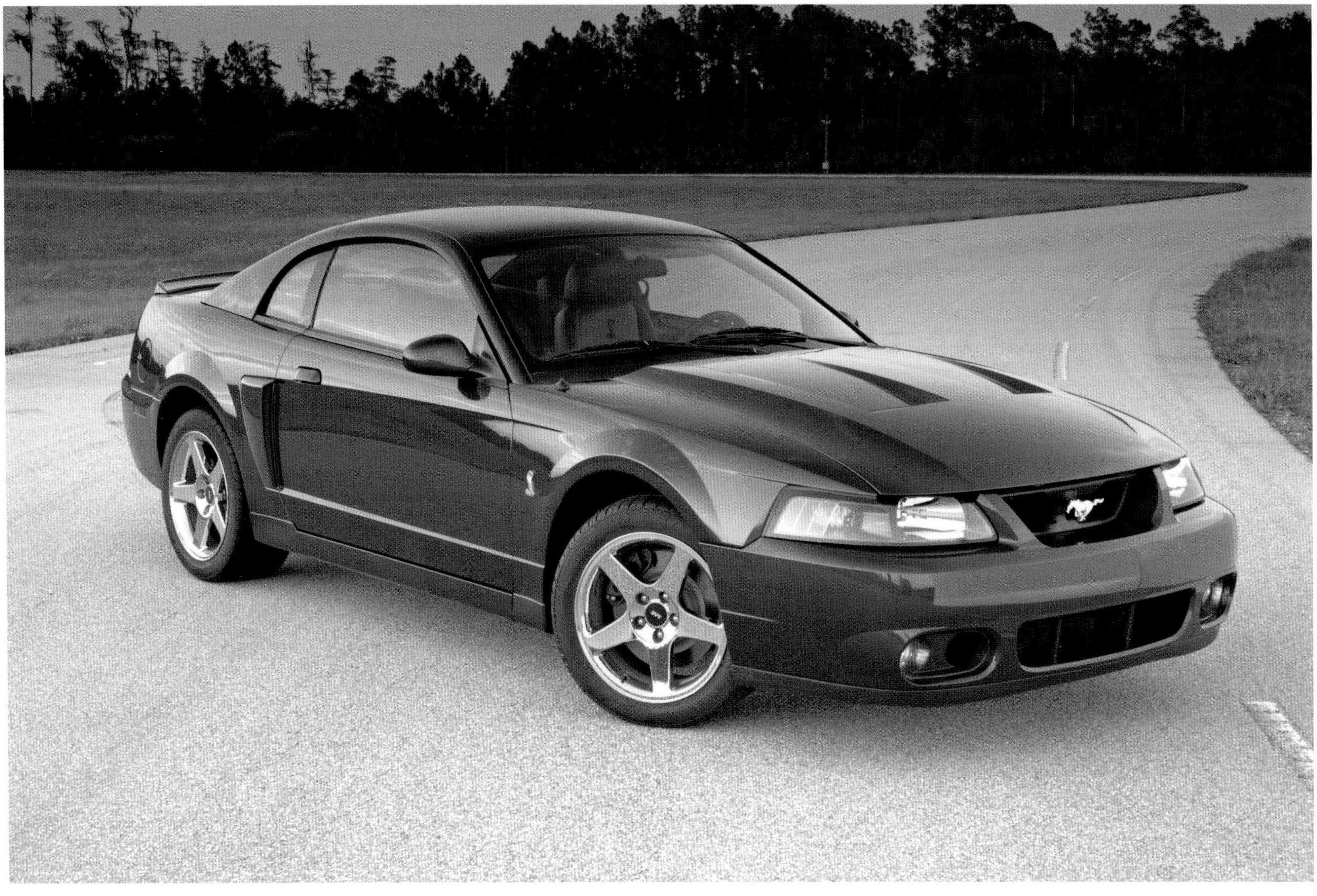

Save for paint choices, no changes were made in 2004 to the Cobra Mustang. Along with the Mystichrome option, new finishes included Competition Orange and Screaming Yellow. Convertible production breakdown by color was 392 in black; 167 in Torch Red; 128 in white; 266 in Silver Metallic; 209 in RedFire; 72 in Competition Orange; and 167 in Screaming Yellow. The list for coupes read 820 in black; 477 in Torch Red; 316 in white; 551 in Silver Metallic; 509 in RedFire; 281 in Competition Orange; and 299 in Screaming Yellow.

Clearly, Coletti wasn't kidding. But he wasn't exactly speaking the truth in 2003 when he said, "Ten years and we're just picking up speed."

2004

The blown Cobra rolled over into 2004 unchanged, but the breed didn't make the jump into the Mustang's next generation for 2005. Coletti retired at the end of 2004, and Ford's Special Vehicle Team basically did the same. Existing more or less in name alone, SVT now sponsors a Mustang that wears the name of an independent entity, Shelby Automobiles, based in Las Vegas. Apparently that "Terminator" code carried more significance than Coletti and crew intended.

As for the last Cobra, the only new news of note involved colors. Two new ones debuted for 2004: Screaming Yellow and Competition Orange. And a third option, the Mystichrome Appearance Package, appeared on a limited run (1,010 cars) of coupes and convertibles, mimicking the Mystic Cobra coupes of 1996.

"Customers loved the original SVT Mustang with Mystic paint," said Tom Scarpello in April 2003. "Even today Mystic cars are still some of the most popular—and most collectible—special editions in SVT's 10-year history. We expect the new Mystichrome Package, with more vibrant colors and one-of-a-kind color-shifting interior trim, to be even more popular with enthusiasts."

That's right: the passenger compartment also changed colors like a chameleon. Both the colored leather inside and the paint outside utilized ChromaFlair light interference pigments, provided by Flex Products of Santa Rosa, California, to do the trick. "The bright, iridescent colors reminded me of chromed exhaust headers blued by intense heat," said Alan Eggly, Ford's color and trim director for North America. Thus he named the effect "Mystichrome."

No Cobra Mustangs appeared in 2005 and 2006. Then along came the Ford Shelby GT500 in 2007. The GT500 got its power from a Romeo-built, SVT-tagged (and autographed) V-8, hence the continuation of the Special Vehicle Team legacy. The special bulging hood vented away under hood heat. *Mike Mueller*

Coiled-snake imagery abounded on the GT500, as did various other bits of nostalgic, traditional Shelby nomenclature. *Mike Mueller*

The only exterior SVT identification came in the center of each wheel, which measured 18 inches across and 9.5 inches wide. Tires were P255/45R units in front and P285/40ZR in back. *Mike Mueller*

2007 Ford Shelby GT500

Model Availability	Two-door coupe and two-door convertible
Wheelbase	107.3 inches
Length	187.6 inches
Width	73.9 inches
Height	54.5 inches
Curb Weight	3,920 pounds
Base Price	$40,930, coupe (plus $1,300 gas-guzzler tax)
Wheels	18x9.5 aluminum
Tires	P255/45R-18, front; P285/45ZR-18, rear
Suspension	Independent reverse-L with MacPherson hydraulic struts, coil springs, and 34-millimeter stabilizer bar in front; three-link solid axle, coil springs, and 24-millimeter stabilizer bar in back
Steering	Power-assisted rack and pinion (15.0:1 ratio)
Brakes	Power-assisted four-wheel vented discs w/ABS (14-inch Brembo front rotors, 11.8-inch rears)
Engine	500-horsepower 5.4-liter V-8
Bore and Stroke	3.552x4.165 inches
Fuel Delivery	Sequential electronic fuel injection with Eaton Roots–type supercharger
Transmission	T-56 six-speed manual
Axle Ratio	3.31:1
Production	10,844; 8,150 coupes, 2,694 convertibles

2007 Ford Shelby GT500

Although no SVT Mustangs were built in 2005 and 2006, pony enthusiasts knew something new was on its way. In March 2005, Ford unveiled an enticing concept vehicle at the New York Auto Show to whet their appetites. This white-striped, red Mustang carried two famous tags: SVT and Shelby.

In August 2003, Dearborn officials announced a new deal with the man who originally proved just how fast a pony car could run. "Carroll Shelby is a legend in the field of performance automotive products," said Chris Theodore, Ford vice president of Advanced Product Creation. "I cannot think of a better person to be partnering with on this endeavor than [him]. Our new partnership with Carroll and his team will create modern-day, world-class performance products that are as potent and coveted as the Shelby Fords from 40 years ago."

"Throughout my career, I have had the privilege of working with several manufacturers in the development of some great automobiles," added Shelby, who turned 80 in 2003. "But my energy and passion for performance products has always been strongest when it involved vehicles from Ford Motor Company. I couldn't be more proud than I am today to have the opportunity to re-create history with the only automotive company that holds the key to my heart."

Try make history. At 500 horsepower, the 2007 Shelby GT500 was far and away the most powerful pony car ever built. "It's one thing to put [500] horsepower in an exotic supercar," said Shelby. "It's another to put that much power in something as

The GT500 came standard with 500 supercharged horses. Producing those horses was a 5.4-liter DOHC Triton V-8 force-fed by an Eaton blower. A six-speed Tremec transmission was standard, too. *Mike Mueller*

affordable as a Mustang." Base price for the latest, by far greatest Shelby Mustang was $40,930, leaving Viper and Z06 owners little choice but to eat their hearts out.

"On paper, the GT500 has enough power and flair to put Chevrolet's base Corvette C6 smack on the trailer," claimed *AutoWeek*. "The Shelby Cobra GT500 is going to be the most capable, the most powerful Mustang that Ford or SVT or Carroll Shelby has ever introduced," added Ford's Advanced Product Creation director Hau Thai-Tang.

Supercharging Ford's 5.4-liter V-8 made those 500 horses possible. An intercooled Eaton blower supplied 8.5 psi of boost, while a Tremec T-56 six-speed manual transmission handled all that power. Brakes were 14-inch vented Brembo discs with four-piston calipers up front, 11.8-inch vented discs with two-piston calipers in back. Wheels were enormous 18x9.5 spokers wearing P255/45R18 rubber at the nose, huge P285/40ZR18 tires at the tail.

And let's not forget all that nostalgic Shelby imagery: those wide white stripes, that exclusive front fascia with its gaping intakes, that ducktail spoiler at the tail. Shelby was using the coiled snakes long before SVT adopted them, and they were present and accounted for inside and out. SVT identification, meanwhile, appeared on the wheels, doorsills, and tachometer, as well as on the traditionally autographed V-8 beneath that bulging, vented hood.

Originally introduced for 2007 in coupe form only, the GT500 was quickly joined by a convertible model wearing only the second cloth top in Mustang history. The first had shown up atop the 2003 Cobra.

Above: Interior adornments included Shelby GT500 identification on the steering wheel center and snake embossing on the seats. SVT lettering lit up at redline on the tachometer face. *Mike Mueller*

Opposite top: Ford introduced the 2008 GT500KR at the 2007 New York auto show. This reborn "King of the Road" Shelby Mustang featured 540 horsepower.

Opposite below: The Red Stripe Package was introduced midyear for the 2007 Shelby GT500. As you might have guessed, this option adds red stripes to a GT500 coupe done in either white or black paint. An upgraded interior with red complements is also included in the deal, priced at $1,650.

Below: A GT500 convertible joined its coupe forerunner in 2007. In place of the Mustang GT's folding vinyl roof, the topless Shelby featured a classy cloth unit. The 2007 GT500 was one of only two Mustang convertibles to sport a cloth top to that point, the other being the 2003 SVT Cobra.

10

Back to the Future

10

2005–2014

- Mustang production moves from Dearborn to the Auto Alliance International (AAI) assembly plant in Flat Rock, Michigan, for the 2005 model year.
- 2005 Mustang first to feature a foundation designed specifically for the pony car application; previous designs all borrowed existing platforms from other Ford models.
- The 2005 GT is the first Mustang to come standard with 300 horsepower.
- The 2005 GT V-8's variable cam timing is a first for rear-driven domestic V-8 models.
- California Special makes an encore appearance in 2007, as does a Hertz Shelby.
- Reborn GT350 introduced by Shelby American for 2011 model year.
- Boss 302 returns for another two-year run (2012 and 2013).
- Carroll Shelby dies in Texas at age 89 on May 10, 2012.
- The Flat Rock plant rolls out its millionth Mustang, a Ruby Red 2014 GT convertible, on Wednesday, April 17, 2013, exactly 49 years to the day after Ford officially introduced its original pony car.
- Design exec J Mays announces his retirement (effective January 1, 2014) in November 2013 after 16 years at Ford.

On January 5, 2003, William Clay Ford Jr. allowed journalists a look at the Mustang's near future, in prototype form, during Detroit's annual North American International Auto Show. At the same time, he also paid homage to a proud legacy that was then nearing its 40th anniversary. "Something old, something new" pretty much said it all about Ford's latest too-cool-for-school concept vehicle, a momentous machine that *AutoWeek*'s editors labeled "Most Significant" at that year's auto show. On the outside, it plain and simply screamed Mustang, thanks to various nostalgic styling cues incorporated into a bold image that, overall, by no means looked like it was lost in the past. Mechanicals certainly were cutting edge, with a supercharged, intercooled DOHC V-8 (making as many as 400 horses) leading the way up front, independent suspension bringing up the rear.

CREATED BY WAY OF COLLABORATIVE EFFORT between Richard Hutting's Ford Design facility in California and chief designer Larry Erickson's studio back east in Dearb orn, the Mustang GT concept was shown off in coupe and convertible forms in 2003 and, like the Mustang II show car of 1963, was based on regular-production developments then well under way. Erickson's team handled all mainstream work on the next new Mustang. Hutting's crew in Valencia, California, took off on a creative tangent, resulting in just the tease Design Group Vice President J Mays was looking for. Unlike so many far-more-farfetched concepts, those two showstoppers weren't meant to be here today and off into the archives tomorrow, a fact Ford people admitted in writing. "The Mustang

Above: The latest, greatest Mustang rolls on a 107.1-inch wheelbase. Overall length is 187.6 inches and height is 54.5 inches. Grabber Orange paint—yet another blast from the past—appeared in vibrant fashion for the 2007 Mustang.

Opposite: Of course the running-horse logo remained in place in the grille to lead the way for the 2005 Mustang. *Mike Mueller*

Previous pages:
Left: The 2005 Mustang featured more standard features than ever. Like its V-8 running mate, this V-6 coupe rolled off the line with power mirrors, interval wipers, and power door locks with remote keyless entry. *Mike Mueller*

Right: A beloved legend, the Boss 302, returned for another brief two-year run in 2012. A 440-hp 5.0-liter V8 was standard for the 2012-13 Boss. *Mike Mueller*

Right: The GT-R concept vehicle appeared at the 2004 New York auto show as part of Ford's celebration of Mustang's 40th birthday. Beneath the hood was a 440-horsepower 5.0-liter DOHC V-8.

Below: Ford, in cahoots with Multimatic Motorsports, introduced its FR500C racing Mustang in 2005 to compete in the Grand-Am Cup series, where it won the first time out at Daytona that year. At the FR500C's heart was a Cammer R-50 V-8 that reportedly made 418 horsepower.

Opposite: Ford promotional people made sure customers noticed the family ties between the 2005 Mustang and its 1967 ancestor. At the same time, they also played up the latest generation's definitely modern appeal. Foglamps were standard for the GT.

GT concepts are strong indications of the next-generation Mustang's design direction," read one press release.

Journalists' predictions then picked up where Ford's words left off. "My suspicions are that the [Mustang] Concept is closer to production than you might think," claimed David Freiburger in *Hot Rod* magazine's March 2003 issue. "The buzz is that the general shape of the car is dead-on."

Damn straight. When Bill Ford returned to the Detroit auto show in January 2004 with Mays' 2005 model, not one witness was left holding the bag wondering whatever happened to those hot-to-trot time machines they'd seen the year before.

Like the original pony cars those two GT concepts mimicked, the truly new 2005 Mustang represented different vehicles to different drivers. Aging baby boomers recognized many bits and pieces of beloved ponies from their pasts. Today's trendsetters couldn't help but feel hipper than hip behind the wheel. And the techno set found more than enough toys to play with. Especially attractive, in any customers' case, was the 2005 GT's newfound performance. As the first Mustang to offer 300 standard horses, this wild horse arguably qualified as the biggest bang for the buck ever heard out of Detroit.

"A pure performer, it's the most affordable 300-horsepower car made and the best rear-drive performance car under $20,000," bragged Phil Martens, group vice president, North America Product Creation. That dollar figure was in reference to the V-6 model, which, with 210 horsepower, was no slouch itself—in 1994, the Mustang GT's 5.0-liter V-8 made only five more horses. Base price for the 2005 V-6 Mustang was $18,785, while its GT running mate began at $24,370.

Balancing that whole retro thing with a thoroughly modern feel was the developmental goal all along, as well as an ideal J Mays stressed. "The new Mustang is pure American Muscle," he said in 2004. "But, rest assured, we're not insisting on history at the expense of our future."

"Yeah, right," claimed some critics who still feel Mays lives too much in the past. At a previous design position with Volkswagen of America, he had been involved with the re-creation of the VW Beetle. After joining Ford in 1997, he had a hand in a run of definitely nostalgic concept cars (most prominently the Ford Forty Nine and 427) and the Ford GT, which more or less was a 1960s GT-40 race car reincarnated. Clearly a trend was present. But Mays remains unfazed by any slings and arrows; he responds with his own pokes at today's fad-conscious designers who feel that absolutely nothing old can ever be new again.

"The new Mustang is pure American Muscle," J Mays said in 2004.

In his humble opinion, heritage can play an important role in modern automotive design and rightfully should have in this case when so much customer loyalty was at stake. "When you're designing a new Mustang, you're the steward of 40 years of automotive history," he says. "If you don't get it right, you've got 8 million Mustang fans to answer to. I think we got it right. By melding the true character of Mustang into a car with fully modern proportions, we ensured that even the uninitiated will instantly recognize these cars as Mustangs."

Modernizing the machine beneath the memories was the job of chief nameplate engineer Hau Thai-Tang, who joined Ford in 1988. During the 1990s, he worked with Ford Racing, then

Right: Bold tri-bar taillights continued the time trip in back, as did the GT's rear wing.

Below: Six more inches of wheelbase made for more room inside the 2005 Mustang's body for driver and passengers. Trunk space increased by 13 percent. Overall torsional stiffness improved, too, by 31 percent in the coupe's case. The convertible shell was 100 percent stiffer compared to its 2004 predecessor.

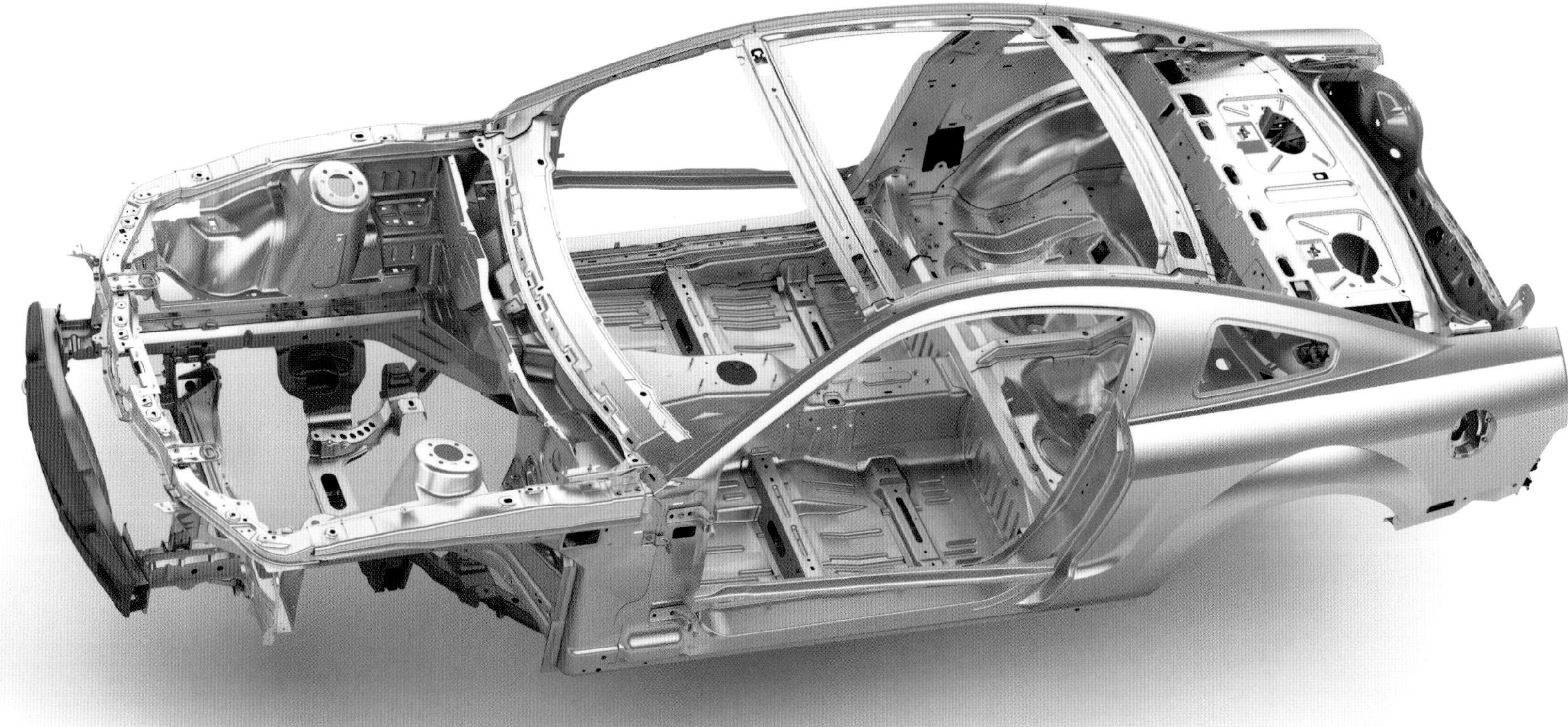

helped develop the 2000 Lincoln LS, a Car of the Year honoree by *Motor Trend*. Next, he shepherded the 2001 Mustang, Cobra, and Bullitt GT models into production.

To get the next-generation Mustang off the ground, Thai-Tang's engineers relied on a foundation that qualified as new despite reports to the contrary. Early prognostications claimed it would be a modified version of the DEW98 platform used by the Lincoln LS and Jaguar S-Type, but Thai-Tang was among the loudest at Ford to say not so. Though the MacPherson strut layout in front resembled that used by the Lincoln LS, that was the closest comparison between the two.

Known internally at Ford as the S197 platform, the new Mustang's structure did share some 30 percent of its makeup with other corporate products, but these family ties were minor. Setting the 2005 chassis further apart from its aging SN95 predecessor were 6 extra inches of wheelbase, which, working in concert with an engine relocated rearward, translated into improved balance. Weight distribution for the 2005 GT, with its three-valve 4.6-liter V-8, was 53 percent in front, 47 in back, compared to about 57/43 for the 2004 GT and Cobra.

And contrary to the Lincoln LS (as well as the GT concepts), the S197 chassis did not feature independent rear suspension. Cost considerations came into play, as a live axle is cheaper and it's also better suited to drag strip–style, dead-off-the-line performance—an aspect designers knew would be just as important to pony car buyers in 2005 as it was 40 years earlier.

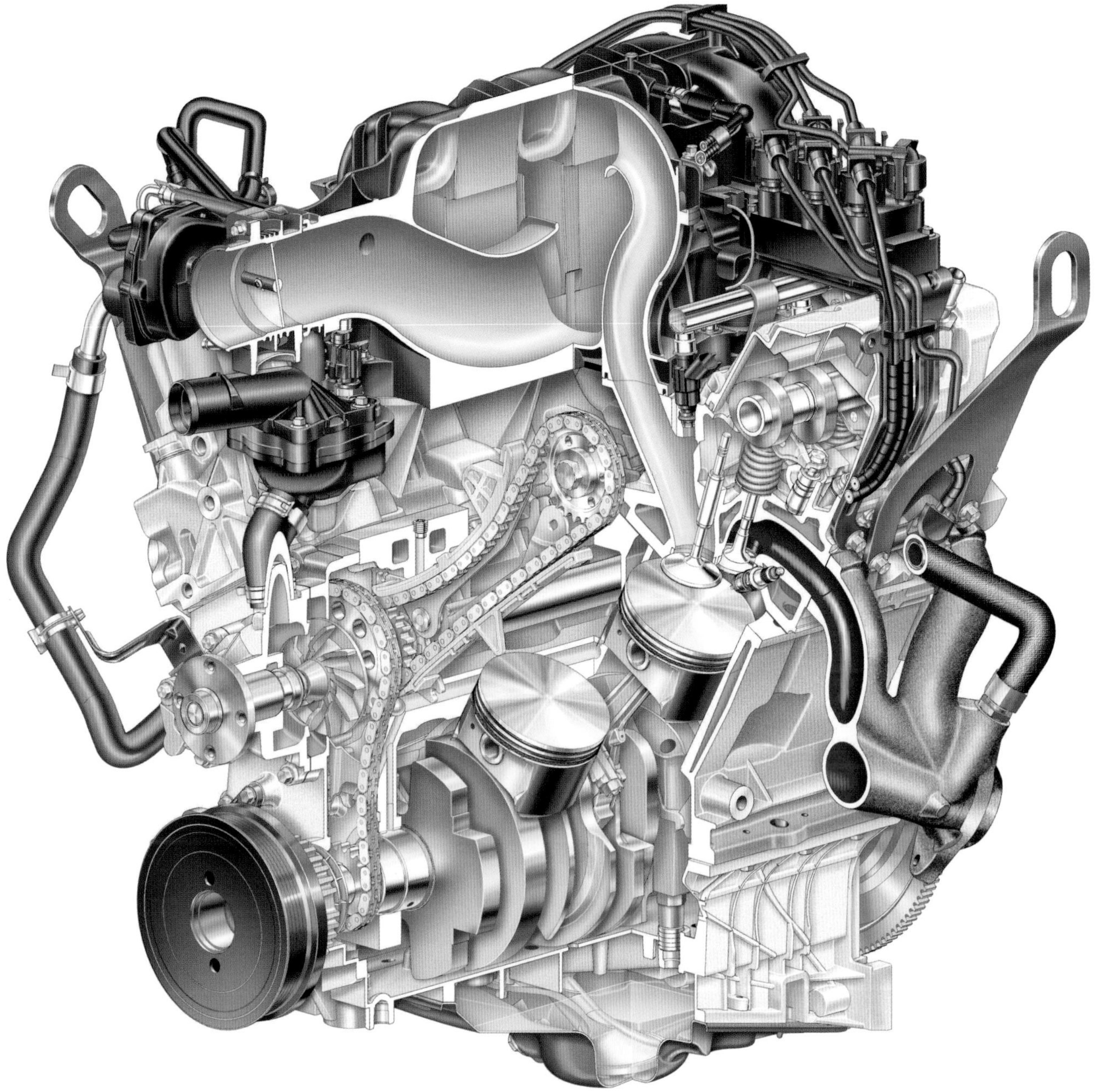

The 2005 Mustang's base V-6 made 210 horsepower, a mere 5 ponies less than the GT's 5.0-liter V-8 was delivering in 1994. This 4.0-liter SOHC engine featured aluminum cylinder heads on a cast-iron block.

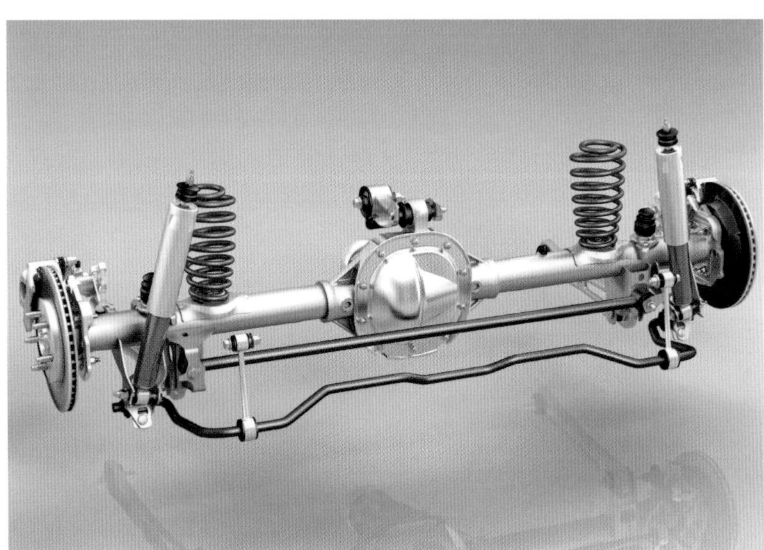

Above: Engineers resisted the temptation to use independent rear suspension (like the SVT Cobra had incorporated from 1999 to 2004) beneath the 2005 Mustang, opting instead to stick with the tried-and-true solid axle in back. A Panhard rod was attached for more precise lateral control of that axle.

Right: MacPherson struts continued to be the norm up front but were now bolted up on the bottom end to lightweight-yet-thoroughly-stiff reverse-L control arms. Rack-and-pinion steering carried over from 2004.

The 2005 GT was the first Mustang to offer 300 standard horsepower. The latest development in Ford's modular engine family, this 4.6-liter SOHC V-8 featured three valves per cylinder—two intakes, one exhaust. The plenum cover here was part of the GT Appearance package that debuted for the 2007 model year.

Right: Modern and nostalgic at the same time, the 2005 Mustang GT interior was enhanced further with the Color Accent Package, which added leather appointments in charcoal and red.

Opposite: A heated rear window and power side glass (with one-touch up on the driver's side) also were standard for the 2005 Mustang. *Mike Mueller*

"We talked to a lot of Mustang owners as we were developing this program," explained Thai-Tang. "They are a very passionate group, and a lot of them told us—very strongly—that the all-new Mustang had to have a solid rear axle."

Even with its old-school live axle in back, the 2005 Mustang's chassis ranked as the best pony car foundation yet. Overall, this superior platform measured 31 percent stiffer compared to the SN95 structure it replaced, and its radical redesign meant this really was the first truly new Mustang since 1979. The original SN95 Mustang may have looked fresh on top in 1994, but it still rolled on what was little more than a modified Fox chassis. Save for its various nostalgic touches, Ford's latest, greatest Mustang carried no leftovers. Guess you can teach an old horse new tricks.

2005

In the beginning, the Mustang was based on the Falcon's existing platform. Then came the Pinto-based foundation for the Mustang II in 1974, followed by the Fairmont-sourced Fox chassis beneath the 1979 redesign. For 2005, we had the first truly new Mustang platform, a ridiculously rigid unit-body structure created specifically for Ford's latest pony car using only a handful of components borrowed from existing parts bins spread around the corporation's global product lines.

According to Hau Thai-Tang, the new platform's convertible rendition had 100 percent more torsional stiffness compared to its 2004 forerunner.

2005

Model Availability	Two-door fastback, two-door convertible
Wheelbase	107.1 inches
Length	187.6 inches
Width	73.9 inches
Height	54.5 inches, fastback;
	55.7 inches, convertible
Curb Weight	3,300 pounds, V-6 manual; 3,345 pounds, V-6 automatic; 3,450 pounds, GT manual; 3,500 pounds, GT automatic
Base Price	Ranged from $18,785 to $27,400
Track	62.3 inches front, 62.5 inches rear
Wheels	16x7 (V-6), 17x8 (GT)
Tires	P215/65SR16 (V-6), P235/55WR17 (GT)
Suspension	Reverse-L independent MacPherson strut with stabilizer bar in front; three-link solid axle with coil springs, Panhard rod, and stabilizer bar (GT only) in back
Steering	Power-assisted rack and pinion (15.7:1 ratio)
Brakes	Four-wheel discs; ABS standard on GT, optional on V-6
Engine	210-horsepower 4.0-liter (245-ci) SOHC V-6 with aluminum heads, base model; 300-horsepower all-aluminum 4.6-liter (281-ci) SOHC V-8 with three valves per cylinder, GT
Bore and Stroke	3.95x3.32 inches (V-6), 3.55x3.51 inches (V-8)
Compression	9.7:1 (V-6), 9.8:1 (V-8)
Fuel Delivery	Sequential electronic fuel injection (66-millimeter single-bore throttle body, V-6; 55-millimeter twin-bore body, V-8)
Transmission	Five-speed manual, standard (T-5, V-6; Tremec 3650, GT); five-speed automatic, optional
Axle Ratio	3.31:1 (V-6), 3.55:1 (GT)
Production	159,587

Right: Shared with the Ford Ranger and Explorer, the latest Mustang's 4.0-liter SOHC V-6 featured electronic throttle control and a composite intake setup exclusive to the pony car application. *Mike Mueller*

Below: In 2006, the Pony Package added a bit of GT flair to the latest-generation V-6 Mustang. This option added fog lamps up front, 17-inch painted aluminum wheels at the corners, and a spoiler in back.

Opposite: The Standard, Deluxe, and Premium pecking order continued for the new Mustang in 2005. Shown here is a 2006 Deluxe coupe, which featured 16-inch bright machined-aluminum wheels and an AM/FM stereo with CD player and four speakers as standard equipment. The 2006 Premium package added chrome spinners to the wheels and superseded the Deluxe's stereo with the mondo Shaker 500 Audio System, which featured eight speakers and MP3 capability.

All this added strength, for both coupe and convertible, meant various things: increased safety, decreased NVH, and improved handling thanks to more precise suspension tuning. Further enhancing the safety aspect was a front structure specially designed to absorb frontal impacts and dissipate threatening forces before they reached the reinforced safety-cage passenger compartment.

"This all-new chassis design does everything better—accelerate, turn, stop—while isolating unwanted noise and making the most of the powerful, new three-valve engine," said Product Creation Group Vice President Phil Martens about the 2005 Mustang. Up front, the new pony's MacPherson struts incorporated high-strength, lightweight coil springs and innovative reverse-L control arms on the bottom end that dampened road shocks better than A-arm or wishbone layouts. In back, the beefed-up 8.8-inch rear axle was held firmly in place by three control arms (one each below at the axle's opposite ends, one atop the differential housing) and a lightweight, tubular Panhard rod, the latter unit added to keep tabs on unwanted lateral motions.

An improved rack-and-pinion unit handled steering chores, while brakes were traditional four-wheel discs with vacuum-controlled power assist. Rotor sizes increased all around for both V-6 and V-8 models, and a new four-channel anti-lock braking system was standard for the latter, optional for the former. Both models used the same 11.8-inch rotors in back, but the GT's front rotors measured 12.4 inches, compared to 11.5 for the V-6. Like ABS, traction control was standard for the GT, optional for the V-6.

The new 210-horsepower V-6 for the 2005 Mustang was a 4.0-liter SOHC unit with a cast-iron cylinder block and aluminum low-profile heads. Made completely of aluminum, the GT's 300-horse 4.6-liter SOHC modular V-8 featured a deep-skirt block that weighed 75 pounds less than its iron counterpart in Ford's conventional 4.6-liter V-8. Its three-valve heads were similar to those seen previously on the 2004 F-150 pickup's 5.4-liter V-8. High-tech additions beneath the 2005 Mustang's hood included electronic throttle control for both engines (a first for the breed) and variable camshaft timing (VCT) for the GT engine, the latter representing the first time this fuel-saving, performance-conscious idea had appeared in an American rear-wheel-drive V-8 application.

Yet another first for the Mustang, a five-speed automatic transmission was optional behind either engine. This close-ratio 5R55S electronic unit was used previously in the Thunderbird and Lincoln LS. Standard behind the V-6 was a Tremec T-5 five-speed manual with a 3.35:1 low gear. A more rugged Tremec 3650 five-speed, with a 3.38:1 low, was standard for the GT.

Additional attractions in 2005 included really trick optional illumination inside. Incorporated into the nostalgic analog instrumentation—when the Interior Upgrade Package was added—was the industry's first color-configurable lighting system, which used green, blue, and red diodes to project a wide range of colors onto the instruments' faces through light piping. These shades could be mixed and matched by the driver, producing more than 125 different backgrounds to, as Ford put it, "suit their personality, mood, outfit or whim."

"During Mustang research clinics, we noticed that many of our customers already were customizing their interiors with different instrument panel features," explained chief Mustang electrical engineer Dean Nowicki. "The concept display was intended to offer choices, and we just decided we wanted all the colors."

If "Purple Haze" was desired, a Mustang driver could turn to the standard 80 watt stereo with single-CD player and four speakers. Two sound systems were optional, beginning with a 500-watt ear-blaster with two subwoofers in the front doors, premium speakers in back, and a six-disc CD changer with MP3 capability. On the top shelf was the mondo 1,000-watt Shaker Audiophile system with its dual 500-watt subwoofers in the trunk. Though still offering every bit as much road-rattling bass as the optional boom box stuffed into 2004 Mustang trunks, the 2005 system took up about one-third less space, meaning some luggage could actually go along for the ride this time around. 'Scuse me while I kiss the sky.

Speaking of trunk space, the larger 2005 body meant cargo capacity in back increased 13 percent to 12.3 cubic feet. Split folding rear seat backs enhanced that convenience further. Drivers too found more personal space as head and shoulder room went up by ½ inch and 1.1 inches, respectively. In back, sculptured buckets allowed passengers 1.1 inches more leg room and 1.2 inches more shoulder room.

"The tallest drivers in our customer base have not been fully happy with previous Mustangs," said package supervisor Keith Knudsen. "We've addressed that in this all-new car, while maintaining the 'cockpit feel' essential to a driver's car. But we wanted to improve comfort for passengers, too. The extra cabin space makes a world of difference on long drives."

2006

The new Mustang's drive grew longer as basically everything rolled over unchanged into 2006. Air conditioning and a CD player remained standard on all models, as did a power fabric top with heated glass for convertibles. Sixteen inch standard wheels for the base V-6, 17-inchers for the GT, were again the norm, and the Interior Upgrade Package with its MyColor instrumentation returned for an optional encore.

As in 2005, both the base Mustang and GT were offered in Deluxe and Premium trim groups, but in 2006 the base model selection was widened to include the more affordable Standard edition. To cut costs, the Standard package traded the flashy alloy wheels for conventional 16-inch rims shod in conservative wheel covers. The 2006 Deluxe V-6 Mustang featured all the Standard's regular attributes plus those 16-inch brightly machined aluminum wheels. Further additions for Premium V-6 models

2006

Model Availability	Two-door fastback, two-door convertible
Wheelbase	107.1 inches
Length	187.6 inches
Width	73.9 inches
Height	54.5 inches, fastback; 55.7 inches, convertible
Curb Weight	3,330 pounds, fastback; 3,476 pounds, GT
Base Price	Ranged from $19,115 (for Standard fastback) to $31,145 (for Premium convertible)
Track	62.3 inches front, 62.5 inches rear
Wheels	16x7 (V-6), 17x8 (GT)
Tires	P215/65R16 (V-6), P235/55ZR17 (GT)
Suspension	Reverse-L independent MacPherson strut with stabilizer bar in front; three-link solid axle with coil springs, Panhard rod, and stabilizer bar (GT only) in back
Steering	Power-assisted rack and pinion (15.7:1 ratio)
Brakes	Four-wheel discs; ABS standard on GT, optional on V-6
Engine	210-horsepower 4.0-liter (245-ci) SOHC V-6 with aluminum heads, base model; 300-horsepower all-aluminum 4.6-liter (281-ci) SOHC V-8 with three valves per cylinder, GT
Bore and Stroke	3.95x3.32 inches (V-6), 3.55x3.51 inches (V-8)
Compression	9.7:1 (V-6), 9.8:1 (V-8)
Fuel Delivery	Sequential electronic fuel injection (66-millimeter single-bore throttle body, V-6; 55-millimeter twin-bore body, V-8)
Transmission	Five-speed manual, standard (T-5, V-6; Tremec 3650, GT); five-speed automatic, optional
Axle Ratio	3.31:1 (V-6), 3.55:1 (GT)
Production	165,762

Above: A 17-inch painted aluminum wheel was standard for the 2006 GT. This 18-inch Premium aluminum rim was optional. A P235/50ZR18 tire came with this five-spoker. *Mike Mueller*

Right: Even though a topless concept car was shown off from the beginning, a new convertible didn't join the 2005 coupe until the spring of 2005. Shown here is a pair of 2006 GT ragtops. *Mike Mueller*

Left: As in 2005, the GT's three-valve, 300-horse V-8 featured variable cam timing and electronic throttle control, both firsts in the pony car field. *Mike Mueller*

Below left: As in 2005, the 2006 GT came standard with a five-speed manual transmission and a limited-slip differential. A five-speed automatic (appearing here) was optional. A Premium 2006 Mustang (shown here) also featured a six-way power driver's seat and leather upholstery. *Mike Mueller*

included the Shaker 500 audio system, a six-way power driver's seat with power lumbar support, and chrome spinners for those 16-inch alloy rims. These spinners were optional for the Deluxe cars.

As in 2005, the 2006 Deluxe GT included the 300-horse V-8, ABS four-wheel discs, traction control, 17-inch painted aluminum wheels, grille-mounted fog lamps, and a rear spoiler. Moving up to the Premium GT meant the Shaker 500 stereo and leather-trimmed sport bucket seats entered into the mix. Those leather seats were optional for all models save for the Standard V-6.

New for 2006 was an optional Pony Package for the Premium V-6 Mustang that added unique fog lamps, 17-inch painted wheels, rear spoiler, ABS brakes, and traction control. Various aluminum wheels were optional for the GT, including a bright aluminum 10-spoke rim and two 18-inch five-spokers: one painted, one polished. V-6 buyers also could've added the Exterior Sports Appearance Package, which included lower-body logo stripes and a rear deck spoiler.

2006 Shelby GT-H

The SVT-developed GT500 went on sale as a 2007 model, but it wasn't the first Shelby variant released to the public. The key phrase here is "to the public."

In early 2006, Shelby announced it would create yet another time machine, this one reminding Mustang fans of warm and fuzzy days back in 1966 when almost anyone could've dropped into a Hertz rental car office and driven away in a Shelby GT350. Shelby American that year prepared about 1,000 GT350H models specially for Hertz, and these "rent-a-racers" today are prized collectibles, to say the least. Forty years later, Shelby and Hertz teamed up again to make it possible for traveling salesmen to move about the countryside in rapid fashion. This time the rental hack was the GT-H.

In January 2006, Hertz launched its Fun Collection, a group of leisure vehicles ranging from sexy convertibles to sporty SUVs, all targeted at rental customers looking for a little excitement after flying from point A to B. Making a Shelby Mustang a member of this collection was a no-brainer, and a limited collection of about 500 GT-H rental cars became available at select major airports that spring.

"Like the original Hertz cars, the Ford Shelby GT-H will be fun to drive," said Carroll Shelby in April 2006. "We started with a terrific Mustang and modified it with some Ford go-fast parts and gave it a distinct look for Shelby-style driving. Whoever gets the opportunity to rent one of these unique cars will get an experience of a lifetime."

As in 1966, that distinctive appearance involved black paint accented with gold stripes, a Hertz tradition dating back to the 1920s. Additional identification included "Shelby GT-H" lettering in the gold rocker stripes, Hertz Edition fender emblems, Hertz Shelby GT-H sill plates, and a numbered dash plaque signed by Carroll Shelby himself. A custom Shelby Performance hood (with tie-down pins), a brushed-aluminum grille, a unique front fascia (like the upcoming California Special's, with a second grille opening across the bottom), and a set of

2006 Shelby GT-H

Model Availability	Two-door fastback only (two-door convertible version introduced for 2007)
Wheelbase	107.1 inches
Length	187.6 inches
Width	73.9 inches
Height	53 inches
Curb Weight	3,536 pounds
Rental Rates	Varied by airport: as much as $174.99 per day and between 29 and 39 cents a mile
Track	62.3 inches front, 62.5 inches rear
Wheels	17-inch five-spoke mag
Tires	235/55SR17
Suspension	Reverse-L independent MacPherson strut with stabilizer bar in front; three-link solid axle with coil springs, Panhard rod, and stabilizer bar in back
Steering	Power-assisted rack and pinion (15.7:1 ratio)
Brakes	Four-wheel discs with ABS
Engine	325-horsepower all-aluminum 4.6-liter (281-ci) SOHC V-8 with three valves per cylinder (features FR1 Power Pack)
Bore and Stroke	3.55x3.51 inches (V-8)
Compression	9.8:1
Fuel Delivery	Sequential electronic fuel injection with 90-millimeter throttle body
Transmission	Five-speed automatic only
Axle Ratio	3.55:1
Production	500

nostalgic bodyside scoops enhanced the image. Out back was a winged spoiler, something the original Hertz Shelby didn't have.

Go-fast parts consisted of various Ford Racing Performance Group components, beginning with the FR1 Power Pack, which boosted the 2006 Mustang's 4.6-liter V-8 to an estimated 325 horsepower by adding a cold air kit (with larger 90-millimeter throttle body), performance calibration for the powertrain control module, and a cat-back exhaust system with tuned mufflers that, according to Ford, emitted a "throaty sound that will make this car unmistakably a Shelby Mustang." Complementing the FR1 parts was the FR3 Handling Pack made up of lowering springs, special sway bars, a strut tower brace, and tuned dampers inspired by the FR500C racing Mustang. Bringing up the rear was a Ford Racing differential containing 3.55:1 gears.

"Any Mustang that traces its roots to a Shelby GT 350H has to boast increased performance and handling over the factory stock configuration," said Ford North American Marketing, Sales and Service Group Vice President Cisco Codina. "Ford Racing's involvement with niche performance Mustang builds like this Hertz project is a natural for us as well as for Hertz and Shelby."

The GT-H Mustang came only with an automatic transmission to hopefully limit a rental customer's excitement. According to *Car and Driver*, the GT-H could toast the quarter-mile in 13.9 seconds at 103 miles per hour. Rest to 60 miles per hour went by in 5.3 clicks, making rental returns even quicker than normally advertised.

All GT-H rental Mustangs were auctioned off after their duties at Hertz were done, with sale prices going as high as $60,000–90,000 right off the bat. Feeding the collector frenzy further was a similarly equipped and dressed-out GT-H convertible, introduced at the New York International Auto Show in April 2007. The first of these went to a Barrett-Jackson auction to help benefit the Carroll Shelby Children's Foundation and the Juvenile Diabetes Research Fund. It was hammered out for $250,000.

It cost quite a bit less to take a 2007 GT-H droptop out for a rental spin. Again, production of these gold-striped, black-painted beauties was limited to 500, all of which also were slated for the auction block at year's end.

2007

The Mustang's Deluxe/Premium pecking order returned for 2007 (the Standard package was dropped), and a digital audio jack became standard inside. Optional heated front seats became available for all models except the Shelby GT500, which was joined this year by the less brutal Shelby

2007

Model Availability	Two-door fastback, two-door convertible
Length	187.6 inches
Width	73.9 inches
Height	54.5 inches, fastback; 55.7 inches, convertible
Curb Weight	3,330 pounds, fastback; 3,476 pounds, GT
Base Price	Ranged from $19,250 (for base Deluxe fastback) to $31,630 (for Premium GT convertible)
Track	62.3 inches front, 62.5 inches rear
Wheels	16-inch machined aluminum, standard (V-6); 17-inch painted aluminum, standard (GT)
Tires	P215/65R16, standard (V-6); P235/55ZR17, standard (GT)
Suspension	Reverse-L independent MacPherson strut with stabilizer bar in front; three-link solid axle with coil springs, Panhard rod, and stabilizer bar (GT only) in back
Steering	Power-assisted rack and pinion (15.7:1 ratio)
Brakes	Four-wheel discs; ABS standard on GT, optional on V-6
Engine	210-horsepower 4.0-liter (245-ci) SOHC V-6 with aluminum heads, base model; 300-horsepower all-aluminum 4.6-liter (281-ci) SOHC V-8 with three valves per cylinder, GT
Bore and Stroke	3.95x3.32 inches (V-6), 3.55x3.51 inches (V-8)
Compression	9.7:1 (V-6), 9.8:1 (V-8)
Fuel Delivery	Sequential electronic fuel injection (66-millimeter single-bore throttle body, V-6; 55-millimeter twin-bore body, V-8)
Transmission	Five-speed manual, standard (T-5, V-6; Tremec 3650, GT); five-speed automatic, optional
Axle Ratio	3.31:1 (V-6), 3.55:1 (GT)
Production	174,417

A 2007 GT with manual transmission came standard with a 3.55:1 limited-slip rear axle, while 3.31:1 gears were standard for automatic transmission models. A limited-slip differential was optional with the latter. Stainless-steel dual exhausts were included in the GT deal too.

Above: The 2007 Mustang convertible featured a Z-fold top that drops down into a low-profile position that took up noticeably less space than the folding roof on the topless 2004 model.

Right: Yet another time machine, the California Special, appeared in 2007. Like its 1968 ancestor, the new GT/CS Mustang featured rear-quarter scoops and bodyside striping. Its exclusive front fascia incorporated a chin spoiler that extends downward more than 1.5 inches compared to the GT's facade. *Mike Mueller*

Opposite: Dark Charcoal leather-trimmed seats (with either Dove or Parchment leather inserts) came standard inside the 2007 California Special. *Mike Mueller*

Officially announced in 2007 Mustang brochures were the various Ford Racing Performance Group's performance enhancements.

GT. Ford also dusted off another old Mustang image for 2007, the California Special, a package offered only for the GT.

Like the original from 1968, the new California Special featured high-profile bodyside stripes and rear quarter side scoops. Also included in the deal were 18-inch polished-aluminum wheels, unique front and rear fascias, bright exhaust tips, Dark Charcoal leather-trimmed seats with Dove or Parchment inserts, and floormats with bright badging. Price for this optional retro dress-up was $1,895.

New too for 2007, the GT Appearance Package could've been combined with the California Special option to really turn heads. Included were a bold hood scoop, bright exhaust tips, and an engine cover featuring the traditional running horse logo. The Pony and Exterior Sport Appearance Packages both returned to dress up the V-6 Mustang with a touch of GT excitement.

Officially announced in 2007 Mustang brochures were the various Ford Racing Performance Group's performance enhancements. The Power Package and Handling Pack as used on the GT-H Shelby were listed, as was the FR Drag Pack, which consisted of a cold-air intake kit, 4.10:1 rear gears (3.73:1 with an automatic transmission), shorty headers, a super short-throw shifter, a performance oil filter, and premium fuel engine calibration.

2007 Shelby GT

Those Ford Racing parts came in especially handy at the Shelby Automobiles shop in Las Vegas again, in this case for a modified Mustang made available for sale to the general public—and this time with a manual transmission. Announced in August 2006, the Shelby GT debuted as a 2007 model for pony fans who didn't want to wait around for the next auction. Or weren't willing to shell out the big bucks the GT-H Mustangs were beckoning.

"We have been overwhelmed at the number of people who want to buy a version of the Shelby GT-H," explained Carroll Shelby. "The Shelby GT will deliver the power and balanced handling of the Shelby GT-H, but with more performance potential, especially due to the available manual transmission."

That's right; the 2007 Shelby GT was offered with either the five-speed automatic or a Hurst-shifted five-speed manual. Most other GT-H mechanicals carried over for the Shelby GT, save for wheels and tires. While the 2006 Shelby GT-H rolled on 17-inch five-spokes, the 2007 GT was fitted with 18-inch five-spokes. Ford also officially certified the FR-enhanced 4.6L V-8 at 319 horsepower for 2007. In addition, while a 2006 GT-H renter wasn't allowed to de-activate traction control (for rather obvious pre-emptive reasons), the Shelby GT's switch, like those on the GT500 and garden-variety GTs, was fully functional, allowing a driver to roast the weenies to his or her heart's content.

2007 Shelby GT

Model Availability	Two-door fastback only
Wheelbase	107.1 inches
Length	187.6 inches
Width	73.9 inches
Height	54 inches
Curb Weight	3,536 pounds
Base Price	$36,970
Track	62.3 inches front, 62.5 inches rear
Wheels	18x8 cast-aluminum five-spoke mag
Tires	235/50ZR18 BFGoodrich g-Force T/A
Suspension	Reverse-L independent MacPherson strut with stabilizer bar in front; three-link solid axle with coil springs, Panhard rod, and stabilizer bar in back
Steering	Power-assisted rack and pinion (15.7:1 ratio)
Brakes	Four-wheel discs with ABS
Engine	319-horsepower all-aluminum 4.6-liter (281-ci) SOHC V-8 with three valves per cylinder (features FR1 Power Pack)
Bore and Stroke	3.55x3.51 inches (V-8)
Compression	9.8:1
Fuel Delivery	Sequential electronic fuel injection with 90-millimeter throttle body
Transmission	Five-speed manual or five-speed automatic
Axle Ratio	3.55:1
Production	500

Above: Unlike the black-only, gold-striped GT-H, the 2007 Shelby GT was offered in two colors (black or white) with silver stripes. *Mike Mueller*

Left: The Shelby GT-H could only be rented through Hertz in 2006, to the dismay of many potential customers who preferred to own one of these gold-striped black beauties. Their demands were met in 2007, when Shelby Automobiles rolled out its Shelby GT. Most everything, save for the hood and wheels, carried over from the GT-H to the new Shelby, including the FR-enhanced 4.6-liter V-8. *Mike Mueller*

"We have been overwhelmed at the number of people who want to buy a version of the Shelby GT-H," explained Carroll Shelby.

Output for the GT-H's V-8 was estimated at 325 horses in 2006. The same engine in the 2007 Shelby GT was officially rated at 319 horsepower. *Mike Mueller*

No rear wing was attached to the GT, and its hood was a standard Mustang's aluminum unit with a riveted-on scoop in place of the GT-H's bulging Shelby lid. Additional differences involved paint choices. The 2007 Shelby GT, offered only in full-roofed form, was available in white or black with silver metallic stripes. White models wore polished wheels, while their black running mates featured black wheel centers. Unlike the GT500, the GT-H and Shelby GT were not SVT-tagged models.

2008

Ford's Mustang remained outstanding in its field all alone through 2007. Then along came a new challenger—literally—after the Dodge boys brought back the good ol' pony car they'd built all-too-briefly from 1970 to 1974. Offered only in Hemi-powered SRT8 form during its first year back on the market, Dodge's reborn 2008 Challenger mimicked Dearborn's latest Mustang redesign with its unmistakable retro look. Once again, time travel seemed wholly possible, not to mention an even quicker trip. Standard for the certainly sexy SRT8 were 425 wild horses and independent rear suspension.

Yet as hot-looking and hard-charging as the new Challenger was, it still had a long way to go to catch the established segment champion, which required little re-grooming to continue turning heads with ease in 2008. No major changes were noted, at least at a glance. New inside were standard side airbags for all models (V-6, V-8, Deluxe, and Premium) to help make an already super safe machine even more occupant friendly in the event of a T-bone accident. Carrying over as part of Ford's 5-Star crash-rated Personal Safety System were dual-stage front air bags, safety belt pretensioners, a weight sensing system for the front passenger seat, and crash severity sensing. A new-for-2008 option, high-intensity discharge (HID) headlights, also helped make nighttime ventures a little less scary.

Driving enjoyment in the dark was enhanced further as available ambient lighting joined the existing MyColor instrumentation option. The mind-altering $295 ambient lighting package allowed drivers to light up their footwells and front cup holders with one of seven shades: red, orange, blue, violet, green, and yellow. More than 125 illumination choices remained available in the MyColor instruments' case, still included as part of the $460 Interior Upgrade deal.

New as well on the 2008 options list were 18-inch alloy rims for V-6 Premium coupes, raising the latest Mustang's available wheel count to eight, up one from 2007. Sixteen-inchers were again standard for V-6 models, 17-inchers for the GT.

2008

Model Availability	Two-door fastback coupe, two-door convertible
Wheelbase	107.1 inches
Length	187.6 inches
Width	73.9 inches
Height	54.5 inches, coupe; 55.7 inches, convertible
Curb Weight	3,352 pounds, manual transmission V-6; 3,345 pounds, automatic V-6; 3,356 pounds, manual transmission V-8; 3,540 pounds, automatic V-8
Track	62.8 front, 63.0 rear, coupe; 62.3 front, 62.5 rear, convertible
Wheels	16x7, V-6; 17x8, GT
Tires	P215/65R16A/S, V-6; P235/55ZR17, GT
Suspension	Reverse-L independent MacPherson strut with stabilizer bar in front; three-link solid axle with coil springs, Panhard rod, and stabilizer bar (GT only) in back
Steering	Power-assisted rack and pinion (15.7:1 ratio)
Brakes	Four-wheel power discs; ABS optional (standard w/GT)
Engine	210-horsepower 4.0-liter (245 cubic inches) SOHC V-6 with aluminum heads, base model; 300-horsepower all-aluminum 4.6-liter (281 cubic inches) SOHC V-8 with three valves per cylinder, GT
Bore and Stroke	3.95x3.32 inches, V-6; 3.55x3.51 inches, V-8
Compression	9.7:1, V-6; 9.8:1 V-8
Fuel Delivery	Sequential electronic fuel injection (66mm single-bore throttle body, V-6; 55mm twin-bore body, V-8)
Transmission	Five-speed manual, standard (Tremec T5, V-6; Tremec 3650, GT); five-speed automatic, optional
Producution	111,125

Base priced at $20,880, the 2008 V-6 Premium coupe could've been further enhanced by the popular Pony Package, which among other things added fog lamps, lower bodystripes, and a rear spoiler.

As before, a vinyl top was standard for the GT convertible in 2008. A cloth top was a $230 option.

Two fresh faces also debuted in 2008: a second-edition Mustang Bullitt and the "Warriors in Pink Edition," the latter created to help raise funds for a definitely great cause, the Susan G. Komen for the Cure fight against breast cancer.

Offered for V-6 Premium coupes and convertibles, the Warriors in Pink package added pink rocker stripes, a unique grille with a chrome bezel and fog lamps, a leather-wrapped aluminum-spoke steering wheel (with contrasting pink stitching), special fender badges, charcoal leather seats, and charcoal floor mats with pink stitching. Portions of Warrior in Pink Mustang sales were slated to go to the Komen for the Cure group. Priced at $1,545, this charitable option also required the installation of the V-6 Pony Package.

Big news down in Vegas in 2008 involved the introduction of a topless Shelby GT (to accompany the carryover coupe) and an even mightier GT500, the KR edition. "The Mustang convertible is the number one selling convertible in the U.S.," said Ford Division Car Marketing manager Robert Parker in June 2007. "[And] since the Mustang program never stands still, we wanted to continue offering consumers what they want, and they told us it was a Ford Mustang Shelby GT convertible."

Ford continued its charitable support of the Susan G. Komen for the Cure breast cancer foundation in 2008 by offering its "Warriors in Pink Edition" Mustang, a limited-edition package that added various pink touches inside and out.

Right: The California Special package, again offered for coupes and convertibles, carried over into 2008. The option's price remained at $1,895.

Below: A topless Shelby GT joined its carryover coupe running mate in 2008. The Shelby GT convertible conversion package cost $11,800.

2008 Mustang Bullitt

Model Availability	Two-door fastback coupe
Wheelbase	107.1 inches
Length	188.0 inches
Width	73.9 inches
Height	55.3 inches
Curb Weight	3,536 pounds
Base Price	$31,075
Track	62.3 front, 62.5 rear
Wheels	18-inch Euro-Flange Bullitt units with charcoal satin finish
Tires	BF Goodrich P235/50ZR-18
Suspension	Reverse-L independent MacPherson strut with stabilizer bar in front; three-link solid axle with coil springs, Panhard rod, and stabilizer bar in back
Steering	Power-assisted rack and pinion
Brakes	12.4-inch vented discs, front; 11.8-inch vented discs, rear
Engine	315-horsepower 4.5-liter SOHC V-8 with open-element induction system and modified H-pipe exhausts
Bore and Stroke	3.55x3.51 inches
Compression	9.8:1
Fuel Delivery	Sequential electronic fuel injection
Transmission	Tremec TR-3650 five-speed manual
Axle Ratio	3.73:1
Production	5,773

Above: Among standard equipment for the GT Deluxe model in 2008 were traction control, a limited-slip differential, ABS brakes, foglights, and a rear spoiler. Along with those goodies, the GT Premium (shown here) also included leather upholstery and an upgraded sound system. The hood scoop was part of the optional GT Appearance Package. *Mike Mueller*

Below: A second Mustang Bullitt appeared in 2008, just in time to mark the Steve McQueen movie's 40th anniversary. Retro-style mags were again part of the Bullitt package, which cost $3,310.

Big news down in Vegas in 2008 involved the introduction of a topless Shelby GT.

"The birth of the Ford Shelby GT was so well received last year, especially by young enthusiasts, that we brought the car back for the 2008 model year," added Shelby Automobiles president Amy Boylan. "The enormous response to the Shelby GT-H convertible [also] convinced us to offer a drop top Shelby GT. And we had so many requests for blue that we decided to make it our signature color in 2008." Beneath that beautiful blue skin were more or less the same mechanicals ably demonstrated by the 319-horse Shelby GT coupe in 2007.

2008 Mustang Bullitt

Not all critics have been quick to take Ford up on its various time travel offers in recent years, implying perhaps that this trick represents a horse long beaten to death. As *AutoWeek*'s Natalie Neff explained in November 2007 concerning Dearborn's second nostalgic tribute to Steve McQueen's 1968 movie *Bullitt*, "We might just as easily dismiss [this car] as one more variation on the

"KR" stood for "King of the Road," an apt label for a pony car able to melt away the quarter-mile in an unworldly 12.1 seconds.

2008 GT500 KR

Model Availability	Two-door fastback coupe
Wheelbase	107.1 inches
Length	187.6 inches
Width	73.9 inches
Height	54.5 inches
Curb Weight	3,920 pounds
Base Price	$79,995
Track	62.3 front, 62.5 rear
Wheels	18-inch multi-spoke
Tires	Goodyear Eagle F1 (P255/45, front; P285/40, rear)
Suspension	Reverse-L independent MacPherson strut with stabilizer bar in front; three-link solid axle with coil springs, Panhard rod, and stabilizer bar in back (modified GT500; lowered and stiffened)
Steering	Power-assisted rack and pinion
Brakes	Power-assisted four-wheel vented Brembo discs
Engine	540-horsepower 5.4-liter 32-valve DOHC V-8 with Ford Racing Power Upgrade Pack
Bore and Stroke	3.552x4.165 inches
Compression	8.4:1
Fuel Delivery	Sequential electronic fuel injection with Eaton Roots-type supercharger
Transmission	Six-speed Tremec TR6060 manual
Axle Ratio	3.73:1
Production	2,300

Mustang theme among a thousand, a simple way for Ford's marketers to milk a few extra bucks from a beloved badge." But even Neff couldn't resist living in the past one more time. "The [Mustang] Bullitt offers up a vision of what it means to be purely Mustang, and wholly cool."

Like its 2001 forerunner, the too-cool-for-school 2008 Bullitt was appropriately offered in Highland Green, with black available optionally. Wheels again mimicked the five-spoke Torq-Thrust mags seen on film in 1968, only this time measuring 18 inches across, compared to 17 in 2001. Gone was the bright aluminum fuel filler door installed that year as the 2008 rendition was made more true to McQueen's rather plain-Jane, de-trimmed movie car. Along with a stock body-colored filler door, the latest Mustang Bullitt also incorporated a blank grille sans the traditional galloping pony—just like McQueen's 1968 GT. Missing too were 2001's hey-look-at-me red brake calipers, replaced by less conspicuous dark grey pieces.

Chassis tweaks included a Ford Racing strut tower brace and Performance Friction Carbon Metallic front brake pads. Limited-slip 3.73:1 gears were standard, as was a modified exhaust system consisting of an H-pipe connection and enlarged 3.5-inch polished stainless-steel tips. Much effort was made to re-create the awesome exhaust note portrayed during *Bullitt*'s equally awesome car chase, and the work apparently paid off. "Remember the sounds you daydreamed about in study hall?" asked *Car and Driver*'s Patrick Bedard. "The [Mustang] Bullitt plays them loud or soft, tracking your foot motions like the needle on an LP."

Those bellowing free-breathing pipes, working in concert with open-element cold-air induction and a revised cam, translated into 15 more horsepower for the 2008 Bullitt's 4.6-liter V-8, bringing the advertised count to 315. A five-speed Tremec gearbox handled those ponies and

Another 40-year anniversary was marked in 2008, this one honoring Carroll Shelby's "King of the Road" GT500, introduced midyear in 1968 to showcase Ford's then-new 428 Cobra Jet big-block V-8. At 540 horsepower, the 2008 GT500KR became the new leader of the high-performance pony car pack.

Left: A single GT500KR coupe was fitted with a special glass roof in 2008, and this black beauty was sent to the Barrett-Jackson auction, with proceeds going to the Juvenile Diabetes Research Foundation. This glass top would become an option for mainstream Mustangs in 2009.

Below: Various Ford Racing power parts helped boost the GT500's supercharged 5.4-liter V-8 from 500 horses to 540 for the new King of the Road Shelby GT500. The 2008 GT500KR was priced at a dizzying $79,995.

again was stirred by a stick sporting a polished 1960s-style shifter ball. Familiar bright accents inside on the dash, door handles, and foot pedals were complemented further with the GT500's sport steering wheel.

According to *Car and Driver*, if McQueen was still alive, he could've pushed the 2008 Mustang Bullitt through the quarter-mile in a smoking 13.6 seconds, topping out at 104 miles per hour. Screaming from rest to 60 miles per hour required 5 seconds flat.

2008 Shelby GT500KR

Like the Shelby GT, the GT500 also rolled over basically unchanged into 2008 and again stood as the meanest, nastiest Mustang ever with its 500 standard horsepower. But not for long. Introduced that spring at the New York Auto Show, Shelby's GT500KR raised the output bar even further to 540 horses.

"The return of the Shelby GT500KR further established Mustang as the true king of the pony car segment," proudly announced Ford marketing manager Robert Parker in March 2008. "With the unveiling of the new KR we are staying true to the promise we made our loyal Mustang fans to continue Mustang's prowess by bringing new, exciting, and more powerful Mustangs to market."

As it did 40 years before, "KR" stood for "King of the Road," an apt label for a pony car able to melt away the quarter-mile in an unworldly 12.1 seconds, hitting 115 miles per hour in the process. In 1968, Shelby's GT500KR was created to showcase Ford's new 428 Cobra Jet big-block; nearly a half century later, the name returned wrapped around a supercharged 5.4-liter V-8 fitted with a Ford Racing Power Upgrade Pack (revised ignition and throttle calibration and cold-air induction) and a denture-rattling Ford Racing exhaust system. Behind that 540-horse beast was a six-speed Tremec box controlled by a Ford Racing short-throw shifter crowned by a nostalgic white ball.

Like the GT500, its KR counterpart was developed by SVT and finished off by Shelby Automobiles in Las Vegas. Big Bembro brakes carried over from the base 500, but the KR's suspension was considerably stiffer and lowered a

"Finding a GT500KR in your garage would be like discovering Charlize Theron in your bathtub."
—Matt Stone

bit. While 20-inch wheels adorned the KR concept seen at the New York Auto Show, Shelby-designed 18-inchers went on production models. Shelby product development vice president Garry Davis also helped fashion a suitable lid for all those horses, a bulging carbon-composite hood featuring two menacing scoops reminiscent of the original KRs. Special commemorative badging marking the 40th anniversary of the 1968 GT500KR, went on the fenders and dash. Headrests also were embroidered with Carroll Shelby's signature.

"This was a great effort between Ford and Shelby Automobiles," said SVT chief designer Doug Gaffka. "The Shelby team and I were in constant contact melding Carroll's classic design cues with some modern concepts and ideas and finessing them into the design of the new KR."

All their sweat translated into almost too much to be believed in the pony car field. "Finding a GT500KR in your garage would be like discovering Charlize Theron in your bathtub," bubbled *Motor Trend*'s Matt Stone. "The KR is a rumbling rocket to drive, a sure-fire collectible, and, much like Charlize, its looks will make you perspire. Such is the privilege of royalty." If you only had a tub.

2009

Ford's basic pony package again carried over almost unchanged into 2009, as did Shelby's GT500 and GT500KR. The King of the Road paraded on without the 40th anniversary badges appropriately applied in 2008, but production plans served to further honor the original KR built four decades back. After rolling out 1,000 KRs in 2008, it was announced that another 746 would follow in 2009 to satisfy worldwide demand. Furthermore, 571 of those were intended for the domestic market, bringing the two-year U.S. total to 1,571, which was the same number of Shelby's Cobra Jet KRs introduced midyear in 1968. How sweet.

2009

Model Availability	Two-door fastback coupe, two-door convertible
Wheelbase	107.1 inches
Length	187.6 inches
Width	73.9 inches
Height	55.4 inches, coupe
Curb Weight	3,336 pounds, base V-6 coupe
Base Price	Ranged from $18,785 to $27,400
Track	62.8 front, 63 rear, coupe; 62.3 front, 62.5 rear, convertible
Wheels	16x7, V-6; 17x8, GT
Tires	P215/65R16A/S, V-6; P235/55ZR17, GT
Suspension	Reverse-L independent MacPherson strut with stabilizer bar in front; three-link solid axle with coil springs, Panhard rod, and stabilizer bar (GT only) in back
Steering	Power-assisted rack and pinion (15.7:1 ratio)
Brakes	Four-wheel power discs; ABS optional (standard w/GT)
Engine	210-horsepower 4.0-liter (245 cubic inches) SOHC V-6 with aluminum heads, base model; 300-horsepower all-aluminum 4.6-liter (281 cubic inches) SOHC V-8 with three valves per cylinder, GT
Bore and Stroke	3.95x3.32 inches, V-6; 3.55x3.51 inches, V-8
Compression	9.7:1, V-6; 9.8:1 V-8
Fuel Delivery	Sequential electronic fuel injection (66mm single-bore throttle body, V-6; 55mm twin-bore body, V-8)
Transmission	Five-speed manual, standard (Tremec T5, V-6; Tremec 3650, GT); five-speed automatic, optional
Production	46,619

Right above: Ford product planners discovered that as much as 62 percent of the sports car segment's customer base showed interest in available sun- or moon-roofs, so they created a glamorous glass roof option for the 2009 Mustang. This tinted transparent top cost $1,995.

Right below: The California Special package was again on coupes and convertibles, in 2009 (before temporarily retiring). This also was the final year for Ford's second-edition Mustang Bullitt.

Left: By 2009 the Mustang GT no longer had the pony-car market to itself. Domestic competitors boasted newer designs and bigger numbers on paper, but the balanced design and genuine value of the Mustang ensured that the original pony car would continue to win comparison tests in all the major car magazines.

Below: Introduced for 2008, Ford Racing's FR500CJ Cobra Jet drag car reappeared in 2010. Like its predecessor, the second-edition Cobra Jet was only available in white. Race-ready wheels and tires were included, as was a full roll cage and a supercharged 5.4-liter V8. FR50CJ models remained available up through 2014.

Mainstream Mustang updates included adding upgraded trim, ambient lighting, and satellite radio to the Premium models' (both V-6 and GT) standard equipment list. Commemorative badging also was created to mark the Mustang's 45th birthday, celebrated by horse lovers of all ages on April 17, 2009, in Birmingham, Alabama.

Easily most notable among new features was an optional glass roof, available atop both V-6 and GT coupes. "Mustang is an icon in our product lineup, and we are committed to keeping Mustang news fresh every year," said Derrick Kuzak, Ford's group vice president of Global Product Development. "As the automotive landscape becomes increasingly competitive, features such as a panoramic glass roof will help differentiate our products from the competition." Or at least it did as long as a Mustang buyer had an extra $1,995 to fork over.

According to Ford, this specially formulated tinted privacy panel reduced both infrared rays and interior cool-down time by 50 percent compared to unprotected automotive glass and also greatly inhibited solar radiation deterioration/discoloration of interior fabrics. An additional layer of vinyl was added to the transparent top to improve interior acoustics and resist exterior noises.

Like various ships passing in the night, the glamorous glass roof option debuted as the California Special, and Mustang Bullitt were making their farewell tours. The Shelby GT had been drydocked after its 2008 passage.

2010

Scheduled for early release in March 2009, the eagerly awaited 2010 Mustang promised to retain the existing foundation, but, according to chief nameplate engineer Paul Randall, would be rewrapped in all-new sheet metal save for the roof panel. "The goal for 2010 was to move the Mustang out of its recent retro past and into the future, still using the platform that debuted in 2004," explained *AutoWeek* senior editor Bob Gritzinger late in 2008. The roof rolled over unchanged only because the plan also called for repeating the jazzy glass-top option, still priced at an eye-opening $1,995.

Purists being purists, this restyle typically represented a cost/benefit proposition. But hardly any customers could deny that Ford's latest, greatest pony still stood as a certainly satisfying selection, as far as overall impressions were concerned. "The 2010 [Mustang] is more than a reskin," proclaimed *Modified Mustangs & Fords* editor Mark Houlahan. "[It] has so much more technology and quality and fit and finish to it that it feels like a completely new car to us."

Newfound beauty beneath that modernized skin included standard ABS and *AdvanceTrac* stability control for all models. Standard wheel sizes also increased, to 17 inches for the V-6, and 18 inches for the GT. Eighteen-inchers were optional for the V-6 Premium, 19-inchers for the GT. In all,

ten attractive alloy wheels were offered in 2010, including two SVT-capped five-spokers for the continuing GT500 coupe and convertible. Ford's voice-activated Sync multimedia integration system also became a factory-installed option.

The GT500KR didn't return for 2010, but in its absence the "base" GT500 was boosted up to 540 horsepower, filling the void nicely. While the yeoman V-6 remained at 210 horsepower, the GT's 4.6-liter V-8 was also pumped up, this time to 315 horses. New beneath the 2010 GT was the

Word came down late in 2009 that Ford's pony car would begin racing the following year on the Nationwide Series, NASCAR's second-tier circuit. A NASCAR Mustang debuted at Daytona on July 2, 2010, and ran a limited schedule from there. Based on the Sprint Cup Series' proven Car of Tomorrow (COT) chassis, this bucking bronco found full-time work in Nationwide competition in 2011.

Bullitt Mustang's enhanced chassis and big 3.5-inch exhaust tips. New on the GT options list was the TrackPack, which among other things added special SVT stabilizer bars and lower control arms, a shock tower brace, performance brake pads, 19-inch wheels, and a 3.73:1 axle.

Quarter-mile numbers, according to a *Motor Trend* test of a pre-production GT, came in at 13.7 seconds and 103.7 miles per hour. "The GT remains the pony car standard-bearer," proclaimed *Motor Trend*'s Edward Loh. "It's a fast and modern muscle car that still demands old-school respect. Detective Lieutenant Frank Bullitt would have it no other way."

Customers who preferred to pound the ground with little or no respect in 2010 could opt for Ford Racing's second edition, race-only Cobra Jet, known around the National Hot Rod Association (NHRA) circuit as the "FR500CJ." Introduced as a new model in November 2008 at Las Vegas' annual Specialty Equipment Market Association (SEMA) convention, the FR500CJ represented the first factory-built drag car from Ford since Dearborn's original race-prepped Cobra Jet Mustang debuted 40 years before. Like their 1968 super-stock ancestors, the 2008 CJ was done only in white, and limited to a 50-unit production run. Power came from a supercharged 400-horse 5.4-liter V-8 backed by a six-speed Tremec manual transmission. A full roll cage was included, as were racing wheels and tires. Upgrades for the 2010 FR500CJ included a strengthened roll cage; improved suspension; lightweight, low-drag brakes; an available automatic transmission; and an optional 475-horsepower Super Cobra Jet 5.4-liter V-8 topped by a Whipple blower.

"The 2008 Cobra Jet was a great car, it did everything we wanted it to," said Ford's North American Motorsports director Brian Wolfe while unveiling its successor at the 2010 SEMA show. "We're really proud of the car, but then again we're always trying to make the next one better. With the 2010 Cobra Jet, we had the luxury of a longer development cycle and the result is absolutely stunning. We are all excited to see the new Cobra Jet in [NHRA] competition."

Also helping wave the blue-oval banner high in competitive circles in 2010 was another Ford Racing product, the Boss 302R, created to both further the successful legacy established by the

2010

Model Availability	Two-door fastback, two-door convertible
Wheelbase	107.1 inches
Length	188.1 inches
Width	73.9 inches
Height	55.6 inches, coupe; 56.1, convertible
Curb Weight	3,572 pounds, GT coupe
Track	62.3 front, 62.9 rear
Wheels	17-inch, V-6; 18-inch, GT
Tires	P215/80R17, V-6; P23550WR18, GT front; P245/50WR18, GT rear
Suspension	Reverse-L independent MacPherson strut with stabilizer bar in front; three-link solid axle with coil springs, Panhard rod, and stabilizer bar in back
Steering	Power-assisted rack and pinion (15.7:1 ratio); AdvanceTrac electronic steering control, standard
Brakes	Four-wheel power discs with ABS & all-speed traction control
Engine	210-horsepower 4.0-liter (245 cubic inches) SOHC V-6 with aluminum heads, base model; 315-horsepower all-aluminum 4.6-liter (281 cubic inches) SOHC V-8 with three valves per cylinder, GT
Bore and Stroke	3.95x3.32 inches, V-6; 3.55x3.51 inches, V-8
Compression	9.7:1, V-6; 9.8:1 V-8
Fuel Delivery	Sequential electronic fuel injection (66mm single-bore throttle body, V-6; 55mm twin-bore body, V-8)
Transmission	Five-speed manual, standard (Tremec T5, V-6; Tremec 3650, GT); five-speed automatic, optional
Production	81,0588

Above: Ford Racing introduced yet another race-prepped pony car, the Boss 302R (left) in December 2009 to help mark the 40th anniversary of Parnelli Jones' 1970 Trans-Am championship, won at the wheel of Ford's original Boss Mustang. Jones' 1970 Boss is represented at right. The 302R served as a rolling test bed for the upcoming street-legal Boss 302, introduced as a 2012 model.

Above right: Reportedly all body panels, save for the roof, were refashioned for the 2010 Mustang (right). New, too, was standard ABS and AdvanceTrak stability control. At the upper left is a 2008 GT for contrast.

FR500C and honor unforgettable racehorses of old. Announced in December 2009, this turn-key, track-ready pony car appeared just in time to mark the 40th anniversary of Parnelli Jones' 1970 Trans-Am title at the wheel of Ford's first Boss Mustang.

"The original Boss 302 was a championship-winning legend and the new Mustang Boss 302R will carry on the tradition," explained Ford Motorsports' Jamie Allison. "The [FR500] road-racing Mustangs and the FR500CJ for drag racing have proven to be great cars for our customers, helping teams win races and championships. We believe that the Boss 302R will provide that same sort of competitive product for our customers with the tradition you can only get from Ford Racing."

Two versions were offered: the basic Boss 302R and the more radical Grand-Am-homologated Boss 302R1, five of which were delivered in time to enter the season-opening Grand-Am event at Daytona in January 2010. Ford promised a production run of 50 Boss 302R Mustangs (as 2011 models), with additional dealer deliveries commencing during 2010's third quarter. All were powered by the 5.0-liter V-8 slated for a regular-production introduction beneath 2011 GT hoods.

Late in 2010, Ford also announced the upcoming debut of a born-again Boss 302 for the street (as a 2012 model) and availability of a second race-only model, the 440-horse Boss 302S, called "an entry-level, purpose-built, road-racing Mustang" by Ford. "Enthusiasts who purchase the Boss 302S will be competitive in both the World Challenge GTS and the NASA American Iron Series," said Ford Racing engineering manager Mark Wilson. "We look forward to adding their names to the Boss 302's racing history."

2011

In 2011, seriously updated power sources hooked with 2010's restyled body. New for base models was the Lincoln MKS/MKT's thoroughly modern 3.7-liter DOHC V-6 with Twin Independent Variable Camshaft Timing (Ti-VCT). Rated at 305 horsepower, this amazing mighty mite was every bit as frugal on fuel as it was rough on the rear treads. Ford reports claimed ratings of 18 to19 miles per gallon in the city, 29 to 30 highway, compared to 16 to 18 and 24 to 26 for the old 4.0-liter SOHC six.

Full dual exhausts, just like the GT's, brought up the 2011 V-6 Mustang's tail. And even more Gran Turismo feel was available by way of the V-6 Performance Package, which added GT suspension and brake components, 3.31:1 gears, 19-inch wheels wearing Pirelli rubber, a front strut tower brace, and revised stability controls.

Even bigger news awaited GT buyers, who found an old friend beneath the hottest 2011 Mustang's hood. Yes, Virginia, the "five-oh" was back, as promised, in place of the tiring 4.6-liter V-8 to remind Mustangers of the good ol' late eighties,

2011

Model Availability	Two-door fastback, two-door convertible
Wheelbase	107.1 inches
Length	188.1 inches
Width	73.9 inches
Height	55.6 inches, coupe; 55.8 inches, convertible
Curb Weight	3,435 pounds, V6 coupe; 3,586 pounds, V6 convertible; 3,605 pounds, GT coupe; 3,720 pounds, GT convertible
Track	62.3 front, 62.9 rear
Wheels (V6)	17x7.0 silver-painted aluminum, std; 17x7.0 dark-painted aluminum w/machined face, optional; 18x8.0 aluminum (in various finishes), optional; 19x8.5 painted aluminum, optional (w/Performance Package)
Wheels (GT)	18x8.0 silver-painted aluminum, std; 18x8.5 aluminum in various finishes, optional; 19x8.5 aluminum, optional (w/California Special); 19x9.0 aluminum, optional (w/Brembo Brake Package)
Tires	P225/60R17 A/S BF Goodrich Radial T/A, std. w/manual trans; P215/65R17 A/S Michelin Energy Saver, std. w/automatic trans std.; P235/50ZR18 A/S Pirelli PZero, optional; P255/40R19 Pirelli PZero Summer-Only, optional (w/Performance Package), V6
Suspension	Reverse-L independent MacPherson strut with stabilizer bar in front; three-link solid axle with coil springs, Panhard rod and stabilizer bar in back; AdvanceTrac electronic stability control, std
Steering	Electric power-assisted (EPAS) rack and pinion (15.7:1 ratio)
Brakes:	Four-wheel power discs with ABS, Four-wheel power-assisted vented discs with 4-sensor, 4-channel ABS & all-speed traction control
Fuel capacity	16 gallons
Engine	305-horsepower 3.7-liter 24-valve DOHC TiVCT V6, base model; 412-horepower 5.0-liter 32-valve DOHC TiVCT V8, GT
Bore & stroke	3.76 x3.41 inches, V6; 3.629x3.649 inches, GT V8
Compression	10.5:1, V6; 11.0:1, GT V8
Fuel Delivery	Sequential electronic fuel injection
Fuel Capacity	16 gallons
Transmission	Six-speed Getrag manual, std.; six-speed automatic with grade-assist "hill mode," optional
Rear axle	2.73:1 limited-slip, std for V6; 3.31:1 limited-slip, std for GT
Production	69,901

This is the view Camaro buyers, not to mention their Challenger comrades, began seeing all too often in 2011. Base prices for the 2011 GT coupe and convertible were $29,645 and $34,645, respectively.

Right: With more standard muscle than its GT running mate offered in 2005, the 2011 V-6 coupe gave many Camaro customers second thoughts. True GT-style dual exhausts brought up the V-6 model's rear.

Below left: Not lost in the limelight cast upon the reborn 5.0-liter V-8 was the 2011 Mustang's equally new V-6, a 305-horsepower 24-valve DOHC wonder borrowed from Lincoln.

Below right: A familiar friend returned for 2011 as the latest GT showcased Ford's "Coyote" V-8, a 412-horse wild animal displacing 5.0 liters, same as the High Output small-blocks that were all the rage on the street scene during the eighties and early nineties.

early nineties. Sharing only its displacement label with its fabled five-liter forerunners, Ford's all-aluminum "Coyote" V-8 relied on the same Ti-VCT technology at the heart of the 3.7L V-6 to help it make 412 definitely healthy horses—just what the doctor ordered, considering Chevy's new Camaro SS featured 426 horsepower. Equally new six-speed transmissions, both manual and automatic, backed up both the 5.0-liter Coyote and the 3.7-liter V-6.

Additional standard updates for 2011 included added noise insulation, a switch to electric (instead of hydraulic) power steering, and Ford's "MyKey" system. Introduced late in 2008 and first offered as standard equipment on the 2010 Focus, MyKey was meant to give ma and/or pa a little peace of mind by allowing them to limit both speed and audio levels whenever their precious and/or precocious offspring went unsupervised behind the wheel. MyKey technology also reminded inexperienced drivers to use their seatbelts, announced low fuel levels earlier, and could be programmed to chime at various rising speed increments. According to Ford, only 36 percent of young drivers polled objected to such parental controls. Sure.

> Yes, Virginia, the "five-oh" was back, as promised.

MyKey proved especially good at preserving parents' sanity whenever junior begged to borrow dad's 2011 GT500, now featuring 550 horsepower. Making those ten extra ponies was an all-aluminum 5.4-liter V-8 created to help reduce the unwanted weight perched over the front wheels of previous

Shelby Mustangs. By cutting loose about 100 pounds under the hood and slightly lowering the suspension, engineers were able to notably improve the handling of the latest GT500.

Adding the new SVT performance package enhanced the GT500 attraction even further. Along with exclusive stripes and a unique rear spoiler, this option included revised springs and shocks, Goodyear Eagle F1 Supercar G:2 rubber on forged aluminum wheels (measuring 19 inches in front, 20 inches in back) and 3.73:1 rear gears. According to *Car and Driver*, the sum of these parts equaled 0 to 60 miles per hour in 4.1 seconds, the quarter-mile in 12.4 clicks at 117 miles per hour. "The combination of less weight, more power, better tires, and a revised suspension turns the [2011] Shelby into the car it always should have been," concluded *Car and Driver*'s Mark Gillies.

2011 GT350

In January 2010, at the annual Barrett-Jackson auction extravaganza in Scottsdale, Arizona, Shelby American officials unveiled their upcoming 45th-anniversary GT350 Mustang, slated to debut as a 2011 model. Unlike the existing GT500, which was built by Ford under a licensing agreement, the commemorative GT350 was a "post-title upgrade" created at the Shelby American plant in Las Vegas. A customer first had to plunk down more than $33,000 for a white-painted 2011 GT coupe, which was then delivered to Nevada directly by Ford or transported personally by said buyer.

Shelby's GT350 transformation cost another $33,995 for a supercharged version, $26,995 for a similar model sans blower. In the former's case, forced induction was supplied by a Ford Racing-sourced Whipple supercharger, which helped boost the GT's new 5.0-liter V-8 to 525 horsepower. An even more radical 5.0-liter also was available, rated at a warrantee-voiding 624 horses.

Familiar Guardsman Blue stripes (vinyl or painted) were predictably included in the deal, as was a long list of exclusive cosmetic treatments and appropriate identification inside and out. Unique fascias went on at both ends, as did specially trimmed taillights in back. GT350 rocker panels incorporated brake-cooling ductwork, and those brakes were six-piston Baer discs in front, ERADISPEED-upgraded units in back. Ford Racing suspension components went underneath, along with an unmistakable Borla center-exiting exhaust system. At the corners were 19-inch alloy rims supplied by Cragar.

An identical GT350 package (without "45th anniversary" identification, of course) was offered for 2012, this time for both coupe and convertible GT Mustangs; color choices were expanded, with the traditional white joined by red, blue, and gold-accented black. The entire Mustang paint palette then became available in 2013, before Shelby American announced the end of the road for its GT350 upgrade.

Vegas-based Shelby American introduced its GT350 "post-title upgrade" (left) as a 2011 model in January 2010, 45 years after Carroll Shelby's original GT350 (right) appeared. In both cases, the only available exterior color was white. *courtesy Shelby American*

2011 GT350

Model availability	Two-door fastback coupe
Wheelbase	107.1 inches
Length	187.6 inches
Width	73.9 inches (discounting mirrors)
Curb weight	3,816 pounds
Wheels	19-inch Cragar
Tires	Goodyear
Suspension	Standard GT layout modified with Shelby/Ford Racing modifications (performance springs, struts, and sway bars; Shelby adjustable camber/caster plate kit)
Steering	Selectable-effort electric power-assisted rack and pinion
Brakes	Power-assisted four-wheel discs w/ABS & all-speed traction control (Shelby/Baer 6-piston front kit w/exclusive nickel-anodized finish; Shelby Baer ERADISPEED rotors and brake pad upgrade in back; front & rear brake ducting and cooling kit
Engine	5.0-liter 32-valve DOHC TiVCT V8 with Shelby/Borla center-exit exhaust system (available with or without Ford Racing Whipple supercharger)
Bore & stroke	3.629x3.649 inches
Fuel delivery	Sequential electronic fuel injection w/Ford Racing Whipple supercharger
Output (supercharged)	525 hp (624 hp for "R-tune" version)
Fuel capacity	16 gallons
Transmission	Gertrag six-speed manual

2012

The Boss 302's reappearance far and away constituted the biggest news this year as the base V-6 Mustang and GT rolled over essentially unchanged from 2011. Arguably most notable among the 2012 updates was adjustable effort settings for the GT's electric power steering, which was introduced the previous year. Dual-illuminated vanity mirrors became standard on all models, as did a universal garage door opener for Premium cars. Lava Red Metallic replaced Sterling Gray Metallic on 2012's palette, and optional Recaro bucket seats became available for the still-strong GT500.

Although no Cobra Jets were built for 2011, Ford Racing did bring the FR500CJ drag package back in 2012, again limiting production to 50 units. Color choices, on the other hand, expanded as Grabber Blue and Race Red joined the rollover Performance White finish.

Initially available for 2007–09 Mustangs, the California Special package returned for both GT coupes and convertibles in 2011, then rolled over into 2012, 2013, and 2014. Like the previous year's rendition, the 2012 GT/CS (shown here) featured a special grille, appropriate body side striping and 19-inch wheels shod in P245/45R tires.

2012

Model availability	Two-door fastback, two-door convertible
Wheelbase	107.1 inches
Length	188.1 inches
Width	73.9 inches (discounting mirrors)
Height	55.6 inches, coupe; 55.8 inches, convertible
Curb weight	3,453 pounds, V6 coupe; 3,586 pounds, V6 convertible; 3,605 pounds, GT coupe; 3,720 pounds, GT convertible
Track (front/rear, in inches)	62.3/62.9
Wheels (V6)	17x7.0 silver-painted aluminum, std; 17x7.0 dark-painted aluminum w/ machined face, optional; 18x8.0 aluminum (in various finishes), optional; 19x8.5 painted aluminum, optional (w/Performance Package)
Wheels (GT)	18x8.0 silver-painted aluminum, std; 18x8.5 aluminum in various finishes, optional; 19x8.5 aluminum, optional (w/California Special); 19x9.0 aluminum, optional (w/Brembo Brake Package)
Tires (V6)	P225/60R17 A/S BF Goodrich Radial T/A, std; P235/50ZR18 A/S Pirelli PZero, optional; P255/40R19 Pirelli PZero Summer-Only, optional (w/ Performance Package)
Tires (GT)	P235/50R18, std; P245/45ZR19 Pirelli PZero, optional (California Special); P255/40R19 Pirelli PZero, optional
Suspension	Reverse-L independent MacPherson strut with stabilizer bar in front; three-link solid axle with coil springs, Panhard rod and stabilizer bar in back; AdvanceTrac electronic stability control, std
Steering	Selectable-effort electric power-assisted (EPAS) rack & pinion (15.7:1 ratio)
Brakes	Four-wheel power-assisted vented discs with 4-sensor, 4-channel ABS & all-speed traction control
Engine	305-horsepower 3.7-liter 24-valve DOHC TiVCT V6, base model; 412-horepower 5.0-liter 32-valve DOHC TiVCT V8, GT
Bore & stroke	3.76 x3.41 inches, V6; 3.629x3.649 inches, GT V8
Compression	10.5:1, V6; 11.0:1, GT V8
Fuel delivery	Sequential electronic fuel injection
Fuel capacity	16 gallons
Transmission	Six-speed Getrag manual, std.; six-speed automatic with grade-assist "hill mode," optional
Rear axle	2.73:1 limited-slip, std for V6; 3.31:1 limited-slip, std for GT
Production	88,392

2012 Boss 302

Ford officially announced the Boss 302's return on August 13, 2010, at the legendary Laguna Seca road course outside Monterey, California, but opted to not release this new pony to the public before its time. "Boss is a hallowed word around here, and we couldn't put that name on a new Mustang until we were sure everything was in place to make this car a worthy successor," explained Mustang chief engineer Dave Pericak. "We were either going to do it right or not do it at all—no one on the team was going to let Boss become a sticker and wheel package."

"The decision to build a modern Boss was not entered into lightly," added Global Product Development Group vice president Derrick Kuzak. "The entire team at Ford felt the time was right and with the right ingredients, the world-class 2011 Mustang could support a successful, race-bred, worthy successor to the original Boss 302."

So it was that the new Boss debuted for 2012, relying on advances made for the 2011 GT working in concert with countless lessons learned since 2010 thrashing the Boss 302R at the track. "The old adage that 'racing improves the breed' held true as we were building the production Boss 302," added Pericak. "Since the 302R used many of our planned production parts, we had the advantage of six months' worth of racing telemetry to add to our standard battery of tests pulled from the 2011 Mustang program."

Fully detailing the Boss 302's impressive parts list is impossible in this tight space, but suffice it to say that a company claim that this was "the quickest, best-handling straight-production Mustang ever offered by Ford" wasn't just bold talk. According to *Car and Driver*'s John Phillips, it was "so agile, so responsive to delicate inputs, it makes the GT500 feel like a FedEx truck." Furthermore, its macho

Above: The Boss was back, in two forms, for 2012. Honoring Dearborn's original 1969–70 Boss 302, the 2012 rendition was available in "base" form (right) or in all-out "Laguna Seca" racing trim, at left. A 444-horse 5.0-liter V-8 was included in both applications, as was a long list of chassis/suspension mods. The Laguna Seca was treated to a special aero package, and its rear seat was traded out in favor of an X-member cross-car brace to stiffen the structure between the rear wheels. A second Boss 302 appeared for 2013 wearing revised exterior graphics.

Right: Modifications to the Boss-specific 5.0-liter V-8 included painstakingly-machined cylinder heads (for superior flow characteristics) and a revised intake (for improved fuel/air delivery). The heads were fashioned from a new high-strength aluminum alloy, and countless other parts were either beefed up for durability or lightened to help make a 7,500-rpm redline possible. Sodium-filled exhaust valves improved heat dissipation.

444-horsepower 5.0-liter V-8 worked equally as well on the street as it did on a track. "The engine revs nearly as quickly as you can flex your right foot," added Phillips, "[and] despite all that cam, it idles as smoothly as a Camry." According to *Motor Trend*, rest to 60 miles per hour required 4.0 seconds; the quarter-mile, 12.3 ticks.

And let's not forget that sound. Beneath the Boss was a quad exhaust system that featured two typical rear-exiting outlets combined with a pair of small sidepipes that released a lesser portion of spent gases just in front of the rear wheels, with the idea being to not necessarily improve flow but to sing a Sirens' song no sailor (nor landlubber) could resist. Critics simply couldn't say enough about said sensual outputs.

"The roar is visceral and intimidating and remains utterly melodious from the depths of idle to the V8's 7500-redline," claimed *Car and Driver*'s clearly smitten Andrew Wendler. "Pin the right pedal, and the sound corrupts like an opiate; one sample and you're hooked, doomed to spend the rest of your days cruising dark streets and freeway tunnels

The 2012-13 Boss 302's unique quad exhaust system featured an extra set of tailpipes that exited just in front of the rear wheels—not to improve on the evacuation of spent gases, but to help make this buckin' bronco wail like no other.

2012 Boss 302

Model availability	Two-door fastback
Wheelbase	107.1 inches
Length	188.1 inches
Width	73.9 inches (discounting mirrors)
Height	55.1 inches
Curb weight	3,621 pounds
Track	(front/rear, in inches) 61.9/62.5
Wheels	Cast aluminum, 9.0x19 in front, 9.5x19 in back (10x19 rear wheels w/Laguna Seca package)
Tires	Pirelli PZero, P255/40ZR19 in front, P285/35ZR19 in back
Suspension	Reverse-L independent MacPherson strut w/stabilizer bar in front; 3-link solid axle w/coil springs, Panhard rod and stabilizer bar in back; AdvanceTrac electronic stability control; adjustable struts and shock absorbers; stiffened springs
Steering	Specially calibrated selectable-effort electric power-assisted (EPAS) rack and pinion (15.9:1 ratio)
Brakes	Four-wheel power-assisted vented discs with specially calibrated ABS & all-speed traction control; 14.0-inch rotors in front, 11.8-inch rotors in back
Engine	444-hp 5.0-liter (302 cid) 32-valve DOHC TiVCT V8 w/quad exhaust system
Bore & stroke	3.629x3.649 inches
Compression	11.0:1
Fuel delivery	Sequential electronic fuel injection
Fuel capacity	16 gallons
Transmission	Close-ratio six-speed manual with heavy-duty clutch
Rear axle	3.73:1 limited-slip (torque-sensitive Torsen differential, optional for Boss 302, standard with Laguna Seca package)
Production	4,016

looking for a suitable place to take another hit of that sweet, thunderous elixir. Drop out of the gas, and the bellow retreats to staccato bursts of bubbles and pops, the engine pulsing against backpressure like Zeus casually farting in his Olympian hot tub." Again, how sweet.

Summed up, the 2012 Boss 302 backed up Ford's boast—and then some. "Nose to tail, this feels like a whole new equine," began John Phillips' conclusion. "Thoroughly sorted, conscientiously massaged, the object of considerable forethought and ambition. As automotive resurrections go, this is a knockout that venerates the original Boss while embarrassing it objectively and subjectively in every meaningful measure. What this is, is the best Mustang ever."

Not so fast. As if the "basic" Boss 302 wasn't big and bad enough, Ford also offered a "Laguna Seca" rendition that featured an even stiffer suspension, an X-member cross-chassis brace in place of the rear seat, and aerodynamic bodywork borrowed from the 302R. Intentions were more than clear.

"The Laguna Seca package puts a race-ready version of the new Mustang Boss 302 directly into enthusiasts' hands," explained Mark Fields, Ford president of The Americas. "Laguna Seca isn't intended for Boss buyers who simply want an exhilarating daily driver. Think of it like a factory-built race car, which we hope avid racers and track-day fans are going to love."

Lust over was more like it.

2013

Like its ancestor, built for 1969 and '70 only, Ford's modern Boss 302 also remained on the scene for an all-too-short two years before taking its place in pony car Valhalla. As in 2012, the Boss production count for 2013 was 4,000 total, including 750 with the Laguna Seca option.

A notably freshened Mustang body, unveiled in November 2011, appeared for 2013, led by a revised front fascia featuring an enlarged grille and high-intensity discharge (HID) headlights. Light-emitting diode (LED) bars complemented those new lamps up front, and LED "ropes" were also incorporated into the traditional three-element taillights (still with sequential turn signals) out back. Further enhancing the light show were available side mirrors that projected the familiar running horse logo on the ground below whenever the doors were unlocked. Body-colored rocker panels also were new, as were functional heat extractors on the GT's hood.

Both the V-6 and GT models were offered with various new wheel treatments, and the latter's 5.0-liter V-8 was bumped up to 420 horsepower. Debuting inside was a 4.2-inch liquid-crystal display (LCD) screen, located between the speedometer and tach, allowing the driver to call up various bits of typical trip information along with Ford's Track Apps, which kept tabs on performance parameters. Recaro bucket seats and a six-speed SelectShift automatic transmission were introduced on the options list. SelectShift allowed drivers to switch from manual to automatic at the press of a button on the shifter.

Previously limited to manual-trans models in 2011 and 2012, the Bembro brake package became available on automatic-equipped Mustangs for the first time in 2013. Along with bigger, better 14-inch vented discs, the Bembro option also included 19-inch wheels, "summer" tires, and a recalibrated stability control system. Another new option, the Track Package, featured all the Bembro stuff, plus upgraded engine cooling, performance brake pads, and the Boss 302's Torsen differential. The Track Package was limited to GT models fitted with optional 3.73:1 rear gears.

In other news, a brutal supercharged 5.8-liter V-8—rated at 662 horsepower—appeared for the 2013 GT500. And a 5.0-liter small-block superseded the previously used 5.4-liter V-8 in that year's FR500CJ package, available in only two colors: black and silver.

Left: A freshened facade, first shown off in November 2011, appeared for the 2013 Mustang, which went on sale in the spring of 2012. GT500 styling cues appeared on both front and rear fascias, with the front unit incorporating new high-intensity discharge (HID) headlamps. The GT (shown here) now offered 420 standard horses.

Below: New, too, were cool side mirrors that incorporated special lighting that projected Ford's familiar galloping horse logo onto the ground beside the car.

2013

Model availability · · Two-door fastback, two-door convertible
Wheelbase · · · · · · · 107.1 inches
Length · · · · · · · · · · · 188.1 inches
Width · · · · · · · · · · · · 73.9 inches (discounting mirrors)
Height · · · · · · · · · · · · 55.6 inches, coupe; 55.8 inches, convertible
Curb weight · · · · · · 3,501 pounds, V6 coupe; 3,586 pounds, V6 convertible; 3,618 pounds, GT coupe; 3,720 pounds, GT convertible
Track · · · · · · · · · · · · (front/rear, in inches) 62.3/62.9
Wheels (V6) · · · · · · · 17x7.0 silver-painted aluminum, std; various 17-, 18- and 19-inch wheels (in differing styles and finishes), optional
Wheels (GT) · · · · · · · 18x8.0 silver-painted aluminum, std; various 17-, 18- and 19-inch wheels (in differing styles and finishes), optional
Tires (V6) · · · · · · · · · P225/60R17 A/S BF Goodrich Radial T/A, std; P235/50ZR18 A/S Pirelli PZero, optional; P255/40R19 Pirelli PZero Summer-Only, optional (w/Performance Package)
Tires (GT) · · · · · · · · · P235/50R18, std; P245/45ZR19 Pirelli PZero, optional (California Special); P255/40R19 Pirelli PZero Summer-Only, optional (Brembo brake package, Performance Package)
Suspension · · · · · · · Reverse-L independent MacPherson strut with stabilizer bar in front; three-link solid axle with coil springs, Panhard rod and stabilizer bar in back; AdvanceTrac electronic stability control, std
Steering · · · · · · · · · · Selectable-effort electric power-assisted (EPAS) rack and pinion (15.7:1 ratio)
Brakes · · · · · · · · · · · Four-wheel power-assisted vented discs with 4-sensor, 4-channel ABS & all-speed traction control
Engine · · · · · · · · · · · 305-horsepower 3.7-liter 24-valve DOHC TiVCT V6, base model; 420-horepower 5.0-liter 32-valve DOHC TiVCT V8, GT
Bore & stroke · · · · · 3.76 x3.41 inches, V6; 3.629x3.649 inches, GT V8
Compression · · · · · · 10.5:1, V6; 11.0:1, GT V8
Fuel delivery · · · · · · Sequential electronic fuel injection
Fuel capacity · · · · · 16 gallons
Transmission · · · · · · Six-speed Getrag manual, std.; six-speed SelectShift automatic (w/manual control selectivity), optional
Rear axle · · · · · · · · · 2.73:1 limited-slip, std for V6; 3.31:1 limited-slip, std for GT
Production · · · · · · · · 84,705

2014

Ford's one-millionth Mustang, a white convertible, rolled off the Dearborn line on February 23, 1966, a mere 23 months and a coupld weeks after Job One was completed on March 10, 1964, a new Detroit record. Building seven digits' worth of fifth-generation pony cars at the Flat Rock assembly plant (home to Mustang production since 2004) took a bit longer, but company officials were equally proud. On Wednesday, April 17, 2013, Flat Rock's millionth—a Ruby Red 2014 GT convertible—was driven off the line by 27-year plant veteran Ed Salna, just in time to help mark Mustang's 49th birthday. Riding shotgun with Salna was Ford's Global Product Development Group vice president, Raj Nair.

"Mustang is one of the most beloved nameplates in the industry, with fans around the world and throughout Ford Motor Company," Nair said during the milestone celebration. "The team here at Flat Rock assembly has built an outstanding reputation for quality while producing one million Mustangs over the last nine years, and we expect that to continue for many years to come."

Right: Two new colors, Deep Impact Blue and Gotta Have It Green (shown here), appeared for 2013. Also depicted here is the Mustang Club of America edition, offered previously in 2011 and 2012. Again offered for V-6 Premium models, the 2013 MCA Package included a billet grille, fog lamps, special stripes, a decklid spoiler, and 18-inch grey-painted wheels.

Below: The SVT-badged GT500 coupe/convertible duo roared on into 2013, now sporting the world's most powerful production V-8, a supercharged 5.8-liter monster that made 662 horsepower.

By then, of course, Mustangers worldwide were eagerly awaiting both the breed's big 50th-anniversary bash and the debut of its sixth generation, surely slated (though not officially announced yet) for 2015. In the meantime, one model run remained for the S197 era, and it predictably played out with few updates, which by no means represented a bad thing. "Even without any dramatic changes, the 2014 Ford Mustang continues to offer style, thrills and value," claimed *Edmunds*. "It's our top pick among muscle cars."

While the Boss 302 didn't return, the ever-present GT500 coupe/convertible duo carried on, as did the FR500CJ drag racing package, now offered only in Gotta Have it Green and Flat Black, the latter a menacing Cobra Jet exclusive. Two new paint choices, Oxford White and the aforementioned Ruby Red metallic, appeared for all other 2014 Mustangs, as 2013's High Performance White, Red Candy metallic, and School Bus Yellow were dropped.

New on the options list were FP6 and FP8 appearance packages for V-6 and GT Mustangs, respectively. Limited to base V-6 coupes (no Premium models), the FP6 option included 18-inch gloss-black wheels, body-colored rear-quarter window louvers, a gloss-black rear spoiler, and gloss-black side mirror caps. The story was similar for the GT's FP8 deal, save for the inclusion of larger 19-inch black-accented wheels.

And so closed the fifth chapter in Ford's long-running pony car tale—time to yet again turn a page.

2014

Model availability	Two-door fastback, two-door convertible
Wheelbase	107.1 inches
Length	188.1 inches
Width	73.9 inches (discounting mirrors)
Height	55.6 inches, coupe; 55.8 inches, convertible
Curb weight	3,501 pounds, V6 coupe w/manual trans; 3,523 pounds, V6 coupe w/automatic trans; 3,630 pounds, V6 convertible w/manual trans; 3,652 pounds, V6 convertible w/automatic trans; 3,618 pounds, GT coupe w/manual trans; 3,675 pounds, GT coupe w/automatic trans; 3,735 pounds, GT convertible w/manual trans; 3,792 pounds, GT convertible w/automatic trans
Track	(front/rear, in inches) 62.3/62.9
Wheels (V6)	17x7.0 silver-painted aluminum, std; various 17-, 18- and 19-inch wheels (in differing styles and finishes), optional
Wheels (GT)	18x8.0 silver-painted aluminum, std; various 17-, 18- and 19-inch wheels (in differing styles and finishes), optional
Tires (V6)	P225/60R17 A/S BF Goodrich Radial T/A, std; P235/50ZR18 A/S Pirelli PZero, optional; P255/40R19 Pirelli PZero Summer-Only, optional (w/Performance Package)
Tires (GT)	P235/50R18, std; P245/45ZR19 Pirelli PZero, optional (California Special); P255/40R19 Pirelli PZero Summer-Only, optional (Brembo brake package, Performance Package)
Suspension	Reverse-L independent MacPherson strut with stabilizer bar in front; three-link solid axle with coil springs, Panhard rod and stabilizer bar in back; AdvanceTrac electronic stability control, std
Steering	Selectable-effort electric power-assisted (EPAS) rack and pinion (15.7:1 ratio)
Brakes	Four-wheel power-assisted vented discs with 4-sensor, 4-channel ABS & all-speed traction control
Engine	305-horsepower 3.7-liter 24-valve DOHC TiVCT V6, base model; 420-horepower 5.0-liter 32-valve DOHC TiVCT V8, GT
Bore & stroke	3.76 x3.41 inches, V6; 3.629x3.649 inches, GT V8
Compression	10.5:1, V6; 11.0:1, GT V8
Fuel delivery	Sequential electronic fuel injection
Fuel capacity	16 gallons
Transmission	Six-speed Getrag manual, std.; six-speed SelectShift automatic (w/manual control selectivity), optional
Rear axle	2.73:1 limited-slip, std for V6; 3.31:1 limited-slip, std for GT
Production	134,082

Flat Rock plant veteran Ed Salna drove the one-millionth S197 Mustang—a Ruby Red 2014 GT convertible—off the line on April 17, 2013, helping mark the breed's 49th birthday in the process. Riding with Salna was Raj Nair, Ford's Global Product Development Group vice president.

Goin' Global

11

2015–2021

- Sixth-generation "S550" Mustang design project kicks off in late 2009.
- Ford's 2015 Mustang is unveiled at six sites around the world on December 5, 2013.
- Mustang Club of America marks the Mustang's 50th birthday with two parties, at Las Vegas Motor Speedway and Charlotte Motor Speedway, lasting for five days beginning April 16, 2014.
- Ford announces return of Shelby GT350 and GT350R on November 17, 2014.
- Sixth-generation Cobra Jet Mustang debuts at SEMA show in November 2015; a 50th anniversary CJ drag package appears in 2018, followed by an electric version in 2020.
- California Special option returns (for GT Premium models) in 2016.
- Reborn GT500 is "teased" in January 2018 at Detroit North American International Auto Show then debuts (as a 2020 model) at 2019 NAIAS.
- Ford announces production of its 10 millionth Mustang on August 8, 2018.
- Repackaged Bullitt Mustang returns for 2019, joined by another California Special after a one-year hiatus.
- Latest, greatest Mach 1 fastback hits the streets in 2021.

Above: Drift racing champion Vaughn Gittin Jr.'s RTR Vehicles teamed up with Ford Performance in 2019 to offer their Series 1 RTR conversion for GT and EcoBoost Mustangs additionally upgraded with Ford's Performance Package option. Aggressive body mods and a tunable suspension were included, and production was limited to 500.

Opposite: What a difference a half-century makes, huh? This 2015 GT convertible features the 50th Anniversary package, which included a chrome-accented grille, 19x8.5 alloy wheels with 255/40R19 tires, an appropriate badge in back, commemorative floor mats inside, and unique stitching for seats and door panels. Both Premium models, EcoBoost and GT, could be adorned in 50th Anniversary garb in 2015. *Mike Mueller*

Previous pages:
Left: Ford Performance and Vaughn Gittin Jr. first went in cahoots in 2018 to build the one-off Eagle Squadron Mustang, the 10th limited-edition model created to benefit the Experimental Aircraft Association following an auction sale. This design honored both the 100th anniversary of the Royal Air Force and the volunteer U.S. pilots who made up the Eagle Squadron, which fought alongside the RAF before America entered World War II in December 1941. At the heart of this beast was a 700-horsepower supercharged 5.0L V-8.

Right: Long rumored, and teased by parent company people more than once, a reborn GT500 finally arrived in 2020, fitted with a supercharged 5.2L V-8 that radiated 760 horsepower. Yes, that was/is a lot—the most in Mustang history, as well as top in its class.

Finding a suitably honored spot in FoMoCo Valhalla for Dearborn's fifth-generation pony car was by no means a tough task. Just ask equine expert Donald Farr, who has been writing about his beloved breed longer than perhaps anyone else out there. "The [10 years] of S197 production may have been the greatest era in Mustang history," claimed the former *Mustang Monthly* editor in April 2014 at mustangandfords.com. "From '05 to '14, Ford produced some of the best, most powerful Mustangs ever. Technology took over, starting with 300 horsepower from a three-valve 4.6-liter modular [V-8] in '05 and ending up with 420 [horses] from a new, high-tech DOHC 'Coyote' 5.0-liter."

HELL, EVEN BASE MODELS were offering more than 300 horses after the S197's original 210-hp 4.0-liter SOHC V-6 was replaced in 2011 with a 3.7-liter six sporting two more overhead cams and twice as many valves and tailpipes. And let's not forget all those special editions: Shelby GT and GT500, both introduced in 2007; Bullitt and GT500 KR in 2008; the Vegas-sourced GT350 in 2011; and the born-again Boss 302 in 2012. For 2013, the latest GT500 not only represented the most muscular pony to date, its 662-hp aluminum heart also ranked as this planet's strongest regular-production V-8. Could it get any better?

It had to.

Accounting for more than 10 percent of all the pony cars released by Ford from 1964 to 2014, those million-plus S197 Mustangs certainly qualified as nothing to sneeze at. But a closer look inside the numbers revealed an infectious trend. After peaking at 166,530 units sold in 2006, calendar-year sales dropped to 134,626 in 2007, 91,251 in 2008, then 66,623 in 2009. Why the sickening slide?

When Flat Rock production began in 2004, Mustang was running alone in its field, thanks to General Motors' decision in 2002 to put its F-body platform—home to Chevrolet's Camaro and Pontiac's Firebird since 1967—out to pasture. Saddled with no competition whatsoever, Mustang sales remained strong from 2003 to 2007, dipping

Above: Bosnian-born, German-educated Kemal Curic was responsible for the 2015 Mustang's basic design. Curic moved from Europe to Michigan in 2010 to become exterior design manager at Ford's Dearborn studio.

Left: Once sketched on paper, the 2015 Mustang's form typically took shape in full-sized three-dimensional form using sculpted clay.

only as low as 129,858 in 2004 before the fifth-gen model emerged to predictably revive cash registers. Then along came the Dodge Boys with their Challenger, last seen in 1974, to once again make a race of things. First-year calendar sales for this retro-styled reborn rival totaled 17,423 in 2008, followed by another 25,852 in 2009, and 36,791 in 2010. Dodge's challenge, however, only partly explained Mustang's stumble.

Helping rein in Ford's long-running stallion even further was a second reincarnated pony car, Chevy's fifth-gen Camaro, which went on sale in April 2009 sporting a 2010 designation. Called a "thoroughly modern interpretation of the 1969 model" by GM Global Design vice president Ed Welburn, the 2010 Camaro relied notably less on nostalgic charm compared to its competitors, hence its greater appeal to younger buyers who couldn't care less about what the breed looked like decades ago. Thus buoyed, the new horse on the block easily eclipsed Challenger and came within 5,000 units of besting Mustang in the segment's 2009 sales sprint before turning the trick (by nearly 7,600 cars) with much fanfare in 2010. The calendar-year count for 2011 then read 88,249 Camaros, 70,438 Mustangs. Ouch.

While the former champion narrowed the calendar-year gap considerably during 2012 and 2013, a close second still was no place for the company that gave America its first pony car, which at the time stood one year short of its much-ballyhooed 50th birthday. Such a momentous occasion obviously merited a major party, and most Mustangers anxiously awaiting that April 2014 event figured Ford surely would have an all-new sixth-gen model gift wrapped by then. After all, Camaro wasn't about to start eating dust by itself.

J Mays wholeheartedly agreed. "With 2014 approaching we have to take a jump forward," proclaimed Ford's worldwide design chief during a question-and-answer session webcast just prior to the opening of the Paris Motor Show in October 2010. "We can't lose the Mustang DNA, which is really important, but we've got to signal that Mustang has got another 50 years of life left in it."

With the technically more-advanced Camaro suddenly leading the way, even Mays was willing to admit that his long-favored nostalgic ideals had run their course, that it was time to live in the now, time to invite a new generation of horse lovers to the party. Ford's first S197 model "was a big hit because we created a nice balance between retro cues and modern styling," he added. "[The] 2010

Ford's pony car finally was fitted with independent rear suspension for 2015. As that modern IRS layout (below) was taking shape, engineers concluded that the front design required updating too, hence the double-ball-joint MacPherson strut setup shown at left. The sixth-generation Mustang's standard brakes were enlarged too.

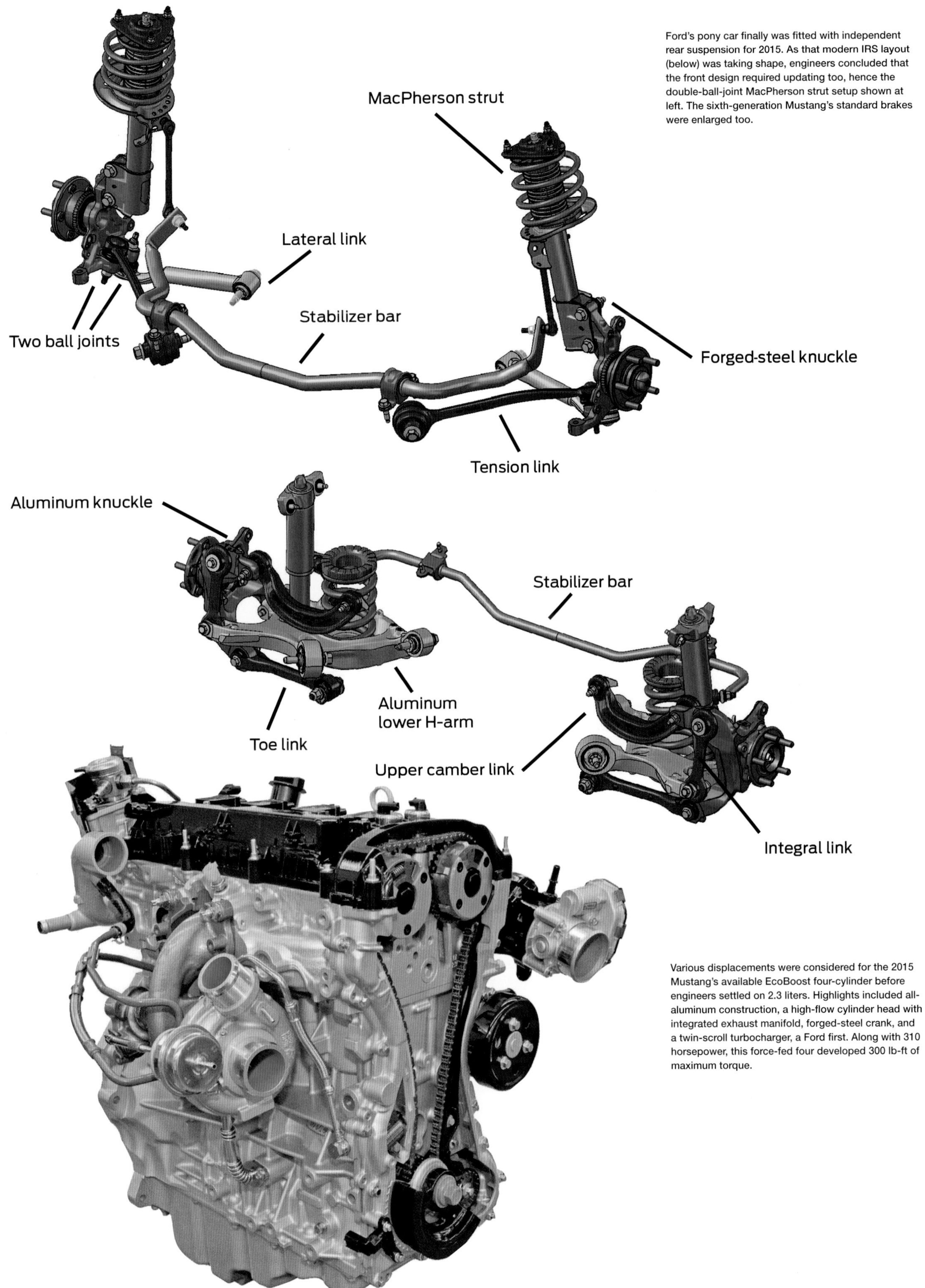

Various displacements were considered for the 2015 Mustang's available EcoBoost four-cylinder before engineers settled on 2.3 liters. Highlights included all-aluminum construction, a high-flow cylinder head with integrated exhaust manifold, forged-steel crank, and a twin-scroll turbocharger, a Ford first. Along with 310 horsepower, this force-fed four developed 300 lb-ft of maximum torque.

After showing off their "kinetic" design concept on the world's auto show stages in 2005, Ford designers came back with an updated theme—"kinetic 2.0," if you will—for their stunning Evos coupe, unveiled at the Frankfurt Motor Show in September 2011. Evos cues then carried over into production for 2013's Fusion.

[update then] drove that message home even more. But now we can't simply do an evolution of the 2005, 2010 cars."

Serious plans to put a majorly modernized Mustang back on track began percolating in late 2009. Given such ample lead time, it was clear Ford's original goal involved introducing the next generation to buyers on or before Mustang's 50th anniversary. This conclusion was echoed in 2010 by various journalists and bloggers, who commonly bandied about a "2014" label for what lay ahead. But rumor-millers stood corrected in 2011 when word leaked out that Ford actually intended to kick off the next generation with a "2015" Mustang, first offered to the public in the spring of the previous calendar year. Sound familiar?

Replicating the breed's original introduction scheme 50 years down the road certainly would've magnified the milestone moment if not for a proverbial wrench finding its way into the works. In 2012, well into the development process, Ford execs curiously decided to return, at least in part, to the drawing board, at a cost of who-knows-how-many-millions. According to Mustang chief engineer Dave Pericak, his group initially had hoped to preserve much of the fifth-gen structure beneath an all-new body, but that plan simply didn't mesh with the project's overriding main goals. "It didn't start out as a clean sheet of paper," he explained to *Time* magazine's Bill Saporito in December 2013. "But it ended up as one."

While reeling in Camaro was clearly among those goals, another reason behind product development executive vice president Raj Nair's do-over decision involved Dearborn's evolving big-picture plans, which would finally encompass its celebrated pony car. "For the first time, the company will produce a Mustang it can sell around the globe," wrote Saporito. "In essence, the next Mustang is designed to be the key to Ford's strategy of producing cars such as Fiesta and Fusion from a limited number of platforms that can be sold profitably from Dearborn to Dubai."

"For the first time" actually wasn't entirely correct, but *Time*'s reporter could be forgiven his half-truth considering Ford's earlier efforts exporting Mustang, which were limited to say the least. Older (or well-read) pony car people will perhaps remember the T-5 models (see page 14), delivered in small numbers to West Germany during the sixties and seventies. According to Ford, a mere 161,000 or so Mustangs had been sold outside of North America prior to 2013, with 4,000 of those finding homes in 36 countries in 2012.

Now the idea was to blanket the planet with a true foreign-friendly product—to officially sell Mustang in more than 110 lands, including long-overlooked China. Factory-built, right-hand-drive models also would be shipped—indeed for the first time—to new markets like the United Kingdom, Australia, Japan, and South Africa. Worldwide research had shown that brand recognition already existed big time in many untapped regions, convincing Ford execs that going global with their next new pony car was definitely doable. And with Mustang's face so widely recognized—if not revered—across so many borders, it also was apparent that any overseas-influenced restyles, minor or otherwise, wouldn't be needed—a good thing considering such unsavory morphs (from a red, white, and blue perspective) surely were out of the question from the get-go. As executive design director (for "The Americas") Moray Callum explained to *Detroit Free Press* business writer Alisa Priddle in December 2013, the goal involved creating "a true American Mustang," not one remolded "to cater to European or Chinese tastes."

Dave Pericak's engineers, on the other hand, had to address various foreign needs and/or wants. Keeping the existing foundation just wouldn't do if the 2015 Mustang was to succeed overseas in places where nimbleness is a priority; mucho muscle beneath the hood isn't. Most notable among foreign-swayed updates was a long-awaited independent rear suspension (IRS) in place of that time-honored, yet-archaic solid axle, considered completely untouchable during the S197 design process (see pages 240–243). And once the rear suspension was revised, the design up front also demanded attention, hence part of the need to rethink where this project was heading.

Clearly, American drag racers no longer had a say in the deal; now it was driving-glove-wearing Europeans who influenced the final product. Or was it Dodge and Chevy engineers, who coincidentally had beaten the Mustang gang to the punch with up-to-date IRS layouts for Challenger and Camaro? Another change of pace also appeared under the hood in the form of a new power source, a fuel-savoring four-cylinder engine, like those preferred in most every other country around the world.

The first four-banger found between Mustang flanks since 1993, this 2.3-liter EcoBoost in-liner, as its name implied, was fitted with a turbocharger to help output reach 310 horses, in turn making it the first force-fed four in the Mustang corral dating back to the last SVO model in 1986. This time, best-in-class fuel economy was promised along with SVO-style excitement.

The 2015 Mustang was introduced worldwide at six sites on December 5, 2013. Standing by proudly during the Barcelona, Spain, event were (left to right) Ford Executive Vice President Stephen Odell, Ford Motor Company chairman Bill Ford, Global Marketing Executive Vice President Jim Farley, and Ford of Europe Chief Operating Officer Barb Samardzich.

Three body styles—a revived "notchback" coupe, fastback, and convertible—initially were considered for the 2015 Mustang, but only the latter two reached reality. An EcoBoost fastback, equipped with the 50th Anniversary appearance package, is shown here. *Mike Mueller*

In the end, after hitting the reset button, Ford had a truly modern Mustang—based on what was now called the "S550" platform—ready for a much larger market than before. "We didn't originally start out as this being all-new," reiterated Pericak. "But it is now an all-new car, meaning there is not a piece of sheet metal, or any other part that hasn't been touched."

Wrapping up the S550 package in a revitalized skin initially involved an international group effort, a first for Mustang but nothing new at Ford. "It is a common process we [presently] use on every vehicle," explained Ford Global Product Development Group vice president Derrick Kuzak in a March 2011 *Automotive News* report. Kuzak was referring to his company's then three-year-old practice of relying on its worldwide talent pool to produce styling proposals for upcoming models. "When we embark on a new product, particularly one that is all new, it involves all of the studios," continued Kuzak.

Hundreds of sketches were whittled down to three before customers were invited to give their feedback to design director Joel Piaskowski's team. The final choice was the work of Bosnian-born, German-educated Kemal Curic, who in 2010 moved from Europe to Michigan to become the Dearborn studio's exterior design manager. "I certainly think we picked the right [submission]," added Moray Callum (a Scotsman, by the by) in Priddle's December 2013 *Detroit Free Press* report. "It was slightly more aggressive and more raw."

Curic, incidentally, also contributed to Ford's Evos concept car, introduced at the Frankfurt Motor Show in September 2011. A two-door coupe, Evos was the first to show off what some called Ford's "kinetic 2.0" exterior. It was an evolution of the Euro-sourced "kinetic" design theme (originally demonstrated by the Iosis concept) unveiled six years before, also at Frankfurt. Kinetic design elements were applied by Ford to various global products beginning in 2007, and parts of the more exciting Evos package also morphed into reality.

Ford's Evos-inspired 2013 Fusion debuted at Detroit's North American International Auto Show in January 2012. Previously built only in Mexico, Dearborn's globally marketed four-door also began sharing Mustang's assembly line in August 2013. Ford eventually invested $555 million updating the Flat Rock facility for production of both the second-generation Fusion and sixth-gen pony car, which borrowed various Evos elements as well.

Once the dust settled, the 2015 Mustang didn't go on sale until fall 2014, about six months late by most counts. Or was it? "We don't gear our business plans, plant switchovers, and engineering programs to birthdays and anniversaries," proclaimed Raj Nair to *Car and Driver*'s Don Sherman in May 2014 after being asked if the sixth-gen could be considered tardy for its own party. "We'll sell the new Mustang when the development program is complete and the car is ready for customers."

At least hopeful horse lovers weren't left holding empty reins. Ford officially unveiled its latest, greatest Mustang on December 5, 2013, at six sites worldwide: Dearborn, New York, Los Angeles, Barcelona, Sydney, and Shanghai. Additional public introductions on U.S. soil followed, including in Flushing Meadows, New York, on April 17, 2014, at the site of the 1964 World's Fair—where Ford's original pony car had debuted to the day a half century before.

Salivating potential customers also were treated to first tastes during the Mustang Club of America's gonzo 50th-anniversary celebration. Beginning on April 16, 2014, and lasting for five days, it was held simultaneously in Las Vegas and Charlotte, North Carolina. Ford officials additionally celebrated by reproducing an October 1965 publicity stunt that involved transporting a white 1966 Mustang convertible in sections via elevators to the Empire State Building's 86th-floor observation deck, where it was put back together and displayed as if it had flown up there. This time, a yellow 2015 convertible was shipped in pieces to New York to make a similar reassembled reappearance 1,000 feet above the bustling streets of Manhattan on April 16–17, 2014.

Talk about your all-new heights.

2015

"Is the new Mustang going to sell in Beijing and Berlin as well as it does in Birmingham?" asked Bill Saporito in December 2013. "No. Ford expects 80 to 90 percent of sales to remain in North America." So why then all the fuss/muss to maybe roll out no more than 15 to 20,000 additional models from Flat Rock?

2015–2017

Model availability	2-door fastback coupe, 2-door convertible
Construction	Unitized welded-steel body w/aluminum hood and front fenders
Wheelbase	107.1 inches
Length	188.3 inches
Width (discounting mirrors)	75.4 inches, 2015; 76.1 inches, 2016–2017
Height	54.4 inches, 2015 coupe; 54.3 inches, 2016–2017 coupe; 54.9 inches convertible
Track (front/rear, in inches)	62.3/64.9
Wheels	17x7.5, std V-6 & EcoBoost; 18x8.0, std GT
Tires	P235/55R H A/S, std V-6 & EcoBoost; P235/50R W A/S, std GT
Suspension	Double-ball-joint independent MacPherson strut w/tubular stabilizer bar, front; integral-link independent w/coil springs, solid stabilizer bar & twin- or mono-tube (depending on application) dampers, rear
Steering	Electric power-assisted rack & pinion (16:1 ratio)
Brakes	4-wheel power discs w/4-sensor, 4-channel ABS & AdvanceTrac electronic stability control (all models)
Brake sizes (base V-6 & EcoBoost)	12.6-inch vented discs w/twin-piston floating aluminum calipers, front; 12.6-inch solid discs w/single-piston floating aluminum calipers & integral parking brake in back
Brake sizes (GT)	13.9-inch vented discs w/4-piston fixed aluminum calipers, front; 13.0-inch vented discs w/single-piston floating iron calipers & integral parking brake in back
Optional brakes (w/EcoBoost Performance Package)	13.9-inch vented discs w/4-piston fixed aluminum calipers in front; 13.0-inch vented discs w/single-piston floating iron calipers in back
Optional brakes (w/GT Performance Package)	15.0-inch vented discs w/Brembo 6-piston fixed aluminum calipers, front; 13.0-inch vented discs w/single-piston floating iron calipers, rear
Engine (base)	3.7-liter (227 cubic inches) 24-valve Ti-VCT DOHC V-6 w/aluminum cylinder block & heads
Engine (EcoBoost)	2.3-liter (140 cubic inches) 16-valve DOHC inline 4-cylinder w/aluminum cylinder block & head
Engine (GT)	5.0-liter (302 cubic inches) 32-valve Ti-VCT DOHC V-8 w/aluminum cylinder block & heads
Output	300 hp, V-6; 310 hp, Ecoboost I4; 435 hp, GT V-8
Bore & stroke (inches)	3.45 x 3.7, EcoBoost I4; 3.76 x 3.41, V-6; 3.63 x 3.65, V-8
Compression	9.5:1, EcoBoost I4; 10.5:1, V-6; 11.0:1, V-8
Fuel delivery	Sequential electronic fuel injection, V-6 & V-8; direct injection, EcoBoost I4
Transmission	6-speed manual w/Hill Start Assist; 6-speed automatic w/paddle shifters, optional
Fuel tank	16 gallons (V-6 & GT); 15.5 gallons (EcoBoost)
Axle ratio (std)	3.15:1, V-6; 3.31:1, EcoBoost & GT (w/manual trans); 3.15:1 (w/automatic)
Optional axle ratio (all models)	3.55:1 (included w/EcoBoost Performance Package)
Optional axle ratio (GT Performance Package)	3.73:1 in Torsen differential

Above: New cylinder heads went atop the all-aluminum 5.0-liter V-8 in 2015, as did an equally new intake manifold. The heads were tweaked for improved intake flow and the manifold featured charge motion control valves that partially restricted intake flow at low rpm for better fuel economy and idle stability, not to mention lower emissions. An oil cooler was standard, as were 435 horses.

Left: Ford was especially proud of the upgraded materials and craftsmanship demonstrated inside the 2015 Mustang. Push-button start, SYNC connectivity, a rearview camera, and eight air bags were standard.

Adding independent rear suspension into the sixth-generation mix helped designers bring back the familiar fastback roofline while increasing interior room at the same time. Another ol' fave—sequential turn signals—also brought back found memories of Mustangs gone by.

As marketing executive vice president Jim Farley told Saporito, "Launching Mustang globally is not about the people who buy it, it's about the people who don't." According to Farley, the main goal involved benefitting the parent company's grand scheme by way of warm/fuzzy associations with what he called "an American automotive icon that symbolizes optimism and freedom for millions of people around the world." As he explained further in *Time,* "the purpose of this exercise is for people to emotionally connect with the Ford brand and Fiestas and Focuses and crossovers in Europe and China and Asia, Australia, Thailand, Russia, Brazil and Argentina. The good feelings [inspired by Mustang] will make them more inclined to buy Fiestas and F-150s."

Stateside customers, meanwhile, simply couldn't help connecting directly with a magical machine still able to turn 'em on in its 50s. "[It] manages well that trick of being entirely new without being unfamiliar," wrote *Car and Driver*'s Jeff Sabatini. "Yet it's unlike any Mustang that came before, loaded with equipment heretofore unseen in the venerable pony car." Twice as many air bags (eight) were now standard, as were a rearview camera and push-button start. A six-speed automatic transmission carried over from 2014 but now incorporated trendy paddle shifters.

Don't forget the EcoBoost turbo four, which joined 2014's two rollover four-valve DOHC engines. While the base model's 3.7-liter V-6 was rerated down slightly to 300 horsepower for 2015, the GT's mildly reworked 5.0-liter V-8 was advertised at 435 horses. A refined Gertrag six-speed manual transmission remained standard behind all three available powerplants.

Also standard for 2015's GT was an electronic line-lock system, an industry first long familiar to drag racers, who may've felt a little left behind after their beloved solid axle was traded for modern IRS. Not at all, assured Ford people, and their line-locking GT was track-ready proof. "Competition has been an integral part of the Mustang lifestyle since its earliest days 50 years ago," said Ford Car marketing manager Steve Ling in April 2014. "We know our customers, and we wanted to provide a unique feature for those wishing to take full advantage of the increased capability offered by [the new] GT at the drag strip." Ford's fine print was quick to point out the obvious: line-lock was meant for off-road competition use only and "racing your vehicle will void your warranty." Duh!

It also went without saying that the sixth-gen's independent rear suspension easily represented the design's most newsworthy technical aspect. Teased by the SVT Cobra's inclusion of IRS from 1999 to 2004, many Mustangers had long wondered when their turn would finally come. Meanwhile, the rest of the Ford world made its transformation from old-school solid axles to full independence. Hopes remained high as the S197 breed was being readied for its 2005 debut only to be dashed, apparently in part by Ford's aforementioned dedication to all those lead-footed weekend warriors out there.

In truth, the decision to stick so long with obsolete technology had less to do with customer loyalty (former chief engineer Hau Thai-Tang's 2005 claims notwithstanding) as it did cost considerations. Reportedly, product development exec Phil Martens had determined late in the S197 design process that Ford could save $100 a car if IRS plans were cancelled, hence the retention of that low-tech live axle. Such money matters, however, apparently mattered less ten years later.

"A decade after Martens' infamous attempt to save [a hundred bucks], Mustang will finally enter the 21st-century," blogged *Motor Trend*'s Scott Evans in August 2011. "Aging drag racers who argued for the live axle's stoplight launch

Above: In November 2014, Ford announced it would repackage its Shelby Mustang in sixth-gen garb. Shown here is the new Shelby GT350 as it turned heads at the Chicago Auto Show in February 2015. Aero-shaped front fenders and hood represented just a few of the mods made to this track-ready pony.

Left: A wilder Shelby, the GT350R, also appeared in 2015 with even more aero touches, plus 19-inch carbon-fiber wheels—a first for a major automaker. Additional weight cuts made the GT350R more than 120 pounds lighter than its GT350 running mate.

Below: Both sixth-gen Shelbys were powered by an unblown 526-hp 5.2-liter V-8—the strongest naturally aspirated Mustang engine ever. Of note, too, was this free-breathing motor's flat-plane crankshaft, a component previously only seen in race machines and exotic sports cars from Europe.

Everything that made 2015's Mustang so great rolled over into 2016. The lineup again included the V-6, EcoBoost, and GT models, with the latter two segregated into base and upscale Premium versions.

advantages gave Ford a handy excuse for the cost-cutting. [But while] Ford has done amazing things with the [solid] axle, that technology's days are past."

While IRS was included in the S550 recipe from day one, a revamped front suspension, as mentioned, didn't get folded in until late in the program. Dave Pericak's engineers responded with an improved double-ball-jointed MacPherson strut layout mounted to a non-isolated full subframe in place of the S197's individual crossmembers. That perimeter subframe both stiffened the front structure and reduced mass, while those double joints (at the steering knuckle's lower end) allowed for the installation of bigger brakes that didn't in turn require excessive wheel offsets (needed to ensure clearance), which negatively affect steering feel.

Effects of rear suspension upgrades also were noticeable on the outside, where the IRS installation, coupled with a widened track in back, allowed Joel Piaskowski's design team to revive the true fastback roofline familiar to original Mustang fans without reducing interior room. Indeed, space inside increased despite that sloping roof, at least for rear ends and shoulders. Per long-running Mustang tradition, backseat headroom still came at a premium—that is unless passengers were ten years old or younger.

Aesthetically speaking, even though modern Evos-inspired touches were clearly present, Ford's all-new pony was more than respectful of its honored legacy. "We crafted this car with the goal of creating a contemporary interpretation of Mustang," said Jim Farley in December 2013. "You only get one chance to make a first impression, and when you see this car, you immediately see a Mustang strong and true," added global design exec Moray Callum.

We also witnessed a new GT350, announced in November 2014, just in time to celebrate Carroll Shelby's original thoroughbred. "Fans of the Shelby brand are among the most passionate in the automotive industry," said Ford Performance marketing manager Henry Ford III in April 2015. "To honor the GT350's 50th anniversary, a limited run of [new] models will be built in 2015."

Limited indeed; only 100 GT350s, plus another 37 GT350Rs, were built for 2015, all of them instant collectibles. Again, duh!

2016

Lightweight, race-ready Shelby Mustangs rolled over into 2016, once more with reshaped aluminum body parts (fenders and hood); bodacious brakes; a brutal, free-breathing 526-hp 5.2-liter V-8; and a massively tweaked chassis that, according to Global Performance Vehicles Chief Engineer Jamal Hameedi, was "tested endlessly on the most challenging roads and tracks in the world." The biggest brakes in Mustang history, those stoppers featured huge (15.5-inches, front; 14.95, rear) cross-drilled rotors clamped by Brembo calipers, six-piston units at the nose, four out back. Cooling ducts additionally helped ensure that brake fade was never an issue, no matter how tough the punishment.

Unlike fifth-gen Shelby V-8s, which were boosted by superchargers, that new 5.2-liter powerplant sucked on its own, and hence represented another milestone: it ranked as Mustang's most powerful naturally aspirated engine to date. Its flat-plane crankshaft—found only in competition machines and sky-high-priced European exotics—was another production-line first for Ford. Conventional engines have long used vibration-nulling 90-degree cranks, which feature rods connected at quarter-turn intervals. Relocating crank journals opposite each other in this case produced a firing order that alternated between cylinder banks, which in turn reduced exhaust pulse overlap, and in the end resulted in improved fuel/air, spent-gas flow at high rpm. Blower? We don't need no stinkin' blower!

Even more weight savings came along as part of the GT350R package, as did additional aero-effectiveness. Also included were steamroller-like 19-inch wheels (11-inch diameter, front; 11.5, rear) made of carbon-fiber—another first, at least for a major automaker.

Above: The popular California Special returned in 2016 for GT Premium fastbacks and convertibles. Along with black-painted 19-inch wheels, the CS/GT deal included blacked-out upper/lower grilles, with the top unit sporting an offset tri-bar pony logo reminiscent of earlier days. This offset logo also appeared in the grille supplied along with the 2016 EcoBoost's new Pony Package.

Left: New for 2016's GT were turn-signal indicators incorporated into the hood's twin vents—an idea first seen in 1967. A California Special application is demonstrated here.

The sum of these parts equaled, in Dearborn's words, the "most track-capable production Mustang ever." According to Ford Performance chief engineer Kerry Baldori, "GT350R's highly efficient aerodynamics, innovative light-weighting, and world-class chassis deliver a truly spectacular driving experience that makes you feel like a professional racing driver."

Back on the street in 2016, Ford people proved they still had ears by bringing back what they called a "heritage cue" first seen in 1967: turn-signal indicators located within the hood's twin vents. "Enthusiasts are not shy about telling us what they want," said marketing manager Melanie Banker in May 2015, "and we're constantly exploring ideas together with our engineering team to develop new features we know our customers will love. These new indicators are a perfect example of us communicating customer feedback to Mustang engineers and the team responding with an exclusive new feature for owners of the 2016 GT."

Topless 5.0 GT fans also were heard, demonstrated by the 2016 convertible's optional Performance Package, offered only for fastbacks in 2015's GT ranks. (But for both fastbacks *and* convertibles in the EcoBoost lineup.) Limited to top-shelf Premium models, this group featured chassis bracing, a larger radiator, heavy-duty springs and rear stabilizer, six-piston Brembo front brake calipers, 19-inch wheels wearing summer tires, and a Torsen limited-slip differential. "The GT fastback with Performance Package has been very popular," added Banker. "Customer feedback indicated a strong desire for the package on the convertible as well, and the 2016 GT delivers."

Yet another old fave, the California Special, returned in 2016 and again featured exclusive identification and deluxe treatments, inside and out. A unique grille (with offset tri-bar pony logo) and 19-inch wheels were included as well in this deal, limited to GT Premium models. Also revived, in this case for EcoBoost Premiums, was an available Pony Package, which added 19-inch polished wheels, side stripes, chrome window highlights, and the CS/GT's grille with offset logo.

New options included a Black Accent Package, for all GTs, and Ford's SYNC 3 communications/entertainment system, available for all Premium Mustangs. The former included 19-inch black-painted wheels, blacked-out trim, and a black decklid spoiler. The latter featured a fast smart-phone-like touch screen, improved voice command, and Applelink functionality.

Really loud news heard in 2016 involved the roaring revival of the drag-strip-dedicated Cobra Jet. The only sixth-gen model fitted with a solid axle, the new FR500CJ was introduced to Ford racers at the SEMA show in November 2015. Dearborn engineers were quick to point out that 75 percent of the CJ's 5.0-liter supercharged V-8 came directly from beneath a GT's hood, and much of the remaining stuff was available from the Ford Performance Parts catalog. "It was important to use production hardware wherever possible to ensure parts are readily available and reasonably priced for racers," said Ford Performance competition manager Jesse Kershaw.

Above: The strip-specific Cobra Jet also returned for the sixth-gen run and was the only 2016 Mustang fitted with a solid axle. Base price for Ford's latest FR500CJ was $99,990. The graphics package shown here was a $1,995 option, and wheelie bars cost another $1,995. Again, production was limited to 50—25 in Oxford White, 25 in Deep Impact Blue.

Below: A supercharged 5.0L V-8 again motivated the new Cobra Jet Mustang in 2016. Output numbers weren't advertised, but Ford did say the car was capable of running 8-second quarter-miles—you do the math. Dearborn people also bragged that 75 percent of the CJ mill's pieces were stock GT items, and most of the remaining 25 percent could be found in the Ford Performance Parts catalog.

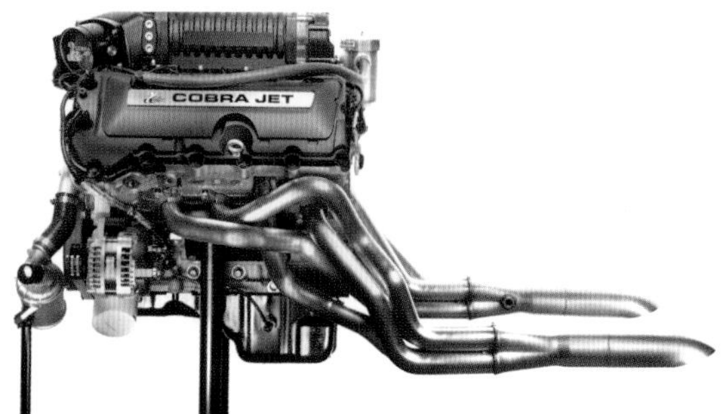

Hertz and Shelby again appeared together in a sentence in 2016, in time to honor the GT350-H "Rent-A-Racer's" 50th birthday. Announced in March that year, a limited run (only 140) of 2016 GT-H Shelbys became available for rent at select airports during the following Memorial Day weekend. A Ford Performance cat-back exhaust system and Ford Racing Handling Pack were part of the deal, as was the traditional gold-accented black finish.

2017

Was it any wonder there was so little to report on 2017's what's-new front? With buyers' desires for Ford's half-century-old horse surging, Dearborn's product planners typically opted to leave nearly everything well enough alone, adding only a few fresh paint choices, dropping a couple other shades, and deleting the barely perceptible turn signal indicators in GT hood vents after only one year's worth of nostalgic winks. Predictable price hikes and a few options tweaks, and that was basically that as far as next-model differentiation was concerned.

So how hot had pony lovers become for the sixth gen? By April 2017, more than 395,000 of them had ridden one home, and not just to American addresses. Per Ford's bigger-picture plan, some 98K of these were shipped outside the US, arriving now in 140 countries on all continents save for Antarctica—if only penguins could drive, right? Six more not-so-cold nations joined the club in 2018.

"The legacy of Mustang continues to grow and in places it never reached before," proclaimed Mustang marketing manager Mark Schaller early in 2017, when the breed's export percentage was expected to nearly double to 30 percent. "We continue to make [Mustang] available in new markets, and drivers [there] continue to respond with resounding approval."

Beating a path into the world's largest auto market, China, in 2015 induced some serious resonance. Mustang exports to Earth's most populous country soared by 74 percent from 2015 to 2016, resulting in Ford's pony earning best-selling sports car status there on the way to supremely claiming the same title in the worldwide arena. Total global Mustang sales surpassed 150K in 2016, up 6 percent from the previous year, an increase plainly spurred on by a corresponding 101 percent surge in exports. Almost 45K second-edition sixth-gen models reached international destinations in 2016.

As for 2017 lineup highlights, both the California Special and the GT350/350R duo returned, with the former remaining just as familiar as this year's base models. GT350 drivers, contrarily, took delivery of a few notable changes, including Ford Performance's now-standard Track Package, a $6,500 option in 2016.

"Ford Performance is always listening to customer feedback" explained the group's global director, Dave Pericak, in April 2016 concerning this upcoming upgrade. "At the end of last year we started offering a back seat option for the Shelby GT350R due to customer demand. Now, we have adjusted the packages available to continue to provide more of what [GT350] customers want."

Along with boosting the base price by nearly 5 G's, 2017's Track Package again added the following into the GT350 mix: aluminum tower-to-tower strut bracing; a high-downforce decklid spoiler; coolers for engine, transmission, and differential lubes; and adaptive MagneRide damping. These competition-ready parts remained included in 2017's GT350R deal, as they had been from the get-go.

Created by Delphi Automotive, then a General Motors subsidiary, MagneRide adaptive suspension was first installed underneath Cadillac's Seville STS

Twenty-sixteen's lineup rolled over unchanged into 2017, with the 435-horsepower GT again leading the way. New paint choices this year included Lightning Blue, White Platinum Metallic Tri-Coat, and Grabber Blue.

A V-6 Mustang was last offered in 2017, again only in base trim. EcoBoost and GT Mustangs continued to appear in base and better-equipped Premium forms this year.

A Tremec six-speed stick and 526 horsepower remained at the heart of 2017's GT350 Shelby and were joined this year by standard MagneRide dampers. New on the topside were three available colors (Ruby Red Metallic, Lightning Blue, and Grabber Blue), which replaced two others (Deep Impact Blue and Competition Orange) that didn't repeat from 2016.

midyear in 2002, then began helping Corvettes hold the road better than ever the following year. Ford's first application of this seemingly magical marvel came in 2015, exclusively for the Shelby twins.

So what's the trick behind this wonderment? Unlike conventional shock absorbers, MagneRide dampers rely on no mechanical valves, nor any other small parts that typically wear out or limit reaction time. Reining in suspension action with cutting-edge aplomb in this case is tasked to four monotubes containing hydraulic fluid impregnated with magnetized iron particles, more technically referred to in some circles as "magnetorheological fluid." On command, electromagnetic coils send a variable current through this juice that reacts with those particles, effectively increasing fluid viscosity in the process. Presto, chango: precisely stiffened damping quicker than you can wave a wand.

Sensors at each wheel, working in concert with an electronic control unit, individually adjust that stiffness literally every 10 milliseconds. And those sensors all but instantly read all inputs, and we mean "all." As vehicle dynamics supervisor Brent Clark explained in May 2015, "the [Shelby's] MagneRide computer system takes into account so many variables—from the obvious ones such as steering angle, pitch and yaw, to some measurements that are a bit more obscure. Even ambient temperature [readings] are fed [in] to ensure optimal performance." Way cool or what?

Additional 2017 Shelby updates involved option revisions. Ford's previously offered Technology Package—originally filled with the SYNC 3 infotainment/navigation system; leather-appointed, heated/cooled power seats; and the Track Pack's strut bracing and MagneRide dampers—was renamed Convenience Package after it was slightly repacked. No need to fiddle with the chassis upgrades now that they came standard. But completely new this year in GT350 terms (it was previously limited to R models) was an optional Electronics Package, which concentrated on the SYNC 3 installation. In all package applications (Convenience, Electronics, and R-installed Electronics), available audio equipment this time featured nine speakers, two more than before. Rock 'em if you got 'em.

2018

When *Car and Driver*'s Tony Markovich reported on the 2017 Mustang in June that year, his article's subhead said it all: "Lying low before the new face arrives for 2018." By then, news of an upcoming "more athletic" exterior was official, this after Dearborn had unveiled an obviously new model early on January 17, 2017, with help from larger-than-life actor Dwayne "the Rock" Johnson. And once the curtain rose on the latest, greatest Mustang, all the ink spared by critics the previous year came in handy, plus a pot-load more. Because a visual makeover wasn't the whole story.

"This is one of the most aggressive refreshes you'll ever see for a vehicle," beamed the breed's chief engineer, Carl Widmann, during Ford's traditional intro that fall. "We identified everything that is important to Mustang fans and delivered across the board, and we couldn't be happier with the end result"

Apparently those devotees no longer cared for the good ol' 3.7-liter V-6, as only the EcoBoost four-holer and bent-eight GT rolled on after 2017. Additionally, the four-cylinder folk must've liked roasting the weenies, too, for electronic line-lock was now standard EcoBoost *and* GT fare after being limited to 5.0 customers for three years. EcoBoosters furthermore were treated to 30 extra pounds of torque as 2018's 2.3-liter turbo four (still rated at 300 horsepower) was recalibrated to better take advantage of more durable driveline hardware.

Like its 5.0 running mate, this year's Ecoboost engine was fitted with a new dual-mass flywheel better able to handle more lb-ft. Beefier clutches

Above: A more aggressive facade that also cut through the wind better than before announced the arrival of 2018's Mustang. New too this year was a state-of-the-art SelectShift 10-speed automatic transmission and available MagneRide dampers.

Left: Electronic line-lock became standard on all Mustangs in 2018 after previously being limited to GT models. EcoBoost buyers furthermore were treated to a new Pony Package, which among other things brought back the traditional "pony corral" grille badge last seen as part of one of 2015's anniversary packages.

were added in both cases, too, with a truly tough twin-disc design debuting in GT ranks. And of course each engine's available six-speed manual transmission also was updated to deal more confidently with additional torque.

The sixth generation's 6-speed automatic, however, followed the V-6 into the archives, replaced by a superior 10-speed Select-Shift unit developed jointly by Ford and General Motors. All those speeds predictably translated into supreme gear spacing for what Dearborn people justly called the best auto-box yet installed between Mustang flanks. Quicker, smoother shifts and that wide ratio span made maximizing acceleration child's play, just what the doctor ordered considering the EcoBoost's newfound muscle.

According to Ford, a supremely equipped 10-speed turbo Mustang could hit 60 miles per hour in less than five seconds in 2018. Oh doctor! And let's not forget this year's GT, which reportedly (again by factory people) now could bust the four-second barrier, establishing a new all-time Mustang best and beating a $94,000 Porsche 911 Carrera in the process. Good night, nurse!

Along with that foolproof 10-speed, a slightly bigger, better 5.0L V-8 helped 2018's GT make those Porsche owners cry like a little . . . well, cry. While that revered metric label remained unchanged, a slight bore job (from 92.2 mm to 93.0) upped Yankee-speak displacement from 302 cubes to 307, and those 5 extra inches were joined by improved cylinder heads and a modernized dual-injection system that featured optimized low-pressure port injectors coupled with new high-pressure direct squirters. The end result was 25 more horses and 20 more lb-ft of torque.

On the surface, 2018's pumped-up athlete was refashioned most notably in front (hood, fenders and grille) to both enhance a "meaner, leaner look" (Ford's words) and improve aerodynamics, thanks to a general lowering and a new truly functional splitter. Meanwhile, front illumination for the first time was supplied by light-emitting diodes as modernized headlamps and turn signals joined the traditional tri-bar taillights in the state-of-the-art LED realm. Those sequential taillamps also were restyled, as was the rear fascia.

Updated seating surfaces inside could be complemented by the optional Premium Plus Package, which among other things added wrapped knee bolsters along with special stitching for the leather seats, console, and dash. And the start button now pulsed red—at 30 times a minute, "like the heart of a resting pony"—to warmly welcome riders into their saddles as soon as the doors unlocked.

The Mustang's first heated steering wheel option appeared for 2018, but even bigger news was the available 12-inch all-digital instrument cluster, included in this year's equally new Premium Plus Package. In part developed by video gamers, this too-cool-for-school feature could be customized to suit countless drivers' whims. Gauge type, readout style, color—you name it, it could be personalized. Fun for the entire family.

Above: Ford Performance marked the Cobra Jet Mustang's 50th birthday in 2018 with another turn-key drag car, announced on August 16 that year. A supercharged 5.2-liter V-8 guaranteed quarter-mile blasts in the 8-second range and a top end exceeding 150 miles per hour. Commemorative graphics also were available for 2018's CJ, limited to a production run of 68 cars in honor of the Cobra Jet's birth year.

Left: The Level 2 Performance Package, which did the carryover GT Performance Pack more than one better, was new for 2018 5.0L manual-trans fastbacks. Representing what Ford considered to be the most track-ready non-Shelby Mustang yet, the Level 2 GT featured MagneRide dampers, Michelin Pilot Sport Cup 2 tires and various aerodynamic upgrades, including a notably enlarged, Boss 302-inspired front splitter.

Above: On August 8, 2018, more than 60 pony car enthusiasts helped commemorate Ford's production of its 10 millionth Mustang by spelling out the news with their beloved rides in the Flat Rock plant's parking lot. The actual milestone model was a 2019 GT convertible—done, of course, in Wimbledon White.

Left: After kicking tail on NASCAR's Infinity circuit for eight years, Mustang graduated up to the Monster Energy Cup series. First came an unveiling for company employees at Ford World Headquarters on August 9, 2018, followed by the car's competition debut at 2019's Daytona 500 the following February.

Hitting the flashing button inside a 2018 GT equipped with another new option, active valve performance exhaust, possibly allowed a 5.0 to go where no 5.0 had gone before: quietly out of the garage. For starters, this addition presented drivers with a choice of four operating modes—"normal," "sport," "track," or "quiet"—each emitting varying decibel levels courteously tailored to fit in appropriately amidst the traffic at hand.

But again that wasn't the whole tale. A fifth choice also was included in this deal: "quiet start," or "Good Neighbor Mode" as Ford engineers called it. One of those better idea guys, Steve von Foerster, dreamed up this industry first after rudely awoken neighbors called the law on him and his bellowing GT350 early one morning as he prepared to head for the office. He wasn't ticketed, nor was he pissed; he completely understood, hence he indeed went right to work.

The fruits of his thoughtful labor involved a timer that made it possible to program a GT to automatically begin the day in quiet mode. No need to consider consideration, just grab the coffee and go, with nary a worry about forgetting that, yes, other ears lived right next door. Then it was let 'er rip once out of a sleepy neighborhood onto wild and/or wooly I-94.

How well did Foerster's scheme keep the peace? Quite, or at least according to exhaust development engineer Matt Flis. "When sounds get up into the upper-70-decibel range, that's typically about when they start to bother people," he said in June 2017. "With quiet start activated, the decibel level of the new GT drops by about 10, to a much more comfortable 72 decibels—about the level of a household dishwasher." Huh, wonder where he buys his kitchen appliances?

Various other Mustang firsts on 2018's options list plainly appealed to safety-conscious techno-crazies, including precollision assist with pedestrian detection and automatic emergency braking, lane-keeping assist, and a driver alert system. Then there were the video gamers, who also must've loved the dazzling 12-inch all-digital instrument cluster (showcased in the aforementioned Premium Plus Package) that now allowed drivers to customize their data readouts in seemingly endless fashions.

A familiar option, the drive mode system offered from the sixth generation's outset, carried over but now featured five choices, as "drag strip" joined the existing "normal," "snow/wet," "sport+," and "track" selections. As one might guess, this fifth mode enhanced straight-line performance by working in electronic cahoots with transmission and tire to not let precious time slip-slide away. Cooperating best with drag mode, in the latter's case, was a North American production car first: Michelin's hottest new rubber, the Pilot Sport 4S summer tire.

These sticky treads were included in yet another rollover option, the twin Performance Packages also listed from the sixth gen's startup for both EcoBoost and GT models. Again, these two Packs added bigger brakes, a beefier suspension, and enlarged wheels to go along with those weather-limited Michelins. And upping the handling ante further were available MagneRide dampers, applied for the first time to non-Shelby Mustangs.

It was those Michelins, 2018's drag mode, and Ford's 10-speed automatic that made the aforementioned record 0–60 runs possible, as Carl Widmann explained in July 2017: "Gearing matters, and in drag strip mode, this car launches better than ever off the line. Typically, when you shift gears, you give up time. In [this] mode, engine torque doesn't drop when you're shifting. You get peak torque and horsepower straight through thanks to our new 10-speed."

Maximizing 5.0 performance off the straight and narrow was made possible by a second GT Performance Package, aptly labeled "Level 2." Let loose for manual-trans GT fastbacks only in the spring of 2018, this option, in Ford parlance, "[bridged] the gap between GT Performance Pack and GT350."

2015–2020 Shelby GT350

Model availability	2-door fastback coupe (GT350 & GT350R)
Construction	Unitized welded-steel body w/aluminum hood, front fenders & bumper
Wheelbase	107.1 inches
Length	188.9 inches, GT350; 189.7 inches, GT350R
Width	75.9 inches (discounting mirrors)
Height	54.2 inches, GT350; 53.6, GT350R
Curb weight	3,791 pounds, GT350; 3,703, GT350R
Track (front/rear, in inches)	63.3/63.7
Wheels, GT350	aluminum 19x10.5, front; 19x11, rear
Wheels, GT350R	carbon-fiber, 19x11, front, 19x11.5, rear
Tires, GT350	Michelin Pilot Super Sport (P295/35ZR19, front; P305/35ZR19, rear) **NOTE:** Michelin Pilot Sport Cup 2 tires (in same sizes) became standard in 2019
Tires, GT350R	Michelin Pilot Sport Cup 2 (P305/30ZR19, front; P315/30ZR19, rear)
Suspension	Double-ball-joint independent MacPherson strut w/1.34-inch tubular stabilizer bar, front; integral-link independent w/coil springs & 0.87-inch tubular stabilizer bar, rear **NOTE 1:** GT350R's rear stabilizer bar featured 0.31-inch shorter arms compared to GT350's **NOTE 2:** MagneRide dampers included with GT350R & 2017–2020 GT350; this system was optional for 2015–2016 GT350
Steering	Electric power-assisted rack & pinion w/selectable effort
Brakes	4-wheel power vented discs w/4-sensor, 4-channel ABS, AdvanceTrac electronic stability control **NOTE:** Smooth rotors replaced cross-drilled units in 2019
Brake sizes	15.5-inch discs w/6-piston aluminum Brembo calipers, front; 15-inch discs w/4-piston aluminum Brembo calipers & drum-in-hat parking brake, rear
Engine	5.2-liter (315 cubic inches) 32-valve Ti-VCT DOHC V-8 w/flat-plane crank & aluminum cylinder block & heads
Output	526 horsepower, 429 lb-ft torque
Bore & stroke (inches)	3.70 x 3.66
Compression	12:1
Fuel delivery	Port fuel injection
Transmission	6-speed Tremec manual w/dual-disc clutch
Fuel tank	16 gallons
Axle ratio (std)	3.73:1 in Torsen differential

You name it—if it worked on a long, winding road course, it was in there. MagneRide dampers and stiffened springs and sway bars. Enlarged front splitter and redesigned rear spoiler. Quicker steering, massive 19-inch wheels (10.5 inches wide in front, 11 in back), and 1.5-inch-wider, lower-profile Michelin Pilot Sport Cup 2 tires that helped drop a Level 2 GT a half-inch closer to the ground. The sum of these parts equaled as track ready a Mustang as ever seen outside the Shelby corral.

Speaking of Shelby, this time it was the GT350/350R duo that stood pat, rolling over identically from 2017 complete with that year's bodywork. Following earlier hints of an upcoming GT500 that had some concluding it would supersede the GT350, Ford further teased pony lovers in January 2018 during Detroit's North American International Auto Show but only with a historical display showcasing a 1967 big-block Shelby. Dohhhh! A real look at a real next-gen GT500 wouldn't come until 2019's NAIAS.

2019

"If it ain't broke, don't fix it" was mostly the motto again for 2019—once more understandably so as Mustang continued its world dominance. More typical color changes and some adjustments to the options list . . . sound familiar?

But there was some intriguing news concerning standard 5.0 mechanicals, as this year's GT six-speed manual was upgraded with rev-matching technology. The trick this time involved automatically matching engine rpm to the next gear change, up or down, to help both smooth out the progression/regression and maximize efficiency, whether on a Sunday drive or pounding the ground with great vigor.

Nearly all other headlines involved options, and much more boldly than in 2017. First, active valve performance exhaust was offered to EcoBoost buyers along with their GT comrades in 2019. And once in quiet mode, all customers could really appreciate the new B&O premium sound system, which replaced the venerable Shaker audio option. Innovators at Bang & Olufsen specifically customized this equipment to blow Mustang riders away (regardless of what was going on beneath the hood) via a 10-channel amplifier that delivered 1,000 head-bangin' watts to 12 higher-than-hi-fidelity (remember that label?) speakers. "Cowabunga" (yet another oldie, goldie) was not a big enough word.

New too for 2019 was yet another California Special package, returning after a one-year hiatus. Again offered for premium GT fastbacks and convertibles, this option produced impressions similar to the 2017–18 rendition and couldn't be combined with either Performance Package, regular or Level 2.

Another blast from the past, 2019's Bullitt Mustang fastback, was announced in January 2018, just in time to help mark the 50th anniversary of the Steve McQueen movie pony lovers still can't forget. Highland Green paint again played a role in the latest Bullitt plot, or buyers could've opted for a Shadow Black finish. Big Brembo brakes, heavy-duty underpinnings, and a Torsen differential were among standard features. But the star of the show was a six-speed-backed, modified 5.0 V-8 that made 480 horsepower. And, yes, a no-nonsense exterior once more was part of the deal.

"This new Bullitt is, as Steve McQueen was, effortlessly cool," said Mustang chief designer Darrell Behmer. "It's my favorite Mustang—devoid of stripes, spoilers, and badges. It doesn't need to scream about anything; it's just cool."

Still hotter than ever, Ford's 526-horsepower Shelby was treated to a fair dose of technical upgrading for 2019. Track experience, coupled with lessons learned during GT500 development, helped engineers heighten the GT350's ability to turn laps quicker than you can say "is that a Camaro back there?" Most notable was a new standard tire, Michelin's Pilot Sport Cup 2, mounted on updated 19-inch aluminum wheels adorned in Ebony paint. Spring rates, sway bar stiffness, and MagneRide damping were recalibrated, as was the ABS system, with the goal being to put those Michelins—they with their GT350-specific tread pattern—to best use. A redesigned spoiler also

Above: New on the EcoBoost front in 2019 was available active valve performance exhaust, a decibel-adjusting option limited to GT Mustangs in 2018. All models this year could be equipped with a booming 12-speaker B&O premium sound system, which superseded the venerable Shaker Pro audio option.

Below: Need for Green paint, one of three new finishes meant to turn heads with what color and materials manager Barbara Whalen called a "confident and youthful attitude," was announced for the upcoming 2019 Mustang in March 2018, just in time for St. Patrick's Day. The others were Velocity Blue and notably nostalgic Dark Highland Green.

Above: Temporarily shelved after 2017, the California Special package returned for GT Premium fastbacks and convertibles in 2019, in familiar fashion. Stripes, an offset grille badge, side scoops, and a rear spoiler again were included, as was a Performance Package splitter in front and high-gloss black-accented 19x8.5 aluminum wheels at the corners.

Left: Yet another anniversary gift appeared in January 2018 as Ford marked the movie *Bullitt*'s 50th birthday with a third-edition commemorative Mustang, done of course in Dark Highland Green paint. Offered for both 2019 and 2020, the latest Bullitt Mustang was powered by a 480-horsepower 5.0L V-8.

was added, the better to cheat the wind like no Mustang before.

Adjustable strut mounts on top were made standard for the GT350R, optional in the GT350's case as part of a new Handling Package, which also included a competition-style Gurney flap to additionally enhance downforce at the tail. The R-model further sported a new steering rack fitted with recalibrated electronic power assist, joined by redesigned steering knuckles (sourced from the GT500 parts bin) that helped revise front suspension geometry. A reborn Technology Package, this time featuring the bonkers B&O sound system, debuted as well for 2019's Shelby, while the familiar Convenience, Electronic, and R-Electronic options didn't return.

Left: Special "Bullitt" identification was predictably included inside the 2019–20 Mustang that again would've made Steve McQueen proud, along with a heated steering wheel and the coveted 12-inch LCD digital dash. And don't forget that nostalgic "cue ball" shift knob.

Below: GT350 wheels and rear spoiler were new for 2019, as was its standard tire: Michelin's Pilot Sport Cup 2. A new option, the Handling Package, added a Gurney flap out back, along with adjustable strut-top mounts.

Above: Three new optional wheels appeared for 2020's Mustang—plus a few more typical paint scheme trade-outs and that was just about that in the latest What's New category. Ford people were proudest of the most crowded pony car lineup in years. Along with the 460-horsepower GT, buyers could choose between EcoBoost, Bullitt, California Special, and now, two Shelbys—the rollover GT350 and its GT500 big-bully brother.

Right: Ford announced yet another new finish suitable for St. Paddy's Day presentation in March 2019, this time for 2020's Mustang/Shelby lineup. "It's lime green on steroids," added pony car palette guru Barb Whalen a year after she painted the Need for Green picture for the press. "This color traces back to a Mustang heritage color while bringing it forward with more modern, dynamic pigments and bold new energy." Translated: this 2020 Shelby's buyer was gonna require shades.

2020

Both the third-edition Bullitt and California Special package encored for 2020 but were completely overshadowed by the long-awaited GT500, discussed a few more column inches down the road here. Changes were fewer than ever, beginning with FordPass Connect technology being made standard across the Mustang board this year after achieving the same status in 2019's Shelby lineup. Previously included in the Premium Plus Package, FordPass connectivity allowed drivers to locate, monitor, lock/unlock, and remote start (in automatic trans applications, of course) their rides using their smartphones.

Above: Two EcoBoost varieties also were offered for the first time in 2020: the 310-horsepower base model and its 2.3L High Performance Package alter ego, fitted with a 330-horsepower turbo four and various GT chassis components.

Left: Along with 20 more horsepower, the 2.3L High Performance option also added a black-painted strut tower brace beneath the hood. Available only for this year's 330-horsepower fastbacks, 2020's EcoBoost Handling Package additionally added MagneRide dampers, premium brakes, Pirelli Corsa summer-only rubber on 19x9.5 wheels, and 3.55:1 Torsen rear gears.

A Heritage Edition Package appeared for the two latest Shelbys to honor the Mustang's 55-year-old racing legacy, predictably bringing with it traditional Wimbledon White paint complemented by Guardsman Blue stripes. But arguably the biggest 2020 news not supplied by the GT500 was made in EcoBoost quarters, where turbo fans were rewarded with the most powerful four-cylinder sports car ever unleashed by an American maker.

Replacing the EcoBoost Performance Pack this year was the widely acclaimed 2.3L High Performance Package, which began life as a Ford Performance "skunkworks" project that involved swapping the defunct RS Focus' hopped-up

2018–2021

Model availability	2-door fastback coupe, 2-door convertible
Construction	Unitized welded-steel body w/aluminum hood and front fenders
Wheelbase	107.1 inches
Length	188.5 inches
Width	76.1 inches (discounting mirrors)
Height	54.3 inches, coupe; 54.9 inches, convertible
Track (front/rear, in inches)	62.4/65.1
Wheels	17x7.5, std EcoBoost; 18x8, std GT
Tires	P235/55R17, std EcoBoost; P235/50RW18, std GT
Suspension	Double-ball-joint independent MacPherson strut w/tubular stabilizer bar, front; integral-link independent w/coil springs, solid stabilizer bar, rear
Steering	Electric power-assisted rack & pinion (16:1 ratio)
Brakes	4-wheel power discs w/4-sensor, 4-channel ABS, AdvanceTrac electronic stability control & electronic line lock
Brake sizes (EcoBoost)	12.6-inch vented discs w/twin-piston aluminum calipers, front; 12.6-inch solid discs w/single-piston aluminum calipers & integral parking brake, rear
Brake sizes (GT)	13.9-inch vented discs w/4-piston fixed aluminum calipers, front; 12.6-inch vented discs w/single-piston floating iron calipers & integral parking brake in back
Optional brakes (w/EcoBoost Performance Package)	13.9-inch vented discs w/4-piston fixed aluminum calipers in front; 15.0-inch vented discs w/single-piston floating iron calipers in back
Optional brakes (w/GT Performance Package)	15.0-inch vented discs w/Brembo 6-piston fixed aluminum calipers, front; 15.0-inch vented discs w/single-piston floating iron calipers, rear
Engine (EcoBoost)	2.3-liter 16-valve DOHC inline 4-cylinder w/aluminum cylinder block & head
Engine (GT)	5.0-liter 32-valve Ti-VCT DOHC V-8 w/aluminum cylinder block & heads
Output	310 hp, Ecoboost I4; 435 hp, GT V-8
Bore & stroke (inches)	3.45 x 3.7, EcoBoost I4; 3.63 x 3.65, V-8
Compression	9.5:1, EcoBoost I4; 12.0:1, V-8
Fuel delivery	Direct injection, EcoBoost I4; dual fuel injection, V-8
Transmission	6-speed manual; 10-speed SelectShift automatic, optional
Fuel tank	16 gallons, GT; 15.5 gallons, EcoBoost
Axle ratio (std)	3.31:1, EcoBoost & GT (w/manual trans); 3.15:1 (w/automatic)
Optional axle ratio (all models)	3.55:1 (included w/EcoBoost Performance Package)
Optional axle ratio (GT Performance Package)	3.73:1 in Torsen differential

turbo-four into a Mustang. A mere 10 months later, this experiment morphed into a production reality, powered by a formidable 2.3-liter mill that now churned out 330 horsepower—enough newfound oomph to push 0–60 runs well down into the four-second range and boost top end to 155 miles per hour.

Mere muscle, however, wasn't the sole focus. GT brakes were included, too, along with suspension and aero goodies copped from the GT Performance Package, including summer-only 255/40R-19 rubber. "Combined with the grippier tires, [these] updates transform the EcoBoost into a road scalpel," concluded *Car and Driver*'s Eric Stafford after encountering what he called the "ghost of Focus RS past."

Promising even sharper cutting-edge performance was 2020's new EcoBoost Handling Package, which added even wider wheels and bigger brakes, 265/40R-19 Pirelli Corsa4 summer-only tires, and MagneRide damping. Available only in concert with the 2.3L High Performance Package, this option was limited to EcoBoost fastbacks, unlike the High Perf Pack, which was available alone in both bodies, with top or without.

2020 GT500

As short press releases go, this one almost didn't make the chart. On June 19, 2019, Dearborn abruptly announced what rumor-mongers had long figured, that the upcoming GT500 would be the most powerful street-legal Ford ever. Among the first paragraph's forty or so words were "760 horsepower" and "625 lb-ft torque," followed by a second one-sentence 'graph that simply read "Enough said." Language artists rested easy; not one word was minced during the making of this historic statement.

Pairing "supercharged" and "Shelby" in the same sentence once again, this reborn GT500 fastback relied on a hand-built, all-aluminum 5.2-liter V-8 to produce those really big numbers. Tucked down nicely between its four-valve, dual-overhead-cam heads was an inverted 2.65-liter Eaton blower that huffed through an air-to-water intercooler. Port fuel injectors shot the juice and stainless-steel tubular headers dealt with the byproducts. In between were forged-aluminum pistons (9.5:1 compression), micro-alloy forged rods, and a forged-steel cross-plane crank. Helping hold things together on the bottom end was an oversized (11-quart) cast-aluminum oil pan that bolted up simultaneously to engine and transmission.

That trans was equally historic, a first-in-class dual-clutch unit, the only choice behind those 760 ponies. This Tremec TR-9070 auto-box featured seven speeds, which it could precisely change in as little as 80 milliseconds. Such inhuman quickness simply can't be put into words, perhaps explaining why Ford folk didn't bother early on.

Among the long list of standard chassis stuff were Brembo brakes (with ventilated rotors), MagneRide dampers, Michelin Pilot Sport 4S tires, and nation-wide 20-inch wheels. Body mods included a big front splitter, wider front fenders, rear spoiler and diffuser, and a bulging hood with tie-downs. One look made it clear that the latest GT500's aerodynamic abilities had reached all-time highs, too.

Even more aero enhancement came via the available Carbon Fiber Track Pack, which added a GT4 wing (predictably done in exposed carbon fiber) and splitter wickers up front. Wheels too were of exposed carbon fiber (along with the instrument panel) and tires were upgraded to Pilot Cup Sport 2 Michelins. Additional GT500 options included its own Technology Package (starring the B&O sound system) and a Handling Package that added a Gurney flap and those splitter wickers.

Above: Enlarging the splitter and rear spoiler on 2020's GT350 made news, as did an available Heritage Package, created to honor the Mustang's 55-year-old racing legacy. Priced at $1,965 (wink, wink), this option starred Wimbledon White paint accented by Guardsman Blue stripes, an unforgettable combo that various rivals watched speed away back in 1965 and '66.

Left: Evidence that a new world indeed was turning arrived in April 2020 in the form of Ford Performance's Cobra Jet 1400 drag car prototype, driven by 1,400 electrically generated horses. Initial tests resulted in a best quarter-mile pass of 8.27 seconds at 168 miles per hour. Later in September, a national television audience was on hand for a match race between electric and fueled Cobra Jets, with the loud, cranky version barely beating its silent-but-deadly cousin by a nose.

Above: Unique GT500 body parts included its hood (with tie-down pins), front fascia, fenders, grille (with large radiator block-off plate), splitter, and rear valance. The standard rear spoiler could be superseded by a big GT4 wing, included in the available Carbon Fiber Track Pack.

Left: The GT500's all-aluminum 5.2L V-8 was crowned with an inverted 2.65-liter Eaton supercharger and a big 92-millimeter throttle body. The only transmission choice behind this monster was a 7-speed dual-clutch Tremec unit that Ford developed in cooperation with General Motors.

2021

Various ships passed in the night as 2020 rolled over into 2021. The EcoBoost's 2.3L High Performance Package returned, but the Level 2 GT Performance Pack didn't. The California Special option continued, but the Bullitt Mustang exited stage right. And the all-powerful GT500 now reigned supreme in Shelby world after the ever-constant GT350/GT350R duo finally retired, as previously rumored, at 2020's end. But, although the elder Shelby was gone, its Tremec six-speed manual trans carried on, with rev-matching, for 2021's GT.

Making news in all Mustang cases in 2021 was the standard installation of Ford's Co-Pilot 360 technology. Enhancing safety was this conglomerate's goal, hence the inclusion of

With its 760 supercharged horses, 2020's new GT500 could hit 60 miles per hour from rest in less than three seconds, world-class performance befitting this planet's best-selling sports car. Quarter-mile times of less than 11 seconds further impressed as other worldly.

2020–2021 Shelby GT500

Model availability	2-door fastback coupe
Construction	Unitized welded-steel body w/sheet-molded-compound (SMC) front fenders & hood
Wheelbase	107.1 inches
Length	189.5 inches
Width	76.6 inches (discounting mirrors)
Height	54.3 inches (53.7 w/Carbon Fiber Track Package option)
Curb weight	4,171 pounds
Track (front/rear, in inches)	63.3/64.3 (63.8/64.4 w/Carbon Fiber Track Package option)
Wheels	20x11 flow-formed aluminum **NOTE:** Carbon Fiber Track Package added exposed carbon-fiber wheels (20x11, front; 20x11.5, rear)
Tires	Michelin Pilot Sport 4S (P305/30R20, front; P315/30R20, rear) **NOTE:** Carbon Fiber Track Package added Michelin Pilot Sport Cup 2 tires in same sizes
Suspension	Double-ball-joint independent MacPherson strut w/1.42-inch tubular stabilizer bar, front; integral-link independent w/coil springs & 0.94-inch tubular stabilizer bar, rear; MagneRide dampers **NOTE:** Carbon Fiber Track Package added thicker (1.39-inch) rear stabilizer bar
Steering	Three-mode electric power-assisted rack & pinion (16:1 ratio)
Brakes	4-wheel power vented discs w/4-sensor, 4-channel ABS, AdvanceTrac electronic stability control
Brake sizes	16.5-inch discs w/6-piston aluminum Brembo calipers, front; 14.6-inch discs w/4-piston aluminum Brembo calipers & electric spot-caliper parking brake, rear
Engine	Supercharged 5.2-liter (315 cubic inches) 32-valve Ti-VCT DOHC V-8 w/aluminum cylinder block & heads
Output	760 horsepower, 625 lb-ft torque
Bore & stroke (inches)	3.70 x 3.66
Compression	9.5:1
Fuel delivery	Port fuel injection & 2.65-liter inverted supercharger
Transmission	7-speed Tremec TR 9070 dual-clutch
Fuel tank	16 gallons
Axle ratio (std)	3.73:1 in Torsen differential

automatic high-beam headlights, a blind-spot information system with cross-traffic alert, lane-keeping assist/alert, precollision assist with automatic emergency braking, and a rearview camera.

The most notable GT500 updates came on 2021's option list, where the Carbon Fiber Handling Package debuted with its black carbon fiber wheels, adjustable strut mounts, Gurney flap, splitter wickers, wheel locks, and a catch can. Last but by no means least amidst 2021's newsmakers was yet another nostalgic revival, now involving the return of the Mach 1 fastback following a 17-year break.

"This is one of those special Mustangs that truly brings a smile to the faces of our owners, enthusiasts, and fans, including me," said Ford chief Jim Farley while announcing his company's latest memory mobile in June 2020. "So there's never been a better time to bring back Mach 1 and have it go global, too."

Familiar imagery was just the beginning. Like so many of its ancestors, 2021's Mach 1 was no slouch when it came time to take flight, its 480-horsepower 5.0L V-8 made sure of that. Various leftover GT350 parts found a home in the Mach 1 engine bay, including its oil cooler, and the Shelby-proven Tremec six-speed manual trans was put to good use, too. Michelin summer-only rubber was predictably part of this deal as well, along with MagneRide damping, 3.73:1 gears in a Torsen differential, and various body modifications.

An optional Handling Package added even more aero improvements, working in concert, of course, with additional chassis beefs. An Elite Package injected the B&O sound into the Mach 1 mix, and an Appearance Package combined Fighter Jet Gray paint with an ebony/orange interior, unique orange-painted brake calipers, and black/orange body striping.

A suitable exclamation point to the Mustang tale's latest, greatest chapter? Damn straight. How many more entries remain? Stay tuned.

Left: Sending pony lovers back in time again was 2021's Mach 1 fastback, powered by a 480-horse 5.0L V-8. Standard mechanicals among other things included Brembo brakes, coolers for engine, transmission, and differential lubes/fluids, an enlarged radiator, beefed-up chassis with MagneRide dampers and active valve performance exhausts. Buyers could chose between the 10-speed SelectShift automatic and a Tremec six-speed stick with rev matching.

Below Left: Unique Mach 1 body mods included front and rear lower fascias; upper, lower, and outboard grillework; and various stripes. Michelin PS4 tires on 19x9.5 wheels were standard. An available Mach 1 Handling Package added fatter rubber on wider (10.5-inch) wheels.

Below Right: Various bits of appropriate identification, complete with chassis number posting, were predictably included inside 2021's Mach 1. As were power seats (six-way, driver; four-way, passenger) and that endlessly entertaining 12-inch digital instrumentation cluster.

Left: On April 26, 2021, Dearborn's Ford Performance Parts group announced availability of aftermarket carbon-fiber exterior components to help trim weight off the GT500. Four options were listed: hood vent and rain tray kit, front splitter with belly pan, front bumper insert (to fit between upper and lower grille intakes), and a rear decklid trim panel. Together these track-targeted upgrades weighed 9 fewer pounds than their stock counterparts.

Appendix
Options

Printed with permission from Mustang Red Book 1964-½–2004, Fourth Edition, MBI Publishing Company, 0-7603-1980-4

1965 Mustang Prices	Retail
2dr Hardtop, 65A	$2,320.96
Convertible, 76A	2,557.64
2+2 Fastback, 63A	2,533.19
200hp 289 V-8 extra charge over 120 hp 6 cyl	105.63
225hp 289 V-8 extra charge over 200 hp V-8	52.85
271hp 289 V-8-without GT Equipment Group	327.92
271hp 289 V-8-with GT Equipment Group	276.34
Cruise-O-Matic automatic transmission with 6 cyl	175.80
Cruise-O-Matic automatic transmission with 200/225hp V-8s	185.39
4-speed manual transmission-6 cyl	113.45
4-speed manual transmission-V-8 engines	184.02
Manual disc brakes-front-8 cyl	56.77
Limited slip differential	41.60
Rally-Pac clock/tachometer	69.30
Special Handling Package-200 & 225 hp V-8s	30.64
GT Equipment Group	165.03
Wheels-styled steel-8 cyl only	119.71
Power brakes	42.29
Power steering	84.47
Power top-convertible	52.95
Emergency flashers	19.19
Padded visors, 65A,76A	5.58
Seatbelts, rear	14.78
Deluxe seatbelts, front (retractable)	7.39
Deluxe seatbelts, front & rear (front retractors)	25.40
Visibility Group	35.83
Accent Group, 65A, 76A	27.11
Accent Group, 63A	13.90
Air conditioner-Ford	277.20
Back-up lamps	10.47
Battery, heavy-duty	7.44
Closed California Emission System	5.19
Console, full-length	50.41
Console, with air conditioner	31.52
Interior Decor Group	107.08
Full-width seat (bench) with center armrest, 65A, 76A	24.42
Glass-tinted with banded windshield	30.25
Windshield only, tinted and banded	21.09
Radio, push-button and antenna	57.51
Rocker panel molding, 65A, 76A	15.76
Steering wheel, deluxe	31.52
Vinyl roof, 65A	74.19
Wheel covers, knock-off hubs	17.82
Magic Aire heater-delete (credit)	(31.52)
Seatbelts-delete (credit)	(10.76)
Tires-6 cyl, extra charge over 6.50x13 4-ply p.r.	
BSW (5) 6.50x13 4-p.r. WSW	33.30
(5) 6.95x14 4-p.r. BSW	7.36
(5) 6.95x14 4 p.r. WSW	40.67
Tires-8 cyl, extra charge over 6.95x14 4-p.r. BSW	
(5) 6.95x14 4-p.r. WSW	33.31
(5) 6.95x14 4-p.r. BSW Nylon	15.67*
(5) 6.95x14 4-p.r. WSW Nylon	48.69*
5) 6.95x14 4-p.r. Dual Red Band Nylon (Std 271hp)	48.97
* NC with 271hp 289 V-8	

1965 Dealer Added Accessories	
Door edge guards	$2.70
Rocker panel molding (set)	19.10
Deluxe with spinner 13-inch wheel covers	28.95
Deluxe with spinner 14-inch wheel covers	28.95
Simulated wire 13-inch wheel covers	58.35
Simulated wire 14-inch wheel covers	58.35
Luggage rack	35.00
Tonneau cover-white	52.70
Tonneau cover-black	52.70
(L.H.) Spotlight	29.95
Vanity mirror	1.95
License plate frame	4.50
Fire extinguisher	33.70
Compass	7.95
AM radio	53.50
Rear seat speaker	11.95
Studio Sonic Sound System (Reverb)	22.95
Round (cone shaped) outside mirror	3.95
Left-hand remote mirror	2.25
Universal (flat) outside mirror	12.75
Matching right-hand mirror	6.75
Inside day/night mirror	4.95
Back-up lights	10.40
Power brakes	47.00
Glove-box lock	2.49
Remote control trunk release	6.95
Windshield washers	14.50
Rally Pac-6 cyl	75.95
Rally Pac-8 cyl	75.95

1965 Shelby Prices	
Street	$4,547.00
Race 5,995.00	

1966 Mustang Prices	Retail
2dr Hardtop, 65A	$2,416.18
Convertible, 76A	2,652.86
2+2 Fastback, 63A	2,607.07
200hp 289 ci V-8 extra charge over 6 cyl	105.63
225hp 289 ci V-8 extra charge over 200hp 289 ci	52.85
271hp 289 ci with GT Equipment Group	276.34
271hp 289 ci without GT Equipment Group	327.92
Cruise-O-Matic automatic transmission-6 cyl	175.80
Cruise-O-Matic automatic transmission-200&225hp V-8s	185.3
Cruise-O-Matic automatic transmission-271hp V-8	216.27
4-speed manual 6 cyl	113.45
4-speed manual 8 cyl	184.02
Power brakes	42.29
Power steering	84.47
Power top, convertible	52.95
Air conditioner, Ford	310.90
AM Radio-Stereosonic Tape System (requires radio)	128.29
Front seat, full with armrest (65A & 76A)	24.42
Luggage rack, rear deck lid (65A & 76A)	32.44
Radio and antenna	57.51
Accent stripe-less rear quarter ornamentation	13.90
Console, full-length	50.41
Console, with air conditioner	31.52
Deluxe steering wheel	32.20
Interior Decor Group	94.13
Vinyl roof-65A	74.36
Wire wheel covers	58.24
Wheel covers, knock-off hubs	19.48
Closed Crankcase emissions system	5.19
Exhaust emission control system (NA 271hp)	45.45
MagicAire heater-delete option	(31.52)
Disc brakes-front-8 cyl (NA with power brakes)	56.77
Limited slip differential	41.60
Rally Pac-clock/tachometer	69.30
Special Handling Package-200 & 225hp V-8s	30.64
GT Equipment Group-with 225 & 271hp V-8s	152.20
Wheels, styled steel-14-inch" (8 cyl. only)	93.84
Battery, heavy-duty-55-amp	7.44
Electric windshield wipers-2 speed	12.95
Seatbelts-Deluxe front & rear (front retractors) and warning light	14.53
Visibility Group (remote mirror, day/night mirror & 2-speed wipers)	29.81
Glass, tinted with banded windshield	30.25
Glass, tinted with windshield only	21.09
Optional tires (except with 271hp 289) Extra charge for:(5) 6.95x14 4-p.r. WSW	33.31
(5) 6.95x14 4-p.r. BSW, nylon (NC with 271hp)	15.67
(5) 6.95x14 4-p.r. WSW, nylon (NC with 271hp)	48.89
(5) 6.95x14 4-p.r. Dual Red Band, nylon	48.97

1966 Shelby Mustang Prices	Retail
High-performance Ford automatic transmission	N/C
Fold-down rear seat	50.00
AM Radio	57.50
Alloy wheels	268.00*
Stripe	62.50
Detroit No-Spin rear axle unit	141.00
Cobra Supercharger (Paxton)	670.00
*Approx.	

1967 Mustang Prices	Retail
2dr Hardtop, 65A	$2,461.46
Convertible, 76A	2,698.14
2+2 Fastback, 63A	2,592.17
289 ci 200hp V-8	105.63
289 ci 225hp V-8	158.48
289 ci 271hp V-8 (with GT Equip. only)	433.55
390 ci 320hp V-8	263.71
Cruise-O-Matic automatic transmission, w/6	188.18
Cruise-O-Matic automatic transmission, w/200 or 225hp V-8	197.89
Cruise-O-Matic automatic transmission with 271 or 320hp	220.17
4-speed manual transmission w/200 & 225hp V-8	184.02
4-speed manual transmission w/271 & 320hp V-8	233.18
Heavy-duty three-speed manual, required with 320hp V-8	79.20
Power front disc brakes	64.77
Power steering	84.47
Power convertible top	52.95
GT Equipment Group (with V-8s only)	205.05
Limited slip differential	41.60
Styled steel wheels (2+2 only)	93.84
Styled steel wheels, all others	115.11
Competition Handling Package (with GT Equip. only)	388.53
Tinted windows and windshield	30.25
Convenience control panel	39.50
Fingertip speed control (requires V-8 & Cruise-O-Matic)	71.30
Remote-control outside mirror (Std 2+2)	9.58
Convertible safety glass rear window	32.44
SelectAire conditioner	356.09
Push-button radio, AM	57.51
Push-button radio, AM/FM	133.65
Stereo-Sonic tape system (AM radio required)	128.49
2+2 folding rear seat and access door (Sport Deck Option)	64.77
Full-width front seat (NA 2+2)	24.42
Tilt-away steering wheel	59.93
Rear deck luggage rack (2+2)	32.44
Comfort weave vinyl trim (NA convertible)	24.53
Center console (requires radio)	50.41
Deluxe steering wheel	31.52
Exterior Decor Group	38.86
Lower back panel grille	19.48
Interior Decor Group (Convertible)	94.36
Interior Decor Group (all others)	108.06
Two-tone paint (Lower back grille)	12.95
Accent Paint stripe	13.90
Vinyl covered roof (hardtop)	74.36
Wheel covers (Std 2+2)	21.34
Wire wheel covers (2+2)	58.24
Wire wheel covers (all others)	79.51
Wide Oval Sports tires (V-8 required)	62.35
Whitewall Tire option (typical)	33.31
Rocker panel molding (Std 2+2)	15.59
MagicAire heater (delete option)	(31.52)

1967 Shelby Mustang Prices	Retail
GT350	$3,995.00
GT500	4,195.00
Power disc brakes	64.77
Power steering	84.47
Shoulder harness	50.76
Select-O-Matic transmission	50.00
Air conditioner-SelectAire	356.09
Exhaust emission control system	45.45
Closed crankcase emission system	5.19
Fold-down rear seat	64.77
Radio, AM push-button	57.51

Deluxe wheels	185.00
Rallye stripe	34.95
Paxton Supercharger (GT350 only)	549.00

1968 Mustang Prices	Retail
2dr Hardtop, 63A	$2,578.60
Convertible	2,814.22
2+2 Fastback	2,689.26
289 ci 195hp V-8	105.63
302 ci 230hp V-8	171.77
390 ci 325hp V-8	263.71
427 ci 390hp V-8	622.00
428 ci 335hp V-8*	434.00
SelectShift Cruise-O-Matic (with 6 cyl)	191.12
SelectShift Cruise-O-Matic (with 195/230hp V-8s)	200.85
SelectShift Cruise-O-Matic (with 325hp V-8)	233.17
4-speed manual transmission (with 195/230hp V-8s)	184.02
4-speed manual transmission (with 325hp V-8)	233.18
Power front disc brakes (V-8s-required with 325hp V-8 onGT Equipment Group)	64.77
Power steering	84.47
Power convertible top	52.95
Convertible glass backlite	38.86
GT Equipment Group (with 230/325hp V-8, NA with SportsTrim Group or optional wheel covers)	146.71
Tachometer (V-8s only)	54.45
Limited slip differential	41.60
Tinted windows and windshield	30.25
Convenience Group (Console required with SelectAire)	32.44
Fingertip Speed Control (with V-8 and SelectShift)	73.83
Remote-control outside mirror (left-hand side)	9.58
SelectAire Conditioner	360.30
Push-button radio (AM)	61.40
AM/FM stereo radio	181.39
Stereo-Sonic tape system (AM radio required)	133.86
Sport deck rear seat (2+2 only)	64.77
Full-width front seat (hardtop & 2+2, NA console)	32.44
Tilt-away steering wheel	66.14
Center console (radio required)	53.71
Interior Decor Group (convertible & full-width front seat)	110.16
Interior Decor Group (all others without full-width seat)	123.86
Two-tone hood paint	19.48
Accept paint stripe	13.90
Vinyl covered roof (hardtop only)	74.36
Wheel covers (NA with GT Group or V-8 Sports Trim Groups)	21.34
Deluxe wheel covers (NA with GT Group or V-8 Sports Trim)	34.33
Wide Oval Tire option (V-8s only)	78.53
Whitewall tire option	33.31

*Available after April 1, 1968

1968 Shelby Mustang Prices	Retail
GT350 Fastback	$4,116.62
GT350 Convertible	4,238.14
GT500 Fastback	4,317.39
GT500 Convertible	4,438.91
GT500KR Fastback	4,472.57
GT500KR Convertible	4,594.09
Power disc brakes	64.77
Power steering	84.47
Shoulder harness	50.76
Fold-down rear seat (fastbacks only)	64.78
Push-button AM radio	57.59
Select-O-Matic Transmission	50.08
Tinted glass (air-conditioned cars only—required)	30.25
Tilt-away steering wheel	62.18

1969 Shelby Mustang Prices	Retail
GT350 SportsRoof	$4,434.00
GT350 Convertible	4,753.00
GT500 SportsRoof	4,709.00
GT500 Convertible	5,027.00
Close ratio 4-speed transmission (GT350 only, standard GT500)	N/C
Automatic transmission	30.54
Air conditioning	374.39
Optional axle ratio	6.13
Traction-Lok Differential	60.97
Drag Package	155.45
Sport Deck Rear Seat (fastback only)	91.51
Tilt-away steering wheel	62.24
Power Ventilation	37.83
AM Radio	57.38
AM/FM Stereo	170.76
Stereo Tape (requires AM radio)	125.64
Intermittent windshield wipers	15.85
Tinted glass	30.54
Heavy-duty batteries (GT350 only) Option #1	7.93
Option #2	15.85
F60x15 Goodyear tires-Extra Heavy-Duty Suspension Package	60.97

1969 Mustang Prices	Retail
Hardtop, 65A	$2,618.00
Convertible, 76A	2,832.00
SportsRoof, 63A	2,618.00
Mach 1, 63C	3,122.00
Grande, 65E	2,849.00
250 ci 155hp 6 cylinder (NA Mach 1)	25.91
302 ci 220hp V-8 (NA Mach 1)	105.00
Extra charge over 302 ci V-8 for:	
351 ci 250hp V-8 (Std Mach 1)	58.34
351 ci 290hp V-8 (except Mach 1)	84.25
Mach 1 over 351 ci 250hp	25.91
390 ci 320hp V-8 (except Mach 1)	58.08
Mach 1 over 351 ci 250hp	99.74
428 ci 335hp V-8 (except Mach 1)	287.53
Mach 1 over 351 ci 250hp	224.12
428 ci 335hp Ram-Air Cobra Jet V-8 (except M1)	420.96
Mach 1 over 351 ci 250hp	357.46
Boss 302 CID 4V 8-cyl engine	676.15
429 ci 4V Cobra Jet HO (Boss 429)	1208.35
SelectShift transmission w/6 cyl	191.13
W/302 & 351 ci V-8s	200.85
W/390 & 428 ci V-8s	222.08
4-speed manual transmission, 302 & 351 ci V-8s	204.64
4-speed manual transmission, 390 & 428 ci V-8s	253.92
Power front disc brake (NA 200 ci six)	64.77
Power steering	94.95
Power convertible top	52.95
Convertible glass rear window	38.86
GT Equipment Group (NA Grande, 6 cyl or 302 V-8)	146.71
Tachometer (V-8 only)	54.45
Limited slip differential (w/250 & 302 V-8)	41.60
Traction-Lok differential (NA 6s & 302 V-8)	63.51
Optional axle ratio	6.53
Intermittent windshield wipers	6.85
High-back bucket seats (NA Grande)	84.25
Color-keyed racing mirrors	19.48
Handling suspension (NA Grande or with 200, 250 & 428)	30.64
Competition Suspension (w/428 only, Std Mach 1)	30.64
Power ventilation (NA w/SelectAire)	40.02
Electric clock (Std Mach 1, Grande)	15.59
Tinted windshield & windows	32.44
Speed control (W/V-8 & SelectShift)	73.83
Remote-control outside mirror (LH)	2.95
SelectAire conditioner (NA 200 ci & 428 ci with 4-speed manual)	379.57
Push-button AM radio	61.40
AM/FM Stereo radio	181.36
Stereo-Sonic tape (AM radio required)	133.84
Rear seat speaker (hardtop & Grande)	12.95
Rear seat deck (SportsRoof & Mach 1)	97.21
Full-width front seat (hardtop, NA console)	32.44
Tilt-away steering wheel	66.14
Rim-Blow deluxe steering wheel	35.70
Console	53.82
Interior Decor Group (NA Mach 1, Grande)	101.10
Interior Decor Group w/color-keyed mirror opt.	88.15
Deluxe Interior Decor Group (Sports Roof & Conv.)	133.44
With color keyed mirror option	120.48
Deluxe seatbelts with warning light	15.59
Vinyl covered roof (Grande & hardtop)	84.25
Wheel covers (NA Mach 1, GT, Grande, std w/Exterior Decor Group)	21.38
Wire wheel covers (Std Grande, NA Mach 1, GT Group)	79.51
Wire wheel covers (W/Exterior Decor Group)	58.27
Exterior Decor Group (NA Mach 1, Grande)	32.44
Chrome styled steel wheels (Std Mach 1, NA Grande & 200-ci six)	116.59
with GT Group	77.73
with Exterior Decor	95.31
Adj. head restraints (NA Mach 1)	17.00
Visibility Group	11.16
Functional adj. rear spoiler (Boss 302)	19.48
Sport Slats (Boss 302)	128.28
Trunk-mounted 85-amp battery (Boss 429)	32.44
Functional front air spoiler (Boss 429)	13.05
Shaker Hood Scoop (351 & 390 engines)	84.25

1970 Mustang Prices	Retail
Hardtop 65A	$2,721.00
SportsRoof 63A	2,771.00
Convertible 76A	3,025.00
Grande 65E	2,926.00
Mach 1 63C	3,271.00
Boss 302	3,720.00
250 cid 155hp Six. Extra charge over 200 CID Six	39.00
302 cid 220hp V-8. Extra charge over 200 CID Six	101.00
351 cid 250hp V-8. Extra charge over 302 CID V-8	45.00
351 cid 300hp V-8. Extra charge over 302 CID V-8	93.00
Mach 1 over 351 CID 250hp	48.00
428 cid 335hp Cobra V-8. Extra charge over 302 CID V-8	356.00
Mach 1 over 351 CID 250hp	311.00
428 cid 335hp Cobra Jet Ram-Air (except Mach 1)	421.00
Mach 1, over 351 CID 250hp	376.00
Boss 429 cid 4V V-8	1,208.00
SelectShift Cruise-O-Matic (except 428)	201.00
with 428 V-8s	222.00
4-speed manual transmission, w/302, 351, 428 V-8s	205.00
Power front disc brakes (NA 200 CID six)	65.00
Power steering	95.00
Air conditioner, SelectAire (NA w/200 CID, Boss 302, 428 cid w/4-speed manual)	380.00
Clock, electric-rectangular (NA Grande, Mach 1, or Decor Group)	16.00
Clock, electric-round (Std Grande, Mach 1) w/Decor Group only	16.00
Console	54.00
Convenience Group w/Grande, Mach 1, Boss 302 & Decor Group	32.00
All others	45.00
Defogger, rear window (2dr hardtops)	26.00
Mirrors, color-keyed dual racing	26.00
Belts, Deluxe with reminder light	15.00
Seat, rear Sport Deck (SportsRoof)	97.00
Steering wheel, Rim-Blow Deluxe	39.00
Steering wheel, tilt	45.00
Windshield wipers, intermittent	26.00
Space Saver spare (Std Boss 302, NA 200 CID Six)	
w/E70 or F70x14 WSW or RWL tires	7.00
w/E78x14 WSW tires	13.00
w/E78x14 BSW tires	20.00
Radio, AM	61.00
Radio, AM/FM	214.00
Stereo-Sonic Tape (AM radio required)	134.00
Bumper Guards, front	13.00
Decor Group, Boss 302 and other models	78.00
Convertibles	97.00
Molding, Rocker Panel (Std with Decor Group, NA Grande, Mach 1, or Boss 302)	16.00
Paint stripes, dual accent, Mach 1	13.00
Roof, vinyl (hardtop & Grande)	26.00
Sport Slats (requires dual racing mirrors)	65.00
Trim rings/hubcaps (Std Boss 302)	26.00
Wheel covers, (Std Grande)	26.00
Wheel covers, Sports, Grande, Boss 302	32.00
All others	58.00
Wheel covers, wire, Grande	53.00
All others	79.00
Wheels, Magnum 500 chrome Boss 302 only	129.00
Wheels, Argent-style steel (NC Mach 1) Grande	32.00
All others	58.00
Axle, Drag Pack, w/428 cid w/3.91:1 & 4.30:1 ratios	155.00
Axle, optional ratio	13.00
Axle, Traction-Lok differential	43.00
Battery, heavy-duty 55-amp	13.00
Battery, heavy-duty 70-amp	13.00
Extra Cooling Package	13.00
Hood scoop, Shaker, Boss 302, 351	65.00
Spoiler, rear deck, SportsRoof models only	20.00
Steering, quick ratio (Std Boss 302)	16.00
Suspension, Competition (NA 6 cyl)	31.00
Tachometer and Trip odometer (NA 6 cyl)	54.00

1971 Mustang Prices	Retail
2dr Hardtop	$2,911.00
2dr SportsRoof	2,973.00
Convertible	3,227.00
2dr Hardtop Grande	3,117.00
2dr SportsRoof Mach 1	3,268.00
2dr SportsRoof Boss 351	4,124.00
302 2V 210hp	N/C
351 2V 240hp	45.00
351 4V 285hp	93.00
429 4V 370hp*	372.00
429 4V 370hp Ram-Air*	436.00
Optional axle ratio (NA Boss 351)	13.00
Heavy-duty 70-amp battery	16.00
Traction-Lok differential (Std Boss 351)	45.00
Drag Pack, 429s only 3.91 & 4.30 w/Traction-Lok	155.00

4.30 w/No-Spin Detroit Locker	207.00
Extra Cooling Package	14.00
Instrumentation Group Mach 1 w/console	37.00
Mach 1 w/o console	54.00
Grande w/o console	62.00
All others	79.00
Dual Ram-Air Induction (NA 250 & 302 engines)	65.00
Competition Suspension	31.00
Rear deck spoiler (SportsRoof only)	32.00
4-speed manual, V-8 engines	216.00
SelectShift Automatic, 250, 302 & 351 engines	217.00
with 429 engine	238.00
Power front disc brakes	70.00
Power steering	115.00
Power windows	127.00
AM radio	66.00
AM/FM stereo radio	214.00
AM/stereo tape system (requires AM radio)	134.00
SelectAire air conditioner	412.00
Front & rear bumper guards (NA Mach 1)	31.00
Console (includes clock), Grande & Mach 1	60.00
All others	76.00
Protection Group, models w/bumper guards	34.00
All others	45.00
Sport Deck seat	97.00
Rim-Blow steering wheel	39.00
Tilt-away steering wheel (requires power steering)	45.00
Trim, Decor Group, Convertible & Boss 351	97.00
All others	78.00
Sports Interior, Mach 1 & SportsRoof	130.00
Boss 351	88.00
Bodyside tape stripe (Mach 1 only, Std Boss 351)	26.00
Vinyl roof, 2dr hardtop (Std Grande)	89.00
Base wheel covers	26.00
Sport wheel covers, Grande	32.00
Mach 1	23.00
All others	58.00
Trim rings/hubcaps, Grande	9.00
All others	35.00
Magnum 500 chrome wheels (requires Competition Suspension, F60x15 RWL tires, and includes Space-saver spare), Grande	129.00
Boss 351 & Mach 1	120.00
All others	155.00
Intermittent windshield wipers	26.00
Rear-window electric defroster	48.00
Color-keyed dual racing mirrors	26.00
Deluxe seatbelts	17.00
Complete tinted glass, Convertible	15.00
All others	40.00
Convenience Group	51.00
Tires	
E78x14 WSW	32.00
E70xl4 Wide Oval WSW over E78x14	39.00
F70x14 Wide Oval WSW over E78x14	68.00
F60x15 Wide Oval BSW/WL over E78x14	99.00
F70xl4 Wide Oval BSW/WL over E70x14 WSW	81.00
F70xl4 Wide Oval WSW over E70x14 WSW	29.00
F70x14 Wide Oval BSW/WL over E70x14 WSW	42.00
F60x15 Wide Oval BSW/WL over E70xl4 WSW	60.00
F70x14 Wide Oval BSW/WL over F70xl4 WSW	13.00
F60x15 Wide Oval BSW/WL over F70x14 WSW	31.00
F60x15 Wide Oval BSW/WL over F70x14 BSW/WL	18.00

*Includes 80-amp heavy-duty battery, Competition Suspension, 55-amp alternator, Extra Cooling Package, dual exhausts, bright engine dress-up with cast-aluminum rocker covers, Mach I hood, plus a 3.50:1 nonlocking axle with Ram-Air and a 3.25:1 nonlocking axle with non-Ram-Air. Requires optional transmission, and Drag Pack when 3.91 or 4.30:1 axle is ordered, plus: Ram-Air—F70x14 Wide Oval belted WSW tires, F70x14 BSW/WL on Mach 1; Non-Ram-Air—E70x14 Wide Oval belted WSW tires except Mach I. Air conditioner not available with Drag Pack and Ram-Air.

1972 Mustang Prices	Retail
6-cyl Models	
2dr Hardtop, 65D	$2,679.00
2dr SportsRoof, 63D	2,736.00
2dr Convertible, 76	2,965 00
Grande Hardtop, 65F	2,865.00
8-cyl Models	
2dr Hardtop, 65D	2,766.00
2dr SportsRoof, 63D	2,823.00
2dr Convertible, 76D	3,051.00
Grande Hardtop, 65F	2,952.00
Mach 1 SportsRoof, 63R	3,003.00
351 cid 2V 8 cyl	40.79
351 cid 4V 8 cyl (includes NASA hood)	115.44
361 cid W HO 8 cyl, with Mach 1	783.00
All others	812.00
SelectShift Cruise-O-Matic transmission	203.73
4-speed manual with Hurst shifter	192.99
SelectAire air conditioner	367.59
Axle, optional ratio	11.66
Axle, Traction-Lok differential	42.64
Battery, heavy-duty 70-amp	13.52
Belts, Deluxe	15.49
Bumper guards, front & rear	28.19
Console, Grande & Mach 1 Sports Interior	53.40
All others	67.96
Convenience Group	45.53
Decor Group	69.79
Door edge guards	5.78
Electric defroster, rear window	42.64
California Emission System	13.87
Extra Cooling Package	12.59
Complete tinted glass, Convertible	13.52
All others	35.94
Hood, NASA-type (Std Mach 1 with 351)	N/C
Instrumentation Group, Grande w/o console	55.24
All others	70.83
Mirrors, outside color-keyed dual racing	23.23
Paint, color-glow	34.90
Power front disc brakes	62.05
Power side windows	113.48
Power steering	102.85
Protection Package	52.06
Radio, AM	59.17
Radio, AM/FM stereo	191.01
Ram Induction NASA hood (with 351 2V only)	58.24
Roof, vinyl	79.51
Roof, 3/4 vinyl	52.35
Seat, Sport Deck rear	86.32
Spoiler, rear deck (SportsRoof models only)	29.12
Sports Interior option, Mach 1	115.44
Steering wheel, Rim-Blow, Deluxe three-spoke	34.90
Steering wheel, tilt	40.79
Stereosonic tape system	120.29
Suspension, competition	28.19
Tape stripe, black or argent bodyside	23.23
Trim rings/hubcaps, Grande	7.86
All others	31.08
Wheel covers	23.23
Wheel covers, Sports, Grande	56.18
Mach 1 & Decor Group	48.33
All others	79.40
Wheels, Magnum 500 Chrome, Grande	115.44
Mach 1 & Decor Group	107.59
All others	138.67
Windshield wipers, intermittent	23.23
Glass, tinted windshield	22.42
Models having (5) E78x14 BSW tires, extra charge for:	
(5) E70x14 WSW	35.28
(5) F70x14 WSW	61.78
(5) F70x14 B/WL	73.57
(4) F60x15 B/WL (includes F78x14 space-saver spare)	90.96
Models having (5) E70x14 WSW tires, extra charge for:	
(5) F70x14 WSW	26.51
(5) F70x14 B/WL	38.36
(4) F60x15 B/WL (includes F78x14 space-saver spare)	55.68

1973 Mustang Prices	Retai
6 cyl Models	
2dr Hardtop, 65D	$2,760.00
2dr SportsRoof, 63D	2,820.00
2dr Convertible, 76D	3,102.00
2dr Hardtop, Grande, 65F	2,946.00
8 cyl Models	
2dr Hardtop, 65D	2,847.00
2dr SportsRoof, 63D	2,907.00
2dr Convertible, 76D	3,189.00
2dr Hardtop, Grande, 65F	3,033.00
2dr SportsRoof Mach 1, 63R	3,088.00
351 cid 2V 8 cyl	40.79
351 cid 4V 8 cyl	107.00
SelectShift Cruise-O-Matic	203.73
4-speed manual with Hurst shifter	192.99
Air conditioner, SelectAire	367.69
Axle, optional ratio	11.66
Axle, Traction-Lok differential	42.64
Battery, heavy-duty 70-amp	13.52
Belts, Deluxe	15.49
Bumper Group, Deluxe	26.00
Bumper Guards, rear	14.00
Console, Grande	53.40
All others	67.95
Convenience Group	45.53
Decor Group	51.00
Door edge guards	5.78
Electric rear-window defroster	57.00
California Emission System	13.87
Extra Cooling Package	12.59
Floor mats, front color-keyed	13.30
Complete tinted glass, Convertible	13.52
All others	35.94
Hood, NASA-type	N/C
Instrumentation Group,	
Grande without console	55.24
All others	70.83
Mirrors, outside color-keyed dual racing	23.23
Paint, Metallic Glow	34.90
Paint, Tu-tone hood (NA w/Dual Ram Induction)	
Mach 1	18.00
All others	34.00
Power front disc brakes	62.05
Power side windows	113.48
Power steering	102.85
Protection Group, Grande	23.38
All others	36.00
Radio, AM	59.17
Radio, AM/FM stereo	191.01
Dual Ram Induction option (w/351 cid 2V only)	58.24
Roof, vinyl	79.51
Roof, 3/4 vinyl	52.35
Seat, Sport Deck rear	86.32
Spoiler, rear deck (SportsRoof & Mach 1)	29.12
Sports Interior option, Mach 1	116.44
Steering wheel, leather-wrapped	23.10
Steering wheel, Rim-Blow, Deluxe 3-spoke	34.90
Steering wheel, tilt	40.79
Stereosonic tape system	120.29
Suspension, competition	28.19
Tape stripe, black or argent bodyside	23.23
Trim rings/hubcaps, Grande	7.86
All others	31.08
Wheel covers	23.23
Wheel covers, sports, Grande	56.18
Mach 1 & Decor Group	48.33
All others	79.40
Wheels, forged aluminum, Grande	118.77
Mach 1 & Decor Group	110.92
All others	142.00
Windshield wipers, interval	23.23
Glass, tinted windshield	22.42
Models having (5) E78x14 BSW tires, extra charge for:	
(5) F78x14 BSW	17.00
(5) E70x14 WSW	35.28
(5) F70x14 WSW	61.78
(5) F70x14 B/WL	73.57
(5) GR78x14 steel-belted radial ply BSW	115.00
(5) GR78x14 steel-belted radial ply WSW	144.00
Models having (5) F78x14 tires, extra charge for:	
(5) F70x14 WSW	46.00
(5) F70x14 B/WL	57.00
(5) GR78x14 steel-belted radial ply BSW	98.00
(5) GR78x14 14 steel-belted radial ply WSW	127.00
Models having E70x14 WSW tires, extra charge for:	
(5) F70x14 WSW	26.51
(5) F70x14 B/WL	38.36
(5) GR78x14 steel-belted radial ply BSW	69.00
(5) GR78x14 steel-belted radial ply WSW	98.00

1974 Mustang II Prices	Retail
4-cyl Models	
2dr Hardtop, 60F	$3,134.00
3dr 2+2, 69F	3,328.00
2dr Ghia, 60H	3,480.00
6-cyl Models	
3dr Mach 1, 69R	3,674.00
Extra charge over 2.3 liter 4 cyl	
2.8 liter V-6	229.00
Credit for 2.3 liter substitution on Mach 1	(229.00)
SelectShift Cruise-O-Matic	212.00

Accent Group	151.00
Air conditioner, SelectAire	390.00
Alarm system, antitheft	75.00
Automatic seatback release	24.00
Axle, Traction-Lok differential	46.00
Battery, heavy-duty	14.00
Belts, color-keyed Deluxe	17.00
Bumper guards, front and rear	37.00
Clock, digital quartz crystal	36.00
Console	53.00
Convenience Group:	
Models with Luxury Interior Group	41.00
Mach 1, models w/Rallye Package or Accent Group	21.00
Ghia, models w/Luxury Interior Group in combination with Rallye Package or Mach 1 in combination with Luxury Interior Group	4.00
All other models	57.00
Electric rear-window defroster	59.00
Emission equipment, Calif.	19.00
Glass, tinted complete	39.00
Light Group	44.00
Luxury Interior Group	100.00
Maintenance Group	44.00
Mirrors, outside color-keyed remote-control	36.00
Molding, rocker panel	14.00
Molding, vinyl insert bodyside	50.00
Paint, glamour	41.00
Pin stripes	14.00
Power front disc brakes	45.00
Power rack-and-pinion steering	107.00
Protection Group, Mach 1	41.00
All others	47.00
Radio, AM	61.00
Radio, AM/FM monaural	124.00
Radio, AM/FM stereo	222.00
Radio with tape player, AM/FM stereo	346.00
Rallye Package (requires 2.8 V-6)	
Mach 1	150.00
3dr 2+2	200.00
All others	244.00
Rear quarter window, flipper (3dr only)	29.00
Roof, vinyl	83.00
Seat, fold-down rear (Std 3dr)	61.00
Steering wheel, leather-wrapped	30.00
Sunroof, manually operated (2dr only)	149.00
Suspension, competition	37.00
Trim, luggage compartment	28.00
Trim, Picardy velour cloth (Ghia)	62.00
Trim rings (w/styled steel wheels)	32.00
Wheels, four forged aluminum:	
Mach 1, models w/Rallye Package, 3dr 2+2 models w/Accent Group	71.00
3dr 2+2 or hardtops with Accent Group	103.00
Ghia	103.00
Hardtop	147.00
Wheels, four styled steel (Std 3dr, models with Rallye Package, and base 2dr with Accent Group) Ghia	N/C
Hardtop	44.00
Models having (5) BR78x13 BSW steel-belted radial tires, extra charge for five:	
BR78x13 steel-belted radial WSW	30.00
BR70x13 Wide Oval steel-belted radial B/WL	59.00
CR70x13 Wide Oval steel-belted radial B/WL	77.00
CR70x13 Wide Oval steel-belted radial WSW	65.00
Credit for five:	
B78x13 BSW	(84.00)
B78x13 WSW	(54.00)
Models having (5) BR78x13 WSW steel-belted radial tires, extra charge for five:	
BR70x13 Wide Oval steel-belted radial B/WL	29.00
CR70x13 Wide Oval steel-belted radial B/WL	47.00
CR70x13 Wide Oval steel-belted radial WSW	34.00
Models having (5) BR70x13 B/WL Wide Oval steel-belted radial tires, extra charge for five:	
CR70x13 Wide Oval steel-belted radial B/WL	17.00
CR70x13 Wide Oval steel-belted radial WSW	5.00

1975 Mustang II Prices	Retail
4-cyl 2.3-liter Models	
2dr Hardtop, 60F	$3,529.00
3dr 2+2, 69F	3,818.00
2dr Ghia, 60H	3,938.00
6-cyl 2.8-liter Model	
3dr Mach 1, 69R	4,188.00
2.8-liter V-6 6 cyl (NA with SelectShift)	272.00
302 cid 2V 8 cyl	
Mach 1 (includes SelectShift transmission)	203.00
All others	217.00
Credit for 2.3-liter substitution from base 2.8 V-6	(272.00)
SelectShift Cruise-O-Matic	239.00
Accent Group, exterior	162.00
Air conditioner, SelectAire	417.00
Antitheft alarm system	76.00
Axle, Traction-Lok differential	46.00
Battery, heavy-duty 53-amp	14.00
Seatbelts, color-keyed Deluxe	17.00
Brakes, power front disc	55.00
Bumper guards, front & rear	35.00
Clock digital quartz crystal	40.00
Console	63.00
Convenience Group (depending on model)	7.00–70.00
Defroster, electric rear window	63.00
California Emission System	41.00
Fuel tank extended range (Std 302 V-8)	19.00
Glass, tinted complete	41.00
Light Group	35.00
Light, fuel monitor warning	19.00
Lock Group, security	15.00
Luxury Interior Group, Hardtop	106.00
3dr 2+2 and Mach 1	89.00
Luxury Group, Ghia Silver	162.00
Maintenance Group	48.00
Mirrors, outside dual color-keyed	39.00
Molding, rocker panel	19.00
Molding, color-keyed vinyl insert bodyside	51.00
Moonroof, silver glass	454.00
Paint, glamour	49.00
Protection Group, Mach 1	20.00
All others	29.00
Radio, AM	65.00
Radio, AM/FM monaural	136.00
Radio, AM/FM stereo	225.00
Radio with tape player, AM/FM stereo	347.00
Rallye Package, Mach 1	141.00
3dr 2+2	195.00
All others	282.00
Roof, vinyl	83.00
Roof, vinyl half, Ghia	N/C
Seat, fold-down rear (Std 3dr)	66.00
Steering, power rack-and-pinion	117.00
Steering wheel, leather-wrapped	32.00
Stripes, pin	24.00
Sunroof, manually operated	210.00
Suspension, Competition, Ghia & Accent Group	43.00
Mach 1	25.00
All others	55.00
Trim, velour cloth, Ghia	88.00
Trim rings	35.00
Wheels, four cast-aluminum spoke	
Mach 1, Rallye Package, 3dr 2+2 with Exterior Accent Group	78.00
3dr 2+2 or Hardtop with Exterior Accent Group	113.00
Ghia	113.00
Hardtop without Exterior Accent Group	158.00
Wheels, four styled steel, Ghia	N/C
Hardtop	45.00
Windows, pivoting rear quarter (3dr)	33.00
Credit for deletion of color-keyed Deluxe seatbelts	(17.00)
Credit for deletion of digital clock	(40.00)
Credit for deletion of tinted glass-complete	(41.00)
Typical tire upgrade	30.00–105.00

1976 Mustang II Prices	Retail
4-cyl 2.3-liter Models	
MPG 2dr Hardtop, 60F	$3,525.00
MPG 3dr 2+2, 69F	3,781.00
MPG 2dr Ghia, 60H	3,859.00
6-cyl 2.8-liter Models	
2dr Hardtop, 60F	3,791.00
3dr 2+2, 69F	4,047.00
2dr Ghia, 60H	4,125.00
3dr Mach 1, 69R	4,209.00
8-cyl 302 cid Models	
2dr Hardtop, 60F	3,737.00
3dr 2+2, 69F	3,992.00
2dr Ghia, 60H	4,071.00
3dr Mach 1, 69R	4,154.00
Credit for 2.3-liter substitution on Mach 1	(272.00)
4-speed manual heavy-duty transmission (required with 302 cid unless Cruise-O-Matic is ordered)	37.00
SelectShift Cruise-O-Matic	239.00
Accent Group, exterior	169.00
Air conditioner, SelectAire (requires power steering)	420.00
Antitheft alarm system	83.00
Axle, optional ratio	13.00
Axle, Traction-Lok differential (requires power front disc brakes)	48.00
Battery, heavy-duty (Std 2.8 & 302 cid)	14.00
Seatbelts, color-keyed Deluxe	17.00
Black Midnight option (Mach 1 only)	83.00
Bracket, front license plate	N/C
Brakes, power front disc	54.00
Bumper guards, front & rear	34.00
Clock, digital quartz crystal	40.00
Clock, electric (NA w/Rallye Package)	17.00
Cobra II Package	325.00
Cobra II Modification Package	287.00
Console	71.00
Convenience Group	35.00
Defroster, electric rear window	70.00
California Emission System	49.00
Fuel tank, extended range	24.00
Ghia Luxury Group	177.00
Glass, tinted complete	46.00
Heater, engine block	17.00
Horn, dual note	6.00
Light Group, models with sunroof or moonroof	28.00
All others	41.00
Light, fuel monitor warning	18.00
Lock Group, security	16.00
Luggage rack deck lid	51.00
Luxury Interior Group	117.00
Mirrors, outside dual color-keyed	42.00
Molding, color-keyed vinyl insert bodyside	60.00
Molding, rocker panel	19.00
Moonroof, glass	470.00
Paint, glamour	54.00
Paint/tape, Tu-tone	84.00
Protection Group, Mach 1 & models w/Black Midnight option	36.00
All others	43.00
Radio, AM	71.00
Radio with tape player, AM	192.00
Radio, AM/FM monaural	128.00
Radio, AM/FM stereo	299.00
Rallye Package, Mach I & w/Cobra II	163.00
All others	237.00
Roof, vinyl	86.00
Roof, half vinyl, Ghia only	N/C
Seat, fold-down rear (Std 3dr)	72.00
Stallion Group, Hardtop & 2+2	72.00
Steering, power rack-and-pinion (required with 302 cid & 2.8 liter w/air conditioning; power front disc brakes also required)	117.00
Steering wheel, leather-wrapped	33.00
Stripes, pin	27.00
Sunroof, manually operated	230.00
Suspension, Competition	29.00
Trim, velour cloth, Ghia only	99.00
Trim rings	35.00
Wheels, four cast-aluminum spoke	
Mach 1, Rallye Package or Cobra II	96.00
Ghia, Stallion Group or Exterior Accent Group	131.00
All others	182.00
Wheels, four forged aluminum	
Mach 1, Rallye Package or Cobra II	96.00
Ghia, Stallion Group or Exterior Accent Group	131.00
All others	182.00
Wheels, four styled steel	
Hardtop & 2+2	51.00
Ghia	N/C
Windows, pivoting rear	33.00
Fleet options:	
Light, luggage compartment	4.00
Mirror, left-hand color-keyed	14.00
Tinted glass, windshield	24.00
Tire upgrade	33.00–208.00

1977 Mustang II Prices	Retail
4-cyl 2.3-liter Models	
2dr Hardtop, 60F	$3,678.00
3dr 2+2, 69F	3,877.00
2dr Ghia, 60H	4,096.00
6-cyl 2.8-liter Models	
3dr Mach 1, 69R	4,332.00
Credit for 2.3-liter substitution on Mach 1	(306.00)

2.8 liter 6 cyl	306.00
302 cid 8 cyl, Mach 1	(12.00)
All others	294.00
SelectShift Cruise-O-Matic (required with 302 cid)	248.00
4-speed manual (NA 302 cid except with Sports Performance Package)	N/C
Appearance Decor Group (NA Mach 1, Ghia, Cobra II)	
Hardtop	151.00
2+2	106.00
Accent Group, exterior, Hardtop	211.00
Air conditioner, SelectAire	443.00
Seatbelts, color-keyed Deluxe	17.00
Brakes, power front disc	57.00
Bumper guards, front & rear	35.00
Clock, digital quartz crystal	42.00
Cloth & vinyl bucket seats, Hardtop & 2+2	12.00
Cobra II Package	689.00
Console	75.00
Convenience Group, 3dr (NA Cobra II & T-roof)	65.00
All others	33.00
Defroster, electric rear window	70.00
Fold-down rear seat (Std 3dr)	84.00
Ghia Sports Group (Ghia only)	398.00
Luxury Interior Group	147.00
Glass, tinted complete	49.00
T-roof convertible option (2+2 & Mach 1)	
2+2 with Cobra II	587.00
All others	629.00
Light Group, w/manually operated sunroof, flip-up open-air roof & T-roof	37.00
All others	42.00
Luggage rack, deck lid	52.00
Mirrors, dual sport	47.00
Molding, color-keyed vinyl insert bodyside	63.00
Molding, rocker panel	20.00
Bodyside molding color-keyed to exterior paint	N/C
Stripes, pin	28.00
Protection Group Models w/front license plate bracket	
Mach 1 & Cobra II	27.00
All others	34.00
Models without bracket	
Mach 1 & Cobra II	23.00
All others	30.00
Radio, AM	65.00
Radio with stereo tape player, AM	192.00
Radio, AM/FM monaural	120.00
Radio, AM/FM stereo, models	
with Deluxe Equipment Group	41.00
All others	161.00
Radio with tape player, AM/FM stereo	
Models with Deluxe Equipment Group	108.00
All others	229.00
Rallye Appearance Package, 2+2	157.00
Rallye Package, Mach 1, Cobra II, Exterior Accent Group & Rallye Appearance Package	54.00
All others	101.00
Seat, 4-way manual driver's	30.00
Sports Performance Package, includes 302 cid V-8 heavy-duty 4-speed manual transmission, power steering, power brakes, and 195/70R WSW (RWL on 2+2 & Mach 1) tires	
Hardtop with Exterior Accent Group	649.00
Hardtop without Exterior Accent Group	686.00
2+2 model with Cobra II Package	516.00
2+2 without Cobra 11 Package	649.00
Ghia	593.00
Mach 1	210.00
Discount, Mach 1	(122.00)
All others	(135.00)
Steering, power rack-and-pinion	125.00
Steering wheel, leather-wrapped sport 2+2 & Mach 1	35.00
All others	51.00
Trim, media velour cloth, Ghia only	102.00
Roof, flip-up open-air, 2dr only	145.00
Sunroof, manually operated, 2dr only	237.00
Roof, full vinyl, Hardtop only	88.00
Paint, metallic glow	57.00
Trim rings, 2+2 only	36.00
Wheel covers, wire, Hardtop	82.00
2+2	40.00
Ghia	63.00
Mach 1, Cobra II, Exterior Accent Group, Appearance Decor Group or Rallye Appearance Package	4.00
Wheels, four lacy spoke aluminum	
(NA Ghia Sports Group) Hardtop	204.00
2+2	161.00
Ghia	184.00
Mach 1, Cobra II, Exterior Accent Group, Appearance Decor Group or Rallye Appearance Package	125.00
Wheels, four forged aluminum (NA Ghia Sports Group) Hardtop	204.00
2+2	161.00
Ghia	184.00
Mach 1, Cobra II, Exterior Accent Group, Appearance Decor Group or Rallye Appearance Package	125.00
Wheels, four white lacy spoke aluminum (NA Ghia Sports Group or Rallye Appearance Package)	
Hardtop	252.00
2+2	210.00
Ghia	233.00
Mach 1, Cobra II, Exterior Accent Group or Appearance Decor Group	173.00
Wheels with trim rings, four styled steel (Std with Mach I and 2+2 [less trim rings]), Exterior Accent Group, Appearance Decor Group and Rallye Appearance Package Hardtop	78.00
Ghia	59.00
Spoiler, front, 2+2 and Mach 1	N/C
Battery, heavy-duty	16.00
Bracket, front license plate	N/C
High-altitude emission equipment	22.00
Emission equipment, Calif.	69.00
Tires, typical upgrade	18.00–185.00
Limited production options	
Heater, engine block immersion	18.00
Light, luggage compartment	4.00
Mirror, inside day/night	7.00
Fleet options	
Mirror, left-hand sport	14.00
Tinted glass, windshield	24.00

1978 Mustang II Prices	Retail
4 cyl 2.3-liter Models	
2dr Hardtop	$3,824.00
3dr 2+2	4,088.00
2dr Ghia	4,242.00
6 cyl 2.8-liter Models	
3dr Mach 1	4,523.00
Credit for 2.3 liter substitution from 2.8 liter, Mach 1	(237.00)
6 cyl 2.8-liter 2V (variable venturi in Calif.)	237.00
8 cyl 5.0-liter (302 cid) Mach 1	148.00
All others	386.00
SelectShift Cruise-O-Matic	292.00
Accent Group, Exterior Hardtop	245.00
2+2	163.00
Air conditioner, SelectAire	469.00
Appearance Decor Group Hardtop	167.00
2+2	128.00
Seatbelts, color-keyed Deluxe	19.00
Bodyside protection, lower	30.00
Bracket, front license plate	N/C
Brakes, power front disc	66.00
Bumper guards, front and rear	39.00
Clock, digital quartz crystal	46.00
Cobra II Package	
Models with 2.3- or 2.8-liter engine	701.00
Models with 5.0 liter engine	724.00
Console	75.00
Convenience Group	
3dr, except Cobra II or T-roof	81.00
All others	34.00
Defroster, electric rear window	80.00
Emission equipment, Calif.	69.00
Emission equipment, high altitude	33.00
Fashion Accessory Package	219.00
Fold-down rear seat	90.00
Ghia Sports Group	386.00
Glass, tinted complete	54.00
Heater, engine block immersion	12.00
Illuminated entry system	49.00
King Cobra option	1,277.00
Light Group	
Models with flip-up roof or T-roof	40.00
All others	62.00
Luxury Interior Group	
Hardtop	167.00
2+2 and Mach 1	161.00
Mirror, left-hand illuminated visor vanity	34.00
Mirrors, dual sport	49.00
Molding, color-keyed vinyl insert bodyside	66.00
Molding, bodyside color-keyed to exterior paint	N/C
Molding, rocker panel	22.00
Paint, Metallic Glow	40.00
Protection Group	
Models with front license plate bracket	
Mach 1	28.00
All others	36.00
Models without front license plate bracket	
Mach 1	24.00
All others	33.00
Radio flexibility option	90.00
Radio, AM	72.00
Radio with 8-track stereo tape player, AM	192.00
Radio, AM/FM monaural	120.00
Radio, AM/FM stereo	161.00
Radio with cassette player, AM/FM stereo	229.00
Radio with 8-track tape player, AM/FM stereo	229.00
Rallye Appearance Package	163.00
Rallye Package	
Mach 1, Exterior Accent Group, Rallye Appearance Package	43.00
All others	93.00
Roof, flip-up open-air	167.00
Roof, full vinyl	99.00
Seat, 4-way manual driver's	33.00
Spoiler, front	8.00
Steering, power rack-and-pinion	134.00
Steering wheel, leather-wrapped sport	
2+2, Mach 1	34.00
All others	49.00
Stripes, pin	30.00
T-roof convertible option	
2+2 without Cobra II, Mach 1	689.00
2+2 with Cobra II	647.00
Trim, cloth & vinyl (Ashton cloth)	12.00
Trim, Willshire cloth	100.00
Trim rings	39.00
Wheel covers, wire	
Hardtop	96.00
2+2	45.00
Ghia	77.00
Mach 1, Cobra II, Exterior Accent Group, Appearance Decor Group, Rallye Appearance Package	12.00
Wheels, four lacy spoke aluminum	
Hardtop	276.00
2+2	224.00
Ghia	257.00
Mach 1, Cobra II, Exterior Accent Group, Appearance Decor Group, Rallye Appearance Package	186.00
Wheels, four forged aluminum Hardtop	276.00
2+2	224.00
Ghia	257.00
Mach 1, Cobra II, Exterior Accent Group, Appearance Decor Group, Rallye Appearance Package	186.00
Wheels, four white lacy spoke aluminum Hardtop	289.00
2+2	237.00
Ghia	270.00
Mach 1, Cobra II, Exterior Accent Group, Appearance Decor Group, Rallye Appearance Package	199.00
Wheels with trim rings, four white styled steel	
Hardtop	90.00
Ghia	71.00
Wheels, four white painted forged aluminum	
Hardtop	289.00
2+2	237.00
Ghia	270.00
Mach 1, Cobra II, Exterior Accent Group, Appearance Decor Group, Rallye Appearance Package	199.00
Typical tire upgrade	23.00–202.00
Limited production options	
Light, luggage compartment	4.00
Mirror, inside day/night	7.00
Mirror, left-hand color-keyed sport	16.00
Tinted glass, windshield	25.00

1979 Mustang Prices**		Retail
Vehicle Order Code		
02	2dr Sedan	$4,494.00
03	3dr Sedan	4,828.00
04	2dr Ghia	5,064.00
05	3dr Ghia	5,216.00
3dr	Pace Car Replica	9,012.00
Y	2.3-liter engine	N/C
Z	2.8-liter 6 cyl	273.00
W	2.3-liter 4 cyl turbocharged	542.00
T	3.3-liter 6 cyl	241.00
F	5.0-liter, with Cobra Package	N/C

	All others	514.00
0	SelectShift automatic	307.00
60Q	Accent Group, exterior	72.00
	Accent Group, interior	
	2dr	120.00
	3dr	108.00
572	Air conditioner, SelectAire	484.00
631	Battery, heavy-duty	18.00
46Q	Belts, color-keyed Deluxe	20.00
61P	Bodyside protection, lower	30.00
63H	Bracket, front license plate	N/C
552	Brakes, power front disc	70.00
443	Cobra Package	1,173.00
17N	Cobra hood graphics	78.00
546	Console	140.00
63Q	Deflectors, mud & stone	23.00
57Q	Defroster, electric rear window	84.00
422	California Emission System	76.00
428	Emission system, high altitude	33.00
43G	Exhaust, sport-tuned	34.00
62Q	Glass, tinted complete	59.00
599	Hood scoop	34.00
641	Light Group, without flip-up open-air roof	37.00
	with flip-up open-air roof	25.00
642	Lock Group, power	99.00
622	Mirror, left-hand remote-control	18.00
625	Mirrors, dual remote	52.00
681	Moldings, narrow vinyl insert bodyside	39.00
68G	Moldings, rocker panel	24.00
771	Moldings, wide bodyside	66.00
	Paint, exterior color	N/C
	Paint, metallic glow	41.00
435	Paint, lower Tu-tone	78.00
61G	Protection Group, with front license plate bracket	36.00
	without bracket	33.00
58V	Radio flexibility option	90.00
582	Radio, AM	84.00
588	Radio, AM, digital clock	131.00
583	Radio, AM/FM monaural	133.00
584	Radio, AM/FM stereo	188.00
587	Radio, AM/FM stereo w/cassette tape	255.00
588	Radio, AM/FM stereo with 8-track tape	255.00
21C	Roof, flip-up open-air	199.00
	Roof, full vinyl	102.00
532	Seat, 4-way manual driver's	35.00
616	Sound system, premium	67.00
	Speakers, dual rear seat	42.00
525	Speed control, fingertip,	
	2dr without Sport option	116.00
	All others	104.00
515	Sport option	175.00
521	Steering, power variable ratio	141.00
524	Steering wheel, leather-wrapped Sport	
	2dr without Sport option	53.00
	All others	41.00
52R	Steering wheel, tilt	
	2dr without Sport option	81.00
	All others	69.00
17A	Stripes, pin (bodyside and deck lid)	30.00
663	Suspension, handling	33.00
	Trim, leather low-back bucket seat	282.00
	Trim Interior colors	N/C
	Trim cloth & vinyl seat	
	Sedan models	20.00
	Ghia models	42.00
	D Trim, accent cloth & vinyl seat	29.00
652	Wheel covers, four turbine	
	3dr or with Sport option	10.00
	All others	39.00
654	Wheel covers, four wire	
	3dr or with Sport option	70.00
	Ghia	60.00
	All others	99.00
65H	Wheels, four cast-aluminum	
	3dr or with Sport option	260.00
	Ghia	251.00
	All others	289.00
65V	Wheels, four forged metric aluminum	
	3dr or with Sport option	269.00
	Ghia models	259.00
	All others	298.00
658	Wheels with trim rings, four styled steel	
	3dr or with Sport option	65.00
	Ghia	55.00
	All others	94.00
591	Windshield wipers, interval	35.00
526	Wiper/washer, rear window	63.00
	Limited-production options	
411	Floor mats, front (color-keyed)	18.00
47A	Heater, engine block immersion	13.00
545	Light, luggage compartment	5.00
62H	Tinted glass, windshield	25.00
	Tires, Models having four B78x13 bias ply BSW as standard equipment, extra charge for:	
1D	B78x13 bias WSW	43.00
15	C78x13 bias BSW	25.00
1E	C78x13 bias WSW	69.00
5A	B78x14 bias WSW	66.00
41	C78x14 bias BSW	48.00
52	BR78x14 BSW	124.00
5B	BR78x14 WSW	167.00
6A	CR78x14 WSW	192.00
6J	CR78x14 RWL	209.00
63	TRX 190/65Rx390 BSW Michelin*	241.00
	Models having four BR78x14 BSW tires as standard equipment, extra charge for:	
5B	BR78x14 WSW	43.00
6A	CR78x14 WSW	69.00
6J	CR78x14 RWL	86.00
63	TRX 190/65Rx390 BSW Michelin*	117.00

*Requires forged metric aluminum wheels
**As of July 4, 1979

1980 Mustang Prices* — Retail

Vehicle Order Code		
02	2dr Sedan	$5,338.00
03	3dr Sedan	5,616.00
04	2dr Ghia	5,823.00
05	3dr Ghia	5,216.00
	A-4 2.3-liter engine	N/C
	B-4 3.3-liter 6 cyl	256.00
	D-0 4.2-liter, with Cobra Package	(144.00)
	All others	338.00
98A	2.3-liter 4 cyl turbocharged	481.00
	SelectShift automatic	340.00
	5-Speed Manual Overdrive	156.00
453	Axle, optional ratio	18.00
60Q	Accent Group, exterior	63.00
60U	Accent Group, interior	
	2dr	134.00
	3dr	120.00
572	Air conditioner, SelectAire	538.00
631	Battery, heavy-duty	20.00
46Q	Belts, color-keyed Deluxe	23.00
61P	Bodyside protection, lower	34.00
63H	Bracket, front license plate	N/C
552	Brakes, power front disc	78.00
475	Cargo area cover	44.00
933	Cobra Package	1,482.00
974	Cobra hood graphics	88.00
184	Console	166.00
17H	Deflectors, mud & stone	25.00
57Q	Defroster, electric rear window	96.00
422	California Emission System	253.00
428	Emission system, high-altitude	36.00
432	Exhaust, sport-tuned with 2.3-liter turbo & auto trans	N/C
	with 4.2-liter (255 cid) engine	38.00
923	Glass, tinted complete	65.00
595	Hood scoop	31.00
943	Light Group	41.00
963	Lock Group, power	113.00
478	Louvers, liftgate	141.00
54J	Luggage carrier, roof-mounted	86.00
622	Mirror, left-hand remote-control	19.00
625	Mirrors, dual remote-control (black)	58.00
68G	Moldings, rocker panel	30.00
681	Moldings, vinyl insert bodysid	43.00
771	Moldings, wide bodyside	74.00
	Paint, exterior color	N/C
	Paint, metallic glow	46.00
954	Paint treatment, lower Tu-tone	88.00
913	Premium sound system	94.00
94H	Protection Group, with front license plate bracket	41.00
	without bracket	38.00
58Z	Radio—delete	(93.00)
583	Radio, AM/FM monaural	53.00
584	Radio, AM/FM stereo	90.00
587	Radio, AM/FM stereo w/cassette tape	179.00
585	Radio, AM/FM stereo with 8-track tape	166.00
58V	Radio flexibility option	63.00
86C	Roof, carriage	625.00
21C	Roof, flip-up open-air	199.00
	Ghia models or w/Light Group	204.00
	All other model	219.00
	Roof, full vinyl	118.00
	Seat, Recaro high-back bucket	531.00
532	Seat, 4-way manual driver's	38.00
	Speakers, dual rear seat	38.00
525	Speed control, 2dr sedan without Sport option	129.00
	All other models	116.00
936	Sport option with carriage roof	168.00
	without carriage roof	186.00
52H	Steering, power	160.00
524	Steering wheel, leather-wrapped	
	2dr without Sport option	56.00
	All others	44.00
52Y	Steering wheel, tilt 2dr without Sport option	90.00
	All others	78.00
93H	Stripes, accent tape with Exterior Accent Group	19.00
	All other models	53.00
953	Stripes, pin (bodyside and deck lid)	34.00
663	Suspcnsion, handling	35.00
88D	Trim, accent cloth & vinyl seat	30.00
	Trim, leather low-back bucket sea	349.00
	Trim Interior colors	N/C
	Trim cloth & vinyl bucket seat Sedan models	21.00
	Ghia models	46.00
88S	Trim, vinyl low-back bucket seat	N/C
652	Wheel covers, four turbine 3dr or with Sport option	10.00
	All others	39.00
654	Wheel covers, four wire 3dr or with Sport option	89.00
	Ghia models	79.00
	All others	121.00
65H	Wheels, four cast-aluminum 3dr or with Sport option	289.00
	Ghia	279.00
	All others	321.00
65V	Wheels, four forged metric aluminum 3dr or with Sport option	323.00
	Ghia models	313.00
	All others	355.00
658	Wheels with trim rings, four styled steel	
	3dr or with Sport option	71.00
	Ghia models	61.00
	All others	104.00
591	Windshield wipers, interval	39.00
526	Wiper/washer, rear window	79.00
	Limited-production options	
12Q	Floor mats, front (color-keyed)	19.00
545	Light, luggage compartment	5.00
922	Tinted glass, windshield	29.00
	Tires, models having four P185/80Rx13 radial ply BSW asstandard equipment, extra charge for:	
2A	P185/80Rx13 WSW	50.00
63	P175/75Rx14 BSW	25.00
6C	P175/85Rx14 WSW	75.00
71	P185/75Rx14 BSW	50.00
7A	P185/75Rx14 WSW	100.00
7J	P185/75Rx14 RWL	117.00
22	TRX 190/65Rx390 BSW	150.00
	Tires, models having four P175/75Rx14 radial ply BSW as standard equipment, extra charge for:	
6C	P175/75Rx14 WSW	50.00
71	P185/75Rx14 BSW	25.00
7A	P185x75Rx14 WSW	75.00
7J	P185/75Rx14 RWL	92.00
22	TRX 190/65Rx390 BSW	125.00

*As of May 5, 1980

1981 Mustang Prices* — Retail

Vehicle Order Code		
P10/14H	2dr S sedan	$5,897.00
P10	2dr sedan	6,363.00
P15	3dr Sedan	6,566.00
P12	2dr Ghia	6,786.00
P13	3dr Ghia	6,901.00
99A	2.3-liter engine	N/C
99B	3.3-liter 6 cyl	213.00
99D	4.2-liter, with Cobra Package	263.00
444	4-speed manual	N/C
445	5-speed manual overdrive	183.00
440	SelectShift automatic	370.00
451	Standard axle	N/C
45A	Traction-Lok	71.00
572	Air conditioner, SelectAire	600.00

631	Battery, heavy-duty	22.00
46Q	Belts, color-keyed Deluxe	24.00
61P	Bodyside protection, lower	39.00
153	Bracket, front license plate	N/C
552	Brakes, power front disc	87.00
422	California Emission System	46.00
428	High-altitude emission system	40.00
475	Cargo area cover	48.00
933	Cobra Package	1,075.00
974	Cobra hood graphics	95.00
956	Cobra tape treatment—delete	(65.00)
184	Console	178.00
17H	Deflectors, mud & stone	27.00
57Q	Defroster, electric rear window	115.00
432	Exhaust, sport-tuned with 4.2-liter (255-cid) engine	39.00
124	Floor mats, front color-keyed	20.00
923	Glass, tinted complete	82.00
595	Hood scoop	32.00
60U	Interior Accent Group	
	2dr sedan	159.00
	3dr sedan	145.00
943	Light Group	45.00
963	Lock Group, power	129.00
478	Louvers, liftgate	154.00
54J	Luggage carrier, roof-mounted	99.00
622	Mirror, left-hand remote-control	22.00
625	Mirrors, dual remote-control (black)	61.00
68G	Moldings, rocker panel (black)	30.00
954	Paint treatment, lower Tu-tone	96.00
952	Paint treatment, special Tu-tone	
	Ghia models	128.00
	All other models	165.00
	Metallic glow paint	50.00
94H	Protection Group, appearance	44.00
583	Radio AM/FM monaural	51.00
584	Radio, AM/FM stereo	88.00
58S	Radio AM, with dual rear-seat speakers	39.00
58T	Radio, AM/FM monaural with dual rear-seat speakers	39.00
583	Radio, AM/FM stereo w/cassette	174.00
584	Radio, AM/FM stereo w/8-track tape	162.00
58V	Radio flexibility option	65.00
58X	Radio flexibility option with dual rear-seat speakers	39.00
58Z	Radio AM—delete	(61.00)
913	Sound system, premium	98.00
86C	Roof, carriage	683.00
21C	Roof, flip-up open-air Ghia models or w/Light Group	227.00
	All other models	241.00
	Roof, full vinyl	127.00
21D	Roof, "T"	916.00
525	Speed control, fingertip	145.00
	Seat, Recaro high-back bucket	776.00
532	Accent cloth & vinyl seat trim	34.00
	Cloth & vinyl bucket seat trim	
	Sedan models	23.00
	Ghia models	51.00
	Leather low-back bucket seat trim	380.00
936	Sport option with Carriage roof	62.00
	without Carriage roof	82.00
52H	Steering, power	176.00
524	Steering wheel, leather-wrapped	
	2dr without Sport option	63.00
	All others	51.00
52Y	Steering wheel, tilt	
	2dr without Sport option	100.00
	All others	88.00
93H	Stripes, accent tape	57.00
953	Stripes, pin	37.00
663	Suspension, handling	46.00
652	Wheel covers, four turbine	46.00
654	Wheel covers, four wire	
	Ghia models	85.00
	All others	132.00
65H	Wheels, four cast-aluminum	
	Ghia	323.00
	All other models	370.00
65V	Wheels, four forged metric aluminum	
	Ghia models	361.00
	All others	407.00
658	Wheels with trim rings, four styled steel	
	Ghia models	67.00
	All others	113.00
64R	Windows, power side	152.00
591	Windshield wipers, interval	44.00
526	Wiper/washer, rear window	94.00
	Limited-production options	
12Q	Floor mats, front (color-keyed)	20.00
922	Glass, tinted (windshield only)	29.00
13H	Heater, engine block immersion	16.00
545	Light, luggage compartment	6.00
	Tires, models having four P175/75Rx14 BSW as standard equipment, extra charge for:	
T6C	P175/75Rx14 WSW	59.00
T71	P185/75/Rx14 BSW	28.00
T7A	P185/75/Rx14 WSW	86.00
T7J	P185/75/Rx14 RWL	107.00
T83	190/65Rx390 TRX BSW	135.00

*As of May 1, 1981

1982 Mustang Prices* — Retail

Vehicle Order Code		
P10	2dr L sedan	$6,345.00
P10	2dr GL sedan	6,844.00
P16	3dr GL sedan	6,979.00
P12	2dr GLX sedan	6,980.00
P13	3dr GLX sedan	7,101.00
P16	3dr GT sedan	8,397.00
99A	2.3-liter engine	N/C
99A/432	2.3-liter F.S.	N/C
99B	3.3-liter 6 cyl	213.00
99D	4.2-liter GT	(57.00)
	All others models	283.00
99F	5.0-liter (Std on GT)	
	With TR Performance Pkg.	494.00
	All other models	544.00
444	4-speed manual	N/C
445	5-speed manual overdrive	196.00
440	SelectShift automatic	411.00
451	Standard axle	N/C
453	Optional ratio	N/C
45A	Traction-Lok	76.00
572	Air conditioner, SelectAire	688.00
631	Battery, heavy-duty	24.00
61P	Bodyside protection, lower	41.00
153	Bracket, front license plate	N/C
552	Brakes, power front disc	93.00
422	California Emission System	46.00
428	High altitude emission system	N/C
475	Cargo area cover	51.00
184	Console	191.00
57Q	Defroster, electric rear window	124.00
923	Glass, tinted complete	82.00
595	Hood scoop	38.00
943	Light Group	49.00
963	Lock Group, power	139.00
478	Louvers, liftgate	165.00
622	Mirror, right-hand remote-control	41.00
954	Paint treatment, lower Tu-tone	116.00
952	Paint treatment, special Tu-tone	
	GL and GLX models	150.00
	L	189.00
	Metallic glow paint	54.00
94H	Protection Group, appearance	48.00
583	Radio AM/FM monaural	76.00
584	Radio, AM/FM stereo	106.00
58S	Radio AM, with dual rear-seat speakers	39.00
58T	Radio, AM/FM monaural with dual rear-seat speakers	39.00
587	Radio, AM/FM stereo w/cassette	184.00
584	Radio, AM/FM stereo w/8-track tape	184.00
58Z	AM radio credit option	(61.00)
913	Sound system, premium	117.00
H	Full vinyl roof	149.00
86C	Roof, carriage	746.00
21C	Roof, flip-up open-air	276.00
21D	Roof, "T"	1,021.00
	Recaro high-back bucket seats	834.00
	Cloth & vinyl seat trim L	29.00
	GL	40.00
	GLX and GT	57.00
	Leather low-back bucket seat trim	415.00
525	Speed control, fingertip	155.00
52H	Steering, power	202.00
524	Steering wheel, leather-wrapped	55.00
52Y	Steering wheel, tilt	95.00
93H	Stripes, accent tape	62.00
953	Stripes, pin	37.00
663	Suspension, handling	50.00
65V	TR Performance Suspension Package	
	L	589.00
	GL and GLX	539.00
	GT	111.00
654	Wheel covers, four wire	
	L models	148.00
	GL and GLX	98.00
	65H Wheels, four cast-aluminum	
	L	404.00
	GL and GLX	354.00
658	Wheels with trim rings, four styled steel	
	L	128.00
	All others	78.00
64R	Windows, power side	165.0
591	Windshield wipers, interval	48.00
526	Wiper/washer, rear window	101.00
	Limited-production options	
12Q	Floor mats, front (color-keyed)	22.00
922	Glass, tinted (windshield only)	32.00
13H	Heater, engine block immersion	17.00
545	Light, luggage compartment	7.00
	Tires, models having four P175/75Rx14 BSW as standard equipment, extra charge for:	
T6C	P175/75Rx14 WSW	72.00
T71	P185/75/Rx14 BSW	36.00
T7A	P185/75/Rx14 WSW	108.00
T7J	P185/75/Rx14 RWL	128.00
	GT model has four P185/75Rx14 BSW as standard equipment, extra charge for:	
T7A	P185/75Rx14 WSW	72.00
T7J	P185/75Rx14 RWL	91.00

*As of June 1, 1982

1983 Mustang Prices* — Retail

Vehicle Order Code		
P26	2dr L sedan	$6,727.00
P26/60C	2dr GL sedan	7,264.00
P28/60C	3dr GL sedan	7,439.00
P26/602	2dr GLX sedan	7,398.00
P27/602	2dr GLX convertible	12,467.00
P28/602	3dr GLX sedan	7,557.00
P28/932	3dr GT sedan	9,449.00
P28/932/99W	3dr Turbo GT	9,714.00
P27/932	GT convertible	13,479.00
99A	2.3-liter engine	N/C
993	3.8-liter V-6 (Std on GLX conv.)	309.00
99F	5.0-liter 4V HO 8-cyl, Std on GT	
	GLX convertible	719.00
	All other models	1,467.00
444	4-speed manual	N/C
445	5-speed manual overdrive	124.00
440	SelectShift automatic	439.00
451	Standard axle	N/C
453	Optional ratio	N/C
45A	Traction-Lok	95.00
572	Air conditioner, SelectAire	737.00
631	Battery, heavy-duty	26.00
61P	Bodyside protection, lower	41.00
153	Bracket, front license plate	N/C
552	Brakes, power front disc	93.00
422	California Emission System	76.00
428	High-altitude emission system	N/C
184	Console	191.00
57Q	Defroster, electric rear window	135.00
923	Glass, tinted complete	105.00
943	Light Group	55.00
963	Lock Group, power	172.00
478	Louvers, liftgate	171.00
622	Mirror, right-hand remote-control	44.00
954	Paint treatment, lower Tu-tone	116.00
952	Paint treatment, special Tu-tone	
	GL and GLX models	150.00
	L 189.00	
	Metallic glow paint	54.00
94H	Protection Group, appearance	39.00
583	Radio AM/FM monaural	82.00
584	Radio, AM/FM stereo 109.00	
587	Radio, AM/FM stereo w/cassette	199.00
584	Radio, AM/FM stereo w/8-track tape	199.00
58Y	AM radio credit option	(61.00)
913	Sound system, premium	117.00
21C	Roof, flip-up open-air	310.00
21D	Roof, "T"	1,074.00
	Cloth sports performance seats	196.00
	Cloth & vinyl seat trim	
	L	29.00
	GL	40.00

	GLX and GT	57.00
	Leather low-back bucket seat trim	415.00
525	Speed control, fingertip	170.00
52H	Steering, power	202.00
524	Steering wheel, leather-wrapped	59.00
52Y	Steering wheel, tilt	105.00
663	Suspension, handling	252.00
652	Wheel covers, four turbine	N/C
654	Wheel covers, four wire	
	L models	148.00
	GL and GLX	98.00
65H	Wheels, four cast-aluminum	
	L	404.00
	GL and GLX	354.00
658	Wheels with trim rings, four styled steel	
	L	128.00
	All others	78.00
64R	Windows, power side	193.00
173	Windshield wipers, interval	49.00
977	Omit standard accent stripe	N/C
	Limited-production options	
12Q	Floor mats, front (color-keyed)	22.00
922	Glass, tinted (windshield only)	38.00
13H	Heater, engine block immersion	17.00
	Tires, models having four P185/75Rx14 BSW as standard equipment, except for GT and models with 5.0-liter Engine Package, extra charge for:	
T7A	P185/75Rx14 WSW	72.00
T7B	P195/75/Rx14 WSW	108.00
T77	P205/70HRx14 BSW	224.00
T84	Michelin TRX P220/55R 390 BSW	551.00
	GT model has four P205/70HRx14 BSW as standard equipment, extra charge for:	
T84	Michelin TRX P220/55R 390 BSW	
	GT	(27.00)
	Models with 5.0-liter Package	327.00
	*As of April 22, 1983	

1984 Mustang Prices*

Vehicle Order Code		Retail
P26	2dr L sedan	$7,089.00
P28	3dr L sedan	7,260.00
P26/602	2dr LX sedan	7,281.00
P28/602	3dr LX sedan	7,487.00
P27/602	2dr LX convertible	11,849.00
P28/932	3dr GT sedan	9,774.00
P27/932	2dr GT convertible	13,247.00
P28/932/99W	3dr Turbo GT sedan	9,958.00
P27/932/99W	2dr Turbo GT convertible	13,441.00
P28/939/99T	3dr SVO	15,585.00
99A	2.3-liter engine	N/C
993	3.8-liter V-6 (Std on LX Conv.)	309.00
99M	5.0-liter 4V HO 8-cylinder, Std on GT	
	LX convertible	727.00
	All other models with VIP	1,372.00
	All other models without VIP	1,574.00
444	4-speed manual	N/C
445	5-speed manual overdrive	N/C
440	SelectShift automatic	439.00
44T	Automatic overdrive	551.00
451	Standard axle	N/C
453	Optional ratio	N/C
45A	Traction-Lok	95.00
572	Air conditioner, SelectAire	743.00
631	Battery, heavy-duty	27.00
61P	Bodyside protection, lower	41.00
153	Bracket, front license plate	N/C
552	Brakes, power front disc	93.00
422	California Emission System	99.00
428	High-altitude emission system	N/C
41C	Competition preparation option (SVO)	(1,253.00)
184	Defroster, electric rear window	140.00
12H	Floor mats, front carpet color-keyed	22.00
923	Glass, tinted complete	110.00
13H	Heater, Engine block immersion	18.00
943	Light/Convenience Group	
	LX and GT	55.00
	All other models	88.00
963	Lock Group, power	177.00
622	Mirror, right-hand remote-control	46.00
954	Paint treatment, lower Tu-tone	116.00
952	Paint treatment, special Tu-tone	
	L and LX models	150.00
	L	189.00
	Metallic glow paint	54.00
584	Radio, AM/FM stereo	109.00
587	Radio, AM/FM stereo w/cassette	
	Use with VIP	113.00
	Use with all others	222.00
58Y	AM radio credit option	(39.00)
913	Sound system, premium	151.00
21C	Roof, flip-up open-air	315.00
21D	Roof, "T" Use with VIP Pkg No. 2 on GT/Turbo GT	760.00
	Use with all others	1,074.00
	Cloth articulated sport seats	366.00
	Vinyl seat trim	
	L	29.00
	LX and GT	29.00
	Leather seat trim (conv. only)	415.00
	Leather seat trim (SVO only)	189.00
525	Steering, power	202.00
524	Steering wheel, leather-wrapped	59.00
52Y	Steering wheel, tilt	110.00
663	Suspension, handling	
	Use with VIP	50.00
	Use without VIP	252.00
654	Wheel covers, four wire style	98.00
65H	Wheels, four cast-aluminum	354.00
T53	Wheels, four metric cast-aluminum	
	L and LX	551.00
	Use with 5.0-liter engine	327.00
	GT	(27.00)
658	Wheels with trim rings, four styled steel	78.00
64R	Windows, power side	
	Convertible models	272.00
	All other models	198.00
173	Windshield wipers, interval	50.00
	Tires, models having four P185/75Rx14 BSW as standard equipment, except for GT, Turbo GT, and SVO and models with 5.0-liter Engine Package, extra charge for:	
T7A	P185/75Rx14 WSW	72.00
T7B	P195/75/Rx14 WSW	109.00
T54	P205/70HRx14 BSW	224.00
	*As of June 4, 1984	

1985 Mustang Prices*

Vehicle Order Code		Retail
P26/602	2dr LX sedan	$6,989.00
P28/602	3dr LX sedan	7,509.00
P27/602	2dr LX convertible	12,237.00
P28/932	3dr GT sedan	10,224.00
P27/932	2dr GT convertible	13,930.00
P28/937	3dr SVO	14,806.00
99A	2.3-liter engine	N/C
993	3.8-liter V-6 (Std on LX Conv.)	454.00
99M	5.0-liter 4V HO 8-cylinder, Std on GT	
	LX convertible	172.00
	LX sedan	1,020.00
444	4-speed manual	N/C
445	5-speed manual overdrive-LX	124.00
440	SelectShift automatic	439.00
44T	Automatic overdrive	
	LX	706.00
	GT	582.00
451	Standard axle	N/C
453	Optional ratio	N/C
45A	Traction-Lok	100.00
572	Air conditioner, manual	762.00
631	Battery, heavy-duty	27.00
153	Bracket, front license plate	N/C
41C	Competition Preparation Option (SVO)	(1,451.00)
422	California Emission System	99.00
428	High-altitude emission system	N/C
184	Console	191.00
57Q	Defroster, rear window	145.00
923	Glass, tinted complete	110.00
13H	Heater, Engine block immersion	18.00
943	Light Group	55.00
963	Lock Group, power	
	LX	215.00
	GT	182.00
954	Paint treatment, lower Tu-tone	116.00
587	Radio, AM/FM stereo w/cassette	148.00
586	Radio, Electronic AM/FM stereo with cassette	300.00
58Y	Radio credit option	(148.00)
913	Sound system, premium	138.00
21C	Roof, flip-up open-air	315.00
21D	Roof, "T"	1,100.00
	Leather articulated sport seats	
	LX convertible	780.00
	GT convertible	415.00
	Vinyl seat trim	29.00
	Leather seat trim (SVO)	189.00
525	Speed control	176.00
964	Spoiler, single wing	N/C
52Q	Steering wheel, tilt	115.00
654	Wheel covers, four wire style	98.00
65M	Wheels, four styled road	178.00
64R	Windows, power side	
	Convertible models	282.00
	All other models	207.00
	Tires, LX has four P195/75Rx14 BSW as standard equipment, extra charge for:	
T7G	P205/70Rx14 WSW	109.00
T54	P205/70VRx14 BSW Performance	238.00
T35	P225/60VRx15 BSW/cast aluminum wheel	665.00
	*As of May 6, 1985	

1986 Mustang Prices*

Vehicle Order Code		Retail
P26	2dr LX sedan	$7,420.00
P28	3dr LX sedan	7,974.00
P27	2dr LX convertible	13,214.00
P28	3dr GT sedan	11,102.00
P27	2dr GT convertible	14,945.00
P28/937	3dr SVO	15,272.00
99A	2.3-liter engine	N/C
993	3.8-liter V-6 (Std on LX Conv.)	565.00
99M	5.0-liter 4V HO 8-cylinder, Std on GT	
	LX convertible	646.00
	LX sedan or hatchback	1,211.00
444	4-speed manual	N/C
445	5-speed manual overdrive-LX	124.00
440	SelectShift automatic	534.00
44T	Automatic overdrive	
	LX	771.00
	LX convertible	237.00
	GT	646.00
451	Standard axle	N/C
572	Air conditioner, manual	788.00
631	Battery, heavy-duty	27.00
153	Bracket, front license plate	N/C
41C	Competition Preparation Option (SVO)	(1,451.00)
422	California Emission System	99.00
428	High-altitude emission system	N/C
184	Console	191.00
57Q	Defroster, rear window	145.00
923	Glass, tinted complete	120.00
13H	Heater, engine block immersion	18.00
974	Hood graphic credit	N/C
943	Light Group	55.00
963	Lock Group, power	
	LX	244.00
	GT	206.00
954	Paint treatment, lower Charcoal accent	116.00
587	Radio, AM/FM stereo w/cassette	157.00
586	Radio, Electronic AM/FM stereo with cassette	310.00
58Y	Radio credit option	(157.00)
913	Sound system, premium	138.00
21C	Roof, flip-up open-air	355.00
21D	Roof, "T"	1,120.00
	Leather articulated sport seats	
	LX convertible	780.00
	GT convertible	415.00
	Vinyl seat trim	29.00
	Leather seat trim (SVO)	189.00
525	Speed control	176.00
964	Spoiler, single wing	N/C
52Q	Steering wheel, tilt	124.00
654	Wheel covers, four wire style	98.00
65M	Wheels, four styled road	178.00
64R	Windows, power side	
	Convertible models	296.00
	All other models	222.00
	Tires, LX has four P195/75Rx14 BSW as standard equipment, extra charge for:	
T7G		

P205/70	Rx14 WSW	118.00
T35	P225/60VRx15 BSW/cast-aluminum wheel	674.00
	* As of July 31, 1986	

1987 Mustang Prices*

Vehicle Order Code		Retail
P40	2dr LX sedan	$8,271.00
P41	3dr LX hatchback	8,690.00
P44	2dr LX convertible	13,052.00
P42	3dr GT hatchback	12,106.00
P45	2dr GT convertible	14,945.00
99A	2.3-liter engine	N/C
99E	5.0-liter 4V HO 8-cylinder, Std on GT	1,885.00
44T	Automatic overdrive	
	LX	515.00
	GT	515.00
572	Air conditioner, manual	788.00
631	Battery, heavy-duty 58-amp	27.00
153	Bracket, front license plate	N/C
422	California Emission System	99.00
428	High-altitude emission system	N/C
57Q	Defroster, rear window	145.00
923	Glass, tinted complete	120.00
13H	Heater, engine block immersion	18.00
943	Light Group	55.00
963	Lock Group, power	
	LX	244.00
	GT	206.00
954	Lower titanium accent treatment	99.00
586	Radio, electronic AM/FM stereo with cassette	310.00
58Y	Radio credit option	(206.00)
913	Sound system, premium	168.00
915	Graphic equalizer	218.00
628	Mirrors, dual electric remote	60.00
677	Mirrors, dual illuminated visor	100.00
979	Bodyside molding insert stripe	49.00
21C	Roof, flip-up open-air	355.00
21D	Roof, "T," LX	1,798.00
	GT	1,618.00
	Leather articulated sport seats	
	LX convertible	780.00
	GT convertible	415.00
	Vinyl seat trim	29.00
525	Speed control	176.00
52Q	Steering wheel, tilt	124.00
654	Wheel covers, four wire style	98.00
65M	Wheels, four styled road	178.00
64R	Windows, power side	
	Convertible models	296.00
	All other models	222.00
	Tires, LX has four P195/75Rx14 BSW as standard equipment, extra charge for:	
T7B	P195/75Rx14 WSW	82.00
T35	P225/60VRx15 BSW/cast-aluminum wheel	
	*As of April 21, 1986	

1988 Mustang Prices*

Vehicle Order Code		Retail
P40	2dr LX sedan	$8,835.00
P41	3dr LX hatchback	9,341.00
P44	2dr LX convertible	13,702.00
P42	3dr GT hatchback	12,745.00
P45	2dr GT convertible	16,610.00
99A	2.3-liter engine	N/C
99E	5.0-liter 4V HO 8-cylinder, Std on GT	2,007.00
44T	Automatic overdrive	
	LX	515.00
	GT	515.00
572	Air conditioner, manual	788.00
631	Battery, heavy-duty 58-amp	27.00
153	Bracket, front license plate	N/C
422	California Emission System	99.00
428	High-altitude emission system	N/C
57Q	Defroster, rear window	145.00
923	Glass, tinted complete	120.00
13H	Heater, engine block immersion	18.00
943	Light Group	55.00
963	Lock Group, power	237.00
954	Lower titanium accent treatment	N/C
586	Radio, electronic AM/FM stereo with cassette	137.00
58Y	Radio credit option	(206.00)
913	Sound system, premium	168.00
915	Graphic equalizer	218.00
677	Mirrors, dual illuminated visor	100.00
628	Mirrors, dual electric remote	60.00
979	Bodyside molding insert stripe	49.00
21C	Roof, flip-up open-air	355.00
	Leather articulated sport seats	
	LX convertible	780.00
	GT convertible	415.00
	Vinyl seat trim	29.00
525	Speed control	182.00
52Q	Steering wheel, tilt	124.00
654	Wheel covers, four wire style	178.00
65M	Wheels, four styled road	178.00
64R	Windows, power side	222.00
	Tires, LX has four P195/75Rx14 BSW as standard equipment, extra charge for:	
T7B	P195/75Rx14 WSW	82.00
T35	P225/60VRx15 BSW/cast-aluminum wheel	
	*As of February 29, 1988	

1989 Mustang Prices*

Vehicle Order Code		Retail
P40	2dr LX sedan	$9,050.00
P41	3dr LX hatchback	9,556.00
P44	2dr LX convertible	14,140.00
P40	2dr LX 5.0-liter Sport sedan	11,410.00
P41	3dr LX 5.0-liter Sport hatchback	12,265.00
P44	2dr LX 5.0-liter Sport convertible	17,001.00
P42	3dr GT hatchback	13,272.00
P45	2dr GT convertible	17,512.00
44T	Automatic overdrive	
	LX	539.00
	GT	539.00
572	Air conditioner, manual	807.00
153	Bracket, front license plate	N/C
422	California Emission System	100.00
428	High-altitude emission system	N/C
57Q	Defroster, rear window	150.00
13H	Heater, engine block immersion	20.00
943	Light Group	55.00
963	Lock Group, power	246.00
	Bodyside molding insert stripe	61.00
954	Lower titanium accent treatment	N/C
586	Radio, electronic AM/FM stereo with cassette and clock	137.00
58Y	Radio credit option	(382.00)
913	Sound system, premium	168.00
677	Mirrors, dual illuminated visor	100.00
	Mirrors, dual electric remote	70.00
21C	Roof, flip-up open-air	355.00
	Leather articulated sport seats	855.00
	LX convertible	489.00
	Vinyl seat trim	37.00
525	Speed control	191.00
52Q	Steering wheel, tilt	124.00
654	Wheel covers, four wire style	193.00
65M	Wheels, four styled road	193.00
64R	Windows, power side	232.00
	Tires, LX has four P195/75Rx14 BSW as standard equipment, extra charge for:	
T7B	P195/75Rx14 WSW	82.00
T35	P225/60VRx15 BSW/cast-aluminum wheel	
	*As of February 29, 1988	

1990 Mustang Prices*

Vehicle Order Code		Retail
P40	2dr LX sedan	$9,753.00
P41	3dr LX hatchback	10,259.00
P44	2dr LX convertible	14,810.00
P40	2 dr LX 5.0-liter Sport sedan	12,222.00
P41	3dr LX 5.0-liter Sport hatchback	13,055.00
P44	2dr LX 5.0-liter Sport convertible	17,796.00
P42	3dr GT hatchback	14,044.00
P45	2dr GT convertible	18,418.00
44T	Automatic overdrive	
	LX 539.00	
	GT 539.00	
572	Air conditioner, manual	807.00
153	Bracket, front license plate	N/C
422	California Emission System	100.00
428	High-altitude emission system	N/C
57Q	Defroster, rear window	150.00
13H	Heater, engine block immersion	20.00
943	Light Group	55.00
963	Lock Group, power	237.00
954	Lower titanium accent treatment	159.00
	Paint, clear coat	91.00
586	Radio, Electronic AM/FM stereo with cassette and clock	137.00
58Y	Radio credit option	(245.00–550.00)
913	Sound system, premium	168.00
677	Mirrors, dual illuminated visor	100.00
21C	Roof, flip-up open-air	355.00
	Vinyl seat trim	37.00
525	Speed control	191.00
52Q	Steering wheel, tilt	124.00
654	Wheel covers, four wire style	193.00
65M	Wheels, four styled road	178.00
64R	Windows, power side	222.00
	Tires, LX has four P195/75Rx14 BSW as standard equipment, extra charge for:	
T7B	P195/75Rx14 WSW	82.00
T35	P225/60VRx15 BSW/Cast-aluminum wheel	
	*As of July 10, 1989	

1991 Prices*

Vehicle Order Code		Retail
P40	2dr LX sedan	$10,702.00
P41	3dr LX hatchback	11,208.00
P44	2dr LX convertible	16,767.00
P40	2 dr LX 5.0-liter Sport sedan	13,815.00
P41	3dr LX 5.0-liter Sport hatchback	14,600.00
P44	2dr LX 5.0-liter Sport convertible	19,787.00
P42	3dr GT hatchback	15,579.00
P45	2dr GT convertible	20,409.00
44T	Automatic overdrive	
	LX 598.00	
	GT 598.00	
572	Air conditioner, manual	807.00
153	Bracket, front license plate	N/C
422	California Emission System	100.00
428	High-altitude emission system	N/C
45C	Cargo tie-down net	65.00
60A	Custom Equipment Group, includes manual a/c, dual illum. mirrors, LX sedan/hatchback	917.00
57Q	Defroster, rear window	160.00
13H	Heater, engine block immersion	20.00
943	Light Group	55.00
963	Lock Group, power	237.00
12H	Floor mats, front	33.00
954	Lower titanium accent treatment	159.00
	Paint, clear coat	91.00
586	Radio, electronic AM/FM stereo with cassette and clock	155.00
58Y	Radio credit option	(245.00–568.00)
913	Sound system, premium	168.00
915	Graphic equalizer, w/premium sound	139.00
	Graphic equalizer, w/o premium sound	307.00
677	Mirrors, dual illuminated visor	100.00
21C	Roof, flip-up open-air	355.00
	Leather articulated sport seats	489.00
	Vinyl seat trim	37.00
525	Speed control	210.00
654	Wheel covers, four wire style	193.00
65M	Wheels, four styled road	193.00
64W	Wheels, cast-aluminum with upsize tires, P205/65Rx15	167.00–360.00
	*As of September 27, 1990	

1992 Mustang Prices*

Vehicle Order Code		Retail
P40	2dr LX sedan	$10,215.00
P41	3dr LX hatchback	11,721.00
P44	2dr LX convertible	16,899.00
P40	2 dr LX 5.0-liter Sport sedan	13,422.00
P41	3dr LX 5.0-liter Sport hatchback	14,207.00
P44	2dr LX 5.0-liter Sport convertible	19,644.00
P42	2dr GT convertible	20,199.00
P44	2dr LX 5.0-liter Sport convertible Vibrant Red	22,727.00
44T	Automatic overdrive	
	LX	595.00
	GT	595.00

572	Air conditioner, manual	817.00
153	Bracket, front license plate	N/C
422	California Emission System	100.00
428	High-altitude emission system	N/C
45C	Cargo tie-down net	65.00
60K	Convenience Group	99.00
57Q	Defroster, rear window	170.00
13H	Heater, engine block immersion	20.00
12H	Floor mats, front	33.00
954	Lower titanium accent treatment	159.00
	Paint, clearcoat	91.00
586	Radio, electronic AM/FM stereo with cassette and clock	155.00
58Y	Radio credit option	(568.00)
217	Seat, 4-way power driver's	183.00
913	Sound system, premium	168.00
915	Graphic equalizer, w/premium sound	139.00
	Graphic equalizer, without premium sound	307.00
677	Mirrors, dual illuminated visor	100.00
21C	Roof, flip-up open-air	355.00
	Leather articulated sport seats	523.00
	Vinyl seat trim	76.00
525	Speed control	224.00
654	Wheel covers, four wire style	193.00
65M	Wheels, four styled road	193.00
64W	Wheels, cast-aluminum with upsize tires, P205/65Rx15	208.00–401.00
	*As of July 15, 1992	

1993 Mustang Prices*		Retail
Vehicle Order Code		
P40	2dr LX sedan	$11,159.00
P41	3dr LX hatchback	11,664.00
P44	2dr LX convertible	17,988.00
P40	2 dr LX 5.0-liter Sport sedan	14,366.00
P41	3dr LX 5.0-liter Sport hatchback	15,150.00
P44	2dr LX 5.0-liter Sport convertible	20,733.00
P42	3dr GT hatchback	16,187.00
P45	2dr GT convertible	21,288.00
P44	2dr LX 5.0-liter Sport convertible	
	Oxford White	21,709.00
	Canary Yellow	22,221.00
44T	Automatic overdrive	
	LX	595.00
	GT	595.00
572	Air conditioner, manual	817.00
153	Bracket, front license plate	N/C
422	California Emission System	100.00
428	High-altitude emission system	N/C
45C	Cargo tie-down net	65.00
60K	Convenience Group	99.00
57Q	Defroster, rear window	170.00
13H	Heater, engine block immersion	20.00
12H	Floor mats, front	33.00
954	Lower titanium accent treatment	159.00
	Paint, clear coat	91.00
586	Radio, electronic AM/FM stereo with CD player	604.00
588	Radio, electronic premium cassette with premium sound	629.00
58Y	Radio credit option	(245.00–584.00)
217	Seat, 4-way power driver's	183.00
913	Sound system, premium	168.00
677	Mirrors, dual illuminated visor	100.00
21C	Roof, flip-up open-air	355.00
	Leather articulated sport seats	523.00
	Vinyl seat trim	76.00
525	Speed control	224.00
654	Wheel covers, four wire style	193.00
65M	Wheels, cast-aluminum with upsize tires, P205/65Rx15	208.00–401.00
	*As of July 15, 1992	

1993 SVT Mustang Cobra Prices		Retail
P42	Cobra hatchback	$18,505.00
PEP	Package 250A	1,455.00
	Mustang Cobra	
	Power Equipment Group	
	Manual air conditioning	
	Front floor mats	
	Clear coat paint	91.00
13C	Flip-open air roof	355.00
	Leather seating surfaces	523.00
57Q	Rear-window defroster	170.00
217	4-way power driver's seat	183.00
585	AM/FM stereo/CD player	629.00
41H	Engine block heater	20.00

1994 Mustang Prices		Retail
P40	Mustang Coupe	$13,365.00
P44	Mustang Convertible	20,160.00
P42	Mustang GT Coupe	17,280.00
P45	Mustang GT Convertible	21,790.00
P42	Mustang Cobra Coupe	21,300.00*
P45	Mustang Cobra Convertible	25,605.00**
44P	4-speed Automatic Overdrive	790.00
422	California Emissions System	95.00
	Leather seats	500.00
672	Air Conditioning, Manual	780.00
552	Anti-lock braking system	565.00
18A	Antitheft system	235.00
45C	Axle, optional ratio (GT only)	N/C
153	Bracket, front license plate	N/C
13T	Convertible hardtop	1,545.00
57Q	Defroster, rear window	160.00
12H	Floor mats, front	30.00
41H	Heater, engine block immersion	20.00
61A	Group 1	505.00
	Includes: Power side windows, Power door locks, Power deckled release	
63A	Group 2	
	w/Mustang Coupe	870.00
	w/Mustang Convertible	775.00
	w/GT Coupe/Convertible	510.00
	Includes: Speed control, Mirrors, dual illuminated visors, Radio, electronic AM/FM stereo/cassette/premium sound	
60K	Group 3	310.00
	Includes: Remote keyless/illuminates entry, Cargo net	
961	Moldings, bodyside	50.00
21Y	Power driver's seat credit	(135.00)
58M	Radio, electronic AM/FM stereo cassette	165.00
586	Radio, Mach 460 electronic AM/FM stereo cassette w/Group 2	375.00
	w/o Group 2	670.00
917	Compact disc player	475.00
64J	Wheels, 15-inch cast-aluminum	265.00
64H	Wheels, unique 17-inch (GT only)	380.00
	*As of October 15, 1993	
	**As of January 12, 1995	

1994 SVT Mustang Cobra Prices*		Retail
P42	Cobra Coupe	$20,765.00
P45	Cobra Convertible	23,535.00
P45	Cobra Conv. Indy Pace Replica	26,845.00
PEP	Package 250A, Coupe	1,185.00
	Air conditioning	
	Rear-window defroster	
	Front floor mats	
	Speed control	
	PEP Package 250A, Convertible	2,285.00
	Air conditioning	
	Rear-window defroster	
	Front floor mats	
	Speed control	
	Remote keyless illuminated entry	
	Mach 460 stereo system	
422	California Emission System	95.00
	Leather seating surfaces (coupe)	500.00
60K	Power Group 3 (includes Power Group 2) Remote keyless illuminated entry and Cargo Net	310.00
912	Mach 460 electronic AM/FM stereo cassette	
917	Compact disc player (requires Mach 460 cassette radio)	475.00
	*As of February 3, 1994	

1995 Mustang Prices		Retail
P40	Mustang Coupe	$14,530.00
P44	Mustang Convertible	20,995.00
P42	Mustang GTS Coupe	16,910.00
P42	Mustang GT Coupe	18,105.00
P45	Mustang GT Convertible	22,795.00
P42	Mustang Cobra Coupe	21,300.00
P45	Mustang Cobra Convertible	25,605.00
44P	4-speed automatic overdrive	815.00
422	California Emission System	95.00
	Leather seats	500.00
217	Power driver's seat	175.00
672	Air conditioning, manual	855.00
552	Anti-lock braking system	565.00
18A	Antitheft system	145.00
45C	Axle, optional ratio (GT/GTS only)	N/C
153	Bracket, front license plate	N/C
13T	Convertible hardtop	1,825.00
57Q	Defroster, rear window	160.00
12H	Floor mats, front	30.00
41H	Heater, engine block immersion	20.00
61A	Group 1	505.00
	Includes: Power side windows, Power door locks, Power deck lid release	
63A	Group 2	
	w/Mustang Coupe	870.00
	w/Mustang Convertible	775.00
	w/GT Coupe/Convertible	510.00
	Includes: Speed control, Mirrors, dual illuminated visors, Radio, electronic AM/FM stereo/cassette/premium sound, Wheels, 15-inch cast-aluminum (NA w/GT)	
60K	Group 3	310.00
	Includes: Remote keyless illuminated entry, Cargo net	
961	Moldings, bodyside	50.00
21Y	Power driver's seat credit	(135.00)
58M	Radio, electronic AM/FM stereo cassette	165.00
586	Radio, Mach 460 electronic AM/FM Stereo cassette w/o Group 2	670.00
585	Compact disc radio/premium sound	
	w/Group 2	140.00
	w/58M	270.00
	w/58F	435.00
912	Compact disc radio/Mach 460 (w/585)	375.00
917	Compact disc player	475.00
64J	Wheels, 15-inch cast-aluminum	265.00
64H	Wheels, unique 17-inch (GT only)	380.00
	*As of January 12, 1995	

1996 Mustang Prices		Retail
P40	Mustang Coupe	$15,180.00
P44	Mustang Convertible	21,060.00
P42	Mustang GT Coupe	17,610.00
P45	Mustang GT Convertible	23,495.00
P47	Mustang Cobra Coupe	24,810.00
P46	Mustang Cobra Convertible	27,580.00
44U	4-speed automatic overdrive	815.00
422	California rmission system	100.00
428	High-altitude emission	N/C
552	Brakes, anti-lock	570.00
217	Power driver's seat	175.00
572	Air conditioning, manual	895.00
18A	Antitheft system	145.00
45C	Axle, optional ratio (3.27 GT only)	200.00
57Q	Defroster, rear window	170.00
12H	Floor mats, front	30.00
41H	Heater, engine block immersion	20.00
143	Keyless entry	270.00
534	Rear spoiler	195.00
677	Mirrors, dual illum.	95.00
961	Molding, bodyside	60.00
58M	Radio, electronic AM/FM stereo cassette & premium sound	165.00
58H	Radio, electronic AM/FM stereo cassette & premium sound	130.00–295.00
586	Radio, Mach 460 electronic AM/FM stereo cassette	395.00–690.00
917	Compact disc player	295.00
61A	Option Group 1 includes: Power side windows/door locks, power deck lid release	505.00
63A	Option Group 2 Includes: Speed control, 15-inch aluminum wheels, AM/FM ETR w/cass. & premium sound	
	Base	775.00
	GT	510.00
65A	Option Group 3 includes: Fog lamps, GT sport seats, leather-wrapped steering wheel, rear spoiler, dual illuminated visors	690.00
64J	Wheels, 15-inch cast-aluminum (base only)	265.00
64Y	Wheels, unique 17-inch (GT only)	400.00
	Leather seats	500.00
	*As of March 7, 1996	

1996 SVT Mustang Cobra Prices*		Retail
P47	Cobra Coupe	$24,810.00
P46	Cobra Convertible	27,580.00
PEP	Package 250A, Coupe	1,335.00
	Mach 460 stereo system, CD player, leather	

	interior, perimeter antitheft system	
422	California Emission System	100.00
534	Rear spoiler	215.00
	*As of March 7, 1996	

1997 Mustang Prices*		Retail
P40	Mustang Coupe	$15,880.00
P44	Mustang Convertible	21,280.00
P42	Mustang GT Coupe	18,525.00
P45	Mustang GT Convertible	24,510.00
P47	Mustang Cobra Coupe	25,335.00
P46	Mustang Cobra Convertible	28,135.00
44U	4-speed automatic overdrive	815.00
422	California Emission System	170.00
428	High-altitude emission	N/C
552	Brakes, anti-lock	570.00
217	Power driver's seat	210.00
525	Speed control	215.00
572	Air conditioning, manual	895.00
18A	Antitheft system	145.00
45C	Axle, optional ratio (3.27 GT only)	200.00
153	Bracket, front license plate	N/C
57Q	Defroster, rear window	190.00
12H	Floor mats, front	30.00
41H	Heater, engine block immersion	20.00
143	Keyless entry	270.00
534	Rear spoiler (Std GT Conv.)	195.00
54A	Sport Appearance Group includes: Rear spoiler, 15-inch polished wheels, Leather-wrapped steering wheel, Lower bodyside accent stripe Base	345.00
677	Mirrors, dual illuminated	95.00
961	Molding, bodyside	60.00
58M	Radio, electronic AM/FM stereo cassette & premium sound	165.00
586	Radio, Mach 460 electronic AM/FM stereo cassette	395.00–690.00
917	Compact disc player	295.00
61A	Option Group 1 includes: Power side windows/door locks, Power deck lid release	565.00
63A	Option Group 2 includes: Speed control, 15-inch aluminum wheels, AM/FM ETR w/cassette & premium sound	
	Base	775.00
	GT	510.00
65A	Option Group 3 includes: Fog lamps, GT sport seats, leather-wrapped steering wheel, rear spoiler, Dual illuminated visors	690.00
64J	Wheels, 15-inch cast-aluminum (base only)	265.00
64Y	Wheels, polished 17-inch (GT only)	500.00
	Leather seats	500.00
	*As of March 12, 1997	

1997 SVT Mustang Cobra Prices		Retail
P47	Cobra Coupe	$25,335.00
P46	Cobra Convertible	28,135.00
PEP	Package 250A, Coupe Mach 460 stereo system, CD Player, Leather interior, Perimeter antitheft system	1,335.00
534	Rear spoiler	195.00
422	California Emission System	100.00

1998 Mustang Prices*		Retail
P40	Mustang Coupe	$16,150.00
P44	Mustang Convertible	20,650.00
P42	Mustang GT Coupe	20,150.00
P45	Mustang GT Convertible	24,150.00
P47	Mustang Cobra Coupe	25,710.00
P46	Mustang Cobra Convertible	28,510.00
44U	4-speed automatic overdrive	815.00
422	California Emission System	170.00
428	High-altitude emission	N/C
552	Brakes, anti-lock	570.00
572	Air conditioning, manual	895.00
18A	Antitheft system	145.00
45C	Axle, optional ratio (3.27 GT only)	200.00
57Q	Defroster, rear window	190.00
41H	Heater, engine block immersion	20.00
534	Rear spoiler (Std GT)	195.00
677	Mirrors, dual illuminated visor	95.00
588	Radio, Mach 460 electronic AM/FM stereo cassette/equalizer	395.00
60C	Convenience Group includes: Front floor mats, rear-window defroster, speed control, power driver's seat	
	Base	495.00
	GT	295.00
54G	GT Sport Group includes: 17-inch 5-spoke aluminum wheels, hood stripe and wraparound fender stripes, leather-wrapped shift knob (manual trans. only), engine oil cooler	595.00
54V	V-6 Sport Appearance Group includes: 16-inch cast-aluminum wheels, rear spoiler, leather-wrapped steering wheel, lower bodyside accent stripe	
	Base	345.00
64Y	Wheels, polished 17-inch (GT Only)	500.00
	Leather seats	500.00
	*As of March 15, 1998	

1998 SVT Mustang Cobra Prices*		Retail
Cobra Coupe, P47		$25,710.00
Cobra Convertible, P46		28,510.00
18A	Antitheft system (requires 54E)	145.00
54E	Electronic Leather/Trim Group, Antitheft system, Mach 460 ETR w/cassette, Leather seating surfaces	
	Coupe	N/C
	Convertible	1,040.00
422	California Emission System	170.00
534	Rear spoiler	195.00
	*As of March 15, 1998	

1999 Mustang Prices		Retail
P40	Mustang Coupe	$16,470
P44	Mustang Convertible	21,070.00
P42	Mustang GT Coupe	20,870.00
P45	Mustang GT Convertible	24,870.00
P47	Mustang Cobra Coupe	27,470.00
P46	Mustang Cobra Convertible	31,470.00
44U	4-speed automatic overdrive	815.00
428	High-altitude emission	N/C
552	Brakes, anti-lock (base)	500.00
553	All-speed traction control	230.00
13K	Rear spoiler (Std GT)	195.00
57Q	Rear window defroster	190.00
677	Mirrors, dual illuminated visor	95.00
588	Radio, Mach 460 electronic AM/FM stereo cassette/equalizer	395.00
54V	V-6 Sport Appearance Group includes: 15-inch cast-aluminum wheels, rear spoiler, leather-wrapped steering wheel, lower bodyside accent stripe	
	Base	310.00
54Y	35th Anniversary Limited Edition Package includes: 17-inch five-spoke aluminum wheels, black tape appliqué on hood, body-color side scoops, rocker panel moldings, rear spoiler, black appliqué between taillamps, black/silver leather/vinyl front seats w/pony logo, silver leatherdoor trim inserts, silver/black floormats with 35th Anniversary logo, aluminum shiftknob (manual trans.)	
	GT	2,695.00
60C	Convenience Group includes: front floor mats, rear-window defroster, speed control, power 6-way driver's seat	
	Base/GT	550.00
63B	Smoker's Package	15.00
64X	Wheels, forged aluminum 17-inch (GT only)	500.00
	Leather seats	500.00

1999 SVT Mustang Prices		Retail
P47	Mustang Cobra Coupe	$27,470.00
P46	Mustang Cobra Convertible	31,470.00
13K	Rear spoiler	195.00
63B	Smoker's Package	15.00

2000 Mustang Prices		Retail
P40	Mustang Coupe	$16,520.00
P44	Mustang Convertible	21,370.00
P42	Mustang GT Coupe	21,015.00
P45	Mustang GT Convertible	25,270.00
P47	Mustang Cobra Coupe	27,605.00
P46	Mustang Cobra Convertible	31,605.00
44U	4-speed automatic overdrive	815.00
428	High altitude emissions	N/C
552	Brakes, anti-lock (base)	500.00
553	All-speed traction control	230.00
57Q	Rear-window defroster	190.00
13K	Rear spoiler (Std GT)	195.00
677	Mirrors, dual illuminated visor	95.00
588	Radio, Mach 460 electronic AM/FM stereo cassette/equalizer	395.00
54V	V-6 Sport Appearance Group includes: 15-inch cast-aluminum wheels, rear spoiler, leather-wrapped steering wheel, lower bodyside accent stripe	
	Base	310.00
60C	Convenience Group includes: Front floor mats, rear-window defroster, speed control, power six-way driver's seat	
	Base/GT	550.00
63B	Smoker's Package	15.00
64X	Wheels, forged aluminum 17-inch (GT only)	500.00
	Leather seats	500.00

2000 SVT Mustang Cobra Prices		Retail
Mustang Cobra Coupe, P47		$27,605.00
Luxury tax 850.00		

2001 Mustang Prices*		Retail
P40	Mustang Standard Coupe	$17,095.00
P40	Mustang Deluxe Coupe	17,660.00
P44	Mustang Deluxe Convertible	22,510.00
P40	Mustang Premium Coupe	18,890.00
P44	Mustang Premium Convertible	25,075.00
P42	Mustang GT Deluxe Coupe	22,730.00
P45	Mustang GT Deluxe Convertible	26,985.00
P42	Mustang GT Premium Coupe	23,880.00
P45	Mustang GT Premium Convertible	28,135.00
P42	Mustang GT Bullitt Coupe	26,230.00
P47	Mustang Cobra Coupe	28,605.00
P46	Mustang Cobra Convertible	32,605.00
44U	4-speed automatic overdrive	815.00
58M	Radio system, Mach 460	550.00
	Seats, leather-surfaced	500.00
	*As of June 4, 2001	

2001 SVT Mustang Cobra Prices		Retail
P47	Mustang Cobra Coupe	$28,605.00
P46	Mustang Cobra Convertible	32,605.00
12H	Floor mats front	30.00
13K	Rear spoiler	195.00
64H	Wheels, polished	395.00

2002 Mustang Prices*		Retail
P40	Mustang Standard Coupe	$17,475.00
P40	Mustang Deluxe Coupe	18,080.00
P44	Mustang Deluxe Convertible	23,000.00
P40	Mustang Premium Coupe	19,195.00
P44	Mustang Premium Convertible	25,585.00
P42	Mustang GT Deluxe Coupe	23,220.00
P45	Mustang GT Deluxe Convertible	27,475.00
P42	Mustang GT Premium Coupe	24,390.00
P45	Mustang GT Premium Convertible	28,645.00
918	Radio system, Mach 1000	1,295.00
589	Radio system, Mach 460	550.00
918	Radio system, Mach 1000	1,295.00
18G	Interior Upgrade Package	315.00
47B	Boot	95.00
	Seats, leather-surfaced	595.00
	*As of March 28, 2002	

2003 Mustang Prices		Retail
P40	Mustang Standard Coupe	$17,720.00
P40	Mustang Deluxe Coupe	18,450.00
P44	Mustang Deluxe Convertible	23,455.00
P40	Mustang Premium Coupe	19,585.00
P44	Mustang Premium Convertible	26,040.00
P42	Mustang GT Deluxe Coupe	23,705.00
P45	Mustang GT Deluxe Convertible	28,045.00
P42	Mustang GT Premium Coupe	24,875.00
P45	Mustang GT Premium Convertible	29,215.00
P42	Mustang Mach 1	28,705.00
P48	Mustang Cobra Coupe	33,460.00
P49	Mustang Cobra Convertible	37,835.00
44U	Automatic transmission	815.00
589	Radio system, Mach 460	550.00
918	Radio system, Mach 1000	1,295.00
18G	Interior Upgrade Package	345.00
47B	Boot	95.00
	Seats, leather-surfaced	595.00

2003 SVT Mustang Cobra Prices		Retail
P48	Mustang Cobra Coupe	$33,460.00
P49	Mustang Cobra Convertible	37,835.00
L59	Gas Guzzler Tax	1,000.00
325A	10th Anniversary Package	1,495.00

13K	Spoiler, (delete)	N/C
18G	Interior Upgrade Package	345.00
64V	Wheels, chrome aluminum	695.00

2004 Mustang Prices		Retail
P40	Mustang Coupe	$17,865.00
P40	Mustang Coupe	$18,595.00
P44	Mustang Deluxe Convertible	23,600.00
P40	Mustang Premium Coupe	19,245.00
P44	Mustang Premium Convertible	25,725.00
P42	Mustang GT Coupe	23,385.00
P45	Mustang GT Deluxe Convertible	27,730.00
P42	Mustang GT Premium Coupe	24,555.00
P45	Mustang GT Premium Convertible	28,900.00
P42	Mustang Mach 1	28,965.00
P48	Mustang Cobra Coupe	34,575.00
P49	Mustang Cobra Convertible	38,950.00
44U	4-speed automatic overdrive	815.00
552	Braking system, anti-lock	730.00
18G	Interior upgrade	345.00
54P	Pony Package	645.00
54V	Sport Appearance Group	175.00
588	Radio, Mach 460	550.00

2004 SVT Mustang Cobra Prices		Retail
P48	Mustang Cobra Coupe	$34,575.00
P49	Mustang Cobra Convertible	38,950.00
L59	Gas Guzzler Tax	1,000.00
76M	Mystichrome Package	3,650.00
13K	Spoiler, (delete)	N/C
64V	Wheels, chrome aluminum	695.00

2005 Mustang Prices		Retail
T80	Base Deluxe Coupe	$19,165.00
T84	Base Deluxe Convertible	23,890.00
T80	Base Premium Coupe	19,990.00
T84	Base Premium Convertible	24,715.00
T82	GT Deluxe Coupe	24,965.00
T85	GT Deluxe Convertible	29,390.00
T82	GT Premium Coupe	26,145.00
T85	GT Premium Convertible	30,570.00
18R	Sport Appearance Package	295.00
18G	Interior Upgraded Package	450.00
68R	Interior Color Accent Package	175.00
44L	5-speed automatic transmission	995.00
43A	Front Side Airbags	370.00
552	Antilock Brakes	775.00
K	Leather Upholestery	695.00
60C	6-way power driver seat	365.00
912	AM/FM radio w/in-dash 6-disk CD/MP3 Changer	665.00
918	Upgraded sound system, Base Premium	
	GT Premium	1,295.00
	GT Deluxe	1,770.00
14A	Theft-deterrent system w/alarm	255.00
59B	Convertible top boot	115.00
13D	Spoiler, delete	N/C
17L	Wheel locking kit	50.00
64D	Bright alloy wheels, Base Deluxe GT 195.00	150.00

2006 Mustang Prices		Retail
T80	Base Deluxe Coupe	$19,215.00
T84	Base Standard Convertible	23,940.00
T80	Deluxe Coupe	19,215.00
T84	Deluxe Convertible	24,040.00
T80	Base Premium Coupe	20,090.00
T84	Base Premium Convertible	24,915.00
T82	GT Deluxe Coupe	25,140.00
T85	GT Deluxe Convertible	29,965.00
T82	GT Premium Coupe	26,320.00
T85	GT Premium Convertible	31,145.00
18R	Sport Appearance Package	195.00
18G	Interior Upgrade Package	460.00
68R	Interior Color Accent Package	175.00
54P	V6 Pony Package	1,195.00
60C	6-way power driver seat	365.00
44L	5-speed automatic transmission	995.00
43A	Front Side Airbags	370.00
552	Antilock Brakes	775.00
K	Leather Upholstery & Sport Buckers	695.00
912	Shaker 500 Audio System	665.00
918	Shaker 1000 Audio System	1,770.00
14A	Theft-deterrent system w/alarm	255.00
59B	Convertible top boot	160.00
13D	Spoiler, delete	N/C
17L	Wheel locking kit	50.00
64D	17" Bright Aluminum Wheels, Base GT 195.00	50.00
64W	18" Premium Aluminum Wheels	825.00
64E	18" Polished Aluminum Wheels	825.00
12H	Rubber floormats	75.00

2007 Mustang Prices		Retail
T80	Base Deluxe Coupe	$19,995.00
T84	Base Deluxe Convertible	24,820.00
T80	Base Premium Coupe	20,990.00
T84	Base Premium Convertible	25,815.00
T82	GT Deluxe Coupe	26,440.00
T85	GT Deluxe Convertible	31,265.00
T82	GT Premium Coupe	27,620.00
T85	GT Premium Convertible	32,445.00
T88	Shelby GT500 Coupe	42,975.00
T89	Shelby GT500 Convertible	47,800.00
T82	Shelby GT Coupe	36,225.00
54C	GT California Special Package	1,895.00
18R	Sport Appearance Package	195.00
18G	Interior Upgrade Package	460.00
68R	Interior Color Accent Package	175.00
53B	Comfort Group	550.00
68B	Premier Trim Package w/Color Accent	395.00
18M	Sport Appearance Package	345.00
54V	Exterior Sport Appearance Package	295.00
18R	Driver Ornamentation Package	195.00
65A	Heated Seats	250.00
54G	GT Appearance Package	245.00
54P	V6 Pony Package	750.00
44L	5-speed automatic transmission	995.00
552	Antilock Braking System	775.00
43A	Front Side Airbags	380.00
K	Leather Upholstery & Sport Buckers	695.00
58X	Navigation System	1,995.00
912	Shaker 500 Audio System	665.00
918	Shaker 1000 Audio System	1,770.00
50S	Sirius Satellite Radio	195.00
67D	Charcoal Instrument Panel	N/C
14A	Theft-deterrent system w/alarm	255.00
86C	Black Cloth Convertible Top	230.00
59B	Convertible soft boot	160.00
13D	Spoiler, delete	N/C
52S	Tape Stripe Delete	N/C
12H	Floor Mat Delete	N/C
41H	Engine Block Heater	35.00
17L	Wheel locking kit	50.00
961	Bodyside Moldings	95.00
455	Limited Slip 3.55 Axle	100.00
64D	17" Bright Machined Aluminum Wheels	195.00
64W	18" Premium Aluminum Wheels	825.00
64E	18" Polished Aluminum Wheels	825.00
17L	Locking Lug Nuts	50.00

2008 Mustang Prices	Retail
Base Deluxe Coupe	$19,850.00
Base Deluxe Convertible	$24,475.00
Base Premium Coupe	$20,880.00
Base Premium Convertible	$25,705.00
GT Deluxe Coupe	$26,240.00
GT Deluxe Convertible	$31,065.00
GT Premium Coupe	$27,420.00
GT Premium Convertible	$32,245.00
Shelby GT500 KR	$79,995.00
Shelby GT500 Coupe	$42,330.00
Shelby GT500 Convertible	$47,155.00
Shelby GT Coupe Package	$9,500.00
Shelby GT Convertible Package	$11,800.00
GT California Special Package (GT Premium)	$1,895.00
Bullitt Package (GT Premium Coupe)	$3,310.00
Safety and Security Package (Base)	$995.00
Exterior Sport Appearance Package (Base)	$295.00
Interior Sport Appearance Package (Base, GT)	$345.00
Interior Upgraded Package (Base Premium, GT)	$460.00
Comfort Group (Base Premium, GT)	$675.00
V-6 Pony Package (Base Premium)	$750.00
V-6 Pony Package w/Polished Aluminum Wheels (Base Premium)	$1,675.00
V-6 Appearance Package (Base Premium Coupe)	$2,395.00
Premier Trim Package (Base Premium, GT Premium)	$395.00
GT Appearance Package	$245.00
Warrior in Pink Package (Base Premium)	$1,545.00
Premium Interior Trim Package (Shelby)	$595.00
5-speed automatic transmission (Base)	$995.00
5-speed automatic transmission (GT Deluxe/Premium)	$645.00
Special Axle Ratio (GT Premium; Not available w/5-speed automatic transmission)	$300.00
Navigation System (Base Premium, GT Premium, Shelby; Required Safety and Security Package w/Base Premium Coupe; Not available w/Shaker 1000 Sound System)	$1,995.00
Leather Upholstery (Base Premium, GT Deluxe)	$695.00
Heated Front Seats (Base Premium, GT; Leather upholstery required w/Base Premium and GT Deluxe)	$250.00
AM/FM radio w/in-dash 6-disc CD/MP3 Changer (Base Premium, GT Premium, Shelby)	$1,295.00
AM/FM radio w/in-dash 6-disc CD/MP3 Changer (GT Deluxe; Included Shaker 1000 Sound System; Required Safety and Security Package w/Base Premium)	$1,770.00
Satellite Radio (Base Premium, GT Deluxe/Premium, Shelby GT500; Required AM/FM radio w/in-dash 6-disc CD/MP3 changer; Not available w/Base Deluxe)	$195.00
IPod Adaptor (Base, GT)	$295.00
Wireless Cell Phone Link (Base/GT Coupe)	$395.00
Ambient Interior Lighting (Base Premium, GT Deluxe, GT Premium, Shelby GT500; Not available w/Base Deluxe)	$295.00
Remote Engine Start (Base, GT)	$295.00
Cargo Net (Base, GT)	$65.00
Rubber Floor Mats (Base, GT)	$75.00
Theft-deterrent system w/alarm (GT)	$325.00
Xenon Headlights (Base Deluxe/Premium, GT Deluxe/Premium, Shelby GT500; Not available w/Base Deluxe Coupe)	$525.00
Cloth Convertible Top (Base Premium, GT)	$230.00
Convertible top boot (Base Premium, GT)	$160.00
Front Car Cover (Base Deluxe/ Premium, GT Deluxe/Premium)	$120.00
Full Car Cover (Base, GT)	$235.00
Full Car Cover (Shelby)	$375.00
Mud Guards (Base, GT)	$80.00
Ambient Lighting (Base Premium, GT Deluxe/Premium, Shelby GT500; Not available w/Base Deluxe)	$295.00
Chrome Exhaust Tips (Base)	$65.00
Chrome Exhaust Tips (GT)	$125.00
Alloy Fuel-Filler Door (Base/GT convertible)	$135.00
Over-the-Top Racing Stripes (Base, GT; Standard w/Shelby Coupe)	$395.00
Over-the-Top Racing Stripes Delete (Shelby Coupe)	$0
Bodyside Stripe Delete (Base, Shelby; Required V-6 Pony Package or Exterior Sport Appearance Package w/Base; Required Over-the-Top Racing Stripes Delete w/Shelby Coupe)	$0
Rear Spoiler, delete (GT)	$0.00
Wheel locking kit (GT; Standard Shelby GT500)	$50.00
Bright Alloy Wheels (Base Premium)	$325.00
Bright Alloy Wheels (GT)	$195.00
18-inch Polished Alloy Wheels (GT; Included 235/50ZR18 tires)	$925.00
18-inch Chrome Alloy Wheels (GT Premium)	$1,185.00

2009 Mustang Prices	Retail
Base Deluxe Coupe	$20,430.00
Base Deluxe Convertible	$25,255.00
Base Premium Coupe	$22,520.00
Base Premium Convertible	$27,345.00
GT Deluxe Coupe	$27,210.00
GT Deluxe Convertible	$32,035.00
GT Premium Coupe	$29,160.00
GT Premium Convertible	$33,985.00
Shelby GT 500KR	$79,995.00
Shelby GT500 Coupe	$43,125.00
Shelby GT500 Convertible	$47,950.00
GT California Special Package (GT Premium)	$1,895.00
Bullitt Package (GT Premium Coupe)	$3,310.00
Safety and Security Package (Base)	$995.00
Exterior Sport Appearance Package (Base)	$295.00
V-6 Pony Package (Base Premium)	$750.00
V-6 Pony Package w/polished aluminum wheels (Base Premium)	$1,675.00
5-speed automatic transmission (Base)	$995.00
5-speed automatic transmission (GT Deluxe/Premium)	$645.00
Plated Satin Aluminum Metallic Fuel-Filler Door (Base, GT)	$135.00

SYNV Voice-activated Communications/ Entertainment System (Base, GT)	$550.00
Comfort Group (Base Premium, GT Premium)	$575.00
17-inch Bright Machined Cast-aluminum Wheels (Base Premium)	$325.00
17-inch Bright Machined Cast-aluminum Wheels (GT)	$195.00
18-inch Premium Polished Forged Wheels (Premium, GT)	$925.00
High-intensity Headlights (Base Premium, GT Premium)	$525.00
Glass Roof (Base/GT Premium Coupe)	$1,995.00
Verona Grain Leather-trimmed Bucket Seats (Base Premium)	$695.00
Shaker 1000 AM/FM Stereo w/6-disc CD/MP3/Sirius (Base/GT Premium)	$1,295.00
Shaker 500 AM/FM Stereo w/in-dash 6-disc CD/MP3 Changer (GT)	$665.00
Tape Stripe Delete (Base Premium)	$0.00
P235/55ZR16AS Tires (Base Premium)	$0.00
P235/50ZR18AS Tires (Base Premium, GT)	$0.00
Touch Screen DVD-based Navigation System (Base/GT Premium)	$1,995.00
Convertible soft boot (Premium, GT)	$160.00
Cloth Convertible Top (Premium, GT)	$230.00
GT Appearance Package	$245.00
GT Security Package	$375.00
Spoiler, delete (GT)	$0.00
Aberdeen-embossed Leather Sport Bucket Seats (GT Deluxe; Standard w/GT Premium Coupe)	$695.00
Premier Trim w/Color Accent Package (GT Premium)	$395.00
3.55:1 Limited Slip Axle Ratio (GT Premium)	$300.00
Leather-trimmed Sport Bucket Seats (GT Premium)	$0.00

2010 Mustang Prices	Retail
V-6 Coupe	$21,395.00
V-6 Convertible	$26,395.00
V-6 Premium Coupe	$24,395.00
V-6 Premium Convertible	$29,345.00
GT Coupe	$28,395.00
GT Convertible	$33,395.00
GT Premium Coupe	$31,395.00
GT Premium Convertible	$36,395.00
Shelby GT500 Coupe	$46,725.00
Shelby GT500 Convertible	$51,725.00
Electronics Package (V-6 Premium, GT Premium, Shelby)	$2,195.00
Exterior Sport Appearance Package (V-6, V-6 Premium)	$295.00
V-6 Pony Package (Premium)	$995.00
Premier Trim w/Color Accent Package (GT Premium)	$395.00
Comfort Package (V-6/GT Premium)	$595.00
TrackPack (GT Premium)	$1,530.00
Accessory Package 1 (V-6/GT Premium Coupe; Included side scoops, quarter window louvers and decklid panel)	$675.00
Accessory Package 2 (V-6/GT Premium Convertible; Same as Package 1 but w/o window louvers)	$450.00
Accessory Package 4 (GT Premium; Included hood scoop, special rear spoiler)	$695.00
Accessory Package 5 (GT Premium Coupe; Included hood scoop, pedestal spoiler, side scoops, decklid face panel and quarter window louvers)	$1,370.00
Accessory Package 6 (GT Premium convertible; Same as Package 5 but w/o window louvers)	$1,145.00
3.73:1 Rear Axle Ratio (GT Base/Premium Coupe)	$495.00
Security Package (V-6, GT)	$395.00
5-speed automatic transmission (V-6, GT)	$995.00
Limited Slip Differential (GT Premium)	$395.00
Limited Slip Differential w/Uprated Brakes (GT)	$495.00
Rearview Camera (V-6/GT Premium)	$385.00
Rearview Camera w/Electronics Package (V-6/GT Premium)	$240.00
Premium Sound System (GT Premium, Shelby)	$1,295.00
Glass Roof Panel (V-6/GT Premium Coupe)	$1,995.00
Remote Engine Start (V-6 Premium, GT; Required 5-speed automatic transmission)	$345.00
Xenon Headlights (V-6/GT Premium, Shelby)	$525.00
Convertible Boot (V-6 Premium)	$160.00
Car Cover (Shelby)	$375.00
Special Paint	$300.00
Over-the-Top Racing Stripes (V-6/GT Premium)	$395.00
Hood and Side Stripes (V-6/GT Premium)	$395.00
Polished Alloy Wheels (GT Premium)	$495.00
18-inch Alloy Wheels (V-6 Premium)	$495.00
19-inch Alloy Wheels (GT Premium)	$895.00
19-inch Bright Alloy Wheels (GT Premium)	$1,095.00

2011 Mustang Prices

P8A	V-6 Coupe	$22,145
P8A	V-6 Premium Coupe	$25,845
P8E	V-6 Convertible	$27,145
P8E	V-6 Premium Convertible	$30,845
P8C	GT Coupe	$29,645
P8C	GT Premium Coupe	$32,845
P8F	GT Convertible	$34,645
P8F	GT Premium Convertible	$37,845
Destination and Delivery (all models)		$850
101A	Equipment Package (V-6)	$295
201A	Equipment Package (V-6 Premium)	$295
202A	Equipment Package (V-6 Premium)	$995
203A	Equipment Package (V-6 Premium)	$995
401A	Equipment Package (GT Premium)	$395
402A	Equipment Package (GT Premium)	$2,475
443	6-Speed Automatic Transmission	$995
453	3.31 Ratio Axle (V-6 Coupe)	$395
455	3.55 Ratio Axle (GT manual transmission only)	$395
457	3.73 Ratio Axle (GT manual transmission only)	$395
64M	18-inch Polished Aluminum Wheels (GT Premium)	$495
64X 1	9-inch Bright Machined Aluminum Wheels (GT Premium)	$995
64V	19-inch Premium Painted Luster Nickel Aluminum Wheels (GT Premium)	$995
67B	V-6 Performance Package	$1,995
59G	Glass Roof	$1,995
51H	HID Headlamps (requires 43S	$525
43S	Security Package	$395
53B	Comfort Group (V-6 & GT Premium)	$595
59B	Convertible Soft Boot	$160
58N	Electronics Package (Nav & DZATC)	$2,340
77C	Rear Video Camera with Electronics Pkg	$240
Rear Video Camera without Electronics Pkg		$385
PU6	Red Candy Specialty Paint	$395
PNQ	Yellow Blaze Metallic Tri-Coat Paint	$495
55D Brembo Brake Package (GT only)		$1,695
974	California Special Car Cover (GT Premium only)	$375
913	AM / FM Stereo CD w/ Clock (Std)	N/C
912	Shaker 500 w/ In-Dash CD, MP3, 8 Speakers (Std Premium)	N/C
918	Shaker 1,000 w/ In-Dash CD, MP3, 10 Speakers (GT Premium only)	$1,295
47A	Over-the-Top Racing Stripe	$475
603	PowerCode Remote Starter (Requires Automatic Transmission)	$345
941	V-6 Coupe Accessory Pkg 1	$720
	GT Convertible Accessory Pkg 2	$720
942	V-6 Convertible Accessory Pkg 2	$480
	GT Convertible Accessory Pkg 2	$480
943	Hood & Side Stripes	$395
944	GT Coupe/Convertible Accessory Pkg 4	$750
945	GT Coupe Accessory Pkg 5	$1,470
946	GT Convertible Accessory Pkg 6	$1,230
18R	Driver Ornamentation Pkg (Fleet Only)	$195
41H	Engine Block Heater (Fleet only)	$35
61R	Daytime Running Lamps (Fleet only)	$45

2012 Mustang Prices

P8A	V-6 Coupe	$22,310
P8A	V-6 Premium Coupe	$26,310
P8E	V-6 Convertible	$27,310
P8E	V-6 Premium Convertible	$31,310
P8C	GT Coupe	$29,710
GT Premium Coupe		$33,710
P8F	GT Convertible	$34,710
GT Premium Convertible		$38,710
P8C	Boss 302	$40,310
Destination and Delivery (all models)		$795
101A	Preferred Equipment Package (V-6)	$295
201A	Preferred Equipment Package (V-6 Premium)	$295
202A	Preferred Equipment Package (V-6 Premium)	$995
203A	Preferred Equipment Package (V-6 Premium)	$995
401A	Preferred Equipment Package (GT Premium)	$395
402A	Preferred Equipment Package (GT Premium)	$1,995
501A	Preferred Equipment Package (Boss 302)	$6,995
443 6-Speed Automatic Transmission		$1,195
453 3.31 Ratio Axle (V-6 Coupe)		$395
455 3.55 Ratio Axle (GT Manual Transmission only)		$395
457 3.73 Ratio Axle (GT Manual Transmission only)		$395
64M	18-inch Polished Aluminum Wheels (GT Premium)	$495
64X	19-inch Bright Machined Aluminum Wheels (GT Premium)	$995
64V	19-inch Premium Painted Luster Nickel Aluminum Wheels (GT Premium)	$995
947	Recaro Cloth Sport Seats & Torsen Differential (Boss 302)	$1,995
59G	Glass Roof	$1,995
43T	HID Headlamps & Security Package	$920
43S	Reverse Sensing System & Security Package	$695
53B	Comfort Group (V-6 & GT Premium)	$595
59B	Convertible Soft Boot	$160
58N	Electronics Package (Nav & DZATC)	$2,340
77C	Rear Video Camera with Electronics Pkg	$240
	Rear Video Camera without Electronics Pkg	$385
PRZ	Red Candy Specialty Paint	$395
PNQ	Yellow Blaze Metallic Tri-Coat Paint	$495
55D	Brembo Brake Package (GT)	$1,695
974	California Special Car Cover (GT Premium)	$375
12A	All Weather Floor Mats	$85
97B	Boss 302 Accessory Package	$475
913	AM / FM Stereo CD w/ Clock (Std)	N/C
912	Shaker 500 w/ In-Dash CD, MP3, 8 Speakers (Std Prem)	N/C
918	Shaker ,1000 w/ In-Dash CD, MP3, 10 Speakers (GT Prem)	$1,295
47A	Over-the-Top Racing Stripe	$475
603	PowerCode Remote Starter (Requires Automatic Transmission)	$345
941	V-6 Coupe Accessory Pkg 1	$720
GT Coupe Accessory Pkg 1		$720
942	V-6 Convertible Accessory Pkg 2	$480
	GT Convertible Accessory Pkg 2	$ 480
943	Hood & Side Stripes	$395
944	GT Coupe/Convertible Accessory Pkg 4	$750
945	GT Coupe Accessory Pkg 5	$1,470
946	GT Convertible Accessory Pkg 6	$1,230
18R	Driver Ornamentation Pkg (Fleet Only)	$195
41H	Engine Block Heater (Fleet only)	$35
61R	Daytime Running Lamps (Fleet only)	$45

2012 Shelby GT 500 Mustang Prices

P8J	Shelby GT500 Coupe	$48,810
P8K	Shelby GT500 Convertible	$53,810
Destination and Delivery (all models)		$795
44E	6-Speed Manual Transmission (Std)	N/C
64W	19-inch Premium Painted Forged Aluminum Wheels (Std)	N/C
T3V	P255 / 40ZR 19-inch Front & P285/ 35ZR 19-inch Rear Wheels (Std)	N/C
21A	6-Way Power Driver Seat (Std)	N/C
Q	Recaro Leather Sport Seats	$1,595
59G	Glass Roof	$1,995
58N	Electronics Package (Nav & DZATC)	$2,340
86C	Cloth Convertible Top (Std)	N/C
971	Full Vehicle Cover	$375
67F	SVT Performance Package	$3,995
912	Shaker 500 w/ In-Dash CD, MP3, 8 Speakers (Std)	N/C
918	Shaker 1,000 w/ In-Dash CD, MP3, 10 Speakers	$1,295

2013 Mustang Prices

P8A	V-6 Coupe	$22,200
P8A	V-6 Premium Coupe	$26,200
P8E	V-6 Convertible	$27,200
P8E	V-6 Premium Convertible	$31,200
P8C	GT Coupe	$30,300
P8C	GT Premium Coupe	$34,300
P8F	GT Convertible	$35,300
P8F	GT Premium Convertible	$39,300
P8C	Boss 302	$42,200
Destination and Delivery (all models)		$795
101A	Equipment Group 101A (V-6)	$295
102A	Equipment Group 102A (V-6)	$1,295
201A	Equipment Group 201A (V-6 Premium)	$295
202A	Equipment Group 202A (V-6 Premium)	$995
203A	Equipment Group 203A (V-6 Premium)	$995
301A	Equipment Group 301A (GT)	$1,195
401A	Equipment Group 401A (GT Premium)	$395
402A	Equipment Group 402A (GT Premium)	$1,995
501A	Equipment Group 501A (Boss 302)	$6,995
443	6-Speed Automatic Transmission	$1,195
453	3.31 Ratio Axle (V-6 Coupe)	$395
455	3.55 Ratio Axle (GT Manual Transmission Only)	$395
457	3.73 Ratio Axle (GT Manual Transmission Only)	$395
64M	18-inch Polished Aluminum Wheels (GT Premium)	$495
64X	19-inch Bright Machined Aluminum Wheels (GT Premium)	$995

64V 19-inch Premium Painted Luster Nickel Aluminum Wheels (GT Premium) $995
U Recaro Cloth Sport Seats (V-6 & GT Coupe) $1,595
S Recaro Leather Sport Seats (V-6 Premium & GT Premium Coupe) $1,595
947 Recaro Cloth Sport Seats & Torsen Differential (Boss 302) $1,995
67B V-6 Performance Package (V-6 & V-6 Premium) $1,995
59G Glass Roof $1,995
43S Reverse Sensing System & Security Package (all models except Boss 302) $695
53B Comfort Group (V6 & GT Premium) $650
59B Convertible Soft Boot (V-6 Premium Convertible) $160
58N Electronics Package (Nav & DZATC) $2,340
77C Rear Video Camera with Electronics Pkg $240
Rear Video Camera w/o Electronics Pkg $385
PRZ Red Candy Specialty Paint (all models except GT Premium & Boss 302) $395
PHD Gotta Have It Green Metallic Tri-Coat Paint (all models except V-6 Premium, GT Premium, Boss 302) $495
55D Brembo Brake Package(GT models only) $1,695
55R GT Track Package (GT Premium) $2,495
974 California Special Car Cover (GT Premium) $375
12A All Weather Floor Mats $85
97B Boss 302 Accessory Package $475
918 Shaker Pro Audio System $1,295
47A Over-the-Top Racing Stripe (V-6 Premium, GT Premium) $475
603 PowerCode Remote Starter (Requires Automatic Transmission) $345
941 V-6 Coupe Accessory Pkg 1 (V-6 models only) $480
GT Coupe Accessory Pkg 1 (GT models only) $480
942 V-6 Convertible Accessory Pkg 2 (V-6 models only) $240
GT Convertible Accessory Pkg 2 (GT models only) $240
943 Hood & Side Stripes (Premium models only) $395
944 GT Coupe/Convertible Accessory Pkg 4 $355
945 GT Coupe Accessory Pkg 5 $835
946 GT Convertible Accessory Pkg 6 $595
18R Driver Ornamentation Pkg (Fleet Only) $195
41H Engine Block Heater (Fleet only) $35
61R Daytime Running Lamps (Fleet only) $45

2014 Mustang Prices

P8A V-6 Coupe $22,510
P8A V-6 Premium Coupe $26,610
P8E V-6 Convertible $27,510
P8E V-6 Premium Convertible $31,610
P8C GT Coupe $31,210
P8C GT Premium Coupe $35,310
P8F GT Convertible $36,210
P8F GT Premium Convertible $40,310
Destination and Delivery (all models) $825
100A Equipment Group 100A (V-6) N/C
102A Equipment Group 102A (V-6)$1,295
200A Equipment Group 200A (V-6 Premium) N/C
201A Equipment Group 201A (V-6 Premium) $295
202A Equipment Group 202A (V-6 Premium) $995
203A Equipment Group 203A (V-6 Premium) $995
300A Equipment Group 300A (GT) N/C
301A Equipment Group 301A (GT) $1,195
400A Equipment Group 400A (GT Premium) N/C
401A Equipment Group 401A (GT Premium) $395
402A Equipment Group 402A (GT Premium) $1,995
443 6-Speed Automatic Transmission $1,195
453 3.31 Ratio Axle (V-6 Coupe) $395
455 3.55 Ratio Axle (GT Manual Transmission Only) $395
457 3.73 Ratio Axle (GT Manual Transmission Only) $395
64M 18-inch Polished Aluminum Wheels (GT Premium) $495
64X 19-inch Bright Machined Aluminum Wheels (GT Premium) $995
64V 19-inch Premium Painted Luster Nickel Aluminum Wheels (GT Premium) $995
U Recaro Cloth Sport Seats (V-6 & GT Coupe) $1,595
S Recaro Leather Sport Seats (Premium models only) $1,595
67B V-6 Performance Package (V-6 & V-6 Premium) $1,995
541 V-6 Appearance Package $795
542 V-8 Appearance Package $995
59G Glass Roof $1,995
43S Reverse Sensing System & Security Package (all models except GT Premium) $695
53B Comfort Group (V-6 & GT Premium) $650
59B Convertible Soft Boot (V-6 Premium Convertible) $160
46D Tape Stripe Delete (V-6 Premium) N/C
13D GT Spoiler Delete (All GT models) N/C
58N Electronics Package (Nav & DZATC) $2,340
77C Rear Video Camera with Electronics Pkg (Premium models only) $240
Rear Video Camera without Electronics Pkg (Premium models only) $385
PRR Ruby Red Metallic Tinted Clearcoat Paint (all models except GT Premium) $395
PHD Gotta Have It Green Metallic Tri-Coat Paint $495
55D Brembo Brake Package—GT (GT, GT Premium) $1,695
55R GT Track Package (GT Premium) $2,495
974 California Special Car Cover (GT Premium) $375
12A All Weather Floor Mats $85
918 Shaker Pro Audio System $1,295
47A Over-the-Top Racing Stripe $475
603 PowerCode Remote Starter (Requires Automatic Transmission) $345
941 V-6 Coupe Accessory Pkg 1 (V-6 Premium) $480
GT Coupe Accessory Pkg 1 (GT models only) $480
942 V-6 Convertible Accessory Pkg 2 (V-6 models only) $240
GT Convertible Accessory Pkg 2 (GT models only) $240
471 Hood & Side Stripes $395
944 GT Coupe/Convertible Accessory Pkg 4 $355
945 GT Coupe Accessory Pkg 5 $835
946 GT Convertible Accessory Pkg 6 $595
41H Engine Block Heater (Fleet only) $35
63B Smoker's Package (Fleet only) N/C
61R Daytime Running Lamps (Fleet only) $45

2014 Shelby GT500 Prices

P8J Shelby GT500 Coupe $55,110
P8K Shelby GT500 Convertible $60,110
Destination and Delivery (all models) $825
820A Shelby GT500 Equipment Group 820A N/C
821A Equipment Group 821A $3,495
Q Recaro Leather Sport Seats $1,595
59G Glass Roof $1,995
58N Electronics Package (Nav & DZATC) $2,340
PHD Gotta Have It Green Metallic Tri-Coat Paint $495
PRR Ruby Red Metallic Tinted Clearcoat Paint $395
46D Tape Stripe Delete - Top & Side Stripe N/C
971 Full Vehicle Cover $375
55S SVT Track Pack $2,995
918 Shaker Pro Audio System $1,295

2015 Mustang Prices

P8A V-6 Fastback $23,600
P8E V-6 Convertible $29,100
P8T EcoBoost Fastback $25,170
P8T EcoBoost Premium Fastback $29,170
P8U EcoBoost Premium Convertible $34,670
P8C GT Fastback $32,100
P8C GT Premium Fastback $36,100
P8F GT Premium Convertible $41,600
P8R GT 50 Years Limited Edition $46,170
Destination and Delivery $825
050A Equipment Group 050A (V-6) N/C
051A Equipment Group 051A (V-6) $995
100A Equipment Group 100A (EcoBoost) N/C
200A Premium Equipment Group 200A (EcoBoost Premium) N/C
201A Equipment Group 201A (EcoBoost Premium) $1,795
300A Equipment Group 300A (GT) N/C
400A Equipment Group 400A (GT Premium) N/C
401A Equipment Group 401A (GT Premium) $1,795
500A Equipment Group 500A (GT 50 Years LE) N/C
443 6-Speed Automatic Transmission $1,195
455 3.55 Ratio Axle (V-6, GT Manual Transmission Only) $395
641 18-inch Foundry Low-Gloss Paint/Machined Aluminum Wheels (EcoBoost and GT) $155
648 19-inch Premium Paint Aluminum Wheels (GT Premium) $995
649 20-inch Bright Machined Aluminum Wheels (all Premium Models) $1,295
3 Recaro Cloth Sport Seats (EcoBoost & GT Coupe) $1,595
S Recaro Leather Sport Seats (all Premium models) $1,595
43S Enhanced Security Package (all models except GT 50 Years LE) $395
60W Wheel & Stripe Package (EcoBoost) $895
67E EcoBoost Performance Package $1,995
68B Premier Trim with Color Accent Group (all Premium models) $395
975 Appearance Package (all Premium models) $1,595
67G GT Performance Package (GT Fastback) $2,495
77R Reverse Park Assist (all models except GT 50 Years LE) $295
66W Spare Wheel and Tire (all models except GT 50 Years LE) $195
13D Spoiler Delete (all models except GT 50 Years LE) N/C
91N Voice-Activated Navigation System (all Premium models) $795
52S Adaptive Cruise Control with Collision Mitigation and Rain Sensing Wipers (GT Premium) $1,195
PRR Ruby Red Metallic Tinted Clearcoat Paint (all models except GT 50 Years LE) $395
PH3 Triple Yellow Tri-Coat Paint (all models except GT 50 Years LE) $495
PL6 Kona Blue Metallic (GT 50 Years LE) N/C
PN4 Wimbledon White (GT 50 Years LE) N/C
12A All Weather Floor Mats (all models except GT 50 Years LE) $95
41H Engine Block Heater (Fleet only) $95

2016 Mustang Prices

P8A V-6 fastback $24,145
P8E V-6 convertible $29,645
P8T EcoBoost fastback $25,645
P8T EcoBoost Premium fastback $29,645
P8U EcoBoost Premium convertible $35,145
P8C GT fastback $32,395
P8C GT Premium fastback $36,395
P8F GT Premium convertible $41,895
Destination and Delivery $900
050A Equipment Group 050A (V-6) NC
051A Equipment Group 051A (V-6 $995
100A Equipment Group 100A (EcoBoost) NC
200A Equipment Group 200A (Eco Boost Premium) NC
201A Equipment Group 201A (EcoBoost Premium) $1,795
300A Equipment Group 300A (GT) NC
400A Equipment Group 400A (GT Premium) NC
401A Equipment Group 401A (GT Premium $1,795
443 6-speed Automatic Transmission $1,195
445 3.55:1 Ratio Axle (V-6, GT Manual Transmission Only $395
641 18-inch Foundry Low-Gloss Paint/ Machined Aluminum Wheels (EcoBoost and GT) $155
648 19-inch Premium Paint Aluminum Wheels (GT Premium) $998
649 20-inch Bright Machined Aluminum Wheels (All Premium Models $1,295
3 Recaro Cloth Sport Seats (EcoBoost & GT Fastbacks) $1,595
S Recaro Leather Sport Seats (All Premium Fastbacks) $1,595
43S Enhanced Security Package (All Models) $395
60W Wheel & Stripe Package (EcoBoost) $895
67E EcoBoost Performance Package
601 Interior & Wheel Package (EcoBoost & GT Fastbacks) $995
68B Premier Trim with Color Accent Group (Premium Models) $395
54P Pony Package (EcoBoost Convertible) $895
54P Pony Package (EcoBoost Fastback) $995
67G GT Performance Package (All GT—Excluding 64F) $2,495
64F Optional GT Performance Package Wheel Finish NC
67G GT Performance Package (All GT—Including 64F) $2,690
60B Black Accent Package (GT Premium) $995
54C California Special (GT Premium) $1,995
21C California Special Car Cover (GT Premium) $375
77R Reverse Sensing System (All Models) $295
66W Spare Wheel and Tire (All Models) $195
13D Spoiler Delete (All Models) NC
91N Voice-Activated Navigation System (Premium Models) $795
52S Adaptive Cruise Control with Collision Warning and Rain Sensing Wipers (GT Premium) $1,195
94B Painted Black Roof (All Fastbacks) $695
47A Over-the-Top Racing Stripe (All Fastbacks) $475
PRR Ruby Red Metallic Tinted Clearcoat Paint (All Models) $395
PH3 Triple Yellow Tri-Coat Paint (All Models) $495
12S All Weather Floor Mats (All Models) $95
41H Engine Block Heater (Fleet Only) $95
63B Smoker's Package (Fleet Only) NC

2017 Mustang Prices

P8A V-6 Fastback $25,185
P8E V-6 Convertible $30,685
P8T EcoBoost Fastback $26,195
P8T EcoBoost Premium fastback $30,195
P8U EcoBoost Premium convertible $35,695
P8C GT Fastback $33,195
P8C GT Premium Fastback $37,195
P8F GT Premium Convertible $42,695
Destination and Delivery $900
050A Equipment Group 050A (V-6) NC
051A Equipment Group 051A (V-6 convertible only) $995
100A Equipment Group 100A (EcoBoost) NC

200A Equipment Group 200A (Eco Boost Premium) NC
201A Equipment Group 201A (EcoBoost Premium) $1,795
300A Equipment Group 300A (GT) NC
400A Equipment Group 400A (GT Premium) NC
401A Equipment Group 401A (GT Premium) $1,795
443 6-speed Automatic Transmission $1,195
455 3.55:1 Ratio Axle (V-6, GT Manual Trans Only) $495
641 18-inch Foundry Low-Gloss Paint/Machined Aluminum Wheels (EcoBoost & GT) $155
648 19-inch Premium Paint Aluminum Wheels (GT Premium) $995
649 20-inch Bright Machined Aluminum Wheels (All Premium Models) $1,295
T3U 20-inch Summer Only Tires (All Premium Models) $295
3 Recaro Cloth Sport Seats (EcoBoost & GT Fastbacks) $1,595
S Recaro Leather Sport Seats (All Premium Fastbacks) $1,595
43S Enhanced Security Package (All Models) $395
60W Wheel & Stripe Package (EcoBoost) $895
67E EcoBoost Performance Package $1,995
601 Interior & Wheel Package (EcoBoost & GT Fastbacks) $995
68B Premier Trim w/Color Accent Group (Premium Models) $395
54P Pony Package (EcoBoost Convertible) $895
54P Pony Package (EcoBoost Fastback) $995
67G GT Performance Package (All GT—Excluding 64F) $2.995
64F Optional GT Performance Package Wheel Finish NC
67G GT Performance Package (All GT—Including 64F) $3,190
60B Black Accent Package (GT Premium) $995
54C California Special (GT Premium) $1,995
21C California Special Car Cover (GT Premium) $375
77R Reverse Sensing System (All Models) $295
66W Spare Wheel & Tire (All Fastbacks) $255
13D Spoiler Delete (All Models) NC
91N Voice-Activated Navigation System (Premium Models) $795
52S Adaptive Cruise Control w/Collision Warning & Rain Sensing Wipers (GT Premium) $1,195
94B Painted Black Roof (All Fastbacks) $695
47A Over-The-Top Racing Stripe (All Fastbacks) $475
PRR Ruby Red Metallic Tinted Clearcoat Paint (All Models) $395
PH3 Triple Yellow Tri-Coat Paint (All Models) $495
PUG White Platinum Tri-Coat Paint (All Models) $495
12A All Weather Floor Mats (All Models) $95
41H Engine Block Heater (Fleet Only) $95
63B Smoker's Package (Fleet Only) NC

2018 Mustang Prices

P8T EcoBoost Fastback $25,680
P8T EcoBoost Premium Fastback $30,695
P8U EcoBoost Convertible $31,180
P8U EcoBoost Premium Convertible $36,195
P8C GT Fastback $35,190
P8C GT Premium Fastback $39,190
P8F GT Premium Convertible $44,690
Destination and Delivery $995
100A Equipment Group 100A (EcoBoost) NC
101A Equipment Group 101A (EcoBoost) $2,000
200A Equipment Group 200A (Eco Boost Premium) NC
201A Equipment Group 201A (EcoBoost Premium) $2,200
300A Equipment Group 300A (GT) NC
301A Equipment Group 301A (GT) $2,000
400A Equipment Group 400A (GT Premium) NC
401A Equipment Group 401A (GT Premium) $2,200
44U 10-speed SelectShift Automatic Transmission $1,595
455 3.55:1 Limited-Slip Rear Axle (Requires 44U) $495
641 18-inch Low-Gloss Ebony Black-Paint Aluminum w/Machined-Face Wheels (EcoBoost & GT) $295
648 19-inch Polished Aluminum Wheels (EcoBoost & GT Premiums) $1,095
64L 19-inch Luster Nickel-Painted Forged-Aluminum Wheels (All EcoBoost) $795
647 19x9-inch (front) & 19x9.5-inch (rear) Luster Nickel-Painted Forged-Aluminum Wheels (All GT) $795
649 20-inch Premium-Painted Aluminum Wheels (All Premium Models) $1,295
583 Shaker Pro Audio System (EcoBoost & GT Premiums) $895
883 Recaro Cloth Sport Seats (EcoBoost & GT Fastbacks) $1,595
88S Recaro Leather-Trimmed Sport Seats (All Premium Fastbacks) $1,595
43S Enhanced Security Package (All Models Except 100A) $395
60B Black Accent Package (All Models) $995
60W Wheel & Stripe Package (EcoBoost) $895
67E EcoBoost Performance Package $2,495
54P Pony Package (EcoBoost Convertible) $895
54P Pony Package (EcoBoost Fastback) $995
68C Carbon Sport Interior Package (w/200A & 400A) $1,195
77S Safe & Smart Package (EcoBoost & GT Premiums) $1,495
673 Performance Package-Level 2 (w/301A & 401A) $6,500
67G GT Performance Package (All GT) $3,995
66W Spare Wheel and Tire (All Fastbacks) $405
96B MagneRide Dampening System (w/101A, 200A, 201A, 300A, 301A, 400A & 401A) $1,695
19B Active Valve Performance Exhaust (w/301A, 400A & 401A) $895
13D Spoiler Delete (All Models) NC
91N Voice-Activated Navigation System (Premium Models) $795
94B Painted Black Roof (All Fastbacks) NC
12A Premium Floor Liners, Front/Rear (All Models) $120
PH3 Triple Yellow Tri-Coat Paint (All Models) $495
PNL Orange Fury Metallic Tri-Coat Paint (All Models) $495
PR3 Royal Crimson Metallic Tinted Clearcoat Paint (All Models) $395
PRR Ruby Red Metallic Tinted Clearcoat Paint (All Models) $395
153 Front License Plate Bracket (All Models) NC
41H Engine Block Heater (Fleet Only) $95
94C Tonneau Caps (Convertible Only) NC

2019 Mustang Prices

P8T EcoBoost Fastback $26,395
P8U EcoBoost Convertible $31,895
P8T EcoBoost Premium Fastback $31,410
P8U EcoBoost Premium Convertible $36,910
P8C GT Fastback $35,355
P8C GT Premium Fastback $39,355
P8F GT Premium Convertible $44,855
P8K Bullitt Fastback $46,595
Destination & Delivery $1,095
100A Equipment Group 100A (EcoBoost) NC
101A Equipment Group 101A (EcoBoost) $2,000
200A Equipment Group 200A (EcoBoost Premium) NC
201A Equipment Group 201A (EcoBoost Premium) $2,200
300A Equipment Group 300A (GT) NC
301A Equipment Group 301A (GT) $2,000
400A Equipment Group 400A (GT Premium) NC
401A Equipment Group 401A (GT Premium) $2,200
500A Equipment Group 500A (Bullitt) NC
44U 10-speed SelectShift Automatic Transmission $1,595
455 3.55:1 Limited-Slip Rear Axle (Requires 44U) $495
641 18-inch Low-Gloss Ebony Black-Paint Aluminum w/Machined-Face Wheels (EcoBoost & GT) $295
648 19-inch Polished Aluminum Wheels (EcoBoost & GT Premiums) $1,095
64L 19-inch Luster Nickel-Painted Forged-Aluminum Wheels (All EcoBoost) $795
647 19x9-inch (front) & 19x9.5-inch (rear) Luster Nickel-Painted Forged-Aluminum Wheels (All GT) $795
649 20-inch Premium-Painted Aluminum Wheels (All Premium Models Except Bullitt) $1,295
3 Recaro Cloth-Trimmed Sport Seats (EcoBoost & GT Premium Fastbacks & Bullitt) $1,595
S Recaro Leather-Trimmed Sport Seats (EcoBoost & GT Premium Fastbacks & Bullitt) $1,595
43S Enhanced Security Package (All Models Except 100A) $395
52B Black Accent Package (All Models) $995
60W Wheel & Stripe Package (EcoBoost) $895
67E EcoBoost Performance Package $2,495
54P Pony Package (EcoBoost Convertible) $895
54P Pony Package (EcoBoost Fastback) $995
68C Carbon Sport Interior Package (w/200A & 400A) $1,195
77S Safe & Smart Package (EcoBoost & GT Premiums) $1,000
673 Performance Package-Level 2 (w/301A & 401A) $6,500
67G GT Performance Package (All GT) $3,995
54C California Special Package (GT Premium) $2,000
67D Bullitt Electronics Package $2,100
47A Over-the-Top Racing Stripe (All Fastbacks Except Bullitt) $475
66W Spare Wheel & Tire (All Fastbacks) $405
96B MagneRide Dampening System (w/101A, 200A, 201A, 300A, 301A, 400A, 401A & 500A) $1,695
19B Active Valve Performance Exhaust (w/301A, 400A & 401A) $895
13D Spoiler Delete (All Models Except Bullitt) NC
91N Voice-Activated Navigation System (Premium Models) $795
12A Premium Floor Liners, Front/Rear (All Models) $120
PNL Orange Fury Metallic Tri-Coat Paint $495
PRR Ruby Red Metallic Tinted Clearcoat Paint $395
153 Front License Plate Bracket (All Models) NC
41H Engine Block Heater $100
583 B&O Play Premium Audio System (Premium Models) $895
94C Tonneau Caps (Convertible Only) NC
21C Full Vehicle Cover (w/500A) $395

2020 Mustang Prices

P8T EcoBoost Fastback $26,670
P8U EcoBoost Convertible $32,170
P8T EcoBoost Premium Fastback $31,685
P8U EcoBoost Premium Convertible $37,185
P8C GT Fastback $35,880
P8C GT Premium Fastback $39,880
P8F GT Premium Convertible $45,380
P8K Bullitt Fastback $46,705
Destination & Delivery $1,195
100A Equipment Group 100A (EcoBoost) NC
101A Equipment Group 101A (EcoBoost) $2,000
200A Equipment Group 200A (EcoBoost Premium) NC
201A Equipment Group 201A (EcoBoost Premium) $2,200
300A Equipment Group 300A (GT) NC
301A Equipment Group 301A (GT) $2,000
400A Equipment Group 400A (GT Premium) NC
401A Equipment Group 401A (GT Premium) $2,200
500A Equipment Group 500A (Bullitt) NC
L59 Gas Guzzler Tax (Bullitt Only) $1,000
44U 10-speed SelectShift Automatic Transmission $1,595
455 3.55:1 Limited-Slip Rear Axle (Requires 44U) $795
641 18-inch Low-Gloss Ebony Black-Paint Aluminum w/Machined-Face Wheels (EcoBoost & GT) $295
64P 19-inch Polished Aluminum Wheels (EcoBoost & GT Premiums) $1,095
64L 19-inch Luster Nickel-Painted Forged-Aluminum Wheels (All EcoBoost) $795
647 19x9-inch (front) & 19x9.5-inch (rear) Luster Nickel-Painted Forged-Aluminum Wheels (All GT) $795
649 20-inch Premium-Painted Aluminum Wheels (All Premium Models Except Bullitt) $1,295
3 Recaro Cloth-Trimmed Sport Seats (GT) $1,595
S Recaro Leather-Trimmed Sport Seats (EcoBoost & GT Premium Fastbacks & Bullitt) $1,595
43S Enhanced Security Package (All Models Except 100A & Bullitt) $395
52B Black Accent Package (All Models Except Bullitt) $995
60L Wheel & Stripe Package (EcoBoost) $895
67E 2.3L High Performance Package (EcoBoost) $4,995
60H EcoBoost Handling Package (All Except 100A) $1,995
54P Pony Package (EcoBoost Convertible) $895
54P Pony Package (EcoBoost Fastback) $995
68C Carbon Sport Interior Package (w/200A & 400A) $1,195
77S Safe & Smart Package (All Models Except Bullitt) $1,000
673 Performance Package-Level 2 (w/301A & 401A) $6,500
67G GT Performance Package (All GT) $5,195
54C California Special Package (GT Premium) $2,000
67D Bullitt Electronics Package $2,100
47A Over-the-Top Racing Stripe (All Fastbacks Except Bullitt) $475
66W Spare Wheel & Tire (All Fastbacks Except Bullitt) $405
96B MagneRide Dampening System (w/300A, 400A, 401A & 500A) $1,695
19B Active Valve Performance Exhaust (w/101A, 200A, 201A, 300A, 301A, 400A & 401A) $895
13D Spoiler Delete (All Models Except 100A & Bullitt) NC
91N Voice-Activated Navigation System (w/101A, 200A, 301A & 400A) $995
12A Premium Floor Liners, Front/Rear (All Models) $170
PCA Twister Orange Tri-Coat Paint $495
PD4 Rapid Red Metallic Tinted Clearcoat Paint $395
153 Front License Plate Bracket (All Models) NC
41H Engine Block Heater $100
583 B&O Play Premium Audio System (Premium Models) $995
94C Tonneau Caps (Convertible Only) NC
21C Full Vehicle Cover (w/500A) $395

2021 Mustang Prices

P8T EcoBoost Fastback $27,205
P8U EcoBoost Convertible $32,705
P8T EcoBoost Premium Fastback $32,225
P8U EcoBoost Premium Convertible $37,725
P8C GT Fastback $36,285
P8C GT Premium Fastback $40,285
P8F GT Premium Convertible $45,785
P8R Mach 1 $52,400
Destination & Delivery $1,195
100A Equipment Group 100A (EcoBoost) NC
101A Equipment Group 101A (EcoBoost) $2,200
200A Equipment Group 200A (EcoBoost Premium) NC
201A Equipment Group 201A (EcoBoost Premium) $2,500
300A Equipment Group 300A (GT) NC
301A Equipment Group 301A (GT) $2,200
400A Equipment Group 400A (GT Premium) NC
401A Equipment Group 401A (GT Premium) $2,400
500A Equipment Group 600A (Mach 1) NC
700A Equipment Group 700A (Mach 1) $1,900

L59	Gas Guzzler Tax (600A & 700A w/Manual Trans 44E)	$1,000
L59	Gas Guzzler Tax (Mach 1 w/Automatic Trans)	NC
44U	10-speed SelectShift Automatic Transmission	$1,595
455	3.55:1 Limited-Slip Rear Axle (Requires 44U)	$795
641	18-inch Machined-Face Aluminum w/Low-Gloss Ebony Black-Painted Pocket Wheels (EcoBoost & GT)	$350
64P	19-inch Polished Aluminum Wheels (EcoBoost & GT Premiums)	$1,150
64L	19-inch Luster Nickel-Painted Forged-Aluminum Wheels (All EcoBoost)	$850
647	19x9-inch (front) & 19x9.5-inch (rear) Luster Nickel-Painted Forged-Aluminum Wheels (All GT)	$850
64S	19-inch Magnetic-Painted Aluminum Wheels (Mach 1)	$450
649	20-inch Premium-Painted Aluminum Wheels (All Premium Models)	$1,350
3	Recaro Cloth-Trimmed Sport Seats (GT & Mach 1)	$1,650
S	Recaro Leather-Trimmed Sport Seats (EcoBoost & GT Premium Fastbacks & Mach 1)	$1,650
43S	Enhanced Security Package (All Models Except 100A & 600A)	$500
43S	Enhanced Security Package w/67D (Mach 1)	NC
67E	2.3L High Performance Package (EcoBoost)	$6,150
60G	Black Accent Package (All Models Except Mach 1)	$995
60H	EcoBoost Handling Package (All Except 100A)	$1,995
60L	Wheel & Stripe Package (EcoBoost)	$895
61D	Rear Seat Delete (Mach 1 only)	$250
18F	Red-Painted Brake Calipers (Mach 1 only)	$495
54A	Mach 1 Appearance Package (700A)	$1,250
67D	Mach 1 Elite Package (700A)	$1,550
60K	Mach 1 Handling Package (600A & 700A)	$3,750
54P	Pony Package (EcoBoost Convertible)	$895
54P	Pony Package (EcoBoost Fastback)	$995
68C	Carbon Sport Interior Package (w/200A & 400A)	$1,195
77S	Ford Safe & Smart Package (w/100A, 101A, 200A, 300A, 301A & 400A)	$725
67G	GT Performance Package (All GT)	$6,500
54C	California Special Package (GT Premium)	$2,000
59C	Stripe Delete (EcoBoost)	NC
47A	Over-the-Top Racing Stripe (All Fastbacks Except Mach 1)	$475
66W	Mini Spare Wheel & Tire (All Fastbacks Except Mach 1)	$415
96B	MagneRide Dampening System (w/301A, 400A, & 401A)	$1,695
19B	Active Valve Performance Exhaust (w/101A, 200A, 201A, 300A, 301A, 400A & 401A)	$995
13D	Spoiler Delete (All Models Except 100A & Mach 1)	NC
91N	Voice-Activated Navigation System (Mach 1 only)	$595
12A	Premium Floor Liners, Front/Rear (All Models)	$170
PCA	Twister Orange Tri-Coat Paint	$495
PD4	Rapid Red Metallic Tinted Clearcoat Paint	$395
153	Front License Plate Bracket (All Models)	NC
41H	Engine Block Heater	$150
583	B&O Play Premium Audio System (Premium Models)	$995
BHQAB	Full Vehicle Cover (Mach 1 only)	$450

Index

Page numbers in italics indicate a photograph or illustration.